Introduction to Risk Management

1st Edition • 2nd Printing

The Institutes
720 Providence Road, Suite 100
Malvern, Pennsylvania 19355-3433

1st Edition • 2nd Printing • November 2012

Library of Congress Control Number: 2012946555

ISBN 978-0-89463-616-5

Introduction to Risk Management

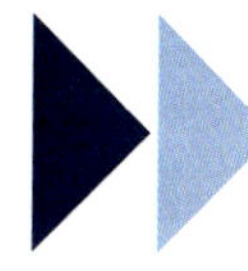

Foreword

The Institutes are the trusted leader in delivering proven knowledge solutions that drive powerful business results for the risk management and property-casualty insurance industry. For more than 100 years, The Institutes have been meeting the industry's changing professional development needs with customer-driven products and services.

In conjunction with industry experts and members of the academic community, our Knowledge Resources Department develops our course and program content, including Institutes study materials. Practical and technical knowledge gained from Institutes courses enhances qualifications, improves performance, and contributes to professional growth—all of which drive results.

The Institutes' proven knowledge helps individuals and organizations achieve powerful results with a variety of flexible, customer-focused options:

Recognized Credentials—The Institutes offer an unmatched range of widely recognized and industry-respected specialty credentials. The Institutes' Chartered Property Casualty Underwriter (CPCU) professional designation is designed to provide a broad understanding of the property-casualty insurance industry. Depending on professional needs, CPCU students may select either a commercial insurance focus or a personal risk management and insurance focus and may choose from a variety of electives.

In addition, The Institutes offer certificate or designation programs in a variety of disciplines, including these:

- Claims
- Commercial underwriting
- Fidelity and surety bonding
- General insurance
- Insurance accounting and finance
- Insurance information technology
- Insurance production and agency management
- Insurance regulation and compliance
- Management
- Marine insurance
- Personal insurance
- Premium auditing
- Quality insurance services
- Reinsurance
- Risk management
- Surplus lines

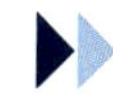

Ethics—Ethical behavior is crucial to preserving not only the trust on which insurance transactions are based, but also the public's trust in our industry as a whole. All Institutes designations now have an ethics requirement, which is delivered online and free of charge. The ethics requirement content is designed specifically for insurance practitioners and uses insurance-based case studies to outline an ethical framework. More information is available in the Programs section of our website, www.TheInstitutes.org.

Flexible Online Learning—The Institutes have an unmatched variety of technical insurance content covering topics from accounting to underwriting, which we now deliver through hundreds of online courses. These cost-effective self-study courses are a convenient way to fill gaps in technical knowledge in a matter of hours without ever leaving the office.

Continuing Education—A majority of The Institutes' courses are filed for CE credit in most states. We also deliver quality, affordable, online CE courses quickly and conveniently through our newest business unit, CEU.com. Visit www.CEU.com to learn more.

College Credits—Most Institutes courses carry college credit recommendations from the American Council on Education. A variety of courses also qualify for credits toward certain associate, bachelor's, and master's degrees at several prestigious colleges and universities. More information is available in the Student Services section of our website, www.TheInstitutes.org.

Custom Applications—The Institutes collaborate with corporate customers to use our trusted course content and flexible delivery options in developing customized solutions that help them achieve their unique organizational goals.

Insightful Analysis—Our Insurance Research Council (IRC) division conducts public policy research on important contemporary issues in property-casualty insurance and risk management. Visit www.ircweb.org to learn more or purchase its most recent studies.

The Institutes look forward to serving the risk management and property-casualty insurance industry for another 100 years. We welcome comments from our students and course leaders; your feedback helps us continue to improve the quality of our study materials.

Peter L. Miller, CPCU
President and CEO
The Institutes

Preface

Introduction to Risk Management is the assigned textbook developed by The Institutes for Temple University's RMI 2101—Introduction to Risk Management course. It is designed to be a "first course" toward the study of risk analysis and risk management.

Risk is everywhere and in everything. If there were no risk, there would likely be no rewards. This text will help learners recognize and manage risk—essential skills for coping with the challenges life presents. It will also help them consider risk as an opportunity to exploit, rather than a danger to avoid.

Assignment 1, "Introduction to and Overview of Risk Management," offers a broad perspective on risk, including how risk can be quantified and classified, facts that exacerbate risk, and the financial consequences of risk. Assignment 2, "The Risk Management Process," offers an intentional approach for assessing and mitigating risk with supporting information on its benefits and goals.

Assignment 3, "Traditional and Enterprise Risk Management," focuses on loss exposures with particular emphasis on liability loss exposures, as well as on how risk management has evolved beyond the treatment of hazard risks. Assignment 4, "Quantitative Methods and Risk Management Applications," discusses the quantitative tools needed to gauge risk and the law of large numbers that underlies risk pooling.

Assignment 5, "Risk Management Alternatives—Loss Control Techniques," examines loss control techniques (which reduce the frequency and/or severity of losses or make losses more predictable) and how to select risk control techniques that are appropriate for meeting an organization's risk control goals. Assignment 6, "Risk Management Alternatives—Loss Financing Techniques," examines risk financing techniques (which generate funds to pay losses) and how to select risk financing techniques that are appropriate for meeting an organization's risk financing goals.

Assignment 7, "Decision Making Under Uncertainty—Risk Management Alternatives," offers a structured approach to making risk management decisions that align with the organization's risk management objectives. Assignment 8, "Definition and Characteristics of Insurance," explains how insurance relies on pooling to be economically feasible and how the principle of indemnity serves as a guide in maintaining the financial integrity of the pool. While insurance is not the only means for treating risk, insurance does have certain advantages over other means.

Assignment 9, "Characteristics of an Insurable Risk," considers insurance from an economic perspective and stresses the importance of an ideally insurable risk, which makes insurance financially feasible. Assignment 10, "Legal Principles Supporting the Insurance Mechanism," considers concepts that support the principle of indemnity and hence the operation of insurance. Assignment 11, "Insurance Policy Provisions," focuses on a limited number of policy provisions that reinforce the principle of indemnity.

Assignment 12, "Introduction to Employer-Provided Benefits," offers an overview of employer-funded benefits that may be granted voluntarily by an employer or that may be required to be provided.

Assignment 13, "Health Risks and Employee Benefits Plans," describes the healthcare indemnity system and the challenges that system is facing. Assignment 14, "Retirement Risks and Employee Benefits Plans," discusses the risk of outliving one's income and the planning and funding needed to mitigate this loss exposure.

Assignment 15, "Mandated/Compulsory Benefits and Social Insurance," describes the safety net that society has created to assist retirees, those who are injured on the job, and individuals who become unemployed.

For this edition of Introduction to Risk Management, The Institutes are grateful for the valuable insight, program design, and curriculum contributions of Dr. Robert B. Drennan, associate professor and chair of the Department of Risk, Insurance, and Healthcare Management at Temple University's Fox School of Business. Additional individuals who were involved in producing this edition of the text are acknowledged on the Contributors page.

For more information about The Institutes' programs, please contact our Customer Service Department at (800) 644-2101, e-mail us at customerservice@TheInstitutes.org, or visit our website at www.TheInstitutes.org.

Mary Ann Cook

Contributors

The Institutes acknowledge with deep appreciation the contributions made to the content of this text by the following persons:

Richard Berthelsen, JD, CPCU, AIC, ARM, AU, ARe, MBA

Pamela J. Brooks, MBA, CPCU, AAM, AIM, AIS

Mary Ann Cook, MBA, CPCU, ARM, AU, AAI

Susan Crowe, CPCU, AIC, ARe

Arthur L. Flitner, CPCU, ARM, AIC

Douglas Froggatt

Connor M. Harrison, CPCU, AU, ARe, AIAF, AAM, ARP

Judith M. Vaughan, CPCU, AIC

Contents

Assignment 1
Introduction to and Overview of Risk Management 1.1
Understanding and Quantifying Risk 1.3
Risk Classifications 1.5
Understanding Hazards 1.9
Financial Consequences of Risk 1.12
Summary 1.15

Assignment 2
The Risk Management Process 2.1
Basic Purpose and Scope of Risk Management 2.3
Benefits of Risk Management 2.4
The Risk Management Process 2.10
Risk Management Program Goals 2.18
Elements of a Loss Exposure 2.25
Identifying Loss Exposures 2.26
Summary 2.36

Assignment 3
Traditional and Enterprise Risk Management 3.1
Types of Loss Exposures 3.3
Legal Liability: Torts, Contracts, and Statutes 3.9
Negligence 3.12
Traditional Risk Management Versus Enterprise Risk Management (ERM) 3.19
Summary 3.27

Assignment 4
Quantitative Methods and Risk Management Applications 4.1
Nature of Probability 4.3
Using Probability Distributions 4.5
Using Central Tendency 4.11
Using Dispersion 4.19
Calculating Alternative Probabilities 4.24
Understanding the Law of Large Numbers 4.29
Understanding Loss Severity 4.33
Summary 4.36

Assignment 5
Risk Management Alternatives—Loss Control Techniques 5.1
Risk Control Techniques 5.3
Risk Control Goals 5.12
Loss Frequency and Loss Severity 5.17
Application of Risk Control Techniques 5.19
Business Continuity Management 5.23
Summary 5.29

Assignment 6
Risk Management Alternatives Loss Financing Techniques 6.1
Risk Financing Goals 6.3
Risk Financing Techniques: Transfer and Retention 6.7
Selecting Appropriate Risk Financing Measures 6.12
Types of Contractual Risk Transfer 6.16
Types of Captive Insurance Plans 6.25
Summary 6.29

Assignment 7
Decision Making Under Uncertainty—Risk Management Alternatives 7.1
Selecting the Proper Tools 7.3
Summary 7.17

Assignment 8
Definition and Characteristics of Insurance 8.1
How Insurance Reduces Risk 8.3
Contract of Indemnity 8.8
Benefits of Insurance 8.10
Summary 8.14

Assignment 9
Characteristics of an Insurable Risk 9.1
Economic View of Insurance 9.3
Economic Issues Related to Insurance Pricing 9.15
Characteristics of an Ideally Insurable Loss Exposure 9.21
Insurability of Commercial Loss Exposures 9.28
Insurability of Personal Loss Exposures 9.40
Government Insurance Programs 9.44
Reinsurance and Its Functions 9.50
Summary 9.54

Assignment 10
Legal Principles Supporting the Insurance Mechanism 10.1
Principle of Indemnity 10.3
Summary 10.7

Assignment 11
Insurance Policy Provisions 11.1
Other-Insurance Provisions 11.3
Insurance to Value 11.9
Coinsurance 11.12
Summary 11.18

Assignment 12
Introduction to Employer-Provided Benefits 12.1
Employer-Funded Employee Benefits 12.3
Rationale for Employer-Provided Benefits 12.6
Characteristics of Employee Benefits Plans 12.8
Tax Treatment of Employer-Provided Benefits 12.11
Advantages and Disadvantages of Group Insurance 12.13
Summary 12.18

Assignment 13
Health Risks and Employee Benefits Plans 13.1
The Healthcare Fee-for-Service Indemnity System 13.3
Health Insurance Plans 13.5
Government-Provided Health Insurance Plans 13.11
Summary 13.18

Assignment 14
Retirement Risks and Employee Benefits Plans 14.1

The Financial Impact of Retirement 14.3

Introduction to Retirement Funding 14.6

Categories of Employer-Sponsored Retirement Plans 14.11

Comparing Employer-Sponsored Retirement Plans 14.16

Retirement Income Choices 14.23

Eligibility Requirements for Retirement Benefits 14.29

Pension Funding 14.31

Summary 14.36

Assignment 15
Mandated/Compulsory Benefits and Social Insurance 15.1

Social Insurance 15.3

Social Security Program (OASDHI) 15.5

Unemployment Insurance 15.10

Workers Compensation Statutes: Purpose, Benefits, and Persons Covered 15.12

Summary 15.19

Direct Your Learning

1

Introduction to and Overview of Risk Management

Educational Objectives

After learning the content of this assignment, you should be able to:

- Describe each of the following in the context of risk:
  - Uncertainty
  - Possibility
  - Possibility compared with probability
- Explain how the following classifications of risk apply and how they help in risk management:
  - Pure and speculative risk
  - Subjective and objective risk
  - Diversifiable and nondiversifiable risk
  - Static and dynamic risk
- Describe the four classifications of hazards.
- Describe the three financial consequences of risk.

Outline

Understanding and Quantifying Risk

Risk Classifications

Understanding Hazards

Financial Consequences of Risk

Summary

Introduction to and Overview of Risk Management

1

UNDERSTANDING AND QUANTIFYING RISK

Although risk may intuitively seem undesirable, it can yield both positive and negative outcomes. Opportunities cannot be pursued, and reward cannot be obtained, without incurring some risk. Because of this risk/reward relationship, individuals and organizations seek to maximize reward while minimizing the associated risk. Risk management helps individuals and organizations to avoid, prevent, reduce, or pay for the negative outcomes of risk so that opportunities for reward can be pursued. Understanding and quantifying risk are the logical starting point for learning how to use risk management.

Risk is a term regularly used by individuals in both their personal and professional lives and is generally understood in context. However, properly defining risk is often difficult because it can have many different meanings. As used in this discussion, risk is defined as the uncertainty about outcomes, with the possibility that some of the outcomes can be negative. Risk can be quantified by knowing the probability of the possible outcomes. See the exhibit "Industry Language—Risk."

Industry Language—Risk

Risk can be used in many contexts in risk management and insurance and can have any of the following meanings:

- The subject matter of an insurance policy, such as a structure, an auto fleet, or the possibility of a liability claim arising from an insured's activities
- The insurance applicant (the insured)
- The possibility of bodily injury or property damage
- A cause of loss (or peril), such as fire, lightning, or explosion
- The variability associated with a future outcome

[DA02845]

Uncertainty and Possibility

The two elements within the definition of risk are these:

- Uncertainty of outcome
- Possibility of a negative outcome

First, risk involves uncertainty about the type of outcome (what will actually occur), the timing of the outcome (when the outcome will occur), or both the type and timing of the outcome. Consider an individual who buys a share of stock in a publicly traded corporation. This individual may experience a positive outcome if the value of the stock increases or a negative outcome if the value of the stock decreases. The timing of either outcome is uncertain because the individual does not know if or when the stock price is going to change or what the new stock price will be. Whether uncertainty involves what will actually happen, when something will happen, or both, it results from the inability to accurately predict the future.

Second, risk involves the possibility of a negative outcome. Possibility means that an outcome or event may or may not occur. The fact that something may occur does not mean that it will occur. For example, it is possible that an individual may be injured while driving to or from work, loading a truck at work, moving some furniture at home, or falling in an icy parking lot at the mall. However, the possibility that these events may occur does not mean that they will occur. Nonetheless, because of the possibility of a negative outcome (injury), risk exists.

Possibility and Probability

The possibility that something may occur does not indicate its likelihood of occurring. Possibility does not quantify risk; it only verifies that risk is present. To quantify risk, one needs to know the **probability** of the outcome or event occurring.

Probability
The likelihood that an outcome or event will occur.

Unlike possibility, probability is measurable and has a value between zero and one. If an event is not possible, it has a probability of zero, whereas if an event is certain, it has a probability of one. If an event is possible, but not certain, its probability is some value between zero and one. Probabilities can be stated as a decimal figure (.4), a percentage (40 percent), or a fraction (four-tenths or two-fifths).

To help understand the difference between possibility and probability, consider the possibility that an individual will be injured in an auto accident while driving to or from work tomorrow. That person will not necessarily be injured in an auto accident tomorrow, and the fact that it is possible does not give any indication of its likelihood. The risk exists and has simply been identified.

Contrast this with there being a 5 percent probability that the same individual will be injured in an auto accident while driving to or from work

tomorrow. This statement not only indicates that it is possible the individual will be injured tomorrow, it gives the likelihood. The risk has now been not only identified but also quantified.

Understanding the probability of various outcomes helps focus risk management attention on those risks that can be appropriately managed. Probability can also be used to help decide which activities (and associated risks) to undertake and which risk management techniques to use.

In the previous example:

- If the probability of injury while driving to or from work was 5 percent, and the probability of injury if the individual took the train to work was 1 percent, the individual may decide to take the train.
- However, if the risk of auto injury was reduced to 1 percent by driving a car with airbags and antilock brakes, and if it was more convenient and quicker to drive, then the individual may decide (cost permitting) to buy a new car with airbags and antilock brakes and then drive to work.

RISK CLASSIFICATIONS

Classifying the various types of risk can help an organization understand and manage its risks. The categories should align with an organization's objectives and risk management goals.

After risks are identified, they should be quantified to the extent possible. Quantifying risks involves determining their likelihood and potential magnitude. Techniques such as benchmarking, probability analysis, and modeling can be used to quantify risks.

Following their quantification, risks can be classified according to a system that best meets the needs of a particular organization. Classification can help with assessing risks because many risks in the same classification have similar attributes. Using results from the quantitative analysis, risks can be prioritized within classifications, and risks in the same classification can be managed with similar techniques. Classification also helps with the administrative function of risk management by helping to ensure that risks in the same classification are less likely to be overlooked.

These classifications of risk are some of the most commonly used:

- Pure and speculative risk
- Subjective and objective risk
- Diversifiable and nondiversifiable risk
- Static and dynamic risk

These classifications are not mutually exclusive and can be applied to any given risk.

Pure and Speculative Risk

Pure risk
A chance of loss or no loss, but no chance of gain.

A **pure risk** is a chance of loss or no loss, but no chance of gain. For example, the owner of a commercial building faces the risk associated with a possible fire loss. The building will either burn or not burn. If the building burns, the owner suffers a financial loss. If the building does not burn, the owner's financial condition is unchanged. Neither of the possible outcomes produces a gain. Because there is no opportunity for financial gain, pure risks are always undesirable. See the exhibit "Classifications of Risk."

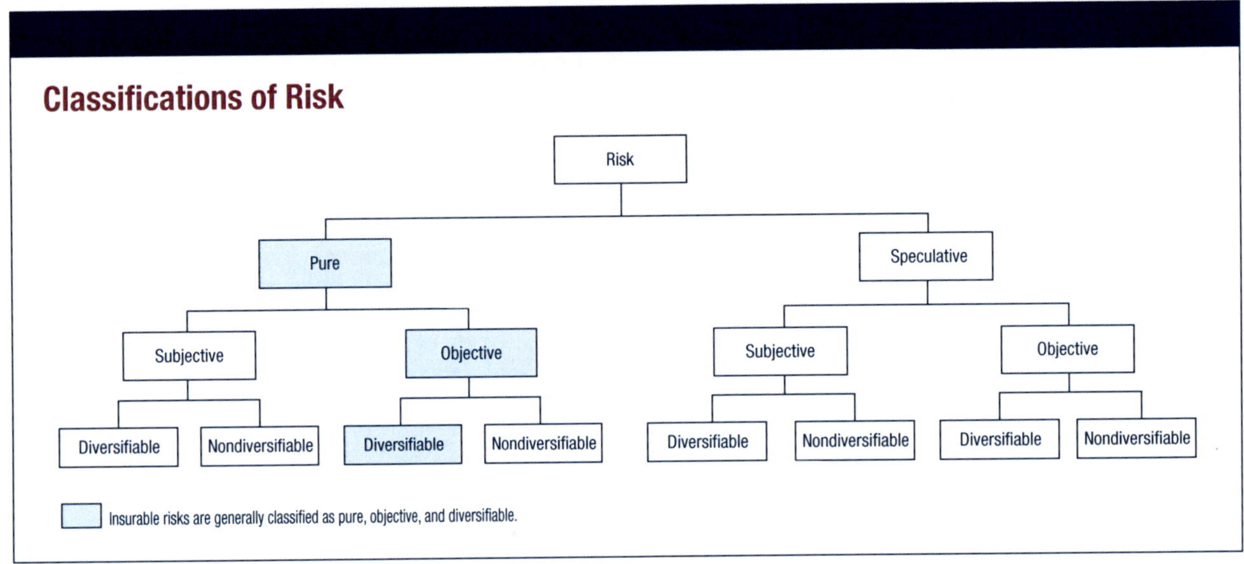

[DA02396]

Speculative risk
A chance of loss, no loss, or gain.

In comparison, **speculative risk** involves a chance of gain. As a result, it can be desirable, as evidenced by the fact that every business venture involves speculative risks. For example, an investor who purchases an apartment building to rent to tenants expects to profit from this investment, so it is a desirable speculative risk. However, the venture could be unprofitable if rental price controls limit the amount of rent that can be charged.

Certain businesses involve speculative risks such as these:

- Price risk—Uncertainty over the size of cash flows resulting from possible changes in the cost of raw materials and other inputs (such as lumber, gas, or electricity), as well as cost-related changes in the market for completed products and other outputs.
- **Credit risk**—Although credit risk is particularly significant for banks and other financial institutions, it can be relevant to any organization with accounts receivable.

Credit risk
The risk that customers or other creditors will fail to make promised payments as they come due.

Financial investments, such as the purchase of stock shares, involve a distinct set of speculative risks. See the exhibit "Speculative Risks in Investments."

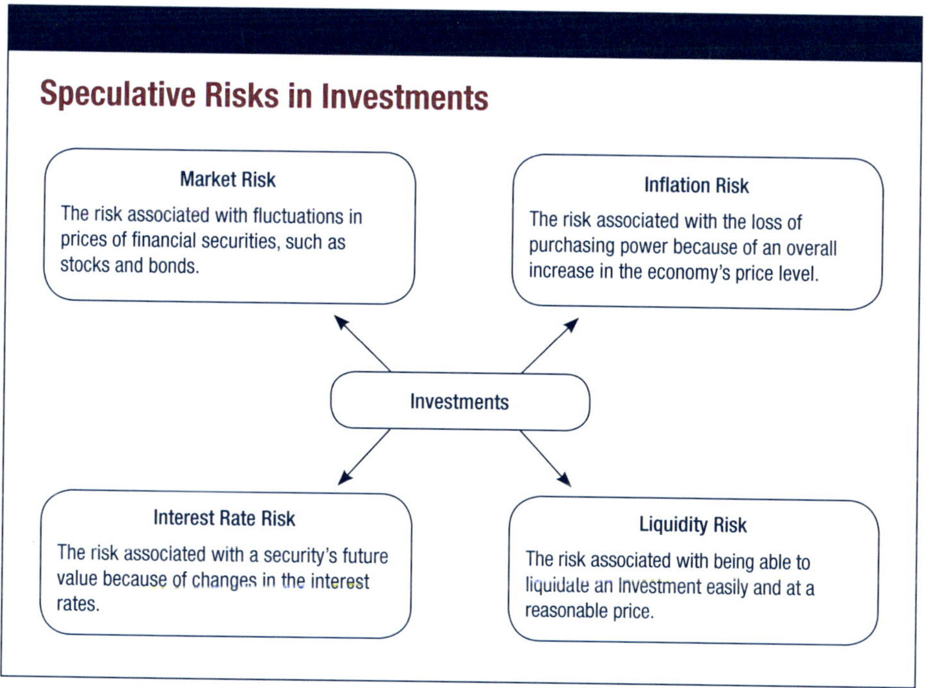

[DA02398]

Insurance deals primarily with risks of loss, not risks of gain; that is, with pure risks rather than speculative risks. However, the distinction between these two classifications of risk is not always precise—many risks have both pure and speculative aspects.

Distinguishing between pure and speculative risks is important because those risks must often be managed differently. For example, although a commercial building owner faces a pure risk from causes of loss such as fire, he or she also faces the speculative risk that the market value of the building will increase or decrease during any one year. Similarly, although an investor who purchases an apartment building to rent to tenants faces speculative risk because rental income may produce a profit or loss, the investor also faces a pure risk from causes of loss such as fire.

To properly manage these investments, the commercial building owner and the apartment owner must consider both the speculative and the pure risks. For example, they may choose to manage the pure risk by buying insurance or taking other measures to address property loss exposures. The speculative risk might be managed by obtaining a favorable mortgage and maintaining the property to enhance its resale value.

Subjective and Objective Risk

When individuals and organizations must make a decision that involves risk, they usually base it on the individual's or organization's assessment of the risk. The assessment can be based on opinions, which are subjective, or facts, which are objective.

Subjective risk
The perceived amount of risk based on an individual's or organization's opinion.

Objective risk
The measurable variation in uncertain outcomes based on facts and data.

Because it is based on opinion rather than fact, **subjective risk** may be quite different from the actual underlying risk that is present. In fact, subjective risk can exist even when **objective risk** does not. The closer an individual's or organization's subjective interpretation of risk is to the objective risk, the more effective its risk management plan will likely be.

Subjective and objective risk can differ substantially for these reasons:

- Familiarity and control—For example, although many people consider air travel (over which they have no control) to carry a high degree of risk, they are much more likely to suffer a serious injury while driving their cars, when the perception of control is much greater.
- Consequences over likelihood—People often have two views of low-likelihood, high-consequence events. The first misconception is the "It can't happen to me" view, which assigns a probability of zero to low-likelihood events such as natural disasters, murder, fires, accidents, and so on. The second misconception is overstating the probability of a low-likelihood event, which is common for people who have personally been exposed to the event previously. If the effect of a particular event can be severe, such as the potentially destructive effects of a hurricane or an earthquake, the perception of the likelihood of deaths resulting from such an event is heightened. This perception may be enhanced by the increased media coverage given to high-severity events.
- Risk awareness—Organizations differ in terms of their level of risk awareness and, therefore, perceive risks differently. An organization that is not aware of its risks would perceive the likelihood of something happening as very low.

Both risk management and insurance depend on the ability to objectively identify and analyze risks. However, subjectivity is also necessary because facts are often not available to objectively assess risk.

Diversifiable and Nondiversifiable Risk

Diversifiable risk
A risk that affects only some individuals, businesses, or small groups.

Diversifiable risk is not highly correlated and can be managed through diversification, or spread, of risk. An example of a diversifiable risk is a fire, which is likely to affect only one or a small number of businesses. For instance, an insurer can diversify the risks associated with fire insurance by insuring many buildings in several different locations. Similarly, business investors often diversify their holdings, as opposed to investing in only one business, hoping those that succeed will more than offset those that fail.

Nondiversifiable risk
A risk that affects a large segment of society at the same time.

Examples of **nondiversifiable risks** include inflation, unemployment, and natural disasters such as hurricanes. Nondiversifiable risks are correlated—that is, their gains or losses tend to occur simultaneously rather than randomly. For example, under certain monetary conditions, interest rates increase for all

firms at the same time. If an insurer were to insure firms against interest rate increases, it would not be able to diversify its portfolio of interest rate risks by underwriting a large number of insureds, because all of them would suffer losses at the same time.

Systemic risks are generally nondiversifiable. For example, if excess leverage by financial institutions causes systemic risk resulting in an event that disrupts the financial system, this risk will have an effect on the entire economy and, therefore, on all organizations. Because of the global interconnections in finance and industry, many risks that were once viewed as nonsystemic (affecting only one organization) are now viewed as systemic. For instance, many economists view the failure of Lehman Brothers in early 2008 as a trigger event which highlighted the systemic risk in the banking sector that resulted in the financial crisis. Further, not understanding the systemic nature of risk posed by the securitization of mortgage obligations was at the root of AIG's risk management failure in writing a large number of collateralized debt obligations to back the securitizations; the high correlation and systemic risk were not recognized or managed.

Systemic risk

The potential for a major disruption in the function of an entire market or financial system.

Static and Dynamic Risk

Static risk, as implied in its name, is risk that is always present for an organization. For most organizations, static risk includes the potential for loss from natural disasters, fire, theft, or employee injury. Different types of organizations will have their own static risks in addition to those that are common to all organizations. For example, manufacturing organizations will always risk exposure to loss from products liability.

Dynamic risk results from economic change and emerging risks. Financial crises—such as the global crisis of 2008, recessions, regulatory changes, increased competition, changes in fuel and other commodity prices, and changes in consumer habits— are examples of economic risks. Emerging risks include climate change, Internet privacy, terrorism, and new technology such as nanotechnology and innovations in energy.

Risk management thought and practice is rapidly evolving because of increased dynamic risk in a global economy with ongoing advances in technology. Traditional risk management applies mainly to static risk. However, the major threats to an organization may relate to dynamic risk.

UNDERSTANDING HAZARDS

Losses result from hazards. The hazard of ice on a highway can lead to accidents. Exceeding the speed limit on an icy highway increases the probability of an accident. Insurers develop an understanding of hazards and how they interact to analyze and predict the financial consequences of loss.

Hazard

A condition that increases the frequency or severity of a loss.

Insurers typically define **hazards** according to these four classifications:

- Moral
- Morale
- Physical
- Legal

Regardless of whether they are moral, morale, physical, or legal, hazards can have a compounding effect. Therefore risk management professionals need to carefully monitor any situations that may involve multiple hazards.

Classification of Hazards

Moral hazard

A condition that increases the likelihood that a person will intentionally cause or exaggerate a loss.

Examples of a **moral hazard** include intentionally causing, fabricating, or exaggerating a loss. For example, one moral hazard incentive is financial difficulty. Someone who is facing overwhelming debt might be tempted to intentionally cause a loss in an attempt to profit from the situation and thereby reduce or eliminate the debt.

Purchasing an insurance policy is another moral hazard incentive—some people might be inclined to behave differently once they enter into a contract that shifts the financial consequences of risk to another party. In insurance, this behavior can include filing false claims, inflating a claim on a loss that did occur, or intentionally causing a loss.

Morale hazard (attitudinal hazard)

A condition of carelessness or indifference that increases the frequency or severity of loss.

Frequency

Number of losses.

Severity

The size of a loss.

Physical hazard

A tangible characteristic of property, persons, or operations that tends to increase the frequency or severity of loss.

Legal hazard

A condition of the legal environment that increases loss frequency or severity.

Driving carelessly, failing to lock an unattended building, or failing to clear an icy sidewalk to protect pedestrians are examples of **morale hazard**.

Both moral and morale hazards are behavior problems that can increase the **frequency** and/or **severity** of losses. The fundamental difference between these two types of hazard is intent. A moral hazard results from a deliberate act; a morale hazard results from carelessness or indifference.

A **physical hazard** is a condition of property, persons, or operations that increases the frequency and/or severity of loss. For example, a slip-and-fall accident is more likely to occur on an icy sidewalk, a fire is more likely to start in a building with defective wiring, and an explosion is more likely to occur in a painting area that has inadequate ventilation. Inadequate ventilation may also create environmental problems for workers and therefore increase the frequency and/or severity of workers compensation claims.

A **legal hazard** is a condition of the legal environment that increases the frequency and/or severity of loss. For example, courts in some geographic areas are much more likely to find in favor of the plaintiff or to grant large damages awards in liability cases than are courts in other areas. Various trends can also be legal hazards. For example, an increasing number of decisions against tobacco manufacturers would present a legal hazard for companies participating in the tobacco industry.

Multiple Hazards

Multiple hazards have a compounding effect. For example, the loss frequency associated with a safe driver in a safe car is increased by either the physical hazard of an unsafe car or the morale hazard of an unsafe driver. The frequency is further increased by the compound effect of an unsafe driver in an unsafe car. Multiple hazards can also affect loss severity. For example, the combination of a moral hazard, such as a person seeking financial gain, and a legal hazard resulting from a lawsuit following a car accident could increase the cost of the loss. Therefore, risk management and insurance professionals need to carefully monitor any situation that may involve multiple hazards. See the exhibit "Loss Frequency and Loss Severity."

Loss Frequency and Loss Severity

Underwriters usually analyze the potential loss exposures of an account in terms of loss frequency and loss severity. Such an analysis should disclose the profit potential of the account and how improvements in the account's profit potential might be achieved.

Loss frequency refers to the number of losses that occur in a particular period. Employees of a garment manufacturer, for example, might suffer a series of minor lacerations caused by cutting and sewing equipment. Likewise, a bakery account with a large fleet of delivery trucks is likely to have multiple minor accidents. Other types of losses, such as those caused by earthquakes, hurricanes, and fire, occur much less frequently.

Underwriters are particularly interested in loss frequency because loss frequency can often be controlled. Frequent puncture-wound losses might be eliminated or reduced by the installation of machine guards or changes in materials-handling procedures. Frequent fender-benders caused by one driver might be controlled by firing that driver or assigning him or her to other work. Underwriters often try to shift the burden of small but frequent losses back to the insured by setting deductibles at such a level that the insured retains these losses.

Loss severity is the dollar amount of damage that results or might result from each loss exposure. Gauging the potential severity of property losses is easier than gauging the potential severity of liability losses. Most property losses have a finite value, and whether the property is partially or completely destroyed, the severity of the loss is usually calculable. The severity of liability exposures is much harder to calculate. If a paint manufacturer, for example, sells paint that produces toxic fumes when applied, the severity of the potential liability loss is almost unlimited.

Underwriters are usually required to make an estimate of an account's loss severity when evaluating an account. Unlike with loss frequency, analysis of past losses is less helpful when evaluating loss severity.

[DA06770]

FINANCIAL CONSEQUENCES OF RISK

Although it may be difficult to precisely calculate the financial consequences of risk, by considering all of its components and at least estimating its financial consequences, an individual or organization is better able to determine where to focus risk management efforts.

The financial consequences of risk faced by individuals or organizations can be broken into three components:

- Expected cost of losses or gains
- Expenditures on risk management
- Cost of residual uncertainty

Expected Cost of Losses or Gains

The first financial consequence of risk is the expected cost of losses or gains. In his seminal work on calculating the expected cost of losses or gains, Herbert W. Heinrich discussed the cost of one specific risk, the cost of risk associated with industrial accidents (pure risk).[1] Industrial accidents can demonstrate the various costs that need to be accounted for when determining expected costs of losses.

Heinrich observed that not only do industrial accidents include the cost of the compensation paid to the injured employee, but they also include other, hidden costs, including these:

- Time lost by the injured employee
- Time lost by other employees who stop work
- Time lost by foremen, supervisors, or other executives
- Time spent on the case by first-aid attendants and hospital department staff (when not paid for by the insurer)
- Damage to the machine, tools, or other property or the spoilage of material
- Interference with production, failure to fill orders on time, loss of bonuses, payment of forfeits, and other similar causes of loss
- Continuation of the injured employee's wages in full after the employee's return to work—even though the employee's services may temporarily be worth less than normal value
- Loss of profit on the injured employee's productivity and on the idle machines
- Lost productivity because of employee excitement or weakened morale resulting from the accident
- Overhead per injured employee, that is, the expense of light, heat, rent, and other items that continue while the injured employee is not productive

Many of these hidden costs are indirect costs and are more difficult to measure than direct accident costs. Consequently, the overall effect of losses is much greater than the direct losses themselves. Therefore, it is important to identify and try to assign a value to hidden costs in order to get a reasonably accurate view of expected costs.

Calculating the expected cost of losses or gains for speculative risks is more complex than calculating pure risk. For example, suppose a manufacturer was considering adding a second plant to its production facilities. The manufacturer would have to consider all of the expected costs associated with all the pure risks of the new plant, including industrial accidents, as well as the costs or gains associated with the speculative risks. Those costs or gains may include the cost of raw materials, the financing costs for the capital to build the plant, the market price at which the manufacturer can sell its goods, or the expected demand for its products. All of these expected costs and/or gains need to be considered with speculative risks.

Expenditures on Risk Management

The second component of the financial consequences of risk is the individual's or organization's expenditures on risk management. The most widely known risk management technique used by individuals is risk financing by purchasing insurance. Homeowners insurance, auto insurance, health insurance, and life insurance are all risk financing measures used by individuals to manage some of the risks they face. Organizations tend to use a wider variety of risk control and risk financing techniques than do individuals. The expenditures on these activities are a financial consequence of risk.

Cost of Residual Uncertainty

The third component of the financial consequences of risk is the cost of residual uncertainty (cost of worry). Residual uncertainty is the level of risk that remains after individuals or organizations implement their risk management plans. This residual uncertainty is also influenced by an individual's or organization's subjective view of the risks to which they are exposed.

For example, if an individual is unduly concerned about a particular risk, he or she may overestimate the frequency or severity of it, resulting in a subjective interpretation of the true objective risk. Residual uncertainty can be minimized, but doing so is costly because more has to be spent on attempts to control or finance the risks involved.

The cost of residual uncertainty may be difficult to measure and is largely ignored in cost of risk studies. However, it may still have a significant effect on the ultimate financial consequences of risk for an individual or organization. For example, because it may be more costly to an employer to hire an employee who is perceived as presenting a high risk (for example, because he or she changes jobs frequently), the employer may not be willing to hire or

will not be willing to pay a high salary for such an individual. This lost salary opportunity is the cost of residual uncertainty for the individual.

For organizations, the cost of residual uncertainty includes the effect that uncertainty has on consumers, investors, and suppliers. Consumers may not be willing to pay as much for products from organizations with a poor safety reputation, investors will require a larger rate of return on their investment from riskier organizations, and suppliers will be less willing to sell their supplies on credit to financially unstable organizations.

Individuals and organizations vary greatly as to how much residual uncertainty they are willing to accept. However, differences in willingness to accept uncertainty (risk) are beneficial to society and economic development. It allows different individuals and organizations to pursue a variety of risky activities that may offer substantial rewards, not just for the investors, but also for society as a whole.

Review Questions

1. Describe the two elements of risk.
2. Describe the difference between possibility and probability.
3. Explain how understanding various outcome probabilities can aid an organization in its risk management efforts.
4. Explain the purpose of classifying risks.
5. Compare pure and speculative risk.
6. Discuss organizations' objective and subjective assessment of risk.
7. Describe diversifiable risk.
8. Describe nondiversifiable risk.
9. Contrast static and dynamic risk.
10. Identify the four classifications of hazards.
11. Compare moral and morale hazards.
12. Describe loss frequency and severity.
13. Explain why underwriters analyze loss frequency and severity.
14. Identify three components that constitute the financial consequences of risk faced by individuals or organizations.
15. List hidden costs that can affect an organization's calculation of expected costs of loss.
16. Describe the costs of residual uncertainty.

Application Questions

1. Atwell Bus Company Inc. (Atwell) is a corporation providing bus transportation to public and private schools in Midland County. Atwell owns 200 new school buses. Its major competitors are two larger bus companies that operate in the same general area. School districts and private schools generally award annual contracts to the lowest bidder from among the bus

companies, but they also consider overall performance and level of service in their evaluations. Explain how the following elements apply to Atwell's risks: a. uncertainty, b. possibility, and c. probability.

2. Mary has purchased a vacation home located in a coastal region of South Florida. Give examples of each of the three financial consequences of risk that Mary is now exposed to with this purchase.

SUMMARY

The word risk can have many different meanings. In this section, risk is defined as the uncertainty about outcomes, some of which can be negative. The two elements within this definition of risk are uncertainty of outcome (uncertainty about what will actually occur, when the outcome will occur, or a combination of the two) and the possibility of a negative outcome.

Possibility means that an outcome or event may or may not occur. This is not the same as probability, which is the likelihood that an outcome or event will occur. Unlike possibility, probability is measurable and has a value between zero and one.

Classifying the various types of risk after they have been quantified can help organizations manage risk. Some of the most commonly used classifications are pure and speculative risk, subjective and objective risk, diversifiable and nondiversifiable risk, and static and dynamic risk.

Insurers use four classifications of hazards: moral, morale, physical, and legal. The presence of multiple hazards increases loss frequency and severity. By understanding hazards and their effects on loss frequency and severity, insurers can predict the likely occurrence and financial consequences of losses.

When managing risk, it is useful to consider the financial consequences of risk. The financial consequences of risk faced by individuals or organizations can be broken into three components: (1) expected cost of losses or gains, (2) expenditures on risk management, and (3) the cost of residual uncertainty.

ASSIGNMENT NOTE

1. Herbert W. Heinrich, *Industrial Accident Prevention*, 4th ed. (New York: McGraw-Hill Book Co., 1959), pp. 51–52. In 1980, a fifth edition of *Industrial Accident Prevention* was published, containing revisions by Dan Peterson and Nester Roos.

Direct Your Learning

2

The Risk Management Process

Educational Objectives

After learning the content of this assignment, you should be able to:

- Describe the basic purpose and scope of risk management in terms of the following:
  - How risk management is practiced by individuals and organizations
  - The basic distinction between traditional risk management and enterprise-wide risk management
- State the benefits of risk management for an organization and the economy.
- Describe each of the steps in the risk management process.
- Summarize pre-loss and post-loss risk management program goals and the conflicts that can arise as they are implemented.
- Describe the three elements of a loss exposure.
- Describe the following methods of loss exposure identification:
  - Document analysis
  - Compliance review
  - Personal inspections
  - Expertise within and beyond the organization

Outline

Basic Purpose and Scope of Risk Management

Benefits of Risk Management

The Risk Management Process

Risk Management Program Goals

Elements of a Loss Exposure

Identifying Loss Exposures

Summary

The Risk Management Process

2

BASIC PURPOSE AND SCOPE OF RISK MANAGEMENT

Risk management involves the efforts of individuals or organizations to efficiently and effectively assess, control, and finance risk in order to minimize the adverse effects of losses or missed opportunities.

Individuals practice risk management to protect their limited assets from losses and to help meet personal goals. For an organization, sound risk management adds value and helps to ensure that losses or missed opportunities do not prevent it from meeting its goals. While many organizations have traditionally focused their risk management efforts on pure risk, the emerging discipline of enterprise-wide risk management is focused on managing all of an organization's pure and speculative risks.

Risk Management for Individuals and Organizations

In its simplest form, **risk management** includes any effort to economically deal with uncertainty of outcomes (risk). For individuals, risk management is usually an informal series of efforts, not a formalized process. Individual or personal risk management may be viewed as part of the financial planning process that encompasses broader matters such as capital accumulation, retirement planning, and estate planning.

Risk management
The process of making and implementing decisions that will minimize the adverse effects of accidental losses on an organization.

Individuals and families often practice risk management informally without explicitly following a risk management process. For example, individuals purchase insurance policies to cover accidental or unexpected losses, or they contribute to savings plans so that they have money available to cover unforeseen events.

In smaller organizations, risk management is not usually a dedicated function, but one of many tasks carried out by the owner or senior manager. In many larger organizations, the risk management function is conducted as part of a formalized risk management program. A risk management program is a system for planning, organizing, leading, and controlling the resources and activities that an organization needs to protect itself from the adverse effects of accidental losses.

Most risk management programs are built around the risk management process. The risk management process is the method of making, implementing, and monitoring decisions that minimize the adverse effects of risk on an organization. Although the exact steps in an organization's risk management process may differ from the process discussed in this section, all risk management processes are designed to assess, control, and finance risk.

Traditional Risk Management and Enterprise-Wide Risk Management

Traditionally, the risk management professional's role has been associated with loss exposures related mainly to pure, as opposed to speculative, risks. This view excludes from the scope of risk management all loss exposures that arise from speculative risk, also referred to as business risk. Therefore, organizational risk management has focused on managing safety, purchasing insurance, and controlling financial recovery from losses generated by hazard risk.

Enterprise-wide risk management (ERM) is the term commonly used to describe the broader view of risk management that encompasses all types of risk. ERM is an approach to managing all of an organization's key risks and opportunities with the intent of maximizing the organization's value.

An ERM approach allows an organization to integrate all of its risk management activities so that the risk management process occurs at the enterprise level, rather than at the departmental or business unit level. How ERM is implemented in practice varies significantly among organizations, depending on their size, nature, and complexity.

BENEFITS OF RISK MANAGEMENT

In a 2008 speech, Ben Bernanke, chairman of the United States Federal Reserve, stated that a significant factor in causing the 2008 financial crisis was risk-management weaknesses at large global financial institutions. He continued, "Given the central role of effective, firm-wide risk management in maintaining strong financial institutions, it is clear that supervisors must redouble their efforts to help organizations improve their risk-management practices."[1]

Traditionally, organizations have recognized the benefits of risk management for hazard risks. Organizations' risk-management techniques, primarily risk mitigation and risk transfer, benefit not only the individual organization, but also the overall economy. For example, insurance can prevent a business failure after a catastrophe and the unemployment that could result from such a failure.

There are also broader risks within individual organizations and the economy. Some of these risks are positive, such as opportunity risk when an organization expands or develops a new product. These risks can result in growth for organizations as well as for the overall economy. However, in the wake of large-scale and well-publicized business failures, such as Enron, and the global financial crisis, many economists are concerned that organizational risk management has not been effective for the broader scope of risks beyond traditional hazard risks. Additionally, Bernanke and other economists believe that risk management must expand to address systemic risk in the economy.

Benefits for an Organization

All organizations face various risks simply by operating. Many risks result in a negative outcome only, such as the possibility of accidental loss, and could prevent an organization from meeting its objectives. Other risks can have either a positive or negative outcome, such as a new product or a financial investment, and could help an organization meet its objectives. There are various benefits to any organization in managing these risks.

Reduce Cost of Hazard Risk

In risk management, an organization's **cost of risk** associated with a particular asset or activity is the total of these:

- Costs of accidental losses not reimbursed by insurance or other outside sources
- Insurance premiums or expenses incurred for noninsurance indemnity
- Costs of risk control techniques to prevent or reduce the size of accidental losses
- Costs of administering risk management activities

Cost of risk
The total cost incurred by an organization because of the possibility of accidental loss.

Risk management aims to reduce the long-term overall cost of risk for the organization without precluding or otherwise interfering with the organization's achieving its goals or engaging in its normal activities. The reduction in the overall cost of risk can increase the organization's profits (or, for a not-for-profit organization, reduce the budget it needs for a particular activity). Risk management also supports safety while minimizing the financial effect of safety measures on the organization's productivity.

Reduce Deterrence Effects of Hazard Risks

The fear of possible future losses tends to make senior management reluctant to undertake activities they consider too risky. Consequently, the organization is deprived of potential benefits. Risk management reduces the deterrence effects of uncertainty about potential future accidental losses by making these

losses less frequent, less severe, or more foreseeable. The resulting reduction in uncertainty benefits an organization in these ways:

- Alleviates or reduces management's fears about potential losses, thereby increasing the feasibility of ventures that once appeared too risky
- Increases profit potential by greater participation in investment or production activities
- Makes the organization a safer investment, and, therefore, more attractive to suppliers of investment capital through which the organization can expand

Many new products and manufacturing processes have become attractive only when better ways of preventing and paying for accidental losses have reduced related uncertainty.

Like an organization's senior managers, those who would provide the organization with funds seek assurances: stockholders or other investors seek assurance that their equity is safe and will generate future income; creditors seek assurance that the money they have loaned will be repaid on time with interest. The security sought by these sources of new capital rests, at least partly, on confidence that the organization will prosper despite any accidental losses that might befall it. Consequently, an organization's ability to attract willing investors depends to a significant degree on the effectiveness of its risk management program to protect investors' capital against the cost of accidental losses.

Reduce Downside Risk

Downside risks, including losses and failures, are an inevitable aspect of any type of business or speculative risk. For example, a company has downside risk whenever it introduces a new product. A financial institution has downside risk every time it makes a loan or an investment. Operational risk is a part of an organization's processes, and the downside risks include delays, errors, cost increases, and the failure of any aspect of the operation. Reducing downside risk provides similar organizational benefits as reducing the deterrence effects of hazard risks.

To reduce downside risks, organizations can use stop-loss limits. This technique has been used successfully in financial firms to reduce market risk, but it also applies to other types of risk. In operational risk, for example, an organization can have triggers in place whenever operations hit a predetermined stop-loss limit. Management can then review what happened and determine the best course of action in view of the organization's risk appetite.[2]

Manage Downside Risk

Although it cannot eliminate downside risk, risk management can help an organization meet its objectives. See the exhibit "Example of Risk Management Failure at Metallgesellschaft."

> **Example of Risk Management Failure at Metallgesellschaft**
>
> In 1992, an American subsidiary of Metallgesellschaft (MG), Metallgesellschaft Refining and Marketing (MGRM), began using a strategy of agreements to sell petroleum products at prices above the current market price over a ten-year period. MGRM hedged these long-term commitments by purchasing short-term energy futures. Their theory was, if oil prices dropped, the fixed-price positions would gain while the futures positions would lose money. Conversely, if oil prices rose, the futures positions would gain while the fixed-price positions would lose. However, when oil prices actually dropped, MGRM had margin calls on the futures positions, which resulted in a cash flow crisis. MG bailed out MGRM at a cost of more than $1 billion.
>
> The risk management failure included failure to recognize funding risk and a mismatch between long and short positions.

James Lam, Enterprise Risk Management: From Incentives to Controls, John Wiley & Sons, Inc., 2003, pp. 12-13. [DA08659]

However, as illustrated in the example of MG and its subsidiary, MGRM, the risk management strategy used must be well thought out so that the risk management itself does not increase risk. Hedging is an example of a risk-management technique that can be used to manage downside risk resulting from market volatility, but it must be well designed and executed.

Intelligent Risk Taking

Successful organizations usually take risks to grow and increase profit. This type of risk can create a positive or a negative outcome. Decisions regarding new opportunities should be based on the organization's **risk appetite**.

Risk appetite
The events or perils and levels of impact an organization intends to retain, treat, and monitor.

A benefit of risk management includes providing the organization with a framework to analyze the risks associated with an opportunity and then to manage those risks. For example, an organization might consider whether to expand into a new product line. Risk management can help the organization decide if the potential rewards are greater than the downside risks. If the organization decides to go forward with the new product line, risk management can assist in designing a process to manage the associated risks.

Maximize Profitability

Risk management can help an organization achieve the optimal risk-adjusted return on capital. If an organization does not take enough risk, its capital may be underutilized. However, if an organization takes on too much risk, it may exceed its capability to withstand potential losses.

Risk management provides an organization with information to evaluate the potential risk-adjusted return on its activities and to manage the risks associated with those activities. For example, an organization may consider whether to increase its dividend to shareholders versus investing in a new product. Although the same amount of capital may be considered for each option, the

risk-adjusted return will not be the same. Risk managers can help the organization evaluate the risks and potential return of each option and their effects on the organization meeting its objectives.

Holistic Risk Management

Traditional risk management was conducted in silos within an organization. For example, a manufacturing organization would typically have the risk-management function manage hazard risk, the finance function manage financial risks such as credit and exchange-rate risk, the operations function manage operational risks such as equipment failures, and the information technology function manage cyber risk. This fragmented approach can miss critical risks to the organization and fails to provide senior management with a picture of the organization's risk portfolio and profile.

In the example of the manufacturing organization, the risk-management function may not be aware of the age and condition of equipment in the plants if this equipment is not insured. Operations may not be aware of the risks presented by some of the older equipment, and its request to senior management for a capital expenditure for new equipment may be turned down. A piece of machinery then malfunctions and causes a fire, rendering the plant unusable for a year and delaying production.

An integrated, holistic approach that manages risk across all levels and functions within an organization presents a more complete picture of an organization's risk portfolio and profile. This picture allows for better decisions and improved outcomes for senior management. In the example of the manufacturing organization, if there was a complete understanding of the risks the equipment presented, senior management may have allocated capital to replacing the equipment instead of making a different investment.

Legal and Regulatory Requirements

Because of the failure of large organizations, such as Enron, and the financial crisis, legislation and regulation in the U.S. require public companies to use and report on risk management. In 2009, the Securities and Exchange Commission (SEC) approved a rule requiring corporate disclosure about risk. The Sarbanes-Oxley Act of 2002 requires both the management of public companies and their auditors to assess and report on financial risk and controls. The Dodd-Frank Act of 2010 requires that financial bank holding companies and certain other public companies have a risk committee, and at least one member of the committee must be a risk-management expert. Basel III and Solvency II in Europe also have risk-management requirements for financial firms and insurers.

One of the benefits of risk management is that organizations with effective risk-management programs will be able to comply with the recent regulatory requirements. Additionally, external auditors will be able to report on these risk-management processes to satisfy the reporting requirements.

Benefits for the Economy

The economy at both local and national levels incurs certain costs associated with risk and its management, as well as uncertainty about future losses. For example, a major hurricane can have widespread effects on the national economy, not just on individual organizations. Beyond a single loss occurrence like a hurricane, the cumulative effect of many smaller losses also adversely affects the national and local economies. For example, many retail stores in a shopping mall would suffer reduced sales if one of the anchor stores were closed because of an accidental loss. Depending on the magnitude of the loss and the length of time required for the anchor store to recover, the local community may sustain lost jobs, reduced tax revenue, and an overall reduction in the quality of life that was enjoyed when the mall was fully operational and thriving.

An economy's cost of risk management includes the resources consumed by or devoted to combating losses. For example, uncertainty throughout the economy causes organizations to be more risk averse. This in turn causes allocation of the economy's resources away from assets or activities that seem to be too risky so that the economy is not as productive as it might otherwise be. Consequently, average living standards can be reduced. Risk management benefits the entire economy by reducing waste of resources, improving allocation of productive resources, and reducing systemic risk.

Reduced Waste of Resources

Any economy possesses a given quantity of resources with which to produce goods and services. If an accidental loss reduces those resources, such as when a fire or an earthquake demolishes a factory or destroys a highway, that economy's overall productive resources are reduced. Risk management prevents or minimizes the waste of these productive resources.

Whenever there is a risk that accidental losses may occur, some portion of the economy's resources must be devoted to risk management. Allocating such resources is a cost because the resources cannot be used for other purposes that could promote growth. However, without such resources the economy would suffer even more in the event of an accidental loss.

Improved Allocation of Productive Resources

Risk management also improves the allocation of productive resources because, when economic uncertainty is reduced for individual organizations, allocating productive resources is improved. Risk management makes those who own or run an organization more willing to undertake formerly risky activities because they are better protected against the downside of risk. That greater willingness frees senior managers, workers, and suppliers of financial capital to pursue activities that maximize profits, returns on investments, and ultimately wages. Such a shift increases overall productivity within an economy and, on balance, improves everyone's average standard of living.

Reduced Systemic Risk

The Dodd-Frank Act, Solvency II, and Basel III all have the purpose of reducing systemic risk. If a systemically important organization does not have an effective risk-management program, that organization's risks can result in failure not only for the organization but also for the economy.

Not only did the financial crisis of 2008-09 cause widespread negative consequences, such as recessions and high unemployment, it also caused many organizations to become risk averse and, therefore, afraid to invest their capital because of uncertainty. The benefits of risk-management programs at systemically important organizations include reducing systemic risk and reassuring investors and the public about reasonable risk taking that can provide economic growth.

THE RISK MANAGEMENT PROCESS

To fulfill the goals of a risk management program, insurance and risk management professionals use the risk management process, a series of six steps that can be applied to any set of loss exposures.

Application of this process can be initiated by events such as an insurance renewal, a serious claim, a merger or an acquisition, or a new law or regulation that affects the organization. However, the risk management process need not be initiated by events such as these, because it is continuous. The last step in the process, monitoring results and revising the existing risk management program, may lead to the identification of new or additional loss exposures. See the exhibit "The Risk Management Process."

Step 1: Identifying Loss Exposures

A wide variety of methods, such as those listed in the "Identifying Loss Exposures" exhibit, can be used to identify the specific loss exposures that could interfere with the achievement of the organization's goals. These methods offer a systematic approach to identifying loss exposures. They also can enable risk management professionals to identify missed opportunities.

Although loss exposure identification methods are applied individually, they can overlap in their use and function. Despite this overlap, using different methods helps the risk management professional avoid overlooking important loss exposures. For example, loss history documents may not reveal the possibility of loss exposures related to flood, but studying a flood insurance rate map or a cause of loss checklist would. See the exhibit "Identifying Loss Exposures."

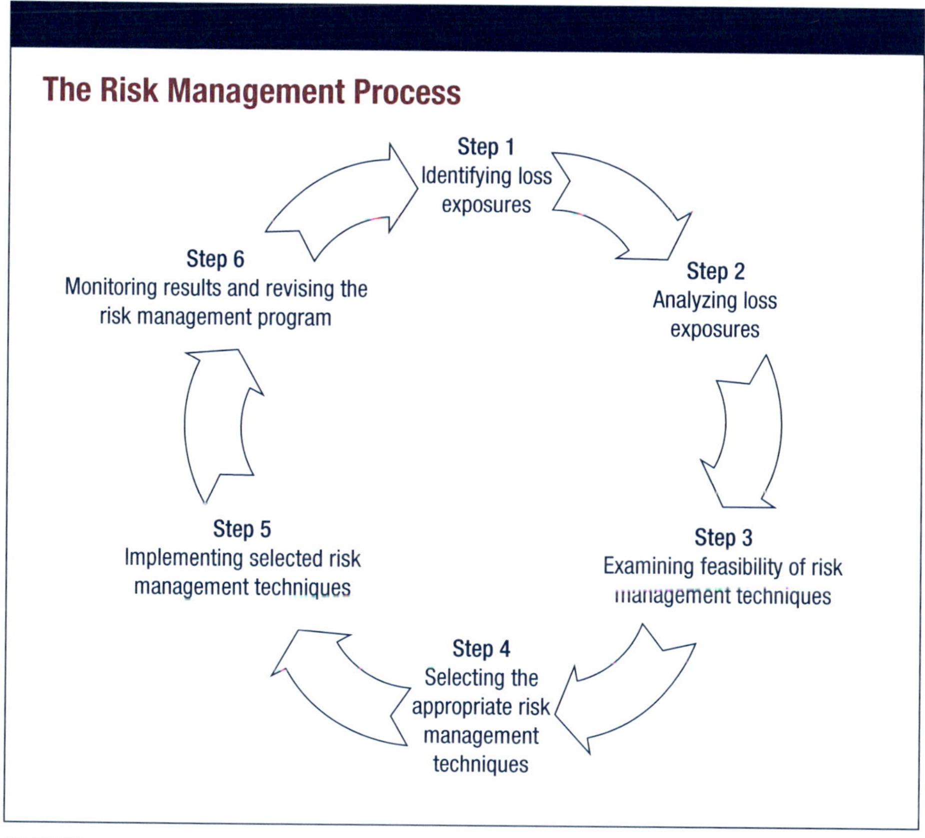

[DA02595]

Step 2: Analyzing Loss Exposures

Analyzing loss exposures is completed by estimating the likely significance of possible losses identified in step one. Together, these two steps constitute the process of assessing loss exposures and are therefore probably the most important steps in the risk management process, because only a properly assessed loss exposure can be appropriately managed. Once a loss exposure has been assessed, the best ways to manage it often become immediately apparent. The remaining steps of the risk management process flow from this assessment.

Loss exposures are analyzed along these four dimensions:

- Loss frequency—the number of losses (such as fires, auto accidents, or liability claims) within a specific time period
- Loss severity—the amount, in dollars, of a loss for a specific occurrence
- Total dollar losses—the total dollar amount of losses for all occurrences during a specific time period
- Timing—when losses occur and when loss payments are made

Identifying Loss Exposures

No single method exists for identifying loss exposures. Risk management professionals may use some or all of the following:

- Document analysis (including any or all of the following):
    - Risk assessment questionnaires and checklists
    - Financial statements and underlying accounting records
    - Contracts
    - Insurance policies
    - Organizational policies and procedures
    - Flowcharts and organizational charts
    - Loss histories
- Compliance reviews
- Inspections
- Expertise within and beyond the organization

[DA02597]

Reviewing these dimensions enables a risk management professional to develop loss projections and prioritize loss exposures so that resources can be properly allocated. Analyzing loss exposures is, in itself, expensive. The cost of risk includes the cost of acquiring risk-related information used in loss forecasts, estimates of future cash flows, and other planning activities. In some cases, this information can actually reduce losses.

For example, recent advances in satellite technology and meteorology provide advance warning that enables people in a hurricane's path to board up windows, evacuate, and implement other loss reduction measures. Such detailed information improves forecast accuracy and can lead to better risk management decisions.

Step 3: Examining the Feasibility of Risk Management Techniques

Loss exposures arise from activities and circumstances that are essential to individuals and to organizations. These loss exposures can be addressed through the risk control techniques and risk financing techniques shown in the "Risk Management Techniques" exhibit. Broadly speaking, risk control techniques are those risk management techniques that minimize the frequency or severity of losses or make losses more predictable. Risk financing techniques are those risk management techniques that generate funds to finance losses that risk control techniques cannot entirely prevent or reduce. See the exhibit "Risk Management Techniques."

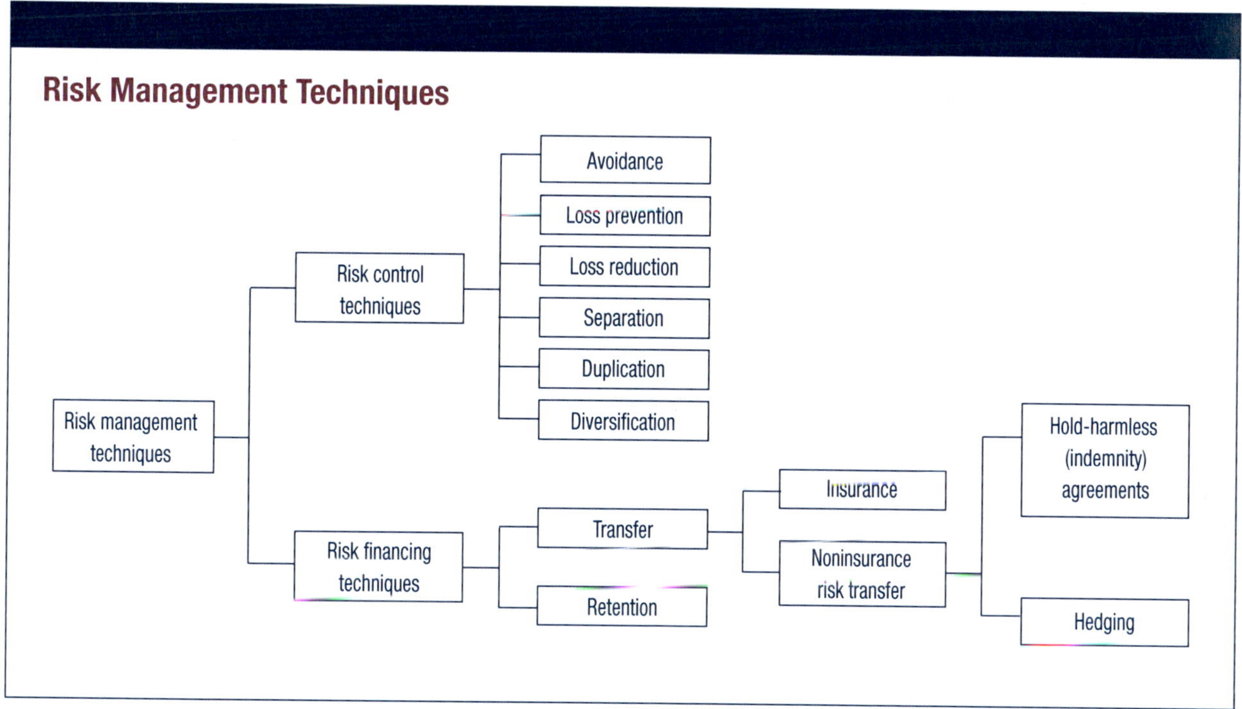

[DA02598]

Risk management techniques are not usually used in isolation. Unless the loss exposure is avoided, organizations typically apply at least one risk control technique and one risk financing technique to each of their significant loss exposures. The risk control technique alters the estimated frequency and severity of loss, and the financing technique pays for losses that occur despite the controls. Most risk control and risk financing techniques can be used with any other control or financing technique.

Step 4: Selecting the Appropriate Risk Management Techniques

Once loss exposures have been identified and analyzed and possible risk management techniques considered, risk management professionals can select those techniques that best prevent or reduce losses and that will adequately finance losses that occur despite prevention and reduction efforts. Selecting the most appropriate mix of risk management techniques is usually based on quantitative financial considerations as well as qualitative, nonfinancial considerations. See the exhibit "Summary of Risk Control and Risk Financing Techniques."

Summary of Risk Control and Risk Financing Techniques

Risk Control Techniques

Avoidance eliminates any possibility of loss. The probability of loss from an avoided loss exposure is zero because an entity decides not to assume a loss exposure in the first place (proactive avoidance) or to eliminate one that already exists (abandonment).

Loss prevention involves reducing the frequency of a particular loss.

Loss reduction involves reducing the severity of a particular loss.

Separation involves dispersing a particular activity or asset over several locations. Separation involves the routine, daily reliance on each of the separated assets or activities, all of which regularly form a portion of the organization's working resources.

Duplication involves relying on backups, that is, spares or duplicates, used only if primary assets or activities suffer loss.

Diversification involves providing a range of products and services used by a variety of customers.

Risk Financing Techniques

Retention involves generating funds from within the organization to pay for losses.

Transfer involves generating funds from outside the organization to pay for losses and includes insurance and noninsurance transfer.

[DA02599]

Financial Considerations

Most private, for-profit organizations choose risk management techniques by using financial criteria—that is, they choose those techniques with the greatest positive (or least negative) effect on the organization's value. The risk management techniques selected should be effective and economical. A technique is effective if it enables an organization to achieve its desired goals, such as to maximize organizational value. A technique is economical if it is the least expensive of the possible effective options.

For all organizations, the potential costs if loss exposures are left completely untreated must be compared with the costs of possible risk management techniques when considering whether a technique is economical. A financial analysis of a risk management technique may be based on three different forecasts.

Based on those considerations, an organization can perform a cost/benefit analysis that identifies the risk management technique, or combination of techniques, that will maximize the organization's value while allowing it to stay within budgetary constraints.

The three forecasts a financial analysis of a risk management technique may be based on are these:

- A forecast of the dimensions of expected losses (frequency, severity, timing of payment, and total dollar losses).
- A forecast, for each feasible combination of risk management techniques, of the effect on the frequency, severity, and timing of these expected losses.
- A forecast of the after-tax costs involved in applying the various risk management techniques. These costs include, for example, the cost of insurance premiums or the expenses associated with installing and maintaining various risk control devices.

Nonfinancial Considerations

Although an organization's goal should be to determine a level of risk management that will maximize its financial value, an organization's value may also stem from ethical and other nonfinancial considerations. Data based on objective risk factors usually are not the only criteria considered in determining appropriate risk management techniques. An organization might also place a great deal of value on maintaining operations or on peace of mind.

An organization's nonfinancial goals can constrain its financial goals, leading to the selection of risk management techniques that, although best for that organization, might be inconsistent with its value maximization goal. For example, a private, family-owned organization might emphasize stability of earnings over time, rather than maximum earnings in any one period. Consequently, the organization might over-invest in loss prevention devices or safety practices rather than absorb the minor losses that these devices or practices are designed to prevent. For similar reasons, a private, family-owned organization would be likely to insure against losses that, from a value maximization standpoint, might be better to retain.

Step 5: Implementing the Selected Risk Management Techniques

After an organization decides which risk management technique(s) to use, the next step is to implement them, which requires cooperation among its departments. Implementing risk management techniques may involve any of these measures:

- Purchasing loss reduction devices
- Contracting for loss prevention services
- Funding retention programs
- Implementing and continually reinforcing loss control programs

- Selecting agents or brokers, insurers, third-party administrators, and other providers for insurance programs
- Requesting insurance policies and paying premiums

Implementing risk management techniques does not necessarily end with the initial implementation of the selected technique. For example, if an organization purchases a building, it almost certainly will also decide to purchase property insurance. However, additional details, such as the exact placement of fire extinguishers, the terms and cost of insurance and noninsurance contract revisions, which insurer to use, the timing of insurance premium payments, or the actual deposit of funds for a retention program or to cover deductibles, must be addressed as the program is implemented.

Step 6: Monitoring Results and Revising the Risk Management Program

Once implemented, a risk management program must be monitored and periodically revised as necessary in order to ensure that it is achieving expected results and to adjust it to accommodate changes in loss exposures and the availability or cost-effectiveness of alternative risk management techniques. Monitoring and revising the risk management program requires four steps: (1) establishing standards of acceptable performance, (2) comparing actual results with these standards, (3) correcting substandard performance or revising standards that prove to be unrealistic, and (4) evaluating standards that have been substantially exceeded.

Establishing Standards of Acceptable Performance

Because of year-to-year variations and the random nature of fortuitous events, the best way to monitor a risk management program may be to combine standards that consider both results and activities. A results standard focuses on actual achievement of goals, regardless of the effort required to achieve them.

For example, a risk management professional might judge a risk management program's performance in terms of a decline in the frequency or severity of employee injuries. However, those results depend largely on fortuitous events, which, by definition, are unpredictable. In contrast, an activity standard focuses on efforts made to achieve a goal regardless of actual results. These independent standards focus mainly on the quality and quantity of the risk management department's activities, such as the installation of new safety equipment designed to protect employees from injury, rather than the actual outcomes.

Risk management professionals often contend that their contribution is as great in years in which there are many losses as in years in which there are few losses, because the losses themselves are beyond their control. In fact, risk management professionals may be even more valuable to their organizations when losses are severe because of the assistance that they can give to

the organization in dealing with those losses. Therefore, risk management professionals have sought performance standards that are not solely dependent on the organization's somewhat uncontrollable loss record. Although results standards are important, activities standards are necessary to obtain a complete picture of the success or failure of a risk management program.

Comparing Actual Results With Standards

A proper standard for evaluating risk management performance includes specifications for how results or performance will be measured. A good standard includes target activity levels or results, or at least desired directions of change.

For example, if an organization had a risk management goal of preventing accidents involving its employees, a results standard could be formulated as a maximum number of accidents per employee hour worked, or at least as a decrease in the number of accidents from one year to the next. A comparison of the actual number of accidents that occur with the number established in the results standard will indicate whether risk management activities are achieving the desired results.

Alternatively, an activity standard relating to the same employee accidents could specify, and provide a schedule for, when an organization's employees should receive safety training updates. The comparison of results against this activity standard would not consider the number of employee accidents, but instead determine whether all employees received the level of training established by the standard.

Correcting Substandard Performance

The risk management professional should also develop a plan for addressing substandard performance. For example, if the number of safety inspections is below that required by the standard, the risk management professional should include a plan to increase their frequency. If retained losses are growing faster than expected, then the risk management professional should determine how retention levels and, perhaps, risk control techniques should be reevaluated.

Substandard performance does not necessarily indicate that the performance itself is the problem. The standard may, in fact, be inappropriate. A risk management program should change when loss exposures change.

Similarly, the standards by which that program is evaluated must be reexamined and possibly altered if the environment within which the risk management program operates also changes. For example, increases in inflation, changes in the volume or nature of an organization's activities, and cyclical or long-term movements in insurance markets or money markets may require adjustments in standards by which acceptable risk management performance is evaluated.

Although changes in risk management standards should not be arbitrary, the continuing need for change should be recognized. Therefore, when monitoring a risk management program, the standards for evaluating that program should also be evaluated, and, when appropriate, revised to accommodate new situations.

Evaluating Standards That Have Been Substantially Exceeded

Performance should ideally meet or exceed a standard. However, if performance substantially exceeds a standard, then the risk management professional should determine why. One reason may be the superior skills of the employee or employees involved in implementing the standard. Another alternative is that the standard is not sufficiently demanding. The risk management professional should, if appropriate, revise the standard so that it more accurately reflects the performance potential of the employees and the organization.

Although monitoring results and revising the risk management program is listed as the final step of the risk management process, it is often the first step for a risk management professional who is taking control of an organization's risk management program. Unless the organization is a start-up, it probably has some (either formal or informal) risk management program in place. Once the risk management program has been properly evaluated, the risk management professional begins the risk management process again. The steps of the risk management process are applied under the revised risk management program, which may now have different program goals or face a new set of organizational risks.

RISK MANAGEMENT PROGRAM GOALS

Senior management support is essential to an effective and efficient risk management program. To gain that support, a risk management program should promote the organization's overall goals. With a clear understanding of the organization's overall goals, a risk management program's goals can be tailored to support the organization's goals.

Risk management program goals are typically divided into two categories: pre-loss goals and post-loss goals. Possible **pre-loss goals** include economy of operations, tolerable uncertainty, legality, and social responsibility. **Post-loss goals** broadly describe the degree of recovery that an organization will strive to reach following a loss. Possible post-loss goals include survival, continuity of operations, profitability, earnings stability, social responsibility, and growth.

Pre-loss goals

Goals to be accomplished before a loss, involving social responsibility, externally imposed goals, reduction of anxiety, and economy.

Post-loss goals

Risk management program goals that should be in place in the event of a significant loss.

Pre-Loss Goals

Regardless of loss experience, every organization has operational goals that are vital to its success that the risk management program should support. Four such operational goals include these:

- Economy of operations
- Tolerable uncertainty
- Legality
- Social responsibility

Although these are not the only possible operational goals, they are typical of the types of operational goals that pre-loss risk management activities are designed to support.

Economy of Operations

A risk management program should operate economically and efficiently; that is, the organization generally should not incur substantial costs in exchange for slight benefits. One way to measure the economy of a risk management program is through benchmarking, in which an organization's risk management costs are compared with those of similar organizations. One such study, conducted annually, is the *Risk and Insurance Management Society (RIMS) Benchmark Survey*.

Tolerable Uncertainty

Tolerable uncertainty involves keeping managers' uncertainty about losses at tolerable levels. Managers should be able to make and implement decisions effectively without being unduly affected by uncertainty. Therefore, risk management professionals typically seek to implement a risk management program that assures managers that whatever might happen will be within the bounds of what was anticipated and will be effectively treated by the risk management program.

Although a risk management program should make all personnel aware of potential loss exposures, the program should also provide assurances through both risk control and risk financing that loss exposures are being managed well.

Legality

The risk management program should help to ensure that the organization's legal obligations are satisfied. These legal obligations will typically be based on:

- Standard of care that is owed to others
- Contracts entered into by the organization
- Federal, state, and local laws and regulations

A risk management professional has an essential role in helping the organization avoid liability by meeting the standard of care that it owes to others. The risk management professional and the organization's legal counsel manage lawsuits brought by others that arise from the organization's wrongful or negligent acts or omissions.

Some public and charitable entities are immune from negligence claims because of long-standing constitutional and other judicial doctrines that exempt them. However, such immunities have eroded over time, and many entities that might be eligible for such immunity choose to purchase liability insurance rather than invoke it.

The risk management professional should be aware of the organization's contractual obligations as well as the contractual obligations that others owe to it. If the organization does not fulfill its obligations under a contract, the other party may bring a lawsuit against the organization for breach of contract. If the other party does not fulfill its obligation and the organization does not pursue the matter, the other party may be relieved of its obligations under the contract.

Risk management professionals also need to be aware of the federal, state, and local laws and regulations that apply to their organizations and should work with other employees to ensure compliance. Examples of laws and regulations of particular concern to the risk management function are occupational health and safety regulations, labeling requirements for consumer products, regulations about hazardous waste disposal, and statutes establishing mandatory insurance requirements.

Social Responsibility

Social responsibility, which is both a pre-loss and a post-loss goal for many organizations, includes acting ethically and fulfilling obligations to the community and society as a whole. Beyond the altruistic interests of the organization's owners, many organizations justify pursuing this goal because of its potential to enhance the organization's reputation.

For public entities and not-for-profit organizations, social responsibility might be the overriding pre-loss goal, even surpassing the need for economy of operations. Public entities exist to fulfill the needs of their constituents, so their purpose is to promote social goals. Similarly, not-for-profit organizations are chartered to meet the needs of members, subscribers, or students, and this often requires a social responsibility focus.

Post-Loss Goals

Post-loss goals are based on the operating and financial conditions that the organization's senior management would consider acceptable after a significant foreseeable loss. These are six possible post-loss goals:

- Survival
- Continuity of operations
- Profitability
- Earnings stability
- Social responsibility
- Growth

After a severe loss, the most basic goal is survival, while the most ambitious goal is uninterrupted growth. The more ambitious a particular post-loss goal, the more difficult and costly it is to achieve.

Survival

Survival is a fundamental post-loss goal. For individuals, survival means staying alive. For organizations, survival means resuming operations to some extent after an adverse event. Survival does not necessarily mean returning to the condition that existed before loss. Within that context, an organization survives a loss whenever that loss does not permanently halt its production and the incomes of those who work for or own it.

Examples of losses that could prevent an organization's survival include these:

- Its only office or plant is destroyed.
- A legal liability judgment or an out-of-court settlement drains its cash and credit resources.
- The death or disability of a key employee (such as an executive or a technician) deprives it of essential leadership or of some vital expertise.

Continuity of Operations

Continuity of operations is an important post-loss goal for many private organizations and an essential goal for all public entities. Although the survival goal requires that no loss (no matter how severe) permanently shut down an organization, the goal of continuity of operations is more demanding. With continuity as a goal, no loss can be allowed to interrupt the organization's operations for any appreciable time.

Within the context of continuity, "appreciable" is a relative term and depends on the goods or services produced. One organization may be unable to tolerate even a few days' shutdown, whereas another organization's output might be continuous even when some of its activities halt for a month or more.

When an organization's senior management sets continuity of operations as a goal, its risk management professional must have a clear, detailed understanding of the specific operations whose continuity is essential and the maximum tolerable interruption interval for each operation.

Any organization for which continuous operation is essential must take steps, and probably incur additional expenses, to forestall an intolerable shutdown. Such steps include these:

- Identify activities whose interruptions cannot be tolerated
- Identify the types of events that could interrupt such activities
- Determine the standby resources that must be immediately available to counter the effects of those losses
- Ensure the availability of the standby resources at even the most unlikely and difficult times

The last step, ensuring the availability of standby resources, is likely to add to an organization's expenses, and, accordingly, achieving the continuity of operations goal tends to be more costly than the more basic goal of survival. However, for organizations that give high priority to continuity of operations, this added cost is preferable to the alternative of business interruption.

For public entities—particularly cities, counties, and other governing bodies, as well as schools and public utilities—maintaining public services without interruption is perhaps the most important risk management goal. Any sustained interruption in police or fire protection, supplies of clean water, removal of trash or sewage, or public education can be catastrophic. The essential purpose of most public entities is to provide some service, and therefore they are willing to commit significant resources to comprehensive contingency plans.

Profitability

As well as considering the physical effects a loss might have on an organization's operations, senior management may also be concerned with how such a loss would affect the organization's profitability. In a for-profit organization, the goal is to generate net income (profit). In a not-for-profit organization, the goal is to operate within the budget. An organization's senior management might have established a minimum amount of profit (or surplus in not-for-profit organizations) that no loss can be allowed to reduce.

To achieve the specified minimum amount of profit, the risk management program is likely to emphasize insurance and other means of transferring the financial consequences of loss so that actual financial results fall within an acceptable range. An organization that requires a minimum profit tends to spend more on risk management, particularly risk financing, than does an organization that is prepared to tolerate an occasional unprofitable financial result.

Earnings Stability

Rather than strive for the highest possible level of profit (or surplus) in a given period, some organizations emphasize earnings stability over time. Striving for earnings stability requires precision in forecasting risk management costs, as well as lower retention levels and a willingness on the part of the organization to spend more on risk transfer mechanisms. A risk management professional focusing on earnings stability would seek ways of creating consistent results over time rather than choose actions that might produce fluctuating results.

Social Responsibility

Losses affect an organization's ability to fulfill its real or perceived obligations to the community and to society as a whole. Organizational disruptions have implications for relationships with customers, suppliers, employees, taxpayers, and other members of the public. These relationships, even though they may not involve legal obligations, are often the focus of the organization's overall mission.

Many not-for-profit organizations and public entities are unable to distinguish between the post-loss goals of survival and social responsibility because of their focus on community service. However, the post-loss goal of social responsibility does not apply only to not-for profit and public entities.

For example, consider an organization with strong ties to the local community that relies heavily on the support of the customers and suppliers in its neighborhood. If such an organization makes a social commitment, such as sponsoring a local charity event, then the failure to honor that commitment could seriously damage its reputation and correspondingly affect its future business operations. Such an organization would want to ensure that its risk management program provided sufficient protection against losses so that the organization's ability to meet its social responsibilities would not be seriously diminished in the event of a loss.

Growth

Emphasizing the post-loss goal of growth—for example, increasing market share, the size and scope of activities or products, or assets—might have two distinctly opposing effects on an organization's risk management program. Those effects depend on the managers' and owners' tolerance for uncertainty.

If striving to expand makes managers and owners more willing to accept greater uncertainty in exchange for minimizing risk management costs, the organization's explicit costs for risk management could be fairly low. Such an organization's risk management professional might find it difficult to obtain a budget adequate to protect against expanding loss exposures. Moreover, if such an organization suffers a severe loss for which it was not adequately prepared, its real cost of risk management—more accurately, its real cost of not

effectively managing loss exposures—might be significant and involve sacrificing much of the growth it has attained.

In contrast, the goal of risk management in a growing organization might be to protect its expanding resources so that its path of expansion is not blocked or reversed by a substantial loss. Risk management costs in this scenario are likely to be high because such an organization might seek increased earnings (growth) rather than survival or earnings stability. Consequently, the organization lowers its tolerance for unanticipated loss and requires greater emphasis on risk control and risk financing.

Conflict Between Goals

Pre-loss and post-loss goals are interrelated and sometimes conflict with each other. Although conflicts may arise between post-loss goals, it is more common for post-loss goals to conflict with pre-loss goals, or for pre-loss goals to compete with each other. Therefore, an organization might discover that fully achieving all risk management program goals simultaneously is impossible.

Achieving any post-loss goal involves expending risk management resources, which may conflict with the pre-loss goal of economy of operations. The more ambitious and costly the post-loss goal, the greater the conflict with the economy of operations goal. The economy of operations goal may also conflict with the tolerable uncertainty goal.

To provide management with the desired level of assurance, the risk management professional must be confident that certain organizational post-loss goals will be achieved. Gaining that confidence requires allocating some of the organization's limited resources, including money, to risk management efforts such as purchasing insurance, installing guards on machinery to prevent industrial accidents, or maintaining duplicate copies of records in case originals are destroyed.

The legality and social responsibility goals may also conflict with the economy of operations goal. Some externally imposed obligations, such as safety standards dictated by building codes, may be nonnegotiable. Therefore, the costs imposed by legal obligations must be accepted as unavoidable, regardless of the economy of operations goal.

Obligations imposed by social responsibility, such as employee benefits subject to collective bargaining agreements, may be negotiable. However, although meeting social responsibility might raise costs in the short term, it can have worthwhile long-term benefits that make the costs acceptable.

ELEMENTS OF A LOSS EXPOSURE

Individuals and organizations incur losses when assets they own decrease in value. Situations or conditions that expose assets to loss are called loss exposures.

Every **loss exposure** has three elements:

Loss exposure
Any condition or situation that presents a possibility of loss, whether or not an actual loss occurs.

- An asset exposed to loss
- Cause of loss (also called a peril)
- Financial consequences of that loss

All three elements can be described for each of these four basic types of loss exposures: property, liability, personnel, and net income.

The three elements are necessary to completely describe a loss exposure. For example, identifying a building (an asset exposed to loss) is not sufficient for describing that building as a loss exposure. It is also necessary to identify the causes of loss associated with that building (such as fire, flood, or hurricane) and the financial consequences of that loss (such as a decline in the market value of the building or in the income produced by the use of the building).

Asset Exposed to Loss

The first element of a loss exposure is an asset exposed to loss. This asset can be anything of value an individual or organization has that is exposed to loss. Assets owned by organizations can include property (such as buildings, automobiles, and office furniture), investments, money that is owed to them, and cash. In addition to these are assets that are often overlooked, including intangible assets (such as patents, copyrights, and trademarks) and human resources.

Individuals may have many of the same assets as organizations (property, money, investments, and so on). In addition, individuals may have intangible assets such as professional qualifications, a unique skill set, or valuable experience.

Cause of Loss

The second element of a loss exposure is cause of loss. Fire, windstorm, explosion, and theft are examples of causes of loss that present a possibility of loss to property. For example, wind-driven fire can burn down a home, causing a total loss to the homeowners' property. A burglar can break into a plumbing supply store, stealing copper fittings, causing a loss to the owner's inventory supply.

Financial Consequences of Loss

The third element of a loss exposure is the financial consequences of the loss. The financial consequences of a loss depend on the type of loss exposure, the cause of loss, and the loss frequency and severity. Some financial consequences can be established with a high degree of certainty; for example, the value of a building that has been damaged by fire.

Other financial consequences may be more difficult to determine, such as the value of business lost while the building damaged by fire is being restored. In addition, although some financial consequences are known as soon as a loss occurs, such as the value of property lost in a robbery, others may take months or years to determine, such as the ultimate value of liability claims regarding a defective product.

IDENTIFYING LOSS EXPOSURES

For individuals, common property and liability exposures can be identified by a property-casualty insurance producer as part of an assessment of insurance needs. Similarly, individuals' net income loss exposures can be identified by life insurance producers as part of a needs assessment for life and health insurance products. For organizations, loss exposure identification is typically more complex, using a variety of methods and sources of information.

The methods of information that enable an organization to take a systematic approach to identifying loss exposures include these:

- Document analysis
- Compliance review
- Inspections
- Expertise within and beyond the organization

Document Analysis

The variety of documents used and produced by an organization can be a key source of information regarding loss exposures. Some of these documents are standardized and originate from outside the organization, such as questionnaires, checklists, and surveys. These standardized documents broadly categorize the loss exposures that most organizations typically face and are completed with information that is exclusive to the organization.

Other documents are organization-specific, such as financial statements and accounting records, contracts, insurance policies, policy and procedure manuals, flowcharts and organizational charts, and loss histories. Although the use and function of the various documents may overlap, causing possible duplication in loss exposure identification, reviewing multiple documents is necessary to avoid failing to identify important loss exposures.

In addition to the documents discussed in this section, virtually any document connected to an organization's operations also reveals something about its loss exposures. For example, Web sites, news releases, or reports from external organizations such as A.M. Best or D&B may indicate something about an organization's loss exposures. Although it is not feasible to review every document that refers to an organization, some of these additional sources may be useful.

Risk Assessment Questionnaires and Checklists

Standardized documents published outside an organization, such as insurance coverage checklists and risk assessment questionnaires, broadly categorize the loss exposures that most organizations typically face. A variety of checklists and questionnaires have been published by insurers, the American Management Association (AMA), the International Risk Management Institute (IRMI), the Risk and Insurance Management Society (RIMS), and others.

Although some organizations or trade associations have developed specialized checklists or questionnaires for their members, most are created by insurers and concentrate on identifying insurable hazard risks. Some focus on listing the organization's assets, whereas others focus on identifying potential causes of loss that could affect the organization.

Checklists typically capture less information than questionnaires. Although checklists can help an organization identify its loss exposures, they do not show how those loss exposures support or affect specific organizational goals. Linking loss exposures with the goals they support can be useful in analyzing the potential financial consequences of loss. Therefore, checklists are of limited benefit in the analysis step of the risk management process.

A questionnaire captures more descriptive information than a checklist. For example, as well as identifying a loss exposure, a questionnaire may capture information about the amounts or values exposed to loss. The questionnaire can be designed to include questions that address key property, liability, net income, and at least some personnel loss exposures.

Questionnaire responses can enable an insurance or a risk management professional to identify and analyze an organization's loss exposures regarding real property, equipment, products, key customers, neighboring properties, operations, and so on. Additionally, the logical sequencing of questions helps in developing a more detailed examination of the loss exposures an organization faces.

Both checklists and questionnaires may be produced by insurers (such questionnaires are known as insurance surveys). Most of the questions on these surveys relate to loss exposures for which commercial insurance is generally available.

Risk management or risk assessment questionnaires have a broader focus and address both insurable and uninsurable loss exposures. However, a disadvantage of risk assessment questionnaires is that they typically can be completed only with considerable expense, time, and effort and still may not identify all possible loss exposures.

Standardizing a survey or questionnaire has both advantages and disadvantages. Standardized questions are relevant for most organizations and can be answered by persons who have little risk management expertise.

However, no standardized questionnaire can be expected to uncover all the loss exposures particularly characteristic of a given industry, let alone those unique to a given organization. Additionally, the questionnaire's structure might not stimulate the respondent to do anything more than answer the questions asked; that is, it will elicit only the information that is specifically requested. Consequently, it may not reveal key information. Therefore, questionnaires should ideally be used in conjunction with other identification and analysis methods.

Because even a thoroughly completed checklist or questionnaire does not ensure that all loss exposures have been recognized, experienced insurance and risk management professionals often follow up with additional questions that are not on the standardized document.

Financial Statements and Underlying Accounting Records

Risk management professionals with accounting or finance expertise sometimes begin the loss exposure identification process by reviewing an organization's financial statements, including the balance sheet, income statement, statement of cash flows, and supporting statements. As well as identifying current loss exposures, financial statements and accounting records can be used to identify any future plans that could lead to new loss exposures.

Balance sheet

The financial statement that reports the assets, liabilities, and owners' equity of an organization as of a specific date.

Income statement

The financial statement that reports an organization's profit or loss for a specific period by comparing the revenues generated with the expenses incurred to produce those revenues.

Statement of cash flows

The financial statement that summarizes the cash effects of an organization's operating, investing, and financing activities during a specific period.

An organization's **balance sheet** is the financial statement that reports the assets, liabilities, and owners' equity of the organization as of a specific date. Owners' equity, or net worth, is the amount by which assets exceed liabilities. Asset entries indicate property values that could be reduced by loss. Liability entries show what the organization owes and enable the risk management professional to explore two types of loss exposures: (1) liabilities that could be increased or created by a loss and (2) obligations (such as mortgage payments) that the organization must fulfill, even if it were to close temporarily as a result of a business interruption.

The **income statement** is particularly useful in identifying net income loss exposures; that is, those loss exposures that reduce revenue or increase expenses.

The **statement of cash flows** (also called the statement of sources and uses of funds) is the financial statement that summarizes the cash effects of an organization's operating, investing, and financing activities during a specific period.

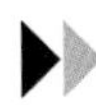

Funds-flow analysis on the statement of cash flows can identify the amounts of cash either subject to loss or available to meet continuing obligations. For example, the statement of cash flows would indicate the amount of cash that is typically on hand to pay for any losses resulting from loss exposures that have been retained by the organization.

Financial statements can reveal that an organization is subject to significant financial risks, such as fluctuations in the value of investments, interest rate volatility, foreign exchange rate changes, or commodity price swings. However, the primary advantage of financial statements from a risk management professional's perspective is that they help to identify major categories of loss exposures.

For example, property loss exposures can be seen in the asset section of the balance sheet. Some liability loss exposures, especially contractual obligations such as loans or mortgages, can be seen in the liabilities section of the balance sheet. The potential effects of net income loss exposures can be seen by comparing revenues with expenses on the income statement.

The major disadvantage of using financial statements for identifying loss exposures is that although they identify most of the major categories of loss exposures (property, liability and net income are identified but personnel loss exposures are not), they do not identify or quantify the individual loss exposures. For example, the balance sheet may show that there is $5 million in property exposed to loss, but it does not specify how many properties make up that $5 million, where those properties are located, or how much each individual property is worth. Moreover, the real and personal property values recorded in financial statements are based on accounting conventions and are not accurate for purposes of insurance or risk management.

Another disadvantage is that financial statements depict past activities—for example, revenue that has already been earned, expenses that have already been incurred, prior valuations of assets and liabilities, and business operations that have already taken place. They are of limited help in identifying projected values or future events. Therefore, even after using financial statements for loss exposure identification, insurance and risk management professionals still need to project what events might occur in the future, determine how these future events could change loss exposures, and analyze and quantify potential losses accordingly.

Contracts

A contract is an agreement entered into by two or more parties that specifies the parties' responsibilities to one another. Analyzing an organization's contracts may help identify its property and liability loss exposures and help determine who has assumed responsibility for which loss exposures. It is often necessary to consult with legal experts when interpreting contracts.

Contract analysis can both identify the loss exposures generated or reduced by an organization's contracts and ensure that the organization is not assuming

liability that is disproportionate to its stake in the contract. Ongoing contract analysis is part of monitoring and maintaining a risk management program.

Entering into contracts can either increase or reduce an organization's property and liability loss exposures. For example, a contract to purchase property or equipment will increase the organization's property loss exposures, whereas a contract to sell property or equipment will reduce property loss exposures.

Hold-harmless agreement (or indemnity agreement)
A contractual provision that obligates one of the parties to assume the legal liability of another party.

Indemnification
The process of restoring an individual or organization to a pre-loss financial condition.

A contract can generate liability loss exposures in two ways. First, the organization can accept the loss exposures of another party through a contract, such as a **hold-harmless agreement** (sometimes referred to as an indemnity agreement). For example, an organization may enter into a hold-harmless agreement with its distributor under which the organization agrees to indemnify the distributor (pay the losses for which the distributor is liable) if the distributor is found liable for a products liability claim. **Indemnification** is the process of restoring an individual or organization to a pre-loss financial condition.

The second way a contract may generate a liability loss exposure is if the organization fails to fulfill a valid contract. For example, if an organization agrees to deliver manufactured goods to a distributor and then fails to deliver those goods, the distributor is entitled to bring a legal claim against the organization. The distributor's claim presents a liability loss exposure for the organization.

Alternatively, an organization can reduce or eliminate liability loss exposures by entering into a contract that transfers its liability to another organization. For example, an organization can enter into a hold-harmless agreement under which the second party agrees to indemnify the organization in the event of a liability claim.

Insurance Policies

Although insurance is a means of risk financing, reviewing insurance policies can also be helpful in risk assessment.

Analyzing insurance policies reveals many of the insurable loss exposures that an organization faces. However, this analysis may either indicate the organization is insured for more loss exposures than it really has, or, alternatively, may not show all the loss exposures the organization faces.

As insurance policies typically are standardized forms, an organization does not necessarily face every loss exposure covered by its policies. Furthermore, the organization may face many other loss exposures that either cannot be covered by insurance policies or are covered by policies the organization has chosen not to purchase.

To identify insurance coverage that an organization has not purchased, and therefore potentially identify insurable loss exposures that have not been insured, a risk management professional can compare his or her organization's coverage against an industry checklist of insurance policies currently in effect.

Organizational Policies and Records

Loss exposures can also be identified using organizational policies and records, such as corporate by-laws, board minutes, employee manuals, procedure manuals, mission statements, and risk management policies. For example, policy and procedure manuals may identify some of the organization's property loss exposures by referencing equipment, or pinpoint liability loss exposures by referencing hazardous materials with which employees come into contact. See the exhibit "Internal Documents as Loss Exposures."

Internal Documents as Loss Exposures

Internal documents, in addition to identifying loss exposures, need to be analyzed to determine their appropriateness and consistency with external publications. An organization's internal documents are not typically written in anticipation that they will be viewed outside the organization. However, many internal documents are used during legal proceedings and therefore may present a potential liability loss exposure to the organization. This illustrates the need for internal documents to be consistent with external information the organization releases.

[DA02555]

As well as identifying existing loss exposures, some documents may indicate impending changes in loss exposures. For example, board minutes may indicate management's plans to sell or purchase property, thereby either reducing or increasing its property loss exposures.

One drawback to using policies and records to identify loss exposures is the sheer volume of documents that some organizations generate internally. It may be virtually impossible to have one employee or a group of employees examine every internal document. In these instances, insurance and risk management professionals would need to examine a representative sample of documents. This makes the task manageable, but increases the likelihood that not all loss exposures will be identified.

Flowcharts and Organizational Charts

A flowchart is a diagram that depicts the sequence of activities performed by a particular organization or process. An organization can use flowcharts to show the nature and use of the resources involved in its operations as well as the sequence of and relationships between those operations.

A manufacturer's flowchart might start with raw material acquisition and end with the finished product's delivery to the ultimate consumer. Individual entries on the flowchart, including the processes involved and the means by which products move from one process to the next, can help identify loss exposures—particularly critical loss exposures.

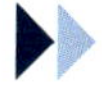

For example, the flowchart might illustrate that every item produced must be spray-painted during the production process. This activity presents a critical property loss exposure, because an explosion at the spray-painting location might disable the entire production line. The simplified flowchart in the exhibit reveals that difficulties with getting the furniture through customs at the Los Angeles Port could disrupt the entire furniture supply chain. See the exhibit "Furniture Manufacturer Flowchart."

Furniture Manufacturer Flowchart

Raw lumber from South America
Raw steel from China
Assembly Plant A Mexico
Assembly Plant B Mexico
Los Angeles Port Customs
Northeast Region Distribution Center
Southeast Region Distribution Center
Midwest Region Distribution Center
West Region Distribution Center

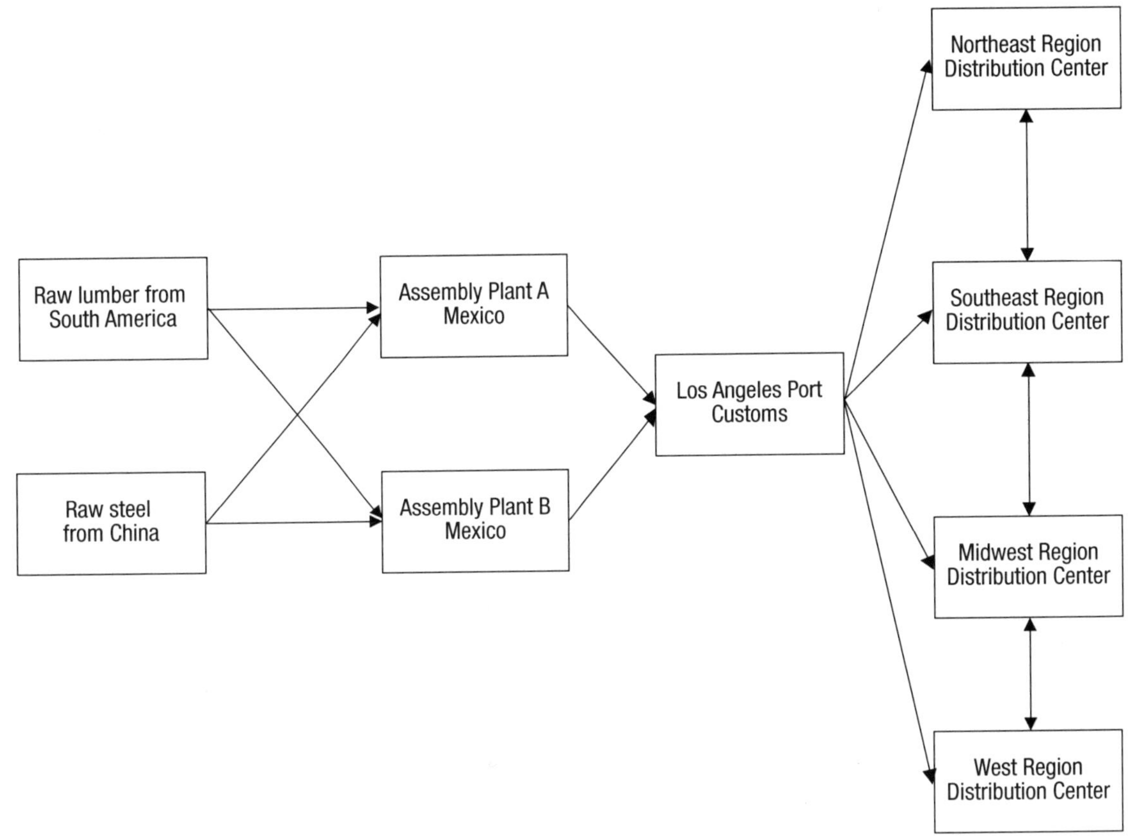

[DA02556]

Information can also be obtained from organizational charts. An organizational chart depicts the hierarchy of an organization's personnel and can help to identify key personnel for whom the organization may have a personnel loss exposure. This chart can also help track the flow of information through an organization and identify any bottlenecks that may exist. Although organizational charts can be fundamental in properly identifying personnel loss exposures, an individual's place on an organizational chart does not guarantee that he or she is a key employee. The organizational chart does not necessarily

reflect the importance of the individual to the continued operation or profitability of the organization.

Loss Histories

Loss history analysis, that is, reviewing an organization's own losses or those suffered by comparable organizations, can help a risk management or an insurance professional to both identify and analyze loss exposures. Loss histories of comparable organizations are particularly helpful if the organization is too small or too new to have a sizeable record of its own past losses, or if the organization's own historical loss records are incomplete.

Any past loss can recur unless the organization has had a fundamental change in operations or property owned. Accordingly, loss histories are often an important indicator of an organization's current or future loss exposures. However, loss histories will not identify any loss exposures that have not resulted in past losses. Therefore, use of loss histories alone is inadequate.

Compliance Review

In addition to document analysis, insurance and risk management professionals may also conduct compliance reviews to identify loss exposures. A compliance review determines an organization's compliance with local, state, and federal statutes and regulations. The organization can conduct most of the compliance review itself if it has adequate in-house legal and accounting resources. Otherwise, it may have to use outside expertise.

The benefit of compliance reviews is that they can help an organization minimize or avoid liability loss exposures. However, a drawback of compliance reviews is that they are expensive and time consuming. Furthermore, because regulations are often changing, remaining in compliance requires ongoing monitoring. As a result, conducting a compliance review simply to identify loss exposures is often impractical. However, because noncompliance is a liability loss exposure, loss exposure identification can be part of the justification of the cost of a compliance review and is an ancillary benefit once a review has been completed.

Personal Inspections

Some loss exposures are best identified by personal inspections, that is, information-gathering visits to critical sites both within and outside an organization. Such visits often reveal loss exposures that would not appear in written descriptions of the organization's operations and therefore should lead to a more complete list of loss exposures.

Personal inspections should ideally be conducted by individuals whose background and skills equip them to identify unexpected, but possible, loss exposures. Additionally, the person conducting the inspection should take

the opportunity to discuss the particular operations with front-line personnel, who are often best placed to identify nonobvious loss exposures. Therefore, a personal inspection can overlap with consulting expertise within and beyond the organization.

Expertise Within and Beyond the Organization

Thorough loss exposure identification should include soliciting expertise both inside and outside the organization. Doing so renders a more complete and objective picture of the organization's loss exposures.

Interviews with employees can be conducted to gather information about their jobs and departments. Whereas an inspection can only reveal what is happening during the inspection, interviews can elicit information about what occurred before the inspection, what might be planned for the future, or what could go or has gone wrong that has not been properly addressed.

Interviews should include a range of employees from every level of the organization. Questionnaires can be designed for use in conjunction with these interviews to ensure that they are comprehensive and are eliciting as much information as possible.

To obtain an external perspective, practitioners in fields such as law, finance, statistics, accounting, auditing, and the technology of the organization's industry can be consulted. The special knowledge of experts in identifying particular loss exposures is an invaluable resource.

Hazard analysis

A method of analysis that identifies conditions that increase the frequency or severity of loss.

One area of specialization that often requires such expert services is **hazard analysis**. For example, a business consultant might identify conditions that cause the organization to overlook opportunities for growth. Alternatively, concerns about environmental hazards might require a specialist to take air or water samples and a specialized laboratory to analyze them. Although hazard analysis is focused on loss exposures that have already been identified, the results of the analysis often identify previously overlooked loss exposures.

Review Questions

1. Explain how risk management practices differ between individuals and organizations.
2. Describe the difference in scope between traditional risk management and enterprise-wide risk management.
3. Explain how the focus of risk management efforts differs for traditional risk management and enterprise-wide risk management.
4. Describe how an organization's total cost of risk associated with an asset or activity is calculated.
5. Describe three benefits to an organization of reducing deterrence effects by risk management.

6. Explain how risk management can help an organization increase intelligent risk taking.
7. Explain how risk management can help an organization maximize its profitability.
8. Describe the benefits of holistic risk management compared with traditional risk management for an organization.
9. Describe three benefits of risk management for the entire economy.
10. List the six steps in the risk management process.
11. Describe four dimensions used to analyze a loss exposure.
12. Describe how an organization uses risk control and risk financing techniques to manage loss exposures.
13. Identify the forecasts an organization might use to analyze the costs of a risk management technique.
14. List the four steps required to monitor and revise a risk management program.
15. Describe four pre-loss operational goals supported by an effective and efficient risk management program.
16. List six possible post-loss goals for an organization after a significant foreseeable loss has occurred.
17. Identify the steps an organization might take to forestall an intolerable shutdown and ensure continuous operations after a loss occurs.
18. Define loss exposure.
19. Identify the three elements of a loss exposure.
20. Identify the types of internal and external documents an organization may use to analyze loss exposures.
21. Describe advantages and disadvantages of using questionnaires in assessing loss exposures.
22. Describe how an organization uses the following documents to identify loss exposures: a. financial statements, b. contracts, c. insurance policies, d. organizational policies and records, e. flowcharts and organizational charts, and f. loss histories.
23. Describe how a compliance review may facilitate the identification of loss exposures.

Application Questions

1. Using the following data, calculate the total cost of risk: costs of accidental losses not reimbursed by insurance, $1.2 million; insurance premiums, $10 million; risk control techniques, $2 million; costs of administering risk management activities, $0.5 million.
2. For each of the following, suggest a standard that a risk management professional might use to gauge performance: a. product shipments to

customers that are damaged in transit, b. customer slip-and-fall injuries in a retail shop, and c. employees injured in warehouse activities.

3. Provide an example of how each of the following risk management program goals can conflict with the pre-loss goal of economy of operations: a. tolerable uncertainty, b. legality, and c. social responsibility.

SUMMARY

Risk management can differ markedly for individuals, small organizations, and large organizations. At whatever level it is practiced, risk management is aimed at dealing economically with risk, whether through an individual's informal efforts or through an organizations's formalized risk management program. Traditionally, risk management has been concerned almost exclusively with pure risk. A new approach, called enterprise-wide risk management, is concerned with all risks, pure and speculative, that an organization faces.

An effective risk-management program provides benefits to an organization in meeting its goals and complying with regulations. Such programs also benefit the economy as a whole by helping to prevent business failures. Additionally, regulators who apply risk-management principles in their functions can help address systemic risk to ensure that risk provides economic benefits rather than negative consequences.

The risk management process consists of six steps that can be applied to any set of loss exposures:

1. Identifying loss exposures
2. Analyzing loss exposures
3. Examining the feasibility of risk management techniques
4. Selecting the appropriate risk management techniques
5. Implementing the selected risk management techniques
6. Monitoring results and revising the risk management program

Risk management program goals are typically divided into two categories: pre-loss goals and post-loss goals. Pre-loss goals include economy of operations, tolerable uncertainty, legality, and social responsibility. Post-loss goals include survival, continuity of operations, profitability, earnings stability, social responsibility, and growth.

Loss exposures are situations or conditions that expose assets to loss. The elements of any loss exposure are an asset exposed to loss, the cause of loss (or peril), and the financial consequences of the loss.

Because identifying loss exposures is the beginning of the risk management process, it should be done thoroughly and systematically. Various methods can be used to identify loss exposures, including document analysis, compliance review, inspections, and expertise within and beyond the organization.

ASSIGNMENT NOTES

1. Ben S. Bernanke, Speech at the Federal Reserve Bank of Chicago's Annual Conference on Bank Structure and Competition, Chicago, May 15, 2008, www.federalreserve.gov/newsevents/speech/bernanke20080515a.htm (accessed February 15, 2012).
2. James Lam, Enterprise Risk Management: From Incentives to Controls, John Wiley & Sons Inc., Hoboken, New Jersey, 2003, pp. 38-39.

Direct Your Learning

3

Traditional and Enterprise Risk Management

Educational Objectives

After learning the content of this assignment, you should be able to:

- Explain how the three elements of a loss exposure apply to the following:
    - Property loss exposures
    - Liability loss exposures
    - Personnel loss exposures
    - Net income loss exposures
- Explain how each of the following can be the basis for legal liability:
    - Torts
    - Contracts
    - Statutes
- Describe negligence claims in terms of:
    - The elements of negligence
    - The required proof of negligence
- Contrast traditional and enterprise risk management.

Outline

Types of Loss Exposures

Legal Liability: Torts, Contracts, and Statutes

Negligence

Traditional Risk Management Versus Enterprise Risk Management (ERM)

Summary

Traditional and Enterprise Risk Management

3

TYPES OF LOSS EXPOSURES

The three elements of loss exposures—the asset exposed to loss, the cause of loss, and the financial consequences of loss—can be applied to each of four different types of loss exposure.

For insurance and traditional risk management purposes, loss exposures are typically divided into these four types:

- Property loss exposures
- Liability loss exposures
- Personnel loss exposures
- Net income loss exposures

Each type is distinguished in relation to how it affects the first element of a loss exposure—that is, the asset exposed to loss.

Property Loss Exposures

A **property loss exposure** is a condition that presents the possibility that a person or an organization will sustain a loss resulting from damage (including destruction, theft, or loss of use) to property in which that person or organization has a financial interest. Property can be categorized as either tangible property or intangible property.

Tangible property is property that has a physical form, such as a piece of equipment. It can be further subdivided into **real property** and **personal property**. **Intangible property** is property that has no physical form, such as a patent or copyright. See the exhibit "Elements of Property Loss Exposures."

Damage to property can cause a reduction in that property's value, sometimes to zero. For example, when property is stolen, the owner suffers a total loss of that property because the owner no longer has use of it. In addition to this loss, property damage can result in a loss of income (net income loss exposure) because the property cannot be used to generate income or because extra expenses are incurred to continue operations.

Property loss exposure
A condition that presents the possibility that a person or an organization will sustain a loss resulting from damage (including destruction, taking, or loss of use) to property in which that person or organization has a financial interest.

Tangible property
Property that has a physical form.

Real property (realty)
Tangible property consisting of land, all structures permanently attached to the land, and whatever is growing on the land.

Personal property
All tangible or intangible property that is not real property.

Intangible property
Property that has no physical form.

Elements of Property Loss Exposures

1. **Asset Exposed to Loss**

- Tangible property
- Real property, such as offices and warehouses
- Personal property, such as office furniture and office equipment
- Intangible property, such as patents, copyrights, trademarks, trade secrets, and customer goodwill

2. **Cause of Loss**

Some of the more frequent causes of loss include the following:

- Lightning or hail
- Tornadoes or high wind
- Water from failure of indoor appliances; heavy rain or flooding; or sewers or drains
- Theft
- Snow or ice
- Fire
- Mold

3. **Financial Consequences of Loss**

The maximum financial consequence of a property loss is limited by the value of the property. However, a property loss may also have an effect on the financial consequences of liability, personnel, or net income losses.

[DA02384]

Liability Loss Exposures

Liability loss exposure
Any condition or situation that presents the possibility of a claim alleging legal responsibility of a person or business for injury or damage suffered by another party.

A **liability loss exposure** results from the claim itself, not necessarily the payment of damages. See the exhibit "Industry Language—Property and Liability Loss Exposures."

Even if a claim is successfully defended, and therefore does not result in payment of damages, the party against whom the claim was made nonetheless incurs defense costs, other claim-related expenses, and potentially adverse publicity, all of which produce a financial loss. See the exhibit "Elements of Liability Loss Exposures."

Personnel Loss Exposures

Personnel loss exposure
A condition that presents the possibility of loss caused by a person's death, disability, retirement, or resignation that deprives an organization of the person's special skill or knowledge that the organization cannot readily replace.

A **personnel loss exposure** is a condition that presents the possibility of loss caused by a key person's death, disability, retirement, or resignation that deprives an organization of that person's special skill or knowledge that the organization cannot readily replace. A key person can be an individual

Industry Language—Property and Liability Loss Exposures

Property

A property loss occurs when a person or an organization sustains a loss as the result of damage (including destruction, taking, or loss of use) to property in which that person or organization has a financial interest. The possibility that such a situation could occur is a property loss exposure.

Insurance professionals often use the term "loss" to mean the event itself. In addition, they often refer to the loss in terms of the applicable property, the cause of loss, the consequences, or the applicable policy.

- When focusing on the type of property, they often refer to a "building loss" or a "personal property loss," regardless of the peril involved.
- When focusing on causes of loss, they often refer to a "fire loss," a "smoke loss," or a "theft loss."
- When focusing on consequences, they often refer to a "business income loss," an "extra expense loss," or an "additional living expense loss," regardless of the type of property or causes of loss involved.
- When focusing on the applicable policy, they often use the policy name or type, such as a "homeowners loss," an "auto loss," or a "business interruption loss."

Similar language is used for loss exposures. Insurance practitioners often refer to a building loss exposure, a fire loss exposure, a homeowners loss exposure, or a business interruption loss exposure.

Liability

Insurance and risk management professionals often refer to specific types of liability losses in terms of the applicable coverage or the activity leading to the loss. For example, a claim for damages arising out of a product defect might be referred to as a "products liability loss," and the possibility of such a claim might be referred to as a "products liability loss exposure." Similarly, owning, operating, maintaining, or using an automobile might be referred to as "auto liability" or "auto liability loss exposures."

[DA02385]

employee, an owner, an officer or a manager of the organization, or a group of employees who possess special skills or knowledge that is valuable to the organization. See the exhibit "Elements of Personnel Loss Exposures."

For example, the possibility that the chief executive officer of an organization can resign to take a position in a more prestigious organization is a personnel loss exposure. The exhibit reviews the three elements of a personnel loss exposure.

If the key person is viewed in terms of his or her family, the loss exposure associated with the loss of that key person is often called a **personal loss exposure** or human loss exposure. Although the terminology is slightly different, the definition is almost the same. For example, a family would face a personal loss exposure with the possibility of the primary wage earner dying.

Personal loss exposure

Any condition or situation that presents the possibility of a financial loss to an individual or a family by such causes as death, sickness, injury, or unemployment.

Elements of Liability Loss Exposures

1. **Asset Exposed to Loss**

The asset exposed to loss for a liability loss exposure is money. Payments that may be required include the following:

- Damages to the plaintiff if the claim is not successfully defended
- Settlement costs if the claim settles out of court
- Legal fees
- Court costs

2. **Cause of Loss**

The cause of a liability loss is the making of a claim or suit against the particular organization by another party seeking damages or some other legal remedy. Even the threat of another party to make such a claim or suit can cause a liability loss in the form of costs the organization incurs to investigate and settle the threatened liability claim or suit.

3. **Financial Consequences of Loss**

In theory, the financial consequences of a liability loss exposure are limitless. In practice, financial consequences are limited to the total wealth of the person or organization. Although some jurisdictions limit the amounts that can be taken in a claim, liability claims can result in the loss of most or all of a person's or an organization's assets, as well as in a claim on future income.

[DA02386]

Net Income Loss Exposures

Net income loss exposure
A condition that presents the possibility of loss caused by a reduction in net income.

A **net income loss exposure** is a condition that presents the possibility of loss caused by a reduction in net income. Net income equals revenues minus expenses and income taxes in a given time period. If income taxes are considered to be part of an organization's expenses, a net income loss is a reduction in revenue, an increase in expenses, or a combination of the two. Both individuals and organizations have net income loss exposures. See the exhibit "Elements of Net Income Loss Exposures."

For example, a fire at an organization's production facilities could not only destroy the facilities (a property loss exposure) but also force the organization to stop operations for a few weeks, resulting in a loss of sales revenue (a net income loss exposure). Similarly, if a tornado damages the retail store of a self-employed business owner, the inability to earn income while the store is being repaired represents a net income loss exposure. The exhibit reviews the three elements of a net income loss exposure.

Net income losses are often the result of a property, liability, or personnel loss (all of which are direct losses). Therefore, net income losses are considered to

Elements of Personnel Loss Exposures

1. **Asset Exposed to Loss**

The asset exposed to loss for a personnel loss exposure is the value that the key person adds to the organization.

2. **Cause of Loss**

Circumstances that can lead to a personnel loss exposure include the following:

- Death
- Disability
- Retirement
- Voluntary separation, such as resignation
- Involuntary separation, such as layoff or firing

3. **Financial Consequences of Loss**

The financial consequences of a personnel loss vary based on the cause of loss and can be partial or total as well as temporary or permanent. For example, the death of a key employee is a total, permanent loss. If the personnel loss is caused by a disability, the loss of value to the organization may only be a partial loss if the employee is able to continue to add some value to the organization. It may also only be temporary, if a full recovery from the disability is expected.

[DA02387]

be indirect losses. A direct loss is a loss that occurs immediately as the result of a particular cause of loss, such as the reduction in the value of a building that has been damaged by fire.

An indirect loss is a loss that results from, but is not directly caused by, a particular cause of loss. For example, the reduction in revenue an organization suffers as a result of fire damage to one of its buildings is an indirect loss. Estimating indirect losses is often challenging because of the difficulty in projecting the effects that a direct loss will have on revenues or expenses. For example, a risk management professional working at a restaurant chain may be able to project the amount needed to settle a lawsuit brought by a customer accusing the restaurant of food poisoning (direct liability loss) with some certainty. However, projecting the effect that any negative publicity relating to the lawsuit would have on future restaurant sales (indirect loss) would be more difficult.

In the insurance industry, the term "net income losses" is usually associated with property losses, and some insurance policies provide coverage for net income losses related to property losses. However, there are many other causes of net income losses.

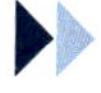

Elements of Net Income Loss Exposures

1. **Asset Exposed to Loss**

The asset exposed to loss for a net income loss exposure is the future stream of net income cash flows of the individual or organization.

2. **Cause of Loss**

Circumstances that can lead to a net income loss exposure include the following:

- Property loss
- Liability loss
- Personnel loss
- Losses stemming from business risks; for example, losses resulting from poor strategic planning

3. **Financial Consequences of Loss**

The financial consequences of a net income loss vary based on the cause of loss. A reduction in revenues, an increase in expenses, or a combination of the two can have financial consequences. The worst case scenario for a net income loss is a decrease in revenues to zero and a significant increase in expenses for a prolonged period.

[DA02388]

Some net income losses are associated with the liability or personnel loss exposures that have traditionally been the focus of risk management. Other net income losses are associated with organizational activities that have not traditionally been the focus of risk management, such as strategic marketing or branding decisions. Besides these, other potential net income losses that may affect individuals or organizations include these:

- Loss of goodwill—Organizations are concerned with maintaining goodwill among customers and other stakeholders. Goodwill can be lost in many ways, including providing poor service, offering obsolete products, or mismanaging operations. For a not-for-profit organization, goodwill is equivalent to reputation. Goodwill has broader implications than just reputation in for-profit organizations, because goodwill may have a monetary value. To maintain goodwill, many organizations choose to pay for certain accidents for which they are not legally responsible. For example, if a guest sustains an injury on an organization's premises, and the organization did not cause or contribute to the injury, that organization might still choose to pay any medical bills in order to maintain goodwill and avoid adverse publicity.
- Failure to perform—Net income losses may occur as a result of some type of failure to perform, including a product's failure to perform as promised,

a contractor's failure to complete a construction project as scheduled, or a debtor's failure to make scheduled payments.

- Missed opportunities—An organization may suffer a net income loss as a result of a missed opportunity for profit. For example, an organization that delays a decision to modify its product in response to changes in market demand might lose market share and profit that it could have made on that updated product.

LEGAL LIABILITY: TORTS, CONTRACTS, AND STATUTES

Every person and all organizations are exposed to liability loss. The possibility of a liability loss is a **liability loss** exposure. To be able to identify, analyze, and properly handle an organization's liability loss exposures, one must understand the concept of **legal liability** and the common sources of liability loss exposures.

Liability loss
Any loss that a person or an organization sustains as a result of a claim or suit against that person or organization by someone seeking damages or some other remedy permitted by law.

Legal liability
The legally enforceable obligation of a person or an organization to pay a sum of money (called damages) to another person or organization.

Anyone who wishes to evaluate an organization's liability loss exposures must understand the various ways in which the organization may become legally liable. Legal liability imposed by civil law can be based on torts, contracts, or statutes.

A liability insurance policy typically obligates the insurer to defend the insured against allegations that, if true, would be covered under the policy. Therefore, an organization can experience a liability loss even as a result of a suit in which it is not legally held liable. In addition, the policy obligates the insurer to pay damages for which the insured is legally liable. In most liability claims in which the insurer believes that its insured is legally liable, it attempts to settle the claim (by offering to pay a certain amount of damages to the claimant) in order to avoid the additional expense of a court proceeding.

Civil Law and Criminal Law

Legal liability can be imposed by **civil law**, **criminal law**, or both. Liability insurance responds to liability imposed by civil law. Insurance for criminal liability is prohibited by law.

Civil law
A classification of law that applies to legal matters not governed by criminal law and that protects rights and provides remedies for breaches of duties owed to others.

Criminal law
The branch of the law that imposes penalties for wrongs against society.

In some instances, a single act can constitute both a civil wrong and a crime. For example, if a driver causes the death of a pedestrian, law enforcement authorities may charge the driver with vehicular homicide, a criminal act. The driver may also be subject to a civil action by the estate of the deceased pedestrian for medical bills, funeral expenses, loss of support, and other damages that the law allows. Insurance coverage would not respond to the criminal charges. It could, however, provide payment for the civil claims.

Civil liability can be based on torts, contracts, or statutes. See the exhibit "Bases for Legal Liability."

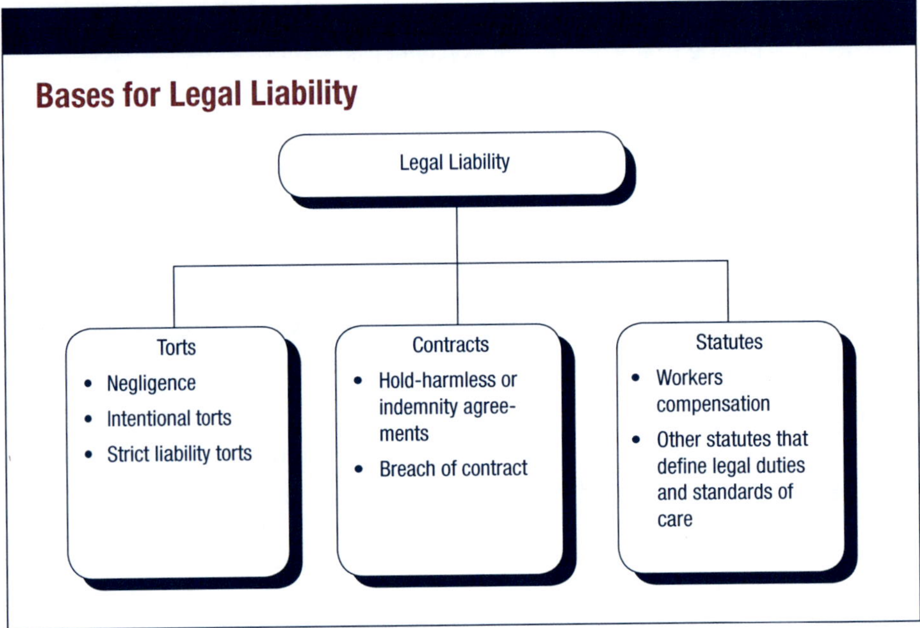

[DA02515]

Legal Liability Based on Torts

Tort
A wrongful act or an omission, other than a crime or a breach of contract, that invades a legally protected right.

Torts may be civil wrongs or private wrongs. Most of the claims covered by liability insurance are based on tort law, which protects the rights of individuals. These rights originally included the rights to security of person, property, and reputation. Over the years, legal changes have established other rights of individuals, such as the right to privacy. Where a right exists, others have a corresponding duty to respect it and to refrain from any act or omission that would impair or damage it. Any wrongful invasion of legally protected rights entitles the injured party to bring an action against the wrongdoer for damages.

The numerous types of torts fall into three broad categories:

- Negligence
- Intentional torts
- Strict liability torts

Negligence
The failure to exercise the degree of care that a reasonable person in a similar situation would exercise to avoid harming others.

Negligence is based on four elements:

- A duty owed to another person
- A breach of that duty
- A close causal connection between the negligent act (breach of duty) and the resulting harm
- The occurrence of actual loss or damage of a type recognized by law and measurable in monetary terms

For example, a motorist who drives at an unsafe and excessive speed and, as a result, causes an accident that injures another motorist has committed the tort of negligence.

An **intentional tort** is a tort committed by a person who foresees (or should be able to foresee) that his or her act will harm another person. The act does not necessarily have to be performed with malicious or hostile intent. An example of an intentional tort is libel, the publication of a false statement that damages a person's reputation.

Intentional tort

A tort committed by a person who foresees (or should be able to foresee) that his or her act will harm another person.

Strict liability (or absolute liability) is liability that is imposed even though the defendant acted neither negligently nor with intent to cause harm. Common examples of strict liability include liability for abnormally dangerous instrumentalities (such as wild animals), ultrahazardous activities (such as blasting), and dangerously defective products (such as malfunctioning smoke detectors).

Strict liability (absolute liability)

Liability imposed by a court or by a statute in the absence of fault when harm results from activities or conditions that are extremely dangerous, unnatural, ultrahazardous, extraordinary, abnormal, or inappropriate.

Strict liability is also used to describe liability imposed by certain statutes, such as workers compensation laws.

Legal Liability Based on Contracts

In addition to torts, **contracts** also impose legal liability. If one party fails to honor the promise, the other may go to court to enforce the contract. Liability based on contracts can arise out of either a breach of contract or an agreement one party has made to assume the liability of another party.

Contract

A legally enforceable agreement between two or more parties in which each party makes some promise to the other.

Breach of contract is a failure to fulfill one's contractual promise. A common type of breach of contract involves the promise (called a warranty) made by a seller regarding its product. If the product fails to fulfill its promise, the warranty has been breached, and the buyer can make claim against the seller. The warranty may be either expressly stated or implied by law. For example, the law implies a warranty that every product is fit for the particular purpose for which it is sold. If the product is unfit for its intended purpose and the buyer is injured as a result, the seller may be held legally liable for damages.

Breach of contract

The failure, without legal excuse, to fulfill a contractual promise.

Liability for injury or damage resulting from a seller's breach of warranty is commonly insurable. Other consequences of breach of contract are not insurable. For example, if a builder fails to complete a new store by the promised date, the store owner's claim for loss of revenue is normally not insurable under the builder's general liability insurance.

A hold-harmless agreement (or indemnity agreement) typically requires one party to "hold harmless and indemnify" the other party against liability arising from the activity or product that is the subject of the contract.

For example, a building's lease may obligate the tenant to hold the landlord harmless against any liability claims made by any person injured on the leased premises. The tenant, in this case, is agreeing by contract to pay claims for which the tenant would not otherwise have been legally liable. Construction

contracts and other types of agreements also often contain hold-harmless agreements. **Contractual liability** is liability assumed through a hold-harmless agreement and is commonly covered under liability insurance policies.

Contractual liability

Liability assumed through a hold-harmless agreement.

Legal Liability Based on Statutes

In addition to torts and contracts, statutes are a third major basis for imposing legal liability. A **statute** is a written law passed by a legislative body, at either the federal or state level. Written laws at the local level are usually referred to as ordinances. Statutes and ordinances can modify the duties that persons owe to others. Thus, the duties imposed by statute or ordinance may be used as evidence of a person's duty of care in a tort action. A statute can also impose legal liability on certain persons or organizations regardless of whether they acted negligently, committed any tort, or assumed liability under a contract.

Statute

A written law passed by a legislative body, at either the federal or state level.

A statute can give certain persons or organizations an absolute legal obligation to compensate other persons if certain events occur. This type of obligation is a form of strict liability, like that previously discussed, except that it is based entirely on requirements imposed by statute rather than on tort law. An important example of liability imposed by statute is the workers compensation system, which requires employers to pay prescribed benefits for occupational injuries or illness of their employees. The employer must pay these benefits even if an employee's injury or illness did not result from the employer's negligence.

NEGLIGENCE

Negligence is an important tort classification for insurance professionals to understand because it is the basis of many property-casualty insurance claims.

Torts are civil (or private) wrongs, as distinguished from crimes, which are public wrongs. Torts are either unintentional or intentional.

Negligence is the broad term used for unintentional torts. All other torts are intentional. A tort results from a **tortfeasor's** breach of duty that results in injury or loss. Describing negligence involves an understanding of two of its aspects:

Tortfeasor

A person or organization that has committed a tort.

- The elements of negligence
- The required proof of negligence

Elements of Negligence

A **plaintiff** in a negligence claim against a **defendant** must establish each of the four essential elements of negligence:

Plaintiff

The person or entity who files a lawsuit and is named as a party.

Defendant

The party in a lawsuit against whom a complaint is filed.

- The defendant owed a legal duty of care to the plaintiff.
- The defendant breached the duty of care owed to the plaintiff.

- The defendant's negligent act was the proximate cause of the plaintiff's injury or damage.
- The plaintiff suffered actual injury or damage.

Legal Duty

The first essential element of negligence is a **legal duty** of care owed by a defendant to a plaintiff. In establishing the existence of a legal duty, the courts ask whether the plaintiff's interests are entitled to legal protection against the defendant's conduct.

Legal duty
An obligation imposed by law for the preservation of the legally protected rights of others.

Legal duties of care are created by statutes, contracts, and the **common law**.

Common law (case law)
Laws that develop out of court decisions in particular cases and establish precedents for future cases.

Consider that many automobile hit-and-run laws impose a duty on drivers involved in accidents to stop and assist injured persons. Failure to obey the statute generally constitutes negligence, and the violator is liable for any damages directly caused by failing to give assistance.

For example, a surgeon has a legal duty to perform surgery properly. If the duty is breached, the patient can sue for negligence.

Failure to perform a contract or performing a contract improperly can violate a legal duty. For example, the subcontractor did not use the concrete formula specified in the contract and the parking garage collapsed. Damage to the garage would be related to a breach of contract. If persons or third-party property were injured or damaged in the collapse, then the subcontractor could also be held liable because of negligence.

Most legal duties arise from the common law. Many such duties are well established; others are defined based on the facts of new cases that raise new legal issues. In response, courts may develop new rules that form compromises between the conflicting positions of plaintiffs demanding protection and defendants claiming they owe no legal duty of care.

For a negligence lawsuit to be successful, the defendant must have owed a duty to the plaintiff. However, the duty need not be owed to a specific person. That the defendant could foresee that harm would occur to someone because of the negligent act or omission is sufficient. Duty extends to all persons and property within the zone of hazard, or area of danger. For example, the duty might extend to an unforeseen plaintiff, such as a guest of the purchaser of a defective product.

A moral obligation to act is not the same as a legal duty. For example, a person who fails to attempt to rescue a drowning child may not be liable for the child's death because he owed her no legal duty, even though he might have had a moral duty to save her.

However, a person who voluntarily undertakes a moral duty has a legal duty to exercise reasonable care in carrying it out. When one volunteers to undertake an act or to perform a service necessary to another's safety, and that person suffers harm in reasonable reliance on the volunteer's performance, the volun-

teer is liable. Having undertaken a task, the volunteer must act as an ordinary, reasonable person would act in performing it.

Breach of Duty

The second essential element of negligence is the defendant's breach of the duty of care owed to the plaintiff; that is, the failure to conform to the standard of care required in the situation. The courts usually apply a **reasonable person test** to determine the standard of care. The question is whether the person's conduct would be the conduct of a reasonable person under the circumstances.

Reasonable person test
A standard for the degree of care exercised in a situation that is measured by what a reasonably cautious person would or would not do under similar circumstances.

The reasonable person test is an external, objective test under which the defendant's individual or personal judgment, or that of other parties involved (subjective factors), is not considered. The test is not based on how jury members would have acted under like circumstances, but only on how the jury perceives that a reasonable person would have acted.

Circumstances further qualify the reasonable person test. For example, if applied to a person with disabilities, the general legal rule would be to consider how a reasonable person with a disability would act under the circumstances. However, the rule varies according to mental incapacity. Courts hold people who are not sane to the same standards as reasonable, sane people and hold people who are intoxicated to the same standards as those who are sober.

The standard applied in cases of professional negligence is the skill and knowledge of reasonably competent members of that profession applied with reasonable care. Professionals are not liable for mere errors in judgment, provided that they have used reasonable care in reaching a judgment. This standard applies to practically all professions and skilled trades, such as lawyers, engineers, accountants, and airline pilots.

The legal standard applied to professionals is usually the standard of professionals in the local community. For example, a rural doctor may not be expected to know about diagnostic machines used only in metropolitan teaching hospitals. The duty is not based on the particular community in which the tort occurred, but on that general type of community in the same geographic area. Doctors coming to the aid of an injured person in a volunteer, or "Good Samaritan," situation are subjected to the standard of care for the doctors in their own community.

The standard or degree of care varies with the nature of the activity. Therefore, the care required of a reasonable person varies according to the possibility of harm involved. As the possibility of harm increases, the party must exercise greater caution, commensurate with the risk. Many courts have established different degrees of care, such as ordinary care or a high degree of care.

A high degree of care is legally necessary in two situations:

- **Common carriers**, those who operate buses, trains, and taxicabs, for example, must exercise the utmost caution characteristic of a very careful person, which is the highest possible care commensurate with the risk or nature of the undertaking.
- People who handle or store dangerous materials, such as explosives, must exercise care commensurate with the risk associated with the materials' dangerous character.

Common carriers
Airlines, railroads, or trucking companies that furnish transportation to any member of the public seeking their offered services.

Proximate Cause

The third essential element of negligence is **proximate cause**. Proof of a wrongful act and harm are not sufficient to prove negligence. The wrongful act must also have been the proximate, or direct, cause of the harm.

Proximate cause
A cause that, in a natural and continuous sequence unbroken by any new and independent cause, produces an event and without which the event would not have happened.

For example, a guest in a hotel is severely injured in a fire and sues the hotelkeeper. At the trial, the plaintiff proves that the hotel did not have legally required sprinklers. This violation of law is not enough to create liability on the hotelkeeper's part. The plaintiff also must prove that the absence of the sprinklers was the proximate cause of the injuries. To illustrate further, the plaintiff might have been at the other end of the hotel with an easy escape route that the plaintiff failed to use.

In determining tort liability, courts have always attempted to place the burden of loss on the person responsible, at the same time recognizing that some limit of liability should exist when the act was so remote as not to be chargeable to the actor. An early case, *Scott v. Shepherd*,[1] known as the "lighted squib" case, illustrates this concept.

In the lighted squib case, the defendant, Shepherd, threw a lighted squib, a type of firecracker, into a crowd. It fell near Y, who picked it up and threw it near Z, who in turn threw it near Scott, where it exploded, injuring Scott. The issue was whether the injury was the result of Shepherd's original act of throwing the squib into the crowd or whether Y or Z, who actually threw the squib near Scott, caused the injury. The court held that Shepherd had set the cause of loss, the squib, in motion and was liable for the resulting injury.

The question in the case was whether, if the squib had been thrown successively by, say, five persons, or had landed in a powder keg rather than near a person in a crowd, Shepherd still would be liable. The controlling doctrine is that one who commits a wrongful act is responsible for the ordinary consequences that can foreseeably flow from the act. The person is not liable for results that could not have been reasonably foreseen, or if an independent intervening cause breaks the chain of causation. Some courts deem proximate cause as a substantial, direct cause, one that would have caused all or at least a substantial part of the injury on its own.

Distance between the act and the injury is not in itself sufficient to make the cause remote. Remoteness is a matter of degree, as the squib case indi-

cates. Likewise, passage of time does not necessarily create remoteness. For example, when a fire damaged a building, and a wall of the building collapsed thirty-eight days later, the fire was still considered the proximate cause of the collapse.

In tort law, rules have evolved to determine proximate cause:

"But for" rule

A rule used to determine whether a defendant's act was the proximate cause of a plaintiff's harm based on the determination that the plaintiff's harm could not have occurred but for the defendant's act.

Substantial factor rule

A rule used to determine proximate cause of a loss by determining which of the acts are significant factors in causing the harm.

- **"But for" rule**—To illustrate the "but for" rule, if Al drove his car onto a sidewalk and injured Bob, it is readily apparent that, but for Al's action, Bob would not have been injured. The act is the proximate cause of Bob's injury.
- **Substantial factor rule**—Sometimes two parties' acts coincide to cause a loss, and the "but for" rule does not produce a satisfactory result. In these situations the substantial factor rule applies. Assume that cars driven by Al and Bob collide at an intersection, and Al's car then swerves onto a sidewalk, injuring Carol. Evidence shows that both Al and Bob are at fault in the collision. If the "but for" rule is applied, the loss would not have occurred "but for" both drivers' negligence; and neither could be held liable. To avoid this unsatisfactory result, the courts have developed the substantial factor rule.
- Proof of defendant's responsibility—An injured person cannot succeed in a lawsuit merely by proving that harm resulted from another person's act. The plaintiff still must prove by a preponderance of the evidence that the defendant caused the harm. When the evidence is clear that it is at least as probable that the act was a third person's responsibility, the plaintiff has failed to win the case.
- **Foreseeability rule**—Under the foreseeability rule, the plaintiff's harm must be the natural and probable consequence of the defendant's wrongful act and such that an ordinarily reasonable person would have foreseen it. However, the defendant need not have foreseen the particular result that followed.

Foreseeability rule

A rule used to determine proximate cause when a plaintiff's harm is the natural and probable consequence of the defendant's wrongful act and when an ordinarily reasonable person would have foreseen the harm.

Intervening act

An act, independent of an original act and not readily foreseeable, that breaks the chain of causation and sets a new chain of events in motion that causes harm.

Concurrent causation (concurrent causation doctrine)

A legal doctrine stating that if a loss can be attributed to two or more independent concurrent causes—one or more excluded by the policy and one covered—then the policy covers the loss.

The defendant is not liable if the harm is caused by an independent, intervening agency, or **intervening act**. The intervening agency, rather than the original cause, then becomes the proximate cause. The intervening agency must be independent of the original act and not readily foreseeable as one that would arise from the original act.

For example, a speeding motorist's negligent driving knocks down a tree on the side of the road. An enterprising motorist the next day stops to cut branches for firewood and injures himself with a hand saw. The act of the enterprising motorist is not connected with the car accident, and it is unlikely that speeding motorist who knocked down the tree could foresee that an enterprising motorist would cut up the tree for firewood. A court might find differently if the local municipal worker tasked to remove the accident's debris was injured cutting up the same tree.

Concurrent causation arises when each of two or more defendants is liable for the entire harm, even though the act of either would not have produced the harm. For example, on a cold, icy day, Jane and Martha, each driving cars at excessive speeds, slide on the ice, collide, go up on the sidewalk, and injure a pedestrian, Kelly. In this case, both Jane and Martha are liable. Their individual acts combined to produce Kelly's injury.

Actual Injury or Damage

The fourth essential element of negligence is actual injury or damage to the plaintiff. For a person to sue successfully for negligence, the negligent act must result in actual injury or damage, or quantifiable harm for which the plaintiff seeks damages. The harm could be bodily injury or financial loss, such as property loss.

Required Proof of Negligence

In a negligence lawsuit, the plaintiff has the burden to prove all the elements of negligence, and the defendant has the burden of proving any defense. The defendant is presumed at the outset of a lawsuit to have used due care until the plaintiff proves otherwise. In some kinds of cases, presumptions favor the plaintiff. For example, a **bailee**, such as a dry cleaner, who returns the plaintiff's property in a damaged condition is presumed to be negligent and has the burden of proving otherwise.

Bailee
The party temporarily possessing the personal property in a bailment.

If the facts are undisputed and point to only one presumption, the court must decide whether, as a matter of law, negligence occurred. If the facts are in dispute or uncertain, or if they are undisputed but are such that fair-minded people might reasonably reach different conclusions, then the court must make findings of fact (supported by the evidence) and may also have to make findings of law (the applicability of a rule of law to the facts of the case) to determine whether negligence occurred.

Negligence Per Se

The law treats certain actions as **negligence per se**, which a court can determine without submitting the question to the jury.

Negligence per se
An act that is considered inherently negligent because of a violation of a law or an ordinance.

Although not all statutes create standards of care for negligence suits, often failure to comply with a statutory standard is negligence *per se*, and proof that the defendant violated the statute is sufficient to establish liability. For example, a victim is killed when his vehicle collides with a disabled truck parked in the fast lane of a divided interstate highway. The truck's location violates traffic regulations requiring that disabled vehicles move immediately from the traveled portion of the highway and provide adequate warning devices to other motorists. Proof that the truck driver neither moved the truck nor provided the warning devices might be sufficient to establish negligence *per se*.

Res Ipsa Loquitur

Res ipsa loquitur

A legal doctrine that provides that, in some circumstances, negligence is inferred simply by an accident occurring.

Res ipsa loquitur, Latin for "the thing speaks for itself," permits an inference of negligence if the action or event causing injury was under the defendant's exclusive control and the accident ordinarily would not have happened if the defendant had exercised appropriate care. The doctrine is based on the conclusion that, in the absence of proof to the contrary, such an accident would likely arise from lack of due care. Although negligence is not actually presumed, the circumstances provide evidence from which a jury might presume negligence.

The *res ipsa loquitur* doctrine involves two factors:

- The probability that, under the given circumstances, the defendant was negligent
- The defendant's duty to rebut the inference of negligence as the party who had **exclusive control** and superior knowledge of the causative circumstances

Exclusive control

The control of only one person or entity; in tort law the control by the defendant alone of an instrument that caused harm.

The exclusive control concept is a flexible one that the courts have adapted to modern manufacturing, packing, shipping, and marketing practices. For example, a plaintiff injured by an exploding carbonated beverage bottle can use the doctrine of *res ipsa loquitur* against the bottler even though the bottle was not in the bottler's physical possession. The bottler could challenge application of the doctrine with evidence that either the plaintiff had mishandled the bottle or that other parties did so after the bottle left the bottler's control. *Res ipsa loquitur* also can apply to airplane crashes because the airlines have control over the equipment and airplane operation.

Courts frequently apply *res ipsa loquitur* in lawsuits by passengers against common carriers. The doctrine also can apply in instances such as bricks that have fallen off buildings, poisonous drugs sold as harmless medicine, and sponges or surgical instruments left inside patients during surgery.

An unexplained injury alone does not mean that *res ipsa loquitur* can be applied. For example, the discovery of a dead person near railroad tracks does not imply in and of itself that the railroad was involved. Several explanations are conceivable other than the railroad's failure to act with due care. See the exhibit "Practice Exercise: Elements of Negligence."

Practice Exercise: Elements of Negligence

Coal Company conducts mountaintop mining operations in the mountains on both sides of a creek. Joseph's house is in the creek valley. Studies have shown that this kind of mountaintop mining can cause flooding in creek valleys if appropriate precautions are not taken, although this valley had a history of flooding caused by spring rains before Coal Company's operations began. In the spring, the valley flooded after unusually heavy rains, destroying Joseph's home in the valley. Joseph sues Coal Company, claiming that its negligence caused the destruction of his home. Describe how the elements of negligence might apply to Joseph's case.

Answer

Joseph must establish that Coal Company owed a legal duty of care to him, and its coal operation in that area probably involves a legal duty to all valley landowners to conduct mining operations so as not to damage their property. Joseph also must establish that Coal Company breached its duty of care by not taking appropriate precautions, and he would need to introduce evidence proving that element. Joseph should have no problem proving that he suffered damage because his home was destroyed. However, proximate cause might be the most difficult negligence element for Joseph to prove if the spring rains would have flooded the valley even without Coal Company's mountaintop mining.

[DA05828]

TRADITIONAL RISK MANAGEMENT VERSUS ENTERPRISE RISK MANAGEMENT (ERM)

Traditional risk management concerns managing hazard risk. Enterprise risk management (ERM) includes traditional risk management, while taking an integrated, holistic approach to risk across all business segments of an organization.

Risk management involves the efforts of individuals or organizations to efficiently and effectively assess, control, and finance risk to minimize the adverse effects of losses or missed opportunities. Individuals practice risk management to protect their limited assets from losses and to help meet personal goals. For an organization, sound risk management adds value and helps to ensure that losses or missed opportunities do not prevent it from meeting its goals.

ERM expands an organization's risk management professional's role to include management of business risk, such as strategic and financial risks. Larger organizations typically conduct risk management through a formalized risk management program that has both pre-loss and post-loss goals that are designed to advance the organization's overall goals and that can be implemented using the risk management process. The risk management process consists of a series of six steps that enable an organization to identify, analyze, and, ultimately, manage its risk.

Risk Management

In its simplest form, risk management includes any effort to economically deal with uncertainty of outcomes (risk). For individuals, risk management is usually an informal series of efforts, not a formalized process. Individual or personal risk management may be viewed as part of the financial planning process that encompasses broader matters such as capital accumulation, retirement planning, and estate planning. Individuals and families often practice risk management informally without explicitly following a risk management process. For example, individuals purchase insurance policies to cover accidental or unexpected losses or they contribute to savings plans so that they have money available to cover unforeseen events.

Risk management program

A system for planning, organizing, leading, and controlling the resources and activities that an organization needs to protect itself from the adverse effects of accidental losses.

Risk management process

The method of making, implementing, and monitoring decisions that minimize the adverse effects of risk on an organization.

In smaller organizations, risk management is not usually a dedicated function, but one of many tasks carried out by the owner or senior manager. In many larger organizations, the risk management function is conducted as part of a formalized risk management program. A **risk management program** is a system for planning, organizing, leading, and controlling the resources and activities that an organization needs to protect itself from the adverse effects of accidental losses.

Most risk management programs are built around the **risk management process**, which is the method of making, implementing, and monitoring decisions that minimize the adverse effects of risk on an organization. Although the exact steps in an organization's risk management process may differ, all risk management processes are designed to assess, control, and finance risk. See the exhibit "Evolving Industry Language: Risk Classification and Risk Categories."

Evolving Industry Language: Risk Classification and Risk Categories

Risk management and insurance professionals often use the terms pure risk and hazard risk interchangeably. They also often use the terms speculative risk and business risk interchangeably. When risk is described as either pure or speculative risk, the description is about the classification of risk. The classification is based on an attribute of the risk—whether there is the potential for gain or not. When risk is described as either hazard or business risk, the description is about a category of risk. The categories are based on terminology that has developed in the risk management industry. Hazard risk has traditionally been managed by risk management professionals, whereas business risk has traditionally been managed outside the risk management department.

The pure or speculative risk classification is important in identifying insurable risks. The hazard or business risk categories are important in understanding the evolution from traditional risk management to enterprise risk management.

Most hazard risks are pure risks, but not all pure risks are hazard risks. Similarly, most speculative risks are business risks, but not all business risks are speculative risks.

[DA08841]

Traditional Risk Management

Traditionally, the risk management professional's role has been associated with loss exposures related to hazard risk. This view excludes from the scope of risk management all loss exposures that arise from business risk. Therefore, organizational risk management has focused on managing safety, purchasing insurance, and controlling financial recovery from losses generated by hazard risk. Risk management professionals have dealt with activities such as monitoring safety programs or processing workers compensation claims, rather than helping achieve organizational gains from exposure to business risk. This has often led traditional risk management departments to be viewed by other departments as cost centers, not as revenue centers—that is, they believe risk management only costs the organization money. This leads to the misconception that risk management does not add value to the organization.

Making sound decisions about individual hazard risks requires a basic understanding of an organization's overall financial condition and its capacity to withstand loss, both of which are influenced by its overall exposure to business risk as well as hazard risk. For example, how much cash an organization can access to pay for unanticipated property losses is directly affected by how well its products are selling and how well its investments are performing. As a result, the traditional role of risk management and of the risk management professional is expanding to include management of a broader array of risks.

Enterprise Risk Management by Organizations

ERM is commonly used to describe the broader view of risk management that encompasses both hazard and business risk. ERM is an approach to managing all of an organization's key risks and opportunities with the intent of maximizing the organization's value. An ERM approach allows an organization to integrate all of its risk management activities so that the risk management process occurs at the enterprise level, rather than at the departmental or business unit level. How ERM is implemented in practice varies significantly among organizations, depending on their size, nature, and complexity. See the exhibit "Enterprise Risk Management in Practice."

Traditionally, risk management is departmentalized. That is, hazard risks are managed in the risk management department, financial risks in the finance department, and so on. Using this approach, an organization rarely makes relative comparisons among its risks to determine how they interact with one another or to evaluate their cumulative effect on the organization. ERM, by coordinating all risk management activities under a single executive, is designed to facilitate these comparisons and evaluations.

For ERM to be effective, an organization must have the culture and infrastructure to manage the risks that most affect its value. Therefore, ERM can be a challenge in organizations that have previously followed a traditional risk management approach.

Enterprise Risk Management in Practice

If ERM is considered a part of a corporate culture in which all risk management decisions are made under the guidance of an individual executive, then it has been practiced by small organizations for years. In a small organization, one individual or a small group of individuals often assesses all risks the organization faces and determines how to allocate limited resources to best manage the risks that have the greatest effect on the organization.

However, ERM is now being implemented by large organizations as well. The risk management professional no longer needs to sell the importance of risk management to senior executives because risk management is no longer viewed as a cost center, but as a way to add value to the organization. In ERM, a risk management executive exhibits top-down control.

One of the barriers to successfully implementing ERM in large organizations involves the balance of control between the various departments. Some departmental managers may be reluctant to relinquish control of risk-related decisions previously made within their departments. For example, the finance department may be reluctant to surrender ultimate control of foreign exchange rate risk. In addition, the internal audit and risk management departments may disagree about who should be in charge of the ERM program.

Mid-size organizations have been slower to adopt ERM, often because they are large enough to need a dedicated risk management function yet do not have the resources to implement a full ERM corporate structure.

[DA08846]

Risk Maps

ERM is a holistic approach to risk management in that it addresses all risks faced by an organization. Although some aspects of risk are qualitative, individual risks can be best compared via a quantitative rating system that incorporates the loss exposures' loss frequency (likelihood of occurrence) and loss severity (significance of loss). One such system of comparison used in ERM programs is a risk map of the type shown in the exhibit.

Risk maps can come in many forms, including geographical maps and two- and three-dimensional charts. Risk maps can also be tailored to show how often the frequency and severity of losses could interfere with achieving specific key business goals. The risk map in the exhibit is a two-dimensional chart created by plotting the organization's risks on a grid relative to one another based on loss frequency (shown on the horizontal axis) and loss severity (shown on the vertical axis). Both frequency and severity are divided into two categories (high and low), yielding four quadrants. The more categories of frequency and severity included in a risk map, the more sectors the map depicts. See the exhibit "Risk Map."

A risk map serves three functions in an ERM program. First, it helps to break down the departmentalization of risk under a traditional risk management program through a central diagram that depicts risks from all sources. Such

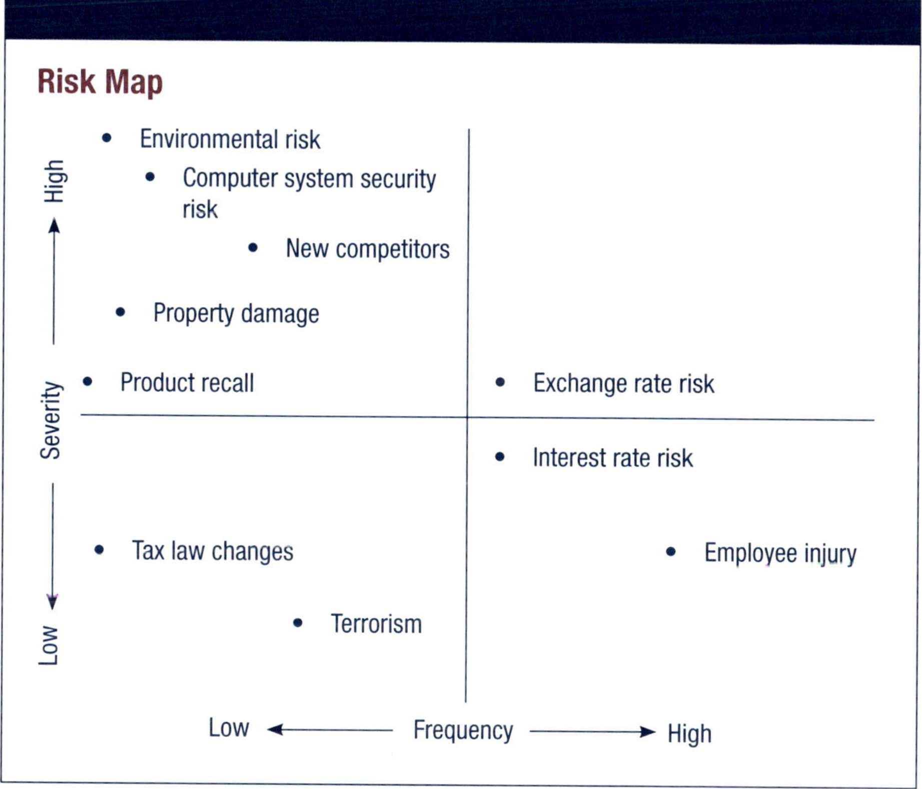

[DA08853]

a depiction enables the comparison of all risks, regardless of the department or area of the organization to which they are assigned. Second, a risk map is an efficient communication tool to help senior management better understand the risks inherent to the organization and can help determine which risks require the most attention and the greatest amount of risk management resources. Finally, risk maps, if tailored to key business goals, rank risks based on their relative effect on those goals. That is, the frequency and severity of the risks are assessed based on how often each would interfere with achieving a specific business goal.

To accommodate the volume and variety of risks organizations face, computerized risk management information systems are frequently used in measuring and rating risks to create risk maps. Because each organization has a different risk profile (risks faced) and risk appetite (risks willing to assume), one organization's risk map will not necessarily apply to another. Therefore, the risks an organization identifies and prioritizes in an ERM program will also vary.

Quadrants of Risk in an Organization

Although no consensus exists about how an organization should categorize its risks, one ERM approach involves dividing them into four risk quadrants: hazard, operational, financial, and strategic. As discussed previously, hazard risks are traditionally managed by risk management professionals. Operational

risks are pure risks that fall outside of the traditional hazard risk category and could jeopardize service-related or manufacturing-related business functions. Financial risks directly affect an organization's financial position via changes in revenue, expenses, business valuation, or the cost or availability of capital. Strategic risks are fundamental to an organization's existence and business plan because they have a current or future effect on earnings or capital arising from adverse business decisions, improper implementation of decisions, or lack of responsiveness to changes in the industry or changes in demand.

The focus of the four risk quadrants is different from the risk classifications: pure and speculative, subjective and objective, diversifiable and nondiversifiable, and static and dynamic. Whereas the classifications of risk focus on some aspect of the risk itself, the four quadrants of risk focus on the source of risk and who has traditionally managed it. Just as a particular loss exposure can fall into more than one classification, a loss exposure can also fall into multiple ERM risk quadrants. For example, intellectual property could be categorized as a strategic risk because protection of intellectual property has often fallen outside of the traditional risk management function. However, because intellectual property is a type of property, it can also be considered a hazard risk.

The quadrant exhibit contains a list of common risks, categorized according to the four ERM risk quadrants. Each of the risks is also classified as either pure or speculative and diversifiable or nondiversifiable. See the exhibit "Causes of Loss Categorized According to the Four Quadrants of Risk."

Causes of Loss Categorized According to the Four Quadrants of Risk

Hazard Risks

Many of these risks are transferred by property-liability insurance policies. Insurance for some of these risks, such as workers compensation, may be mandated by law.

Examples include:

- Property damage (pure, diversifiable)
- Third-party liability (pure, diversifiable)
- Directors and officers (D&O) liability (pure, diversifiable)
- Health and safety (pure, diversifiable)
- Natural hazards, such as flood or earthquake (pure, nondiversifiable)
- Asbestos (pure, diversifiable)
- Terrorism (pure, diversifiable)

Operational Risks

Although many operational risks are pure risks, traditional risk management deals less frequently with operational risks.

Examples include:

- Product recall (pure, diversifiable)
- Discrimination (pure, diversifiable)
- Embezzlement (pure, diversifiable)
- Workplace violence (pure, diversifiable)
- Kidnap (pure, diversifiable)
- Turnover (pure, diversifiable)
- Service provider failures, such as phone or utility service (pure, diversifiable)
- Supplier business interruption (pure, diversifiable)

Financial Risks

Financial risks are traditionally handled by the treasury or chief financial officer (CFO) function. These risks are normally speculative and can sometimes be managed with financial tools such as options or futures.

Examples include:

- Debt rating (speculative, diversifiable)
- Liquidity/cash (speculative, diversifiable)
- Asset valuation (speculative, diversifiable)
- Legislative changes (speculative, nondiversifiable)
- Commodity prices, such as fuel prices (speculative, nondiversifiable)
- Interest rates (speculative, nondiversifiable)
- Currency/foreign exchange rates (speculative, nondiversifiable)
- Economic growth/recession (speculative, nondiversifiable)

Strategic Risks

Many strategic risks are directly linked to management decisions.

Examples include:

- Intellectual property (speculative, diversifiable)
- Ethics (speculative, diversifiable)
- Planning (speculative, diversifiable)
- Technology (speculative, diversifiable)
- Union relations (speculative, diversifiable)
- New competitors (speculative, diversifiable)
- Media coverage (speculative, diversifiable)
- Industry consolidation (speculative, diversifiable)
- Product design (speculative, diversifiable)

[DA08854]

Traditional Risk Management Contrasted With ERM

Enterprise risk management is an extension of traditional risk management. However, the following significant differences exist between the two:

- Strategic application—ERM is integrated into an organization's strategic business decisions. Organizations that practice ERM typically place an executive in charge of risk management, sometimes called a chief risk officer (CRO), to ensure that risk is effectively managed across the organization. Because ERM is applied enterprise-wide, it supersedes departmental or functional autonomy that could impede risk management

efforts. In contrast, traditional risk management focuses only on hazard risk without examining risk in other functional areas. For example, if an organization practices traditional risk management, then a decision about purchasing property insurance on a production facility would be made by its risk management professional, whereas a decision to hedge exchange rate risk would be made by the financial manager. The risk management professional and the financial manager would have little, if any, interaction about these two decisions. If the same organization practiced ERM, then both of these decisions would be included in the risk management function.

- Risks considered—ERM involves managing all risks affecting an organization's ability to meet its goals, regardless of whether the risks are hazard or business. As shown in the quadrant exhibit, traditional risk management normally considers only hazard risks that involve fortuitous losses—that is, losses over which the organization has no control. ERM considers all risks that an organization faces, regardless of their source or potential outcomes. For example, traditional risk management would have focused on property loss exposures related to the fire cause of loss, whereas ERM would focus on those as well as the likelihood of the failure of new products.
- Performance metrics—ERM emphasizes results-based performance measurement. Results indicate whether a risk management technique helped achieve an underlying business goal, such as total sales or return on investment. In traditional risk management, success can be measured on both an activity and results basis. That is, in addition to measuring the success of risk management efforts based on results such as fewer property losses, traditional risk management also evaluates based on activity, such as the number of safety drills held in a year.

All forms of risk management are intended to help minimize the adverse effects of losses and missed opportunities. Understanding the specific benefits that risk management offers can help an individual or organization determine which risk management activities to undertake.

Review Questions

1. Identify the assets that are exposed to loss in each of these types of loss exposures: a. property loss exposure, b. liability loss exposure, c. personnel loss exposure, and d. net income loss exposure.
2. Distinguish between these types of property: a. tangible property, b. intangible property, c. real property, and d. personal property.
3. Describe a financial loss that an organization or individual might experience resulting from these types of loss exposures: a. property loss exposure, b. liability loss exposure, c. personnel loss exposure, and d. net income loss exposure.
4. Howard, the chief executive officer (CEO) of Joste Technology, a software development organization, voluntarily resigns to take a job as CEO of an

automobile manufacturer. Explain how the three elements of a loss exposure apply to Howard's voluntary resignation.

5. What costs, covered under general liability policies, might result from a liability claim?
6. Explain how a business can experience a liability loss even if it is found not to be legally liable.
7. Identify the elements of the tort of negligence.
8. Define and give an example of each of the following types of torts: a. intentional tort and b. strict (absolute) liability.
9. Give an example of each of the following: a. breach of contract and b. hold-harmless agreement.
10. Identify the elements of negligence.
11. At the outset of a lawsuit, what presumption favors the defendant?
12. Describe the difference in scope between traditional risk management and ERM.
13. Identify three functions of a risk map in an ERM program.
14. Describe the four quadrants of risk an organization uses when implementing an ERM approach.

Application Questions

1. Agnes owns and operates an exotic pet store. Her most popular pets include varieties of poisonous spiders, scorpions, and snakes. Agnes is meticulous about stocking only legal pets and checking the background of buyers before every sale. One day, a scorpion that she sold to a customer escapes from the customer's home and injures a neighbor. For Agnes, on what type of tort might any potential liability be based?
2. Describe how these factors differ between ERM and traditional risk management approaches: a. strategic application, b. risks considered, and c. performance metrics.
3. Melissa, the risk manager for Millwright Hockey Supply (MHS), was promoted to chief risk officer when MHS adopted an ERM approach. Describe some of the new risks Melissa must now consider.

SUMMARY

The three elements of loss exposures apply to each of the four types of loss exposures: property loss exposures, liability loss exposures, personnel loss exposures, and net income loss exposures.

A liability loss exposure is the possibility of experiencing a liability loss. A liability loss includes all costs to an organization as the result of a specific legal claim or suit against that organization. The person making claim or suit against the organization (the claimant) ordinarily attempts to prove that the organization is legally liable to pay damages.

Anyone who wishes to evaluate an organization's liability loss exposures must understand the various ways in which the organization could become legally liable. Broadly speaking, civil liability (in contrast with criminal liability) can be based on torts, contracts, or statutes.

Negligence is a broad term used for unintentional torts. Describing negligence involves an understanding of two of its aspects: the elements of negligence (including duty, breach of duty, proximate cause, and actual injury or damage) and the required proof of negligence.

Traditional risk management concerns managing hazard risk, whereas enterprise risk management (ERM) expands an organization's risk management to include an integrated, holistic approach to risk across all business segments of an organization—including strategic and financial risks. An ERM approach allows an organization to integrate all of its risk management activities at the enterprise level, rather than at the departmental or business unit level, as in traditional risk management. ERM uses tools to compare and analyze risk, such as a risk map or a quadrant approach. Traditional risk management contrasts with ERM in its strategic application, the risks considered, and its emphasis on performance metrics.

ASSIGNMENT NOTE

1. *Scott v. Shepherd*, 96 Eng. Rep. 525 (1773).

Direct Your Learning

4

Quantitative Methods and Risk Management Applications

Educational Objectives

After learning the content of this assignment, you should be able to:

- Describe the nature of probability with respect to theoretical and empirical probability and the law of large numbers.
- Explain how the information provided in a simple probability distribution can be used in making basic risk management decisions.
- Describe the various measures of central tendency and how they can be used in analyzing the probabilities associated with risk.
- Describe the measures of dispersion and how they can be used in analyzing the probabilities associated with risk.
- Calculate the alternative probability of the following:
  - Two mutually exclusive events
  - Two nonmutually exclusive events
- Describe the law of large numbers and, in particular, the conditions needed for its optimal operation.
- Describe loss severity in the context of maximum possible versus maximum probable loss.

Outline

Nature of Probability

Using Probability Distributions

Using Central Tendency

Using Dispersion

Calculating Alternative Probabilities

Understanding the Law of Large Numbers

Understanding Loss Severity

Summary

Quantitative Methods and Risk Management Applications

4

NATURE OF PROBABILITY

The probability of an event is the relative frequency with which the event can be expected to occur in the long run in a stable environment. Determining the probability that a certain event will occur can be an important part of exposure analysis in the risk management process.

Concepts affecting the basic nature of probability include theoretical probability, empirical probability, and the law of large numbers.

Theoretical Probability and Empirical Probability

Any probability can be expressed as a fraction, percentage, or decimal. For example, the probability of a head on a coin toss can be expressed as 1/2, 50 percent, or .50. The probability of an event that is totally impossible is 0 and the probability of an absolutely certain event is 1.0. Therefore, the probabilities of all events that are neither totally impossible nor absolutely certain are greater than 0 but less than 1.0.

Probabilities can be developed either from theoretical considerations or from historical data. **Theoretical probability** is probability that is based on theoretical principles rather than on actual experience. Probabilities associated with events such as coin tosses or dice throws can be developed from theoretical considerations and are unchanging. For example, from a description of a fair coin or die, a person who has never seen either a coin or a die can calculate the probability of flipping a head or rolling a four.

Theoretical probability
Probability that is based on theoretical principles rather than on actual experience.

Empirical probability is probability that is based on actual experience. For example, the probability that a sixty-two-year-old male will die in a particular year cannot be theoretically determined, but must be estimated by studying the loss experience of a sample of men aged sixty-two. The empirical probabilities deduced solely from historical data may change as new data are discovered or as the environment that produces those events changes.

Empirical probability (a posteriori probability)
A probability measure that is based on actual experience through historical data or from the observation of facts.

Empirical probabilities are only estimates whose accuracy depends on the size and representative nature of the samples being studied. In contrast, theoretical probabilities are constant as long as the physical conditions that generate them remain unchanged.

Although it may be preferable to use theoretical probabilities because of their unchanging nature, they are not applicable or available in most of the situations that insurance and risk management professionals are likely to analyze, such as automobile accidents or workers compensation claims. As a result, empirical probabilities must be used.

Law of Large Numbers

Probability analysis

A technique for forecasting events, such as accidental and business losses, on the assumption that they are governed by an unchanging probability distribution.

Probability analysis is particularly effective for projecting losses in organizations that have (1) a substantial volume of data on past losses and (2) fairly stable operations so that (except for price level changes) patterns of past losses presumably will continue in the future. In organizations with this type of unchanging environment, past losses can be viewed as a sample of all possible losses that the organization might suffer.

The larger the number of past losses an organization has experienced, the larger the sample of losses that can be used in the analysis. Consequently, the forecasts of future losses are more reliable (consistent over time) because the forecast is based on a larger sample of the environment that produced the losses. This is an application of the **law of large numbers**.

Law of large numbers

A mathematical principle stating that as the number of similar but independent exposure units increases, the relative accuracy of predictions about future outcomes (losses) also increases.

As an example, suppose an urn holds four marbles. One of the marbles is red and three are black. Assume that the number of red or black marbles is not known. The task is to estimate the theoretical probability of choosing a red marble on one draw (sample) from the urn by repeatedly sampling the marbles and replacing each in the urn after the sampling.

After twenty samples a red marble has been chosen eight times, which yields an empirical frequency of 40 percent (8/20). However, this estimate is inaccurate because the theoretical probability is 25 percent (1/4), given that only one of the four marbles is red.

According to the law of large numbers, the relative inaccuracy between the empirical frequency (40 percent in this case) and the theoretical probability (25 percent) will decline, on average, as the sample size increases. That is, as the number of samples increases from 20 to 200 or 2,000, the empirical frequency of choosing a red marble gets closer and closer to 25 percent.

The law of large numbers has some limitations. It can be used to more accurately forecast future events only when the events being forecast meet all three of these criteria:

- The events have occurred in the past under substantially identical conditions and have resulted from unchanging, basic causal forces.
- The events can be expected to occur in the future under the same, unchanging conditions.
- The events have been, and will continue to be, both independent of one another and sufficiently numerous.

USING PROBABILITY DISTRIBUTIONS

Once empirical probabilities are determined, probability distributions can be constructed. The information provided by probability distributions can be instrumental in analyzing loss exposures and making risk management decisions.

A properly constructed **probability distribution** always contains outcomes that are both mutually exclusive and collectively exhaustive. There are two forms of probability distributions: discrete and continuous. Discrete probability distributions have a finite number of possible outcomes and are typically used as frequency distributions. Continuous probability distributions have an infinite number of possible outcomes and are typically used as severity distributions.

Probability distribution
A presentation (table, chart, or graph) of probability estimates of a particular set of circumstances and of the probability of each possible outcome.

Outcomes of a Properly Constructed Probability Distribution

Both theoretical probabilities (such as those involving tossing coins or rolling dice) and empirical probabilities (such as those involving the number or size of losses) have outcomes that are mutually exclusive and collectively exhaustive. For example, on a particular flip of a coin, only one outcome is possible: heads or tails. Therefore, these outcomes are mutually exclusive.

Similarly, these two outcomes are the only possible outcomes and, therefore, are collectively exhaustive. A properly constructed probability distribution always contains outcomes that are both mutually exclusive and collectively exhaustive. For example, the exhibit shows the hypothetical probability distribution of the number of hurricanes making landfall in Florida during any given hurricane season. Each outcome (hurricane) is mutually exclusive and the sum of the outcomes is 1.0, so they are collectively exhaustive. See the exhibit "Number of Hurricanes Making Landfall in Florida During One Hurricane Season."

The second exhibit shows the distribution as a pie chart. See the exhibit "Probability of Hurricanes Making Landfall in Florida During One Hurricane Season."

Theoretical Probability Distributions

Consider the probability distribution of the total number of points on one throw of two dice, one red and one green. There are thirty-six equally likely outcomes (green 1, red 1; green 1, red 2; … green 6, red 6). The exhibit shows

Number of Hurricanes Making Landfall in Florida During One Hurricane Season

Number of Hurricanes Making Landfall	Probability
0	.300
1	.350
2	.200
3	.147
4	.002
5+	.001
Total Probability	1.000

[DA02572]

Probability of Hurricanes Making Landfall in Florida During One Hurricane Season

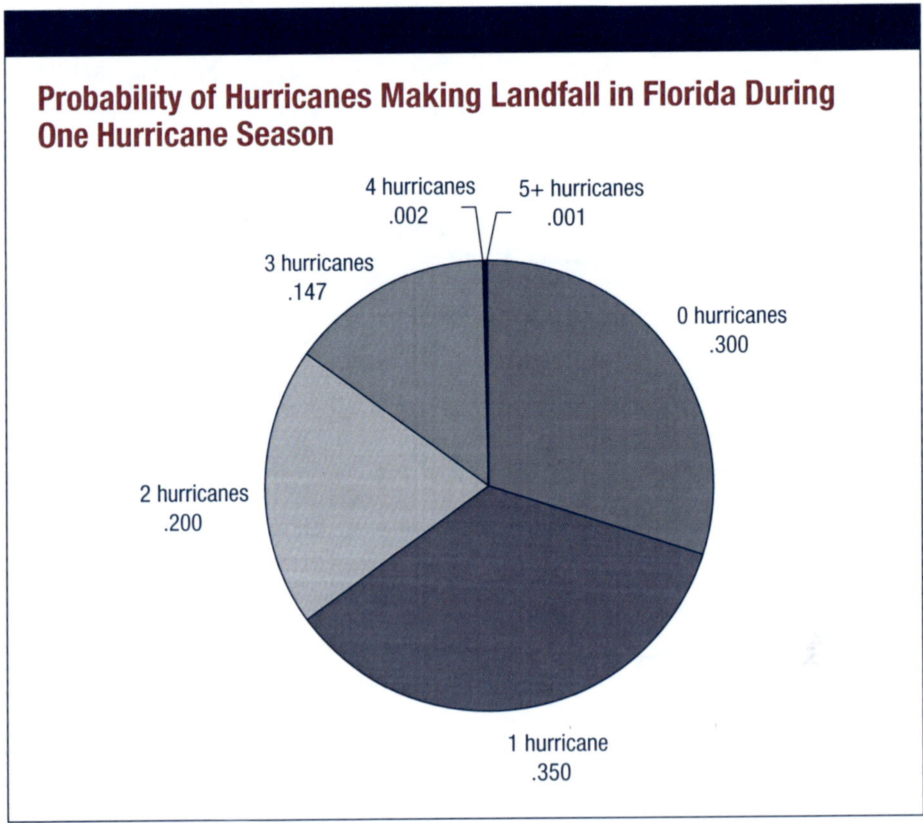

[DA02573]

three alternate presentations of this probability distribution—a table, a chart and a graph.

- All possible outcomes are accounted for (they are collectively exhaustive), and the occurrence of any possible outcome (such as green 1, red 1) excludes any other outcome.
- Eleven point values are possible (ranging from a total of two points to a total of twelve points), and the probability of each of these eleven possible point values is proportional to the number of times each point value appears in the table of outcomes.
- As the chart in the exhibit indicates, the probability of a total of two points is 1⁄36 because only one of the thirty-six possible outcomes (green 1, red 1) produces a total of two points.
- Similarly, 1⁄36 is the probability of a total of twelve points. The most likely total point value, seven points, has a probability of 6⁄36, represented in the table of outcomes by the diagonal southwest-northeast row of sevens. When the outcomes are presented as a graph, the height of the vertical line above each outcome indicates the probability of that outcome.

Although insurance and risk management professionals work with theoretical distributions on occasion, relatively few of the loss exposures they analyze involve theoretical probabilities. Therefore, most of the work they do involves empirical probability distributions. See the exhibit "Probability Distribution of Total Points on One Roll of Two Dice."

Empirical Probability Distributions

Empirical probability distributions (estimated from historical data) are constructed in the same way as theoretical probability distributions. The exhibit shows a hypothetical empirical probability distribution for auto physical damage losses. See the exhibit "Estimated Probability Distribution of Auto Physical Damage Losses."

Because the first requirement of a probability distribution is that it provide a mutually exclusive, collectively exhaustive list of outcomes, loss categories (bins) must be designed so that all losses can be included. One method is to divide the bins into equal sizes, similar to the exhibit, with each bin size being a standard size (in this case, $5,000).

The second requirement of a probability distribution is that it define the set of probabilities associated with each of the possible outcomes. The exhibit shows empirical probabilities for each size category in Column 3.

To determine the empirical probabilities in Column 3, the number of losses for each category (Column 2) is divided by the total number of losses. The sum of the resulting empirical probabilities is 100 percent (that is, the outcomes are collectively exhaustive) and any given loss falls into only one category (the outcomes are mutually exclusive). Therefore, the empirical

Probability Distribution of Total Points on One Roll of Two Dice

A. Table of Outcomes

		Red Die					
		1	2	3	4	5	6
Green Die	1	2	3	4	5	6	7
	2	3	4	5	6	7	8
	3	4	5	6	7	8	9
	4	5	6	7	8	9	10
	5	6	7	8	9	10	11
	6	7	8	9	10	11	12

B. Chart Format

Total Points Both Dice	Probability				
2	1/36	or	.028	or	2.8%
3	2/36	or	.056	or	5.6
4	3/36	or	.083	or	8.3
5	4/36	or	.111	or	11.1
6	5/36	or	.139	or	13.9
7	6/36	or	.167	or	16.7
8	5/36	or	.139	or	13.9
9	4/36	or	.111	or	11.1
10	3/36	or	.083	or	8.3
11	2/36	or	.056	or	5.6
12	1/36	or	.028	or	2.8
Total	36/36	or	1.000	or	100.0%

Note: Total may not sum to 1 or 100% because of rounding.

C. Graph Format

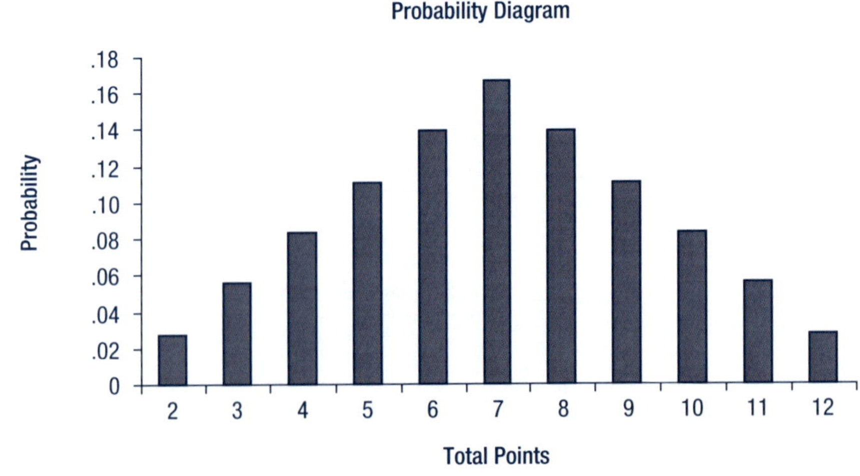

[DA02574]

Estimated Probability Distribution of Auto Physical Damage Losses

(1) Size Category of Losses (bins)	(2) Number of Losses	(3) Percentage of Number of Losses	(4) Dollar Amount of Losses	(5) Percentage of Dollar Amount
\$0–\$5,000	7	36.84%	\$18,007	10.64%
\$5,001–\$10,000	7	36.84	51,448	30.39
\$10,001–\$15,000	2	10.53	27,298	16.13
\$15,001–\$20,000	1	5.26	15,589	9.21
\$20,001–\$25,000	1	5.26	21,425	12.66
\$25,001+	1	5.26	35,508	20.98
Total	19	100.00%	\$169,275	100.00%

Mean dollar amount = \$8,909

[DA02575]

probability distribution for losses is described by Columns 1 and 3 and satisfies all the requirements of a probability distribution.

The empirical probability distribution for auto physical damage losses presented in the exhibit differs in two ways from the theoretical probability distributions of the dice rolls shown in the "Probability Distribution of Total Points on One Roll of Two Dice" exhibit:

- First, the outcomes shown in Column 1 of the auto physical damage exhibit (size categories of losses) are arbitrarily defined boundaries, whereas the outcomes of a roll of dice are specific and observable.
- Second, whereas the maximum possible dice total is twelve, the largest size of auto physical damage losses (\$25,000+) has no evident upper limit.

Discrete and Continuous Probability Distributions

Probability distributions come in two forms: discrete probability distributions and continuous probability distributions. Discrete probability distributions have a finite number of possible outcomes, whereas continuous probability distributions have an infinite number of possible outcomes.

Discrete probability distributions are usually displayed in a table that lists all possible outcomes and the probability of each outcome. These distributions are typically used to analyze how often something will occur; that is, they are shown as frequency distributions. The number of hurricanes making landfall in Florida (shown in the "Number of Hurricanes Making Landfall in

Florida During One Hurricane Season" exhibit) is an example of a frequency distribution.

Discrete probability distributions have a countable number of outcomes. For example, it is impossible to have 2.5 outcomes. In contrast, continuous probability distributions have an infinite number of possible outcome values and are generally represented in one of two ways: either as a graph or by dividing the distribution into a countable number of bins (shown in the "Estimated Probability Distribution of Auto Physical Damage Losses" exhibit).

The "Continuous Probability Distributions" exhibit illustrates two representations of continuous probability distributions. The possible outcomes are presented on the horizontal axes, and the likelihood of those outcomes is shown in the vertical axes. The height of the line or curve above the outcomes indicates the likelihood of that outcome. The outcomes in a continuous probability distribution are called probability density functions. Continuous probability distributions are typically used for severity distributions—they depict the value of the loss rather than the number of outcomes.

Figure (a) in the "Continuous Probability Distributions" exhibit, which has a flat line above the interval $0 to $1,000, illustrates that all of the outcomes between $0 and $1,000 are equally likely. Figure (b), which has a curve that starts at $0 and increases until it reaches a peak at $500 and then declines to $0 again at $1,000, illustrates that the very low (close to $0) and very high (close to $1,000) outcomes are unlikely and that the outcomes around $500 are much more likely. See the exhibit "Continuous Probability Distributions."

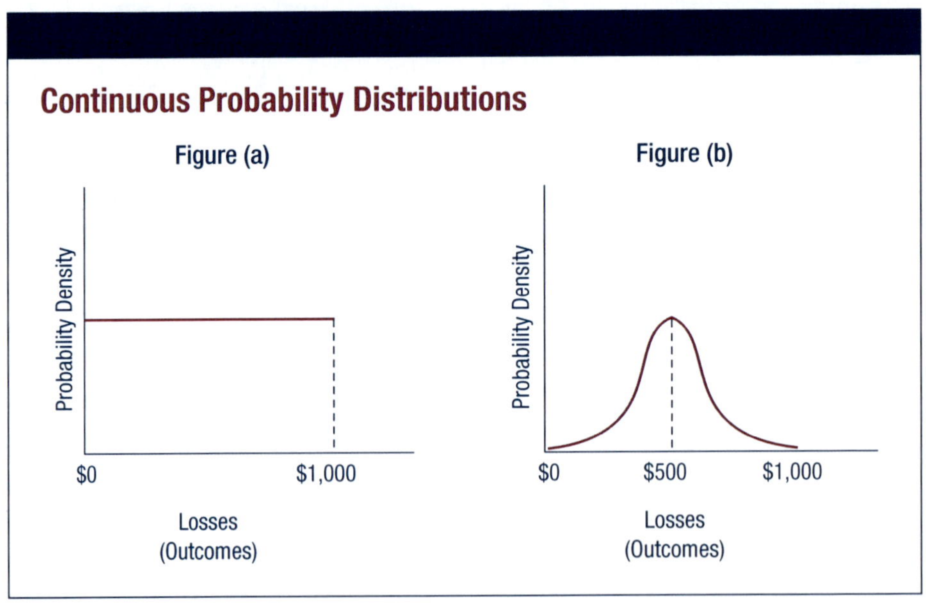

[DA02576]

The other way of presenting a continuous probability distribution is to divide the distribution into a countable number of bins. The "Estimated Probability

Distribution of Auto Physical Damage Losses" exhibit displays auto physical damage losses in a continuous probability distribution that has been divided into six bins described by various ranges of losses. Although the auto physical damage distribution is a continuous probability distribution, the dividing of the losses into bins makes the continuous distribution resemble a discrete probability distribution with several outcomes.

In continuous probability distributions used as severity distributions, the value lost can take any value between $0 and some upper limit (such as $1,000,000). By definition, continuous probability distributions have an infinite number of possible outcomes (otherwise they are discrete distributions). Therefore, the probability of any given outcome is zero, as there are an uncountable number of other outcomes.

As a result, an insurance or risk management professional has to divide the continuous distribution into a finite number of bins. When divided into bins, a probability of an outcome falling within a certain range can be calculated.

For example, in a discrete frequency distribution, the probability of a high-rise office building not having a fire (zero fires) may be .50, of having one fire—.35, and of having two fires—.15. If a fire occurs, the damage may be anywhere between $0 and $1,000,000,000, which is a continuous severity distribution.

It is almost impossible for an insurance or risk management professional to assign a probability to the likelihood of having a loss amount of $35,456.32. However, if the severity distribution is divided into a finite number of bins, $0–$1,000,000, $1,000,001–$2,000,000, and so on, it is possible to assign a probability to each bin.

For example, the probability of the damage being between $0 and $1,000,000 is .25, and the probability of the damage being between $1,000,001 and $2,000,000 is .30. By dividing a continuous distribution into bins, the insurance or risk management professional simplifies the analysis necessary to develop a forecast of future losses using frequency and severity distributions.

USING CENTRAL TENDENCY

In analyzing a probability distribution, the measures of central tendency represent the best guess as to what the outcome will be. For example, if a manager asked an underwriter what the expected losses from fire would be on a store that the underwriter had insured, the underwriter's best guess would be one of the measures of central tendency of the frequency distribution multiplied by one of the measures of central tendency of the severity distribution. So, if the expected number of fires was two, and each fire had an expected severity of $5,000, the underwriter would expect $10,000 in losses.

Central tendency
The single outcome that is the most representative of all possible outcomes included within a probability distribution.

After determining empirical probabilities and constructing probability distributions, the insurance or risk management professional can use **central**

tendency to compare the characteristics of those probability distributions. Many probability distributions cluster around a particular value, which may or may not be in the exact center of the distribution's range of values. The three most widely accepted measures of central tendency are the expected value or mean, the median, and the mode.

Expected Value

Expected value
The weighted average of all of the possible outcomes of a probability distribution.

The **expected value** is the weighted average of all of the possible outcomes of a theoretical probability distribution. The weights are the probabilities of the outcomes. The outcomes of a probability distribution are symbolized as $x1$, $x2$, $x3$, ... xn (xn represents the last outcome in the series), having respective probabilities of $p1$, $p2$, $p3$, ... pn. The distribution's expected value is the sum of ($p1 \times x1$) + ($p2 \times x2$) + ($p3 \times x3$) + ... ($pn \times xn$). See the exhibit "Calculating the Expected Value of a Probability Distribution—The Two Dice Example."

Calculating the Expected Value of a Probability Distribution—The Two Dice Example

(1) Total Points—Both Dice (x)	(2) Probability (p)	(3) $p \times x$	(4) Cumulative Probability (sum of p's)
2	1/36	2/36	1/36
3	2/36	6/36	3/36
4	3/36	12/36	6/36
5	4/36	20/36	10/36
6	5/36	30/36	15/36
7	6/36	42/36	21/36
8	5/36	40/36	26/36
9	4/36	36/36	30/36
10	3/36	30/36	33/36
11	2/36	22/36	35/36
12	1/36	12/36	36/36, or 100%
Total	36/36 = 1	252/36 = 7.0	

Expected Value = 252/36 = 7.0
Median = 7 (There is an equal number of outcomes (15) above and below 7.)
Mode = 7 (The most frequent outcome.)

[DA02577]

In the example of a probability distribution of total points on one roll of a pair of dice, the distribution's expected value of 7.0 is shown in the exhibit as the sum of the values in Column 3.

The procedure for calculating the expected value applies to all theoretical discrete probability distributions, regardless of their shape or dispersion. For continuous distributions, the expected value is also a weighted average of the possible outcomes. However, calculating the expected value for a continuous distribution is much more complex and therefore is not discussed here.

Mean

Probabilities are needed to calculate a theoretical distribution's expected value. However, when considering an empirical distribution constructed from historical data, the measure of central tendency is not called the expected value, it is called the **mean**. In other words, the mean is the numeric average. Just as the expected value is calculated by weighting each possible outcome by its probability, the mean is calculated by weighting each observed outcome by the relative frequency with which it occurs.

Mean
The sum of the values in a data set divided by the number of values.

For example, if the observed outcome values are 2, 3, 4, 4, 5, 5, 5, 6, 6, and 8, then the mean equals 4.8, which is the sum of the values, 48, divided by the number of values, 10. The mean is only a good estimate of the expected outcome if the underlying conditions determining those outcomes remain constant over time.

Unlike the expected value, which is derived from theory, the mean is derived from experience. If the conditions that generated that experience have changed, the mean that was calculated may no longer be an accurate estimate of central tendency. Nonetheless, an insurance or a risk management professional will often use the mean as the single best guess as to forecasting future events.

For example, the best guess as to the number of workers compensation claims that an organization will suffer in the next year is often the mean of the frequency distribution of workers compensation claims from previous years.

Median and Cumulative Probabilities

Another measure of central tendency is the **median**. In order to determine a data set's median, its values must be arranged by size, from highest to lowest or lowest to highest. In the array of nineteen auto physical damage losses in the exhibit, the median loss has an adjusted value of $6,782. This tenth loss is the median because nine losses are greater than $6,782 and nine losses are less than $6,782. See the exhibit "Array of Historical and Adjusted Auto Physical Damage Losses."

Median
The value at the midpoint of a sequential data set with an odd number of values, or the mean of the two middle values of a sequential data set with an even number of values.

A probability distribution's median has a cumulative probability of 50 percent. For example, seven is the median of the probability distribution of points in

Array of Historical and Adjusted Auto Physical Damage Losses

(1) Date	(2) Historical Loss Amount	(3) Adjusted Loss Amount*	(4) Rank
09/29/X3	$ 155	$ 200	19
04/21/X3	1,008	1,300	18
03/18/X4	1,271	1,500	17
12/04/X3	1,783	2,300	16
07/27/X5	3,774	4,000	15
06/14/X6	4,224	4,224	14
04/22/X6	4,483	4,483	13
02/08/X5**	5,189	5,500	12
05/03/X3	4,651	5,999	11
01/02/X6**	6,782	6,782	10
07/12/X4	6,271	7,402	9
05/17/X5**	7,834	8,303	8
08/15/X4	7,119	8,403	7
06/10/X6	9,059	9,059	6
12/19/X5	12,830	13,599	5
08/04/X5	12,925	13,699	4
11/01/X4	13,208	15,589	3
01/09/X6	21,425	21,425	2
10/23/X6	35,508	35,508	1

* Adjusted amount column is the historical loss amount adjusted to current year dollars using a price index.

** Loss for which adjustment of historical amount to current year dollars changes ranking in array.

[DA02578]

rolling two dice because seven is the only number of points for which the probability of higher outcomes (15/36) is equal to the probability of lower outcomes (15/36). That is, there are fifteen equally probable ways of obtaining an outcome higher than seven and fifteen equally probable ways of obtaining an outcome lower than seven.

The median can also be determined by summing the probabilities of outcomes equal to or less than a given number of points in rolling two dice, as in the "Calculating the Expected Value of a Probability Distribution—The Two Dice Example" exhibit. The cumulative 50 percent probability (18/36) is reached in the seven-points category (actually, in the middle of the seven-point class of results). Therefore, seven is the median of this distribution.

The cumulative probabilities in Column 4 of the exhibit indicate the probability of a die roll yielding a certain number of points or less. For example, the cumulative probability of rolling a three or less is 3/36 (or the sum of 1/36 for rolling a two and 2/36 for rolling a three). Similarly, the cumulative probability of rolling a ten or less is 33/36, calculated by summing the individual Column 2 probabilities of outcomes of ten points or less.

With probability distributions of losses, calculating probabilities of losses equal to or less than a given number of losses or dollar amounts of losses, individually and cumulatively, can be helpful in selecting retention levels. Similarly, calculating individual and cumulative probabilities of losses equal to or greater than a given number of losses or dollar amounts can help in selecting upper limits of insurance coverage.

The "Cumulative Probabilities" exhibit shows how to derive a cumulative probability distribution of loss sizes from the individual probabilities of loss size in the exhibit. See the exhibit "Cumulative Probabilities That Auto Physical Damage Losses Will Not Exceed Specified Amounts."

Column 3 of the "Cumulative Probabilities" exhibit indicates that, on the basis of the available data, 36.84 percent of all losses are less than or equal to $5,000 and that another 36.84 percent are greater than $5,000 but less than or equal to $10,000. Therefore, the probability of a loss being $10,000 or less is calculated as the sum of these two probabilities, or 73.68 percent, as shown in Column 4 of the "Cumulative Probabilities" exhibit. Similarly, as shown in Column 7 of the same exhibit, individual losses of $10,000 or less can be expected to account for 41.03 percent of the total dollar amount of all losses.

Understanding the cumulative probability distribution will enable an insurance or risk management professional to evaluate the effect of various deductibles and policy limits on insured loss exposures. For example, if an insurance policy has a $5,000 deductible, the insurance or risk management professional would know that 36.84 percent of losses covered by that policy would be below the deductible level and therefore would not be paid by the insurer.

The summed probabilities in Column 4 of the "Cumulative Probabilities" exhibit indicate that the median individual loss is between $5,001 and $10,000, the category in which the 50 percent cumulative probability is reached. This result is consistent with the $6,782 median loss found by examining the "Array of Historical and Adjusted Auto Physical Damage Losses" exhibit.

Mode

Mode
The most frequently occurring value in a distribution.

In addition to mean and median, a further measure of central tendency is the **mode**. For a continuous distribution, the mode is the value of the out-

Cumulative Probabilities That Auto Physical Damage Losses Will Not Exceed Specified Amounts

(1) Loss Size Category	(2) Number of Losses	(3) Percentage of Number of Losses	(4) Cumulative Percentage of Number of Losses Not Exceeding Category	(5) Dollar Amount of Losses	(6) Percentage of Dollar Amount	(7) Cumulative Percentage of Dollar Amount of Losses Not Exceeding Category
$0–$5,000	7	36.84%	36.84%	$18,007	10.64%	10.64%
$5,001–$10,000	7	36.84	73.68	51,448	30.39	41.03
$10,001–$15,000	2	10.53	84.21	27,298	16.13	57.16
$15,001–$20,000	1	5.26	89.47	15,589	9.21	66.37
$20,001–$25,000	1	5.26	94.74	21,425	12.66	79.02
$25,001+	1	5.26	100.00	35,508	20.98	100.00
Total		100.00%			100.00%	

[DA02579]

come directly beneath the peak of the probability density function. In the distribution of total points of two dice throws, the mode is seven points. In the empirical distribution of auto physical damage losses shown in the "Cumulative Probabilities" exhibit, the mode is the $0–$5,000 range or the $5,001–$10,000 range, because those ranges have the highest frequency of losses (seven).

Knowing the mode of a distribution allows insurance and risk management professionals to focus on the outcomes that are the most common. For example, knowing that the most common auto physical damage losses are in the $0–$10,000 range may influence the risk financing decisions regarding deductible levels for potential insurance coverages.

The relationships among the mean (average), median, and mode for any data set are illustrated by the distribution's shape. The shape of a particular relative frequency or severity probability distribution can be seen by graphing a curve of the data as shown in the "Typical Shapes" exhibit and can be either symmetrical or asymmetrical. See the exhibit "Typical Shapes of Symmetrical and Skewed Distributions Showing Relative Locations of Mean, Median, and Mode."

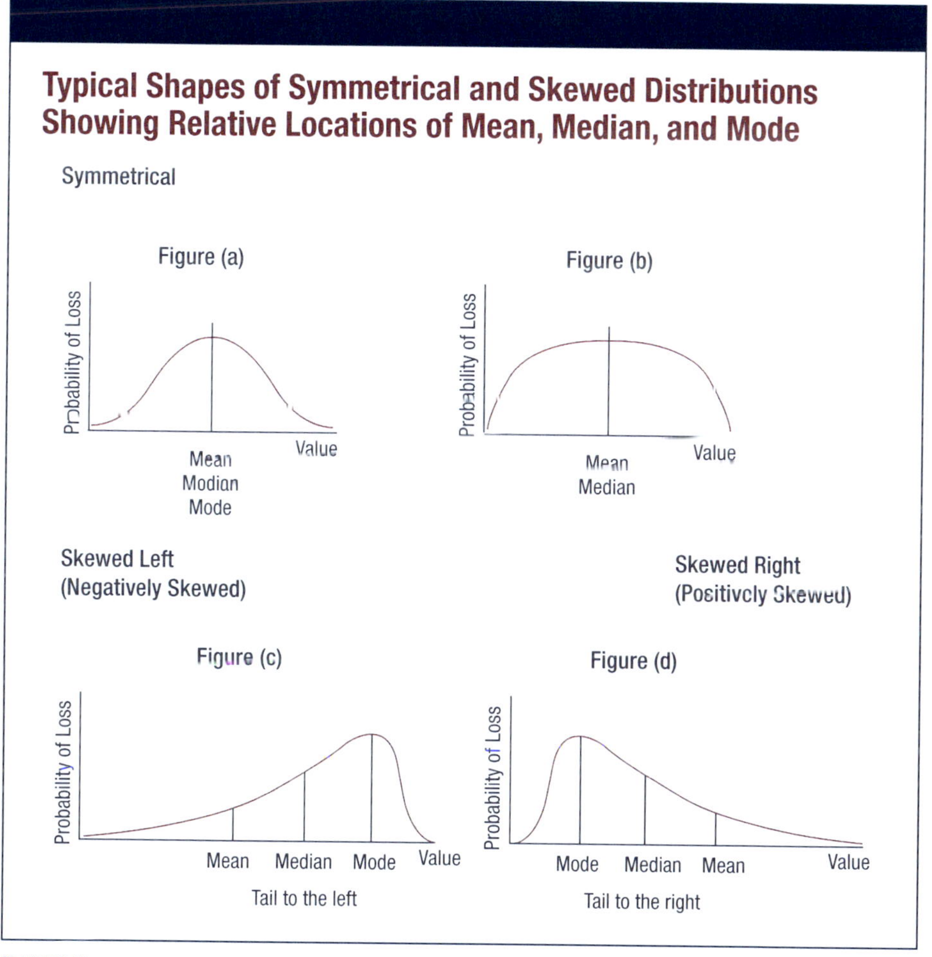

[DA02581]

In a symmetrical distribution, one side of the curve is a mirror image of the other. The distribution in Figure (a) of the exhibit is the standard (normal) distribution commonly called a bell-shaped curve, but the distributions in both Figure (a) and Figure (b) are symmetrical. In a symmetrical distribution, the mean and median have the same value. In a standard bell-shaped distribution, the mode also has the same value as that of the mean and the median.

If a distribution is asymmetrical, it is skewed. Skewed distributions are shown in both Figure (c) and Figure (d) of the exhibit. Many loss distributions are skewed because the probability of small losses is large whereas the probability of large losses is small. Asymmetrical distributions are common for severity distributions where most losses are small losses but there is a small probability of a large loss occurring. If the distribution is skewed, the mean and median values will differ and the median value of the distribution is often a better guess than the mean as to what is most likely to occur.

For example, if the distribution of workers compensation claims was skewed by two years in which an organization experienced an unusually high level of claims, the mean would be higher than the median. In that situation, the median is more likely a better estimate of next year's claims than the mean. See the exhibit "Practice Exercise."

Practice Exercise

Based on the mean of the total workers compensation losses for each year, the risk manager of an airline company expects the total amount of such losses next year to be $2 million. The chief financial officer has assured the risk manager that the company can afford to retain half of that amount ($1 million) in an effort to reduce the insurance premium. Using the values provided in the chart, what is the highest aggregate annual deductible the risk manager should consider?

Loss Size Category	Dollar Amount of Losses	Percentage of Total Dollar Amount of Losses
$0 – $10,000	$500,000	25%
$10,001 – $20,000	$300,000	15%
$20,001 – $50,000	$300,000	15%
$50,001 – $100,000	$400,000	20%
$100,001 +	$500,000	25%
Total	$2,000,000	100%

Answer

By adding the percentages of total dollar amounts to obtain cumulative percentages (shown in the new column, far right), the risk manager can see that 50 percent, or $1 million, will likely be retained by the company if it chooses a deductible of slightly less than $50,000. The risk manager may want to resize the loss size categories to derive a more accurate number.

Loss Size Category	Dollar Amount of Losses	Percentage of Total Dollar Amount of Losses	Cumulative Percentage of Dollar Amount of Losses Not Exceeding Category
$0 – $10,000	$500,000	25%	25%
$10,001 – $20,000	$300,000	15%	40%
$20,001 – $50,000	$300,000	15%	55%
$50,001 – $100,000	$400,000	20%	75%
$100,001 +	$500,000	25%	100%
Total	$2,000,000	100%	

[DA05840]

USING DISPERSION

When analyzing probability distributions, insurance and risk management professionals use measures of dispersion to assess the credibility of the measures of central tendency used in analyzing loss exposures.

Measures of central tendency for a distribution of outcomes include the expected value (or mean), which can provide useful information for compar-

Dispersion

The variation among values in a distribution.

ing characteristics of distributions. However, another important characteristic of a distribution is its **dispersion**. Dispersion describes the extent to which the distribution is spread out rather than concentrated around the expected value. The less dispersion around the distribution's expected value, the greater the likelihood that actual results will fall within a given range of that expected value.

Therefore, less dispersion means less uncertainty about the expected outcomes. Insurance professionals may be able to use measures of dispersion around estimated losses to determine whether to offer insurance coverage to a possible insured. Dispersion also affects the shape of a distribution. The more dispersed a distribution (larger standard deviation), the flatter the distribution. A less dispersed distribution forms a more peaked distribution. Two symmetrical distributions with the same mean but with different standard deviations are shown in the "Dispersion" exhibit. See the exhibit "Dispersion."

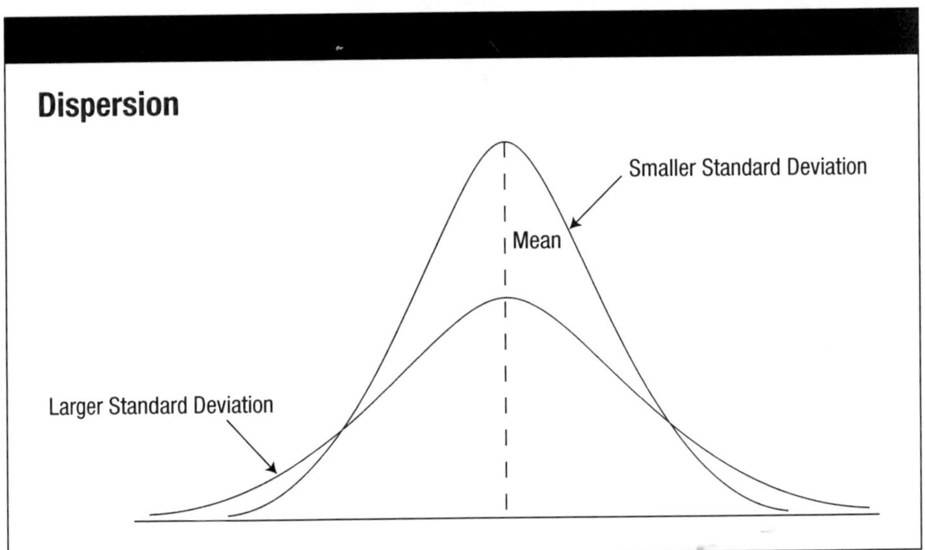

[DA02582]

For example, if an underwriter is choosing between two accounts, both with the same expected loss, but one account has more variation in possible losses then the other, the underwriter will likely choose to insure the account with less variation (lower dispersion). In general, the less dispersion around the central tendency, the less risk is involved in the loss exposure.

There are two widely used statistical measures of dispersion:

- Standard deviation
- Coefficient of variation

Standard Deviation

The **standard deviation** is the average of the differences (deviations) between the values in a distribution and the expected value (or mean) of that distribution. The standard deviation therefore indicates how widely dispersed the values in a distribution are.

Standard deviation

A measure of dispersion between the values in a distribution and the expected value (or mean) of that distribution, calculated by taking the square root of the variance.

To calculate the standard deviation of a probability distribution, one must perform these steps:

1. Calculate the distribution's expected value or mean
2. Subtract this expected value from each distribution value to find the differences
3. Square each of the resulting differences
4. Multiply each square by the probability associated with the value
5. Sum the resulting products
6. Find the square root of the sum

The "Calculation of Standard Deviation of the Probability Distribution of Two Dice" exhibit illustrates how to calculate a standard deviation for the distribution of values in rolling two dice. The distribution's expected value or mean is seven. See the exhibit "Calculation of Standard Deviation of the Probability Distribution of Two Dice."

The standard deviation of auto physical damage losses can be estimated using the individual loss amounts shown in Column (1) of the "Calculation of Standard Deviation of Individual Outcomes" exhibit. Calculating a standard deviation using a sample of actual outcomes is done in much the same way as for a probability distribution. To calculate the standard deviation using the actual sample of outcomes, it is not necessary to know the probability of each outcome, just how often each outcome occurred. See the exhibit "Calculation of Standard Deviation of Individual Outcomes."

The steps for calculating the standard deviation of a set of individual outcomes not involving probabilities are these:

1. Calculate the mean of the outcomes (the sum of the outcomes divided by the number of outcomes).
2. Subtract the mean from each of the outcomes.
3. Square each of the resulting differences.
4. Sum these squares.
5. Divide this sum by the number of outcomes minus one. (This value is called the variance.)
6. Calculate the square root of the variance.

The "Calculation of Standard Deviation of Individual Outcomes" exhibit illustrates how to calculate a standard deviation using actual loss data rather than a theoretical probability distribution. Insurance and risk management professionals use measurements of dispersion of the distributions of potential outcomes to gain a better understanding of the loss exposures being analyzed.

Calculation of Standard Deviation of the Probability Distribution of Two Dice

(1) Points (x_i)	(2) Probability (p)	(3) Step 1 EV	(4) Step 2 $x_i - EV$	(5) Step 3 $(x_i - EV)^2$	(6) Step 4 $(x_i - EV)^2 \times p$
2	1/36	7	–5	25	25/36
3	2/36	7	–4	16	32/36
4	3/36	7	–3	9	27/36
5	4/36	7	–2	4	16/36
6	5/36	7	–1	1	5/36
7	6/36	7	0	0	0
8	5/36	7	1	1	5/36
9	4/36	7	2	4	16/36
10	3/36	7	3	9	27/36
11	2/36	7	4	16	32/36
12	1/36	7	5	25	25/36
			Step 5	Total	210/36
			Step 6	$\sqrt{(210/36)}$ =	2.42*

*Rounded

[DA02583]

For example, knowing the expected number of workers compensation claims in a given year is important, but it is only one element of the information that can be gleaned from a distribution. The standard deviation can be calculated to provide a measure of how sure an insurance or risk management professional can be in his or her estimate of number of workers compensation claims.

Coefficient of Variation

Coefficient of variation

A measure of dispersion calculated by dividing a distribution's standard deviation by its mean.

The **coefficient of variation** is a further measure of the dispersion of a distribution. For example, the coefficient of variation for the distribution of total points in rolling two dice equals 2.4 points (the standard deviation of the distribution) divided by 7.0 points (the mean or expected value), which is 0.34. Similarly the coefficient of variation of the sample of outcomes in the "Calculation of Standard Deviation of Individual Outcomes" exhibit is $8,430 divided by $8,909, or approximately 0.95.

In comparing two distributions, if both distributions have the same mean (or expected value), then the distribution with the larger standard deviation

Calculation of Standard Deviation of Individual Outcomes

(1) Adjusted Loss Amount (ALA)	(2) Step 1 Mean Loss (ML)	(3) Step 2 ALA-ML	(4) Step 3 $(ALA\text{-}ML)^2$
$ 200	$8,909	$–8,709	$ 75,846,681
1,300	8,909	–7,609	57,896,881
1,500	8,909	–7,409	54,893,281
2,300	8,909	–6,609	43,678,881
4,000	8,909	–4,909	24,098,281
4,224	8,909	–4,685	21,949,225
4,483	8,909	–4,426	19,589,476
5,500	8,909	–3,409	11,621,281
5,999	8,909	–2,910	8,468,100
6,782	8,909	–2,127	4,524,129
7,402	8,909	–1,507	2,271,049
8,303	8,909	–606	367,236
8,403	8,909	–506	256,036
9,059	8,909	150	22,500
13,599	8,909	4,690	21,996,100
13,699	8,909	4,790	22,944,100
15,589	8,909	6,680	44,622,400
21,425	8,909	12,516	156,650,256
35,508	8,909	26,599	707,506,801
Step 4	Sum		$1,279,202,694
Step 5	Variance [sum ÷ (n – 1)]		71,066,816
Step 6	Standard deviation (sqrt variance)		$8,430

[DA02584]

has the greater variability. If the two distributions have different means (or expected values), the coefficient of variation is often used to compare the two distributions to determine which has the greater variability relative to its mean (or expected value).

For insurance and risk management professionals, comparing two distinct distributions with different means and standard deviations is difficult. In the example of an underwriter trying to determine to which account to offer coverage, if the means are the same, all else being equal, the underwriter should choose the account with the lower standard deviation. If the accounts have different means and standard deviations, the underwriter could compare the two accounts using the coefficient of variation and choose the account with the lower coefficient of variation.

Insurance and risk management professionals can use the coefficient of variation to determine whether a particular loss control measure has made losses more or less predictable (that is, whether the distribution is more or less variable).

For example, an insurance or a risk management professional may calculate that an organization's theft losses have a severity distribution with a mean of $3,590 and a standard deviation of $3,432 for a coefficient of variation of 0.96. If the organization installs a new security system, the theft losses may have a severity distribution with a mean of $2,150 and a standard deviation of $2,950 for a coefficient of variation of 1.37.

Although the security system has reduced the mean severity, it has actually made the losses less predictable because the new severity distribution is relatively more variable than the old distribution without the security system.

The coefficient of variation is useful in comparing the variability of distributions that have different shapes, means, or standard deviations. The distribution with the largest coefficient of variation has the greatest relative variability. The higher the variability within a distribution, the more difficult it is to accurately forecast an individual outcome.

CALCULATING ALTERNATIVE PROBABILITIES

Alternative probability
The probability that any one of two or more events will occur within a given period.

Alternative probability is the probability that any one of two or more events will occur within a given period. The formula for calculating alternative probabilities is determined by whether the events involved are mutually exclusive. Examples that will be used in this section, to calculate alternative probabilities, are the probability that either a three or a five will come up in one roll of one die (mutually exclusive events), the probability that a card drawn from a deck will be either a five or a club (not mutually exclusive), and the probability that Galston Transport will suffer either a fire loss or a burglary loss within the next year.

The formula for calculating alternative probabilities is determined by whether the events involved are mutually exclusive. Two or more events are mutually exclusive if the occurrence of one makes the other impossible. For example, rolling a three on a die makes it impossible to roll a five (or any other number) on the same roll, so three and five on one roll of one die are mutually exclusive events.

Similarly, the probabilities that Galston will suffer no collision loss in a particular year, that it will suffer only one collision loss, that it will suffer only two collision losses, and that it will suffer more than two collision losses are

probabilities of four mutually exclusive events, because in no one year can the number of collision losses fall into any two or more of these categories.

Examples of events that are not mutually exclusive include drawing a five or a club from a deck of cards on one draw (because the five of clubs may be drawn) and Galston suffering both collision and snow closure losses in a particular year (because in one year, Galston could experience both of these causes of loss).

Mutually Exclusive Events

For mutually exclusive events, the probability that any one of them will occur is the sum of their separate probabilities:

$$p(A \text{ or } B) = p(A) + p(B)$$

Therefore, the probability of rolling either a three or a five on one roll of one die is

$$p(3 \text{ or } 5) = {}^{1}/_{6} + {}^{1}/_{6} = {}^{2}/_{6} \text{ (or } {}^{1}/_{3}\text{)}$$

Another set of mutually exclusive events concerns the dollar amounts of individual losses. Because a given loss can be only one particular dollar amount, no individual loss can fall into two loss severity categories. A loss is, for example, either:

1. Less than $5,000
2. Equal to or more than $5,000

In a probability distribution of losses by size (severity distribution), the probability of a loss equal to or less than a given figure is the sum of the probabilities of losses up to this figure. As mentioned previously, the sum of the probabilities of all possible mutually exclusive events—events that are both mutually exclusive and collectively exhaustive—is one.

Probabilities of mutually exclusive events are also relevant to risk management situations in which loss can be caused by one of two causes of loss but not by more than one. For example, Galston Transport might lose a particular truck by fire or by flood, but not by both causes of loss. In other words, the truck being lost by fire and the truck being lost by flood are mutually exclusive events. Suppose that the probability that a given truck will be destroyed by fire in a given year is .04 and that the probability of this truck being lost to flood in that year is .06. The probability of the truck being lost to either fire or flood during that year is expressed as:

$$\begin{aligned} p(\text{flood or fire}) &= p(\text{flood}) + p(\text{fire}) \\ &= .06 + .04 \\ &= .10 \end{aligned}$$

Nonmutually Exclusive Events

When two or more events can occur within a specified time period, they are not mutually exclusive. For such events, the probability that at least one, and possibly both or all of them, will occur is the sum of their separate probabilities minus the joint probability that they will both or all occur. For two nonmutually exclusive events, A and B, this can be expressed as:

$$p(A \text{ or } B \text{ or both}) = p(A) + p(B) - p(A \text{ and } B)$$

or

$$p(A \text{ or } B \text{ but not both}) = [p(A) \times p(\text{not } B)] + [p(B) \times p(\text{not } A)]$$

With more than two events that are not mutually exclusive, the calculations become more complex. Therefore, this discussion of alternative probabilities for nonmutually exclusive events is restricted to cases involving only two events. For example, the probability of drawing a five from a deck of cards without jokers is $^1/_{13}$, the probability of drawing a club is $^1/_4$, and the probability of drawing the five of clubs is $^1/_{52}$. Therefore, the probability of drawing a five or a club is calculated as:

$$\begin{aligned} p(\text{five or club}) &= p(\text{five}) + p(\text{club}) - p(\text{five and club}) \\ &= {}^1/_{13} + {}^1/_4 - {}^1/_{52} \\ &= {}^4/_{52} + {}^{13}/_{52} - {}^1/_{52} \\ &= {}^{16}/_{52} \\ &= {}^4/_{13} \end{aligned}$$

Subtracting the joint probability of events that are not mutually exclusive is necessary to avoid overstating the probability of the alternative events by double-counting the five of clubs as both a five and a club.

The problem of double-counting becomes more serious with events that have large probabilities. Suppose that the climate in a particular area is such that the probability of rain at noon on any given day is .50 and that the probability that the noon temperature will exceed 70 degrees is .80. On some days, it is both raining and warmer than 70 degrees at noon, so rain and heat above 70 degrees are not mutually exclusive. In this example, rain and heat are assumed to be independent. If the joint probability of rain and heat is not subtracted, the probability of either rain or heat, or both, is mistakenly calculated as p(rain or heat or both) = .50 + .80 = 1.30. This is an impossible result because, by definition, no probability can exceed 1.0. The following is the proper calculation:

$$\begin{aligned} p(\text{rain or heat or both}) &= p(\text{rain}) + p(\text{heat}) - p(\text{rain and heat}) \\ &= p(\text{rain}) + p(\text{heat}) - [p(\text{rain}) \times p(\text{heat})] \\ &= .50 + .80 - (.50 \times .80) \\ &= .50 + .80 - .40 \\ &= .90 \end{aligned}$$

Therefore, the probability that at noon it will be raining, or the temperature will exceed 70 degrees, or both is .90.

Calculating Alternative Probabilities

Calculating the alternative probability of two events, but not both, when one does not know the probability of both, involves:

1. Identifying each of the mutually exclusive ways that the events may occur
2. Calculating the probability of each of these ways
3. Adding the resulting probabilities

For two nonmutually exclusive events, A and B, this can be expressed as:

$$\begin{aligned} p(A \text{ or } B \text{ but not both}) &= [p(A) \times p(\text{not } B)] + [p(B) \times p(\text{not } A)] \\ &= [p(A) \times (1-p(B))] + [p(B) \times (1-p(A))] \end{aligned}$$

For example, the probability of heat or rain but not both at noon on a particular day is equal to the probability of heat and no rain plus the probability of rain plus no heat. Those two combinations of circumstances are the only two ways of having rain or heat but not both. Because the probability of rain is .50 and the probability of heat is .80, the alternative probability of the two events is calculated as:

$$\begin{aligned} p(\text{rain and no heat}) &= p(\text{rain}) \times p(\text{no heat}) \\ &= p(\text{rain}) \times [1-p(\text{heat})] \\ &= .50 \times (1 - .80) \\ &= .50 \times .20 \\ &= .10. \end{aligned}$$

$$\begin{aligned} p(\text{heat and no rain}) &= p(\text{heat}) \times p(\text{no rain}) \\ &= p(\text{heat}) \times [1-p(\text{rain})] \\ &= .80 \times (1 - .50) \\ &= .80 \times .50 \\ &= .40. \end{aligned}$$

Therefore:

$$\begin{aligned} p(\text{rain or heat but not both}) &= p(\text{rain and no heat}) + p(\text{heat and no rain}) \\ &= .10 + .40 \\ &= .50 \end{aligned}$$

In risk management, alternative probabilities of nonmutually exclusive events arise when dealing with two or more causes of loss that can each occur either independently or simultaneously. For example, the cargo inside one of Galston's trucks could be affected by both water damage (by less than total flooding) and theft (of less than an entire truck load). Assume, for example, that the probability of theft loss (pilferage) to a shipment is .09 and that the

probability of water damage is .06. The probability of loss by pilferage or water damage or both is calculated as:

$$p(A \text{ or } B \text{ but not both}) = [p(A) \times p(\text{not } B)] + [p(B) \times p(\text{not } A)]$$
$$= [p(A) \times (1 - p(B))] + [p(B) \times (1 - p(A))]$$

Calculating the probability of theft or water damage but not both requires summing the probabilities of the two mutually exclusive ways that this result can occur. Those are the probabilities of (1) pilferage but no water damage and (2) water damage but no pilferage. The calculation is shown:

$$p(\text{pilferage but no water damage}) = p(\text{pilferage}) \times [1 - p(\text{water damage})]$$
$$= .09 \times (1 - .06)$$
$$= .09 \times .94$$
$$= .0846$$

$$p(\text{water damage but no pilferage}) = p(\text{water damage}) \times [1 - p(\text{pilferage})]$$
$$= .06 \times (1 - .09)$$
$$= .06 \times .91$$
$$= .0546$$

$$p(\text{pilferage or water damage but not both}) = .0846 + .0546$$
$$= .1392$$

The probability of either kind of damage but not both is smaller than the probability of either kind of damage and possibly both because the former excludes the chance of both happening. See the exhibit "Summary of Probability Calculations."

Summary of Probability Calculations

m = the number of occurrences of the event whose probability is sought.

n = the number of opportunities for the event to occur (exposure units or exposures).

The probability that an event, A, will occur in a given period:

$$p(A) = m \div n$$

The expected number of events in a given period:

$$E\text{(total number of events)} = n \times p\text{(single event)}.$$

The probability that an event, A, will not occur in a given period:

$$p(\text{not } A) = 1 - p(A)$$

The probability that both event A and event B will occur in a given period:

If A and B are independent: $p(A \text{ and } B) = p(A) \times p(B)$

If A is dependent on B: $p(A \text{ and } B) = p(B) \times p(A|B)$

If A is sequentially dependent on B: $p(B \text{ followed by } A) = p(B) \times p(A \text{ following } B)$

The probability of events that are independent of each other occurring multiple times:

$$p(A \text{ occurring x times}) = p(A)^x$$

The probability that either event A or event B will occur in a given period:

If A and B are mutually exclusive:

$$p(A \text{ or } B) = p(A) + p(B)$$

If A and B are not mutually exclusive:

$$p(A \text{ or } B \text{ or both}) = p(A) + p(B) - p(A \text{ and } B)$$

or:

$$p(A \text{ or } B \text{ but not both}) = [p(A) \times p(\text{not } B)] + [p(B) \times p(\text{not } A)].$$

[DA01957]

UNDERSTANDING THE LAW OF LARGE NUMBERS

The law of large numbers is the mathematical principle that serves as the foundation for insurance pricing.

The law of large numbers makes risk transference possible. By transferring risk to an insurer, members of a group or pool exchange the uncertainty of an unspecified economic loss for the certainty of a definite insurance premium payment. Insurance is able to reduce the uncertainty of the individual members of the pool by increasing the predictability of the pool as a whole.

Operation of the Law of Large Numbers

The law of large numbers explains how pooling increases predictability and the conditions that must be met for it to operate properly. According to the law of large numbers, adapted for insurance purposes, as the number of similar, independent **exposure units** increases, the relative accuracy of predictions about future losses based on these exposure units also increases.

Exposure unit

A fundamental measure of the loss exposure assumed by an insurer.

For example, actuaries use car year as the exposure unit for auto insurance—one auto insured for a twelve-month period. In simple terms, actuaries divide total losses and loss adjustment expenses by the number of exposure units to determine loss costs per unit of exposure. While car year is the appropriate exposure unit, or exposure base, for auto insurance, other lines of insurance use exposure bases that are responsive to the characteristics of the insurance being provided. Rating manuals used by underwriters and underwriting technicians for individual account pricing often use the term "exposure basis" interchangeably with "**premium base**." See the exhibit "Pooling and Insurance Rates."

Premium base

The unit in which the exposure is measured, such as gross sales or payroll.

Underwriting account selection activities are critical to the proper operation of the law of large numbers. In addition to having a large number of exposure units, viable risk transfer requires exposure units to be independent and homogeneous. Underwriters, through exposure analysis and classification, help ensure that these conditions are met. See the exhibit "The Law of Large Numbers—Insurance Example."

Homogeneity

The operation of the law of large numbers is predicated on the exposure units' being similar or **homogeneous**, but not necessarily identical. Homogeneity is ensured through classification systems and the refinement of those systems.

Homogeneous

Units of exposure that face approximately the same expected frequency and severity of loss.

Insurance classification systems group risks that share similar characteristics and that usually have the same likelihood of loss. Categories created by separate lines of business, such as general liability and commercial property, also help improve the homogeneity of events that might cause a loss.

Actuaries and underwriters try to identify additional attributes that affect or reflect potential frequency and severity of loss. Actuaries are often able to use this information to create a more-refined classification system that produces more accurately priced accounts. Underwriters look for these attributes during the underwriting process so that they can select superior accounts within a classification.

The goal of actuaries and underwriters when designing a rating system is to make each class as homogeneous as possible without sacrificing the predictive accuracy that large numbers create. The level of confidence an actuary has in projected losses (and the resulting rates) increases as the number of exposure units increases. Actuaries call this confidence level credibility. Credibility

Pooling and Insurance Rates

Pooling is a fundamental risk management concept that is essential to the operation of insurance. Understanding how insurance reduces risk through pooling helps risk management and insurance professionals evaluate the effectiveness of insurance relative to other risk management techniques. In the context of risk financing, a pool is a financial arrangement that combines the loss exposures and financial resources of individuals or organizations within a group to share losses experienced by members of the group.

Insurance involves sharing losses experienced by those insured through an insurer. The insurer pools premiums paid by insureds, and insureds who incur covered losses are paid from the insurer's pooled funds. The total cost of losses is thereby spread (or shared) among all insureds. Insurers estimate the total cost of future losses, based on past loss experience, to determine how much they must collect from insureds in premiums.

The amount of premium collected from an insured is determined by multiplying the number of the insured's exposure units by the insurance rate. The insurance rate is the amount charged per unit of exposure and has several components. The largest component is established to pay for expected losses of the insureds. It is referred to as the pure premium and is the average amount of money an insurer must charge per exposure unit to be able to cover the total expected losses (including loss adjustment expenses) for an insurer's line of business, such as homeowners insurance.

Another component of the insurance rate is the risk charge. This is an amount collected in addition to the expected loss component of the premium (the pure premium) to compensate the insurer for taking the risk that actual losses might be higher than expected. Even with a sufficient number of similar, independent exposure units to make the law of large numbers operate effectively, the expected losses of a pooled group of insureds rarely equal the group's actual losses. Estimates of expected losses vary in their credibility. The higher the confidence in the estimate, the lower the risk charge.

A third component of the insurance rate is funds for the administrative costs to sell and service the insurance coverage as well as the insurer's overhead costs. Administrative costs are usually charged as a percentage of the overall insurance rate. The overall insurance rate—which includes the rate components of pure premium, risk charge, and administrative costs—is referred to as the gross premium.

[DA08856]

factors are used to minimize variations in rates that result from purely chance variations in losses. Credibility factors range from zero (no credibility at all) to one (full confidence). One simple way of applying credibility is to multiply the projected rate change by the credibility factor. For example, if the credibility factor is 0.30 and the data indicate that a rate increase of 10 percent is needed, a rate increase of 3 percent (10 × 0.30) is warranted. This same approach is appropriate for rate reductions.

The Law of Large Numbers—Insurance Example

Assume that the chance of any one Businessowner (BOP) insured's experiencing a loss (frequency of loss) is 1 percent (or 1 in 100). Further assume that Insurer A sells one BOP policy in each of ten different cities, for a total of ten policies. If none of the ten policyholders experiences a loss, the group has no losses (a 0 percent frequency of loss). If one policyholder experiences a loss, the group's actual loss frequency is 10 percent (1 in 10). Similarly, if two policyholders suffer losses, the group's actual loss frequency is 20 percent (2 in 10). The group's performance (0 percent, 10 percent, and 20 percent) differs significantly from the expected loss frequency of 1 percent for BOP insurance.

As Insurer A sells more BOP policies, the size of the group of insureds will increase. As the group's size increases, Insurer A can anticipate that the performance of the group will get closer and closer to the expected loss frequency of 1 percent because of the operation of the law of large numbers. If Insurer A sells 1,000 policies, this larger group may include five policyholders who suffer losses (0.5 percent, or 5 in 1,000), ten who suffer losses (1 percent, or 10 in 1,000), or twenty who suffer losses (2 percent, or 20 in 1,000). These performances (0.5 percent, 1 percent, and 2 percent) are much closer to the expected loss frequency of 1 percent than the performance of the group that included only ten policyholders. As Insurer A sells more policies, it could expect the group of policyholders' losses to get closer and closer to the expected loss frequency of 1 percent.

Although the law of large numbers allows insurers to predict expected loss levels for large groups of policyholders, there is no such method to determine which individual policyholders actually will suffer a loss. For example, if Insurer A sells 1,000 BOP policies, it can statistically expect ten policyholders from that group to have losses (based on the 1 percent expected frequency rate). The law of large numbers does not, however, allow the insurer to predict specifically which policyholders will suffer those losses. It can only indicate that approximately ten policyholders from within that group can be expected to experience a loss.

[DA06769]

Independence

Independence

A situation in which the occurrence of one event has no effect on the likelihood of the occurrence of any other event.

For the law of large numbers to operate properly, events should be independent of one another. **Independence** is not maintained when more than one exposure unit is exposed to the same loss-causing event. For example, one catastrophic event—such as an earthquake, a hurricane, or a flood—can affect many exposure units. Insurers often insure multiple buildings that are adjacent to one another. Because of this proximity, a fire in one building could spread to the other structures, thereby violating the condition of independence. Insurers consider independence to be one characteristic of an ideally insurable loss exposure.

Although the condition of independence is frequently violated, underwriters have an important role in evaluating the independence of exposure units insured. Insurers usually use information systems to track the geographic location of properties insured. In addition to designating the geographic location

of each insured property, underwriters are usually required to determine an **amount subject** for each location. Insurers differ in their approach to calculating each account's amount subject, but the objective is to determine potential loss severity.

Amount subject
The total value exposed to loss at any one location from any one event.

For example, an insurer might require its underwriters to assume a total loss and determine the maximum dollar amount that could possibly be paid for all responding coverages. Insurers aggregate this information using catastrophe-modeling computer software to determine total amounts subject to various types of catastrophes. Underwriters use this information to limit their exposures in certain geographic areas or to obtain catastrophe **reinsurance**.

Reinsurance
The transfer of insurance risk from one insurer to another through a contractual agreement under which one insurer (the reinsurer) agrees, in return for a reinsurance premium, to indemnify another insurer (the primary insurer) for some or all of the financial consequences of certain loss exposures covered by the primary's insurance policies.

UNDERSTANDING LOSS SEVERITY

Analyzing loss severity helps insurance and risk management professionals develop loss projections and, therefore, also helps them prioritize loss exposures so that risk management resources can be concentrated where they are needed most.

The purpose of analyzing loss severity, which is the dollar amount of loss for a specific occurrence, is to determine how serious a loss might be. For example, how much of a building could be damaged in a single fire? Alternatively, how long might it take for an organization to resume operations after a fire?

Insurance and risk management professionals use several terms to describe the largest loss that can reasonably be expected. Some insurance and risk management professionals use terms such as maximum possible loss and maximum probable loss when gauging loss severity.

Maximum Possible Loss

Effectively managing risk requires identifying the worst possible outcome of a loss. The maximum possible loss is the total value exposed to loss at any one location or from any one event. For example, in the case of fire damage to a building and its contents, the maximum possible loss is typically the value of the building plus the total value of the building's contents.

To determine maximum possible loss for multiple exposure units, such as a fleet of cars, an insurance or a risk management professional may consider factors such as whether multiple vehicles travel together (a circumstance that could cause one event, such as a collision, to affect several vehicles at once) or whether several vehicles are stored in the same location (a circumstance that could cause one event, such as a fire, flood, or theft, to affect several vehicles). This helps determine the maximum number of vehicles that could be involved in any one loss and, therefore, the event's maximum possible loss.

Although maximum possible property losses can be estimated based on the values exposed to loss, this estimation is not necessarily appropriate or possible for assessing maximum possible liability losses. In theory, liability losses

are limited only by the defendant's total wealth. Therefore, some practical assumptions must be made about the maximum possible loss in liability cases to properly assess that loss exposure. Instead of focusing on the defendant's total wealth, a common assumption is that the maximum amount that would be exposed to liability loss 95 percent (or 98 percent) of the time in similar cases is the maximum possible loss.

Maximum Probable Loss

Maximum probable loss is an insurance or risk management professional's estimate of the largest loss likely to occur. Because it is a generally subjective measure, maximum probable loss is challenging to quantify. However, many insurance professionals choose not to provide simply "guess work" and have devised methodology that they can apply consistently to the loss exposures they are assuming.

For example, some insurers would diminish their expectation of loss severity from the maximum possible loss amount if a building contained fire divisions that would stop a fire in one part of the building from spreading. Some methodologies consider whether the building is multistory, has a sprinkler system, or is built of fire-resistant construction. As arbitrary as the methodology may be, insurance companies frequently maintain maximum probable loss estimates as a means to evaluate loss severity.

Review Questions

1. Explain the difference between theoretical and empirical probabilities.
2. Identify two conditions in which probability analysis is effective for projecting losses.
3. List three criteria necessary to accurately forecast future events based on the law of large numbers.
4. Identify outcome characteristics common to both theoretical and empirical possibility distributions.
5. List two requirements to construct an empirical probability distribution.
6. Describe the following two forms of probability distributions and how they are used in analyzing future losses: a. discrete probability distributions and b. continuous probability distributions.
7. Describe mean, median, and mode and how a risk management professional uses them in assessing loss exposures.
8. Explain how calculating the expected value is similar to calculating the mean.
9. Explain what knowing the mode of a distribution allows insurance and risk management professionals to do.
10. Describe standard deviation and how insurance and risk management professionals use it in assessing loss exposures.

11. Describe coefficient of variation and how insurance and risk management professionals use it in assessing loss exposures.
12. Describe the steps used for calculating the standard deviation of a set of individual outcomes not involving probabilities.
13. Explain what insurance and risk management professionals can use the coefficient of variation for when evaluating a particular loss control measure.
14. Explain how the calculation of mutually exclusive events and the calculation of nonmutually exclusive events differ. Explain.
15. In one draw of one card from a standard deck containing no jokers, calculate the following: a. the probability of drawing a five, b. the probability of drawing a five or a jack, and c. the probability of drawing a diamond or a spade.
16. In one draw of one card from a standard deck containing no jokers, calculate the probability of drawing a five or a spade.
17. Explain how the law of large numbers is used to increase the accuracy of loss predictions.
18. Explain how homogeneity in exposure units is ensured.
19. Explain how independence in exposure units is maintained.
20. Explain what factors insurance or risk management professionals may consider when determining the maximum possible loss for multiple exposure units, such as a fleet of cars.
21. Describe maximum probable loss.
22. Explain how damage to property on floors of a building that were not reached by a fire can occur and how such damage affects the maximum probable fire loss.

Application Questions

1. The underwriter at Millwright Insurance must choose between two accounts to provide insurance coverage. Both accounts have provided a probability distribution based on past losses. Account A's distribution has a mean of $8,500. Account B's distribution has a mean of $10,000. Which account has higher expected losses?
2. The underwriter at Millwright Insurance must choose between two accounts to provide insurance coverage. Both accounts have provided a probability distribution based on past losses. Account A's distribution has a mean of $8,500 and a standard deviation of $17,000. Account B's distribution has a mean of $10,000 and a standard deviation of $18,000. Which account has greater variability relative to its mean?
3. Sam is a risk management professional for a department store chain that operates two warehouses in his state. One warehouse is centrally located in a rural area with little infrastructure development nearby, including fire protection; the other is in the largest city of the state. The warehouses

are hundreds of miles apart. Explain whether these two warehouses are homogenous and independent in terms of their exposure to fire.

4. Jennifer is a risk management professional for the owner of a high-rise office building. The owner has asked her to calculate the maximum probable loss of a fire loss at the building. The building has fire-detection equipment that notifies the local fire department directly, as well as an automatic sprinkler system and fire doors that close in the event of a fire. How will these lines of defense be included in Jennifer's calculation of the maximum probable loss?

SUMMARY

Concepts affecting the use of probability in risk analysis include theoretical probability, empirical probability, and the law of large numbers. Although it may be preferable to use theoretical probabilities because of their unchanging nature, theoretical probabilities are not applicable or available in most situations that insurance and risk management professionals are likely to analyze. Applying the law of large numbers to probability reveals that a forecast of future losses will be more reliable if the forecast is based on a larger sample of the losses used in the analysis.

A properly constructed probability distribution always contains outcomes that are both mutually exclusive and collectively exhaustive. All probability distributions can be classified as either discrete or continuous.

The central tendency is the single outcome that is the most representative of all possible outcomes included within a probability distribution. The three most widely accepted measures of central tendency are expected value or mean, median, and mode.

Dispersion, which is the variation between values in a distribution, can be used as well as central tendency to compare the characteristics of probability distributions. The less dispersion around a distribution's expected value, the greater the likelihood that actual results will fall within a given range of that expected value. Two widely used statistical measures of dispersion are standard deviation and the coefficient of variation.

For alternative probabilities of any one of two or more events occurring within a given period, one must determine whether the events are mutually exclusive—that is, whether the happening of one event does, or does not, make the happening of other events impossible.

These calculations enable risk managers to determine or estimate the likelihood that an organization will experience various combinations of losses in one year or another time period. Arithmetic trending techniques can also improve these loss forecasts.

The law of large numbers is the mathematical principle that serves as the foundation for insurance pricing. This law states that the accuracy of loss predictions increases as the number of exposure units increases.

Effective risk management requires analyzing loss severity. A future severe loss can be estimated and expressed in terms of maximum possible loss and maximum probable loss. The maximum possible loss is the total value exposed to loss at any one location or from any one event. The maximum probable loss is an insurance or a risk management professional's estimate of the largest loss likely to occur. Maximum possible loss is used to convey the concept of a loss larger than the maximum probable loss.

Direct Your Learning

5

Risk Management Alternatives—Loss Control Techniques

Educational Objectives

After learning the content of this assignment, you should be able to:

- Describe the six categories of risk control techniques in terms of the following:
  - Whether each reduces loss frequency, reduces loss severity, or makes losses more predictable
  - How each can be used to address a particular loss exposure
  - How they differ from one another
- Explain how an organization can use risk control techniques and measures to achieve the following risk control goals:
  - Implement effective and efficient risk control measures
  - Comply with legal requirements
  - Promote life safety
  - Ensure business continuity
- Explain how an insurance or risk management professional evaluates the effects of proposed risk control measures on loss frequency and loss severity.
- Explain how risk control techniques can be applied to property, liability, personnel, and net income loss exposures.
- Describe business continuity management in terms of its scope, the process used to implement it, and the contents of a typical business continuity plan.

Outline

Risk Control Techniques

Risk Control Goals

Loss Frequency and Loss Severity

Application of Risk Control Techniques

Business Continuity Management

Summary

Risk Management Alternatives—Loss Control Techniques

5

RISK CONTROL TECHNIQUES

To select the most appropriate risk management techniques, insurance and risk management professionals consider the various techniques available so that they can then determine which of those techniques most effectively address an organization's or individual's loss exposures.

All risk management techniques fall into one of two categories: risk control or risk financing. The focus of this section is on **risk control**. Risk control techniques can be classified using these six broad categories:

- Avoidance
- Loss prevention
- Loss reduction
- Separation
- Duplication
- Diversification

Risk control

A conscious act or decision not to act that reduces the frequency and/or severity of losses or makes losses more predictable.

Each of the techniques in these six categories aims to reduce either loss frequency or severity, or make losses more predictable. See the exhibit "Target of Risk Control Techniques."

Avoidance

The most effective way of managing any loss exposure is to avoid the exposure completely. If a loss exposure has successfully been avoided, then the probability of loss from that loss exposure is zero.

The aim of **avoidance** is not just to reduce loss frequency, but also to eliminate any possibility of loss. Avoidance should be considered when the expected value of the losses from an activity outweighs the expected benefits of that activity. For example, a toy manufacturer might decide not to produce a particular toy because the potential cost of products liability claims would outweigh the expected revenue from sales, no matter how cautious the manufacturer might be in producing and marketing the toy.

Avoidance

A risk control technique that involves ceasing or never undertaking an activity so that the possibility of a future loss occurring from that activity is eliminated.

Avoidance can either be proactive or reactive.

Proactive avoidance seeks to avoid a loss exposure before it exists, such as when a medical student chooses not to become an obstetrician because he or she wants to avoid the large professional liability (malpractice) claims associated with that specialty.

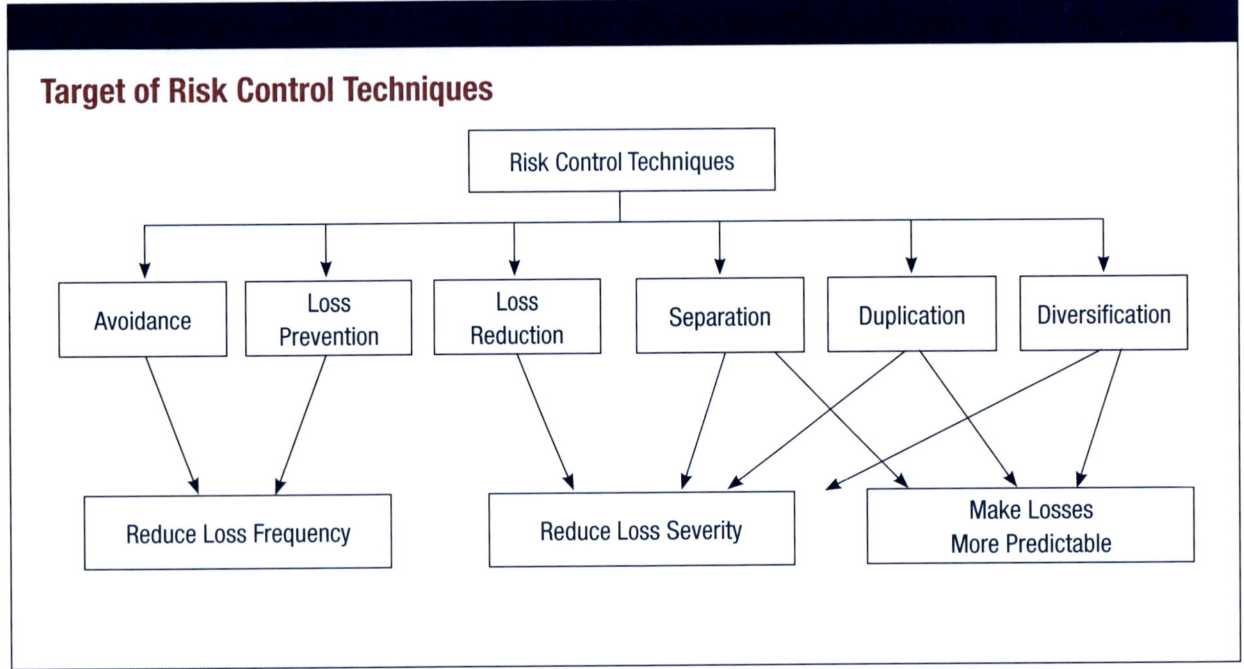

[DA02648]

Reactive avoidance seeks to eliminate a loss exposure that already exists, such as when manufacturers of hand-held hair dryers stopped using asbestos insulation in their dryers once the cancer-causing properties of asbestos became known.

Reactive avoidance, that is, discontinuing an existing activity, avoids loss exposures from future activities but does not eliminate loss exposures from past activities. For example, the hair dryer manufacturer may avoid claims from consumers who purchase the hair dryers produced after asbestos is no longer used, but would remain legally liable for associated harm suffered by prior consumers.

Because loss exposures do not exist in a vacuum, avoiding one loss exposure can create or enhance another. For example if an individual is concerned about dying in an airplane crash, he or she can choose not to travel by air. However, by avoiding air travel, the individual increases the loss exposure to injury or death from the other means of transport chosen in its place.

Complete avoidance is not the most common risk control technique and is typically neither feasible nor desirable. Loss exposures arise from activities that are essential to individuals and to organizations. Therefore, it is not possible to avoid these core activities. For instance, if a manufacturer's principal product is motorcycle safety helmets, it could not stop selling them in order to avoid liability loss exposures. Similarly, an organization cannot decline to occupy office space in order to avoid property loss exposures. Nonfinancial concerns also can render avoidance impossible. For example, a municipality cannot arbitrarily stop providing police protection or water to its inhabitants in order to avoid the associated liability loss exposures.

Loss Prevention

Loss prevention is a risk control technique that reduces the frequency of a particular loss. For instance, pressure relief valves on a boiler are intended to prevent explosions by keeping the pressure in the boiler from reaching an unsafe level. The valve is a type of loss prevention, not avoidance, because a boiler explosion is still possible, just not as likely.

Loss prevention
A risk control technique that reduces the frequency of a particular loss.

To illustrate a loss prevention measure, consider a hypothetical manufacturing company, Etchley Manufacturing (Etchley). Etchley has 500 employees working at a single plant. The workers' compensation loss history for this plant shows a significant number of back injuries. Etchley is considering hiring a back injury consultant to host a series of educational seminars for its employees. The consultant estimates that, based on the results of his past seminar series, Etchley will see a 20 percent reduction in the frequency of back injuries. See the exhibit "Example of a Loss Prevention Measure: Etchley Manufacturing."

Example of a Loss Prevention Measure: Etchley Manufacturing

Probability
0.1
0.075
0.05
0.025
0
Mean = 24
Standard Deviation = 4.20
Coefficient of Variation
= 4.20 ÷ 24 = 0.1750
Mean = 30
Standard Deviation = 5.48
Coefficient of Variation
= 5.48 ÷ 30 = 0.1827
1 3 5 7 9 11 13 15 17 19 21 23 25 27 29 31 33 35 37 39 41 43 45 47 49
Number of Injuries per Year
- - - - - - Probability of Injury Without Seminar
——— Probability of Injury With Seminar

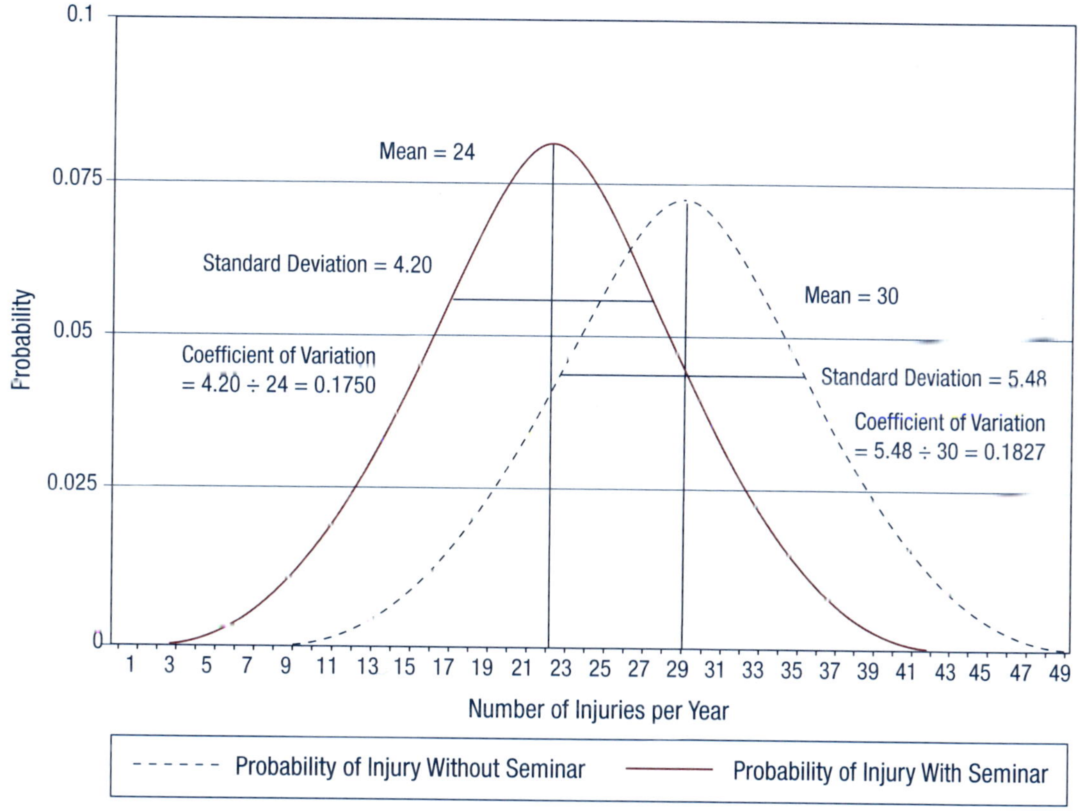

[DA02649]

The chart in the exhibit shows the frequency distributions of back injuries both with and without the educational seminar in order to demonstrate the estimated effect of this loss prevention measure. The frequency distribution without the educational seminar has a mean of 30, a standard deviation of 5.48 and a coefficient of variation of 0.1827.

The frequency distribution with the educational seminar has a lower mean of 24, a lower standard deviation of 4.20, and a lower coefficient of variation of 0.1750. Based on these figures, not only would the consultant's educational seminar reduce the expected frequency of back injuries, it would also reduce their variability from year to year, which would allow Etchley to budget more effectively for those injuries that do occur.

Loss prevention measures that reduce frequency may also affect the loss severity of the specified loss exposures. For example, as a result of the educational seminar, both the number of back injuries that occur and their severity may be reduced.

Generally, a loss prevention measure is implemented before a loss occurs in order to break the sequence of events that leads to the loss. Because of the close link between causes of loss and loss prevention, determining effective loss prevention measures usually requires carefully studying how particular losses are caused.

For example, according to Heinrich's domino theory, as described in the exhibit, most work-related injuries result from a chain of events that includes an unsafe act or an unsafe condition. Workplace safety efforts have therefore focused on trying to eliminate specific unsafe acts or unsafe conditions to break this chain of events and prevent injuries.

As is the case with avoidance, a loss prevention measure may reduce the frequency of losses from one loss exposure but increase the frequency or severity of losses from other loss exposures. For example, a jewelry store that installs security bars on its windows would likely reduce the frequency of theft. These same bars, however, might make it impossible for firefighters to enter the building through the windows or might trap employees inside the store if a fire occurs. See the exhibit "Heinrich's Domino Theory."

Loss Reduction

Loss reduction

A risk control technique that reduces the severity of a particular loss.

Loss reduction is a risk control technique that reduces the severity of a particular loss. Automatic sprinkler systems are a classic example of a loss reduction measure; sprinklers do not prevent fires from starting, but can limit or extinguish fires that have already started. Some loss reduction measures can prevent losses as well as reduce them.

For example, using burglar alarms is generally considered a loss reduction measure because the alarm is activated only when a burglary occurs. However, because burglar alarms also act as a deterrent, they can prevent loss as well as reduce it.

Heinrich's Domino Theory

In 1931, H. W. Heinrich published the first thorough analysis of work injuries caused by accidents. He determined that work injuries were actually a result of a series of unsafe acts and/or mechanical or physical hazards (dominoes) that occurred in a specific order. Furthermore, he concluded that if any one of these dominoes could be removed from the chain, the work injury could be prevented. Heinrich's theory included the following five dominoes: (1) social environment and ancestry, (2) the fault of persons, (3) personal or mechanical hazards, (4) the accident, and (5) the injury. For example, if risk control measures could minimize mechanical hazards, the domino chain would be broken and fewer injuries would occur. Many of the principles that Heinrich outlined in his publication became the basis of modern risk control measures.

H.W. Heinrich, Industrial Accident Prevention, 4th edition (New York: McGraw-Hill, 1959). [DA02650]

As an example of a loss reduction measure, assume the consultant Etchley hired to conduct the educational seminars suggested that Etchley provide back braces for all of its employees because back braces help prevent back injuries and reduce the severity of back injuries that do occur.

The exhibit contains the original severity distribution for Etchley and the new severity distribution with all employees using back braces. As with most severity distributions, the severity distribution for back injuries is not symmetrical, but skewed. Most back injuries are grouped in the left-hand portion of the distribution (lower severity values), with some very serious injuries grouped as outliers to the right. This positively skewed distribution pulls the tail of the distribution to the right and increases the mean.

Note the difference between the means and modes with and without back braces. The use of back braces lowers the average severity (mean) by $15,792 ($29,800 – $14,008 = $15,792) as well as the severity of the injuries that would occur most often (mode) by $5,000 ($8,000 – $3,000 = $5,000).

The two broad categories of loss reduction measures are pre-loss measures, applied before the loss occurs, and post-loss measures, applied after the loss occurs. The aim of pre-loss measures is to reduce the amount or extent of property damaged and the number of people injured or the extent of injury incurred from a single event.

For example, Etchley's use of back braces is a pre-loss measure erecting firewalls to limit the amount of damage and danger that can be caused by a single fire is also a pre-loss measure. See the exhibit "Example of a Loss Reduction Measure: Etchley Manufacturing."

Post-loss measures typically focus on emergency procedures, salvage operations, rehabilitation activities, public relations, or legal defenses to halt the spread or to counter the effects of loss. An example of a post-loss loss reduction measure is to temporarily move an organization's operations to a new location following a fire so that operations can continue while the main premises is repaired, thus reducing loss severity.

Example of a Loss Reduction Measure: Etchley Manufacturing

[DA02651]

Disaster recovery plan
A plan for backup procedures, emergency response, and post-disaster recovery to ensure that critical resources are available to facilitate the continuity of operations in an emergency situation.

Disaster recovery planning is a specialized aspect of loss reduction. A **disaster recovery plan**, also called catastrophe recovery plan or contingency plan, is a plan for backup procedures, emergency response, and post-disaster recovery to ensure that critical resources are available to facilitate the continuity of operations in an emergency situation. For many organizations, disaster recovery planning is especially important in addressing the risks associated with those systems without which the organization could not function. Disaster recovery plans typically focus on property loss exposures and natural hazards, not on the broader array of risks and associated loss exposures that may also threaten an organization's survival.

Separation

Separation
A risk control technique that isolates loss exposures from one another to minimize the adverse effect of a single loss.

Separation is appropriate if an organization can operate with only a portion of these separate units left intact. If one unit suffers a total loss, the portion of the activity or assets at the other unit must be sufficient for operations to continue. Otherwise, separation has not achieved its risk control goal.

Separation is rarely undertaken for its own sake, but is usually a byproduct of another management decision. For example, few organizations build a second warehouse simply to reduce the potential loss severity at the first warehouse. However, if an organization is considering constructing a second warehouse to expand production, the risk control benefits of a second warehouse could support the argument in favor of the expansion.

The intent of separation is to reduce the severity of an individual loss at a single location. However, if an organization is considering constructing a second warehouse to expand production, the risk control benefits of a second warehouse could support the argument in favor of the expansion. The intent of separation is to reduce the severity of an individual loss at a single location. However, by creating multiple locations, separation most likely increases loss frequency. For example, using two distantly separated warehouses instead of one reduces the maximum possible loss at each individual location, but increases loss frequency, because two units are exposed to loss. The insurance or risk management professional should be confident that the benefits of reduced loss severity from separation more than offset the increased loss frequency.

As an example of separation, consider a hypothetical organization, Ryedale Shipping Company (Ryedale), which has to decide between these options for shipping its clients' products:

- Option A—use one central warehouse
- Option B—use two warehouses

Under Option A, the central warehouse would contain $500,000 worth of merchandise and have a 5 percent chance of experiencing a fire in any given year. For simplicity, assume that only one fire per year can occur and that if a fire occurs, all of the warehouse's merchandise is completely destroyed. Under Option B, the two warehouses would each have the same probability of a fire (5 percent), but would each house $250,000 worth of merchandise. For simplicity, assume that the two locations are independent of one another. See the exhibit "Example of Separation: Ryedale Shipping Company."

The exhibit shows the severity distributions for these options and how the expected loss is calculated.

Under Option A, the severity distribution is just the single outcome of a loss of $500,000. There are two possible outcomes in any one year: a fire at the central warehouse or no fire at the central warehouse. Given a probability of fire of .05 (5 percent), Ryedale would expect a $500,000 loss 5 percent of the

Example of Separation: Ryedale Shipping Company

Option A

	Central Warehouse
Value of merchandise	$500,000
Probability of a fire	.05

Severity distribution (maximum loss in a fire)	**$500,000**
Probability of a fire in the central warehouse	.05
Expected loss (.05 × $500,000)	**$25,000**

Option B

	Warehouse 1 (W1)	Warehouse 2 (W2)
Value of merchandise	$250,000	$250,000
Probability of a fire	.05	.05

Severity distribution (maximum loss in a fire)	**$250,000**
Probability of fire at W1 and fire at W2 (.05 × .05)	.0025
Probability of fire in W1 but not W2 [.05 × (1 – .05)]	.0475
Probability of fire in W2 but not in W1 [(1 – .05) × .05]	.0475
Probability of one fire in either W1 or W2 (.0475 + .0475)	.095
Probability of zero fires (1 – .05) × (1 – .05)	.9025
Expected loss [(.0025 × $500,000) + (.095 × $250,000)]	**$25,000**

[DA02652]

time and a $0 loss 95 percent of the time. Therefore, the expected loss in any given year is $25,000 (.05 × $500,000 = $25,000).

Under Option B, only $250,000 worth of merchandise is at risk in any one fire. Therefore, having two warehouses reduces Ryedale's severity distribution from $500,000 to $250,000.

Increasing the number of warehouses increases the number of possible outcomes. One of these situations will occur:

- No fire at either location.
- There will be a fire at the first warehouse (W1) but not at the second warehouse (W2).
- There will be a fire at W2 but not at W1.
- There will be a fire at both W1 and W2.

The probability of each of these possible outcomes is shown in the exhibit. Given a probability of fire of .05, Ryedale would expect these outcomes:

- $500,000 loss (fires at both W1 and W2) 0.25 percent of the time
- $250,000 loss at W1 4.75 percent of the time
- $250,000 loss at W2 4.75 percent of the time
- $0 loss 90.25 percent of the time

The expected loss remains $25,000, but the likelihood of suffering a $500,000 loss has fallen from 5 percent to 0.25 percent, whereas the likelihood of suffering a $250,000 loss has increased from 0 percent to 9.5 percent.

This results in a total claims distribution for Option B that has a lower standard deviation than the total claims distribution for Option A. The standard deviation of losses under Option A would be $108,973, and the standard deviation for Option B falls to $77,055.18, which makes losses under Option B more predictable than Option A.

Duplication

Duplication is a risk control technique that uses backups, spares, or copies of critical property, information, or capabilities and keeps them in reserve. Examples of duplication include maintaining a second set of records, spare parts for machinery, and copies of keys.

Duplication
A risk control technique that uses backups, spares, or copies of critical property, information, or capabilities and keeps them in reserve.

Duplication differs from separation in that duplicates are not a part of an organization's daily working resources. Duplication is only appropriate if an entire asset or activity is so important that the consequence of its loss justifies the expense and time of maintaining the duplicate.

For example, an organization may make arrangements with more than one supplier of a key raw material. That alternative supplier would be used only if a primary supplier could not provide needed materials because of, for example, a major fire at the primary supplier's plant.

Like separation, duplication can reduce an organization's dependence on a single asset, activity, or person, making individual losses smaller by reducing the severity of a loss that may occur. Duplication is not as likely as separation to increase loss frequency because the duplicated unit is kept in reserve and is not as exposed to loss as is the primary unit. For example, a duplicate vehicle that is ordinarily kept garaged is not as vulnerable to highway accidents as the primary vehicle.

Duplication is likely to reduce the average expected annual loss from a given loss exposure because it reduces loss severity without increasing loss frequency. Similar to separation, duplication can also make losses more predictable by reducing the dispersion of potential losses.

There are several measures an organization can implement that are similar to duplication and that incorporate nonowned assets.

One option is for an organization to contractually arrange for the acquisition of equipment or facilities in the event that a loss occurs. For example, a plant that manufactures aircraft can pay an annual fee for a contract in which a supplier agrees to deliver within thirty days the hydraulic tools and scaffolding required to continue operations in a rented hangar if the manufacturer's assembly plant incurs a loss. In this way, the aircraft manufacturer can continue operations with minimal business interruptions and avoid the expense associated with the ownership or storage of the duplicate equipment.

Diversification

Diversification

A risk control technique that spreads loss exposures over numerous projects, products, markets, or regions.

Although **diversification** closely resembles the risk control techniques of duplication and separation, it is more commonly applied to managing business risks, rather than hazard risks.

Organizations engage in diversification of loss exposures when they provide a variety of products and services that are used by a range of customers.

For example, an insurer might diversify its exposures by type of business and geographically by selling both personal and commercial insurance and both property-casualty and life insurance in multiple regions. Investors employ diversification when they allocate their assets among a mix of stocks and bonds from companies in different industry sectors. An investor might diversify investments by purchasing stock in a bank and stock in a pharmaceutical manufacturer. Because these are unrelated industries, the investor hopes that any losses from one stock might be more than offset by profits from another.

As with separation and duplication, diversification has the potential to increase loss frequency, because the organization has increased the number of loss exposures. However, by spreading risk, diversification reduces loss severity and can make losses more predictable.

Organizations implement risk control techniques and the measures that support them to address one or more specific loss exposures. Each measure should be tailored to the specific loss exposure under consideration. Furthermore, the application of risk control techniques should serve to support an organization's overall goals, pre-loss and post-loss risk management goals, and risk control goals.

RISK CONTROL GOALS

Individuals and organizations have a variety of goals when implementing a risk management program. Just as the risk management program goals support the overall organizational goals, risk control goals support the risk management program goals. See the exhibit "Risk Management Goals."

Insurance and risk management professionals therefore seek to apply risk control techniques through specific risk control measures that most effectively and efficiently support the risk management program and thereby help the organization achieve its goals.

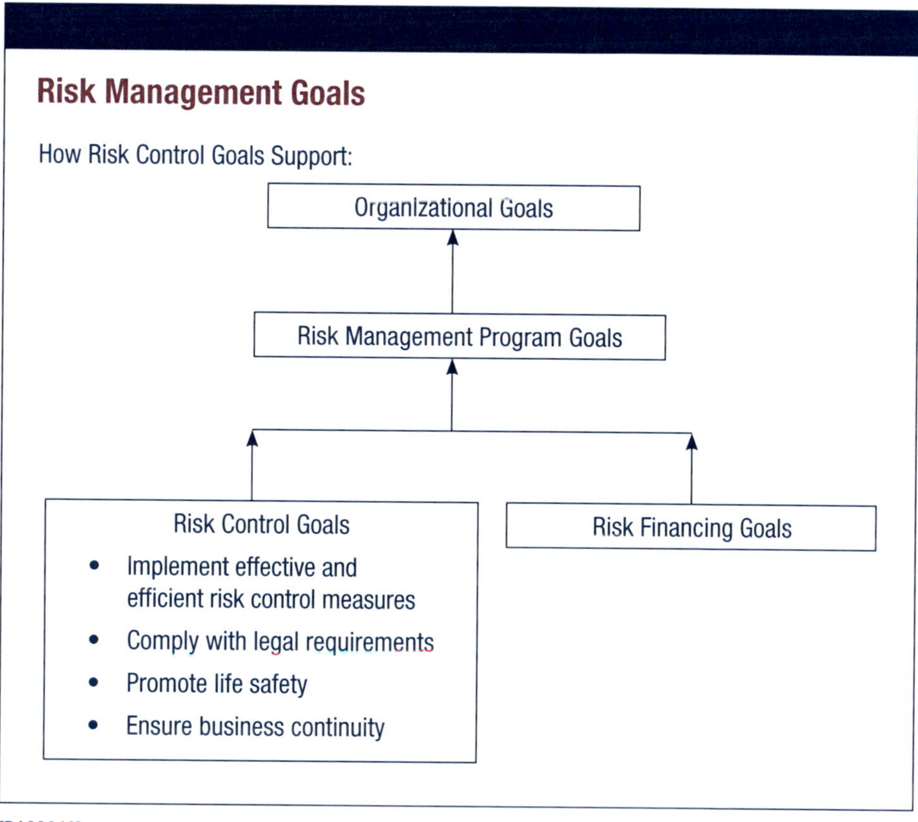

[DA02646]

To this end, risk control techniques are used to support these risk control goals: implement effective and efficient risk control measures, comply with legal requirements, promote life safety, and ensure business continuity.

Implement Effective and Efficient Risk Control Measures

An individual or organization generally undertakes risk control measures that have a positive financial effect. Most risk control measures are implemented at a cost to the individual or organization. These costs are typically cash outlays, like the costs of the losses they aim to control, and are considered part of the cost of risk. However, so that risk control does not unduly increase the cost of risk, one of the goals of risk control is to employ measures that are effective and efficient.

A measure is effective if it enables an organization to achieve desired risk management goals, such as the pre-loss goals of economy of operations, tolerable uncertainty, legality, and social responsibility or the post-loss goals of survival, continuity of operations, profitability, earnings stability, growth, and social responsibility.

Some risk control measures will be more effective than others. For example, both a sprinkler system and employees patrolling a warehouse with fire extinguishers may be effective risk control measures. However, a sophisticated sprinkler system with heat and flame sensors will likely be more effective than employee patrols.

The effectiveness of various risk control measures is often based on both quantitative and qualitative standards. For example, determining whether measures to ensure worker safety are effective may rely not only on statistics regarding workers compensation claims, but also on employee satisfaction with the measures taken.

As well as being effective, a risk control measure should be efficient. A measure is efficient if it is the least expensive of all possible effective measures. This does not necessarily mean an organization should choose the measure that entails the least initial cash outlay.

The long-term effects should also be examined to determine which measure can be implemented with the least overall cost to the organization.

For example, consider an organization that needs to improve security at night. The organization's risk management professional determines that a new security system and stationing a night security guard are both equally effective measures from a financial perspective, but needs to determine which of these methods is most efficient. See the exhibit "Using Cash Flow Analysis to Determine the More Efficient Risk Control Measure."

There are several methods available for this comparison, one of which is cash flow analysis. Given a loss exposure and the effective alternative risk control measures, the risk management professional can use cash flow analysis to determine which measure will be most efficient. The "Using Cash Flow Analysis" exhibit illustrates a cash flow analysis of these two security measures.

In this example, both the security system and the security guard are equally effective; they both reduce annual losses by $40,000. Cash flow analysis shows that although the security system requires a larger initial investment, it costs less to operate and maintain each year.

If the risk management professional examines these choices over a ten-year period, the annual cost of the security guard eventually eclipses the initial investment required for the security system, making the security system ultimately more efficient.

The major advantage of using cash flow analysis for selecting risk control measures is that it provides the same basis of comparison for all value-maximizing decisions and thereby helps the organization achieve its value-maximization goal. It is also very useful for not-for-profit organizations that want to increase their efficiency by reducing unnecessary expenditures on risk control.

Using Cash Flow Analysis to Determine the More Efficient Risk Control Measure

Security System

Net Cash Flow *(NCF)* Calculations		
Reduction in annual losses:		$40,000
Less: Differential cash expenses		
System annual monitoring fees	$ 4,200	
System annual maintenance expenses	$ 400	($ 4,600)
Before-tax *NCF*:		$35,400
***NCF* Analysis**		
Factors:		
Initial investment	$200,000	
Life of system	10 years	
Differential annual cash flow	$ 35,400	
Minimum acceptable rate of return (annual)	10.00%	
Net Present Value *(NPV)* Analysis		
PV of differential annual cash flow ($35,400 × 6.145)	$217,533	
Less: *PV* of initial investment	($200,000)	
Net present value:	$ 17,533	

Annual savings by installing a security system.

The system's initial cost must be considered in cash flow analysis.

To discount cash flows for ten years at 10 percent discount rate, the equivalent net present value factor is 6.145.

Installing a security system would be effective, in that the cost of the risk control measure is less than the savings in prevented losses. In present value terms, the security system would save the organization over $17,000.

Security Guard

***NCF* Calculations**		
Reduction in annual losses:		$40,000
Less: Differential cash expenses		
Security guard salary and benefits	$ 38,000	($38,000)
Before-tax *NCF*:		$2,000
***NCF* Analysis**		
Factors:		
Initial investment	$0	
Life of system	10 years	
Differential annual cash flow	$ 2,000	
Minimum acceptable rate of return (annual)	10.00%	
***NPV* Analysis**		
PV of differential annual cash flow ($2,000 × 6.145)	$ 12,290	
Less: *PV* of initial investment	($0)	
Net present value:	$ 12,290	

Annual savings by hiring security guard.

The security guard does not have upfront costs like the cost of the security system.

Hiring a security guard would be effective, in that the cost of the risk control measure is less than the savings in prevented losses. However, it is not as efficient as the security system.

[DA02647]

The disadvantages of cash flow analysis include the weaknesses of the assumptions that often must be made to conduct the analysis and the difficulty of accurately estimating future cash flows. Moreover, cash flow analysis works on the assumption that the organization's only goal is to maximize its economic value and does not consider any of the nonfinancial goals or selection criteria. For example, legality and social responsibility goals are not directly considered in cash flow analysis.

Comply With Legal Requirements

An organization may be required to implement certain risk control measures if a state or federal statute mandates specific safety measures, such as protecting employees from disability or safeguarding the environment against pollution. These risk control measures are a means of implementing the risk control techniques of avoidance, loss prevention, and loss reduction and they also support the risk management program pre-loss goal of legality. The cost of adhering to legal requirements becomes part of the cost of risk.

Many laws and regulations require organizations to implement specific risk control measures.

For example, the fire safety code mandates certain fire safety procedures, environmental regulations govern the nonuse or use and disposal of toxic material, workers' compensation laws require employers to provide a safe working environment, and disability laws require organizations to make certain accommodations for people with disabilities. All of these examples would include risk control measures that support avoidance (ban of some toxic substances), loss prevention (safety procedures for machinery usage), and loss reduction (fire suppression systems).

Some laws and regulations are amended fairly frequently, so it is important for the risk management professional to stay apprised of these amendments. For example, the privacy issues and enforcement regulations regarding the Health Insurance Portability and Accountability Act of 1996 (HIPAA) continue to evolve. Failure to comply with legal requirements exposes the individual or organization to additional fines, sanctions, or liability.

Promote Life Safety

Life safety

The portion of fire safety that focuses on the minimum building design, construction, operation, and maintenance requirements necessary to assure occupants of a safe exit from the burning portion of the building.

Safeguarding people from fire has grown in importance from a risk control perspective because of the emphasis legislative bodies have placed on health and safety issues and because of the increasing frequency and severity of liability claims. In the context of risk control, **life safety** is the portion of fire safety that focuses on the minimum building design, construction, operation, and maintenance requirements necessary to assure occupants of a safe exit from the burning portion of the building.

Life safety must consider both the characteristics of the people who occupy buildings and the types of building occupancies (such as residences, office

work, or manufacturing). Consideration of the general characteristics of both building occupants and occupancy has led to the development of specific fire safety standards for buildings. These standards are codified in the Life Safety Code® published by the National Fire Protection Association (NFPA) and cover the risk control techniques of avoidance, loss prevention, and loss control.[1]

Promoting life safety can be expanded beyond fire safety to incorporate any cause of loss that threatens the life of employees or customers. Therefore, organizations must be concerned about other causes of loss, such as product safety, building collapse, industrial accidents, environmental pollution, or exposure to hazardous activities that may create the possibility of injury or death. For example, a toy manufacturer should have an established product recall procedure in the event that a safety issue arises with one of its toys. Alternatively, a car manufacturer should install appropriate safety guards on machinery, equip employees with appropriate safety gear, and give employees sufficient training to enable them to carry out their jobs in reasonable safety.

Ensure Business Continuity

In addition to implementing effective and efficient measures, complying with legal requirements, and promoting safety, risk control should aim to ensure business continuity—that is, minimize or eliminate significant business interruptions, whatever their cause. Business continuity is designed to meet both the primary risk management program post-loss goal of survival and the post-loss goal of continuity of operations.

Loss exposures and their associated losses vary widely by industry, location, and organization. Some organizations are more susceptible to terrorism, some are more susceptible to information technology problems, and others are more susceptible to natural disasters. Because each organization is unique in its potential losses, each must also be unique in its application of risk control measures to promote business continuity.

For example, there are many causes of loss, such as fire, theft or vandalism, that can be prevented through appropriate loss prevention measures. If left untreated, these causes of loss could easily result in a business interruption. However, there are other causes of loss (including natural disasters such as hurricanes or earthquakes) that an organization may not be able to avoid or prevent. Nonetheless, the organization may be able to minimize any business interruption that could occur during and after a natural disaster through appropriate loss reduction techniques.

LOSS FREQUENCY AND LOSS SEVERITY

To properly evaluate the effect of risk control measures on loss frequency and loss severity, the insurance or risk management professional should conduct an analysis of the effect that each measure will have both on the specified loss exposure and on any other loss exposures.

Risk control goals are designed to support the risk management program goals, which in turn support the individual's or organization's goals.

Effect of Risk Control Measures

A particular risk control measure may reduce the loss frequency of the specified loss exposure but increase its loss severity. Conversely, a risk control measure could reduce loss severity but increase loss frequency. For example, an organization may be concerned that a fire or flood at its only warehouse would destroy its entire inventory. Accordingly, the organization may choose to acquire a second warehouse in a different location. Although this separation decreases the loss severity at each of the two warehouses, it doubles the loss exposure units, which may increase the frequency of loss occurrence for the organization. See the exhibit "Inverse Relationship Between Loss Frequency and Loss Severity."

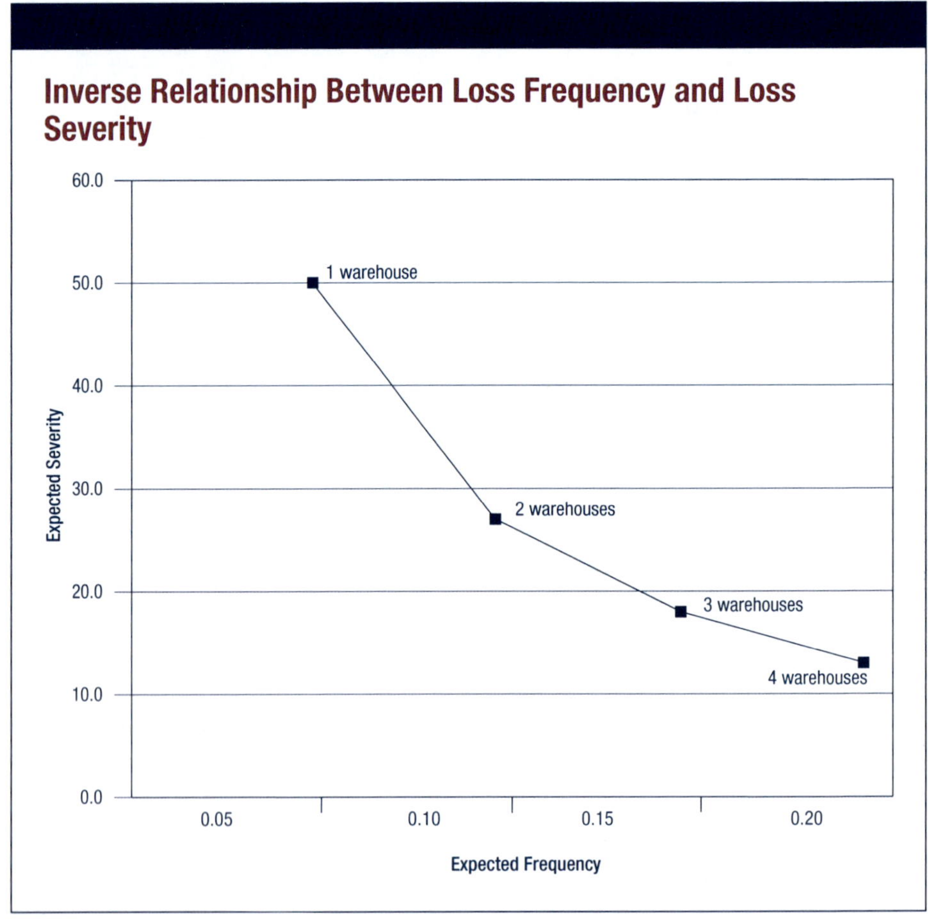

[DA02645]

The exhibit shows the inverse relationship between loss frequency and loss severity as the number of exposure units increases. In this exhibit, as the number of warehouses increases from one to four, the expected severity at each location declines, while the potential frequency increases.

Externalities

In addition to this inverse relationship between loss frequency and loss severity, a measure to control one kind of loss exposure may alter the frequency and severity of other loss exposures. When a risk control measure has implications outside of its intended purpose in this way, it is described as having externalities. Externalities can be either positive or negative.

A positive externality exists when a risk control measure implemented for one particular loss exposure reduces the loss frequency or loss severity related to another loss exposure. For example, an organization may institute random drug testing to lower the frequency of employee injuries. The organization may also find a positive externality exists, such as that drug testing also reduces the incidences of employee theft.

Conversely, if a risk control measure increases loss frequency or loss severity for another loss exposure, it is described as having a negative externality. For example, if an organization installs a sprinkler system, the sprinkler system can reduce losses resulting from fire, but it has a negative externality in that it might also increase losses caused by sprinkler leakage.

The existence of negative externalities does not necessarily rule out a risk control measure. For example, if the expected damage (losses) from sprinkler leakage were less than the expected damages resulting from fire, the danger of sprinkler leakage should not necessarily prevent the organization from installing a sprinkler system.

APPLICATION OF RISK CONTROL TECHNIQUES

After considering alternative risk control techniques, insurance and risk management professionals decide which techniques are appropriate for a particular loss exposure and which are not.

In performing this part of the risk management process, the insurance or risk management professional can benefit from knowing which risk control techniques are usually applicable to each of these loss exposures:

- Property
- Liability
- Personnel
- Net income

Property Loss Exposures

Property loss exposures are generally divided into two categories—tangible property loss exposures (covering real property, such as land and buildings, and tangible personal property) and intangible property loss exposures. The risk control techniques that are most applicable to property loss exposures

vary based on the type of property as well as the cause of loss threatening the property. For example, risk control measures to prevent or reduce damage caused by fire are substantially different than those to prevent or reduce damage resulting from theft.

Because of the broad array of property loss exposures and causes of loss, all of the categories of risk control techniques can be applied in some way to property loss exposures. Insurance producers and underwriters commonly examine commercial property loss exposures based on construction, occupancy, protection, and external exposure (known by their acronym—COPE). Each factor inherent in COPE can be addressed through the application of risk control techniques, as demonstrated in the exhibit. See the exhibit "Applications of Risk Control Techniques to COPE."

Applications of Risk Control Techniques to COPE

COPE Factor	Description	Risk Control Technique
Construction	Construction materials and techniques range from simple frame construction (least resistive to fire) to fire-resistive construction (most fire resistive), with a wide variety of choices in between.	Loss prevention and loss reduction through construction techniques designed to minimize frequency and severity of losses.
Occupancy	There are nine different classifications of occupancy, ranging from residential to industrial, with each classification presenting its own unique risk to real property.	Loss reduction through safety training and emergency evacuation procedures.
Protection	There are two categories of protection, internal or external. Internal protection refers to what the organization does to protect its own real property. External protection refers to what fire departments and other public facilities do to safeguard the general public, including the organization, from fire and other causes of loss.	Two loss reduction measures used for internal fire protection are fire detection and suppression. External protection could involve security systems and security guard services.
External Exposure	A building is exposed to many hazards from outside sources, such as neighboring buildings. COPE factors are used to evaluate neighboring buildings' fire risk and the risk of transfer to the organization's real property.	The loss prevention and reduction measures may include relocation away from external hazards and fire protection to the exterior of the property to prevent or reduce the likelihood of fire from another building to the organization's property.

[DA02643]

Liability Loss Exposures

To implement effective risk control for liability losses, individuals and organizations need to understand the bases of legal liability. Legal actions can be brought under torts, contracts, or statutes. The liability loss exposures facing most individuals and organizations are presented in the exhibit. Three risk control techniques can be used to control liability losses: (1) avoid the activity that creates the liability loss exposure, (2) decrease the likelihood of the losses occurring (loss prevention), and (3) if a loss does occur, minimize its effect on the organization (loss reduction). The other risk control techniques of separation, duplication, and diversification are not as effective in treating liability loss exposures. See the exhibit "Typical Liability Loss Exposures."

Typical Liability Loss Exposures

Liability Loss Exposure	Description
Premises liability	Created by having visitors to an organization's premises.
Operations liability	Created by conducting operations either on or away from an organization's premises.
Products liability	Created by manufacturing or distributing products.
Workers compensation liability	Created by state statutes to cover employees for work-related injuries and illnesses.
Professional liability	Created by common law, which imposes a higher duty of care on professionals. A professional owes a duty of care to refrain from an action that carries an undue risk of causing harm to someone else.
Completed operations liability	Created because organization is responsible for bodily injury or property damage caused by completed work when the work is completed away from the organization's premises.
Automobile liability	Created because drivers and owners of autos owe a duty to others to use their autos in a reasonable, prudent manner and to exercise care for the safety of others.
Watercraft liability	Created because drivers and owners of watercraft owe a duty to others to use their watercraft in a reasonable, prudent manner and to exercise care for the safety of others.
Management liability	Created by the various duties that those in positions of trust owe to those they serve. Directors, officers, and managers hold such positions.

[DA02644]

Although avoidance is sometimes an effective risk control technique for liability losses, particularly proactive avoidance, it is often either not practicable or not possible to avoid undertaking the activity or activities that can lead to liability losses. Therefore, loss prevention and loss reduction measures are more typically used.

The most common loss prevention measure is to control hazards (conditions that increase loss frequency or severity). Limiting the number or magnitude of hazards surrounding the loss exposures can prevent losses from occurring.

For example, to limit liability claims arising from employee or customer injuries that occur in a parking lot, an organization could implement loss prevention measures such as clearing ice and snow, providing adequate signs, repairing potholes and cracks in walking surfaces, or conducting periodic inspections.

After a liability loss has occurred, individuals and organizations can implement loss reduction measures to reduce the severity of the liability loss. Such measures can include these:

- Consulting with an attorney for guidance through the legal steps necessary to resolve liability claims.
- Properly responding to the liability claim and to the claimant in order to avoid feelings of ill will that may increase the claimant's demands.
- Participating in alternative dispute resolution. Litigation is a long and costly process. Some forms of alternative dispute resolution, such as mediation or arbitration, often help to resolve liability claims more quickly and more economically than litigation.

Personnel Loss Exposures

Personnel loss exposures are unavoidable, because all organizations have key employees. These loss exposures can arise from events both inside and outside the workplace.

The risk control measures that organizations find most cost-effective are those that can be instituted in the workplace. Therefore, most risk control measures regarding personnel loss exposures involve preventing and reducing workplace injury and illness.

Loss prevention measures used to control work-related injury and illnesses typically involve education, training, and safety measures. An organization may also attempt to prevent personnel causes of loss that occur outside the workplace by controlling key employees' activities through employment contracts; for example, placing restrictions on hazardous activities such as sky diving, flying personal aircraft, riding motorcycles, and so on. Alternatively, organizations may use a form of separation, such as restricting the number of key employees who can travel on the same aircraft.

Loss reduction measures include emergency response training and rehabilitation management. Although all organizations must comply with federally mandated safety measures issued by OSHA (the Occupational Safety and Health Administration), additional training and safety precautions are often cost-effective.

Net Income Loss Exposures

Net income loss exposures can be associated with property, liability, or personnel loss exposures. Therefore, any of the risk control measures that control these three categories of loss exposures also indirectly control net income loss exposures. For example, to prevent a net income loss associated with a property loss exposure, an organization needs to prevent the property loss from occurring.

In addition to reducing the immediate effect of property, liability, or personnel losses on net income, risk control efforts must also control long-term effects, such as a loss of market share that can result from the net income loss. For example, if a manufacturer conducts a product recall, that manufacturer loses sales in the short term, causing a temporary loss of revenue. If the manufacturer's customers switch to purchasing products from other organizations, permanent market share could be lost, which is a long-term effect that translates into permanent revenue loss.

Two risk control measures that are directly aimed at reducing the severity of net income losses are separation and duplication. Separation and duplication enable an organization to reduce net income losses by maintaining operations or quickly resuming operations following a loss. Diversification is also a viable risk control technique for many because it helps to ensure that an organization's entire income is not dependent on one product or customer.

BUSINESS CONTINUITY MANAGEMENT

Business continuity management is a risk control process for identifying potential threats to an organization and ensuring the organization's continued business operations. By minimizing or avoiding significant business interruptions, business continuity management is aimed at meeting the organizational post-loss goals of survival and continuity of operations.

To help ensure the survival of the organization, business continuity management relies on the business continuity process to develop and implement a business continuity plan. The business continuity process assesses the threats to critical functions and develops a methodology for handling those threats. The business continuity plan is the planned response an organization will follow once a survival-threatening loss has occurred. By assessing threats to critical functions and pre-determining the organization's response to losses associated with those threats, business continuity management maximizes the probability of an organization's survival of a critical loss.

Scope of Business Continuity Management

Business continuity management, developed during the 1990s, typically focused on information technology (IT) concerns that could disrupt operations at organizations. Business continuity management has developed beyond its initial IT focus to encompass issues such as terrorism; corporate scandals; and economic developments that have led to more outsourcing, less duplication in production, greater reliance on just-in-time delivery, and more interdependence between organizations and key suppliers or buyers. Business continuity management plans have been expanded to help an organization handle interruptions from these:

- Property losses
- IT problems
- Human failures (such as fraud, sabotage, or terrorism)
- Loss of utility services or infrastructure
- Reputation losses
- Human asset losses (personnel losses)

These risks vary widely by industry, location, and organization. Some organizations are more susceptible to a particular loss exposure than others. Because each organization is unique in its loss exposures, it will also have to be unique in its application of business continuity management.

Business Continuity Process

The business continuity process provides a systematic approach to developing and implementing a business continuity plan. The process involves these six steps:

1. Identify the organization's critical functions
2. Identify the risks (threats) to the organization's critical functions
3. Evaluate the effect of the risks on those critical functions
4. Develop a business continuity strategy
5. Develop a business continuity plan
6. Monitor and revise the business continuity process

These steps are similar to the six steps of the risk management process and are designed to assess and control risks that are significant enough to warrant special attention because of the effect they can have on the organization's survival.

The process involves identification of both the critical functions (processes) of the organization and the risks that could have a substantial effect on those functions. The duration of interruption necessary to produce a substantial effect depends on the function. For example, even a very brief loss of electricity to a hospital can seriously impede the staff's ability to provide basic

medical care. After the risks have been identified and evaluated, a business continuity strategy and plan are developed to establish how to maintain critical functions during a survival-threatening loss. Finally, similar to the risk management process, the entire process must be monitored and evaluated to ensure that it is functioning properly.

The business continuity process provides organizations with the framework to develop a systematic response to a variety of risks that could potentially threaten their future viability. Although following this process cannot ensure the survival of an organization, it can help to minimize the scope of threats that can cause its demise. See the exhibit "Business Continuity Management in Practice."

Business Continuity Management in Practice

Organizations that have implemented business continuity management face some common issues. One issue is deciding whether to outsource business continuity management to an organization that specializes in business continuity on a consulting or implementation basis. Another issue is determining the location of a backup site. Ideally, the backup site is close enough to the primary site so that employees can access the site quickly, but far enough away from the primary site so that the cause of the crisis cannot affect both locations simultaneously. The backup site would ideally have different telecommunications, power, and utilities from the primary site, in case the original cause of the crisis prevented those from functioning properly. A third issue is deciding the amount of detail that should be in a business continuity plan. The plan needs to be simple enough to follow in an emergency, but detailed enough to provide guidance in a wide variety of scenarios that may evolve. Finally, organizations need to be concerned about cost. How much time, energy, and money should be invested in business continuity is difficult to determine and is unique to each organization.

[DA02641]

Business Continuity Plan

A business continuity plan details the activities the organization will take in response to an incident that interrupts its operations. An important part of the business continuity process is to develop such a plan before a significant loss occurs that disrupts business. The plan should be designed with the understanding that it is going to be used during a crisis; that is, it should be clear and able to be quickly read and understood. All relevant parties should have a copy of the plan and should receive appropriate training, including periodic rehearsals of crisis procedures. See the exhibit "Emergency Management Considerations."

Emergency Management Considerations

- Direction and Control
  - Emergency Management Group (EMG)
  - Incident Command System (ICS)
  - Emergency Operations Center (EOC)
  - Planning Considerations
  - Security
  - Coordination of Outside Response
- Communications
  - Contingency Planning
  - Emergency Communications
  - Family Communications
  - Notification
  - Warning
- Life Safety
  - Evacuation Planning
  - Evacuation Routes and Exits
  - Assembly Areas and Accountability
  - Shelter
  - Training and Information
  - Family Preparedness
- Property Protection
  - Planning Considerations
  - Protection Systems
  - Mitigation
  - Facility Shutdown
  - Records Preservation
- Community Outreach
  - Involving the Community
  - Mutual Aid Agreements
  - Community Service
  - Public Information
  - Media Relations
- Recovery and Restoration
  - Planning Considerations
  - Continuity of Management
  - Insurance
  - Employee Support
  - Resuming Operations
- Administration and Logistics
  - Administrative Actions
  - Logistics

Adapted from "Emergency Management Guide for Business and Industry," FEMA 141, section 2, www.fema.gov/pdf/business/guide/bizindst.pdf (accessed January 15, 2010). [DA02642]

Although business continuity plans vary widely by organization, some content is fairly general. Most business continuity plans contain these:

- Strategy the organization is going to follow to manage the crisis
- Information about the roles and duties of various individuals in the organization
- Steps that can be taken to prevent any further loss or damage
- Emergency response plan to deal with life and safety issues
- Crisis management plan to deal with communication and any reputation issues (reputation management) that may arise
- Business recovery and restoration plan to deal with losses to property, processes, or products
- Access to stress management and counseling for affected parties

The exhibit contains the emergency management considerations developed by a public-private partnership with the Federal Emergency Management Association (FEMA). Ultimately, both business continuity management and risk control are aimed at enabling an individual or organization to not only deal with hazards and loss exposures, but to deal with them in the most efficient and cost-effective way in order to reduce the exposure to, and cost of, risk.

Review Questions

1. Explain how proactive and reactive avoidance differ in reducing loss frequency of a loss exposure.
2. Describe the purpose of the following loss reduction measures in controlling losses: a. pre-loss measures and b. post-loss measures.
3. Describe the purpose of a disaster recovery plan.
4. Identify circumstances in which each of the following techniques would be an effective choice for loss reduction: a. separation, b. duplication, and c. diversification.
5. Describe the advantages of using cash flow analysis for the selection of risk control measures.
6. Describe the disadvantages of using cash flow analysis for the selection of risk control measures.
7. List the types of state or federal statutes an organization may need to consider when selecting risk control measures in order to comply with legal requirements.
8. Identify possible consequences an organization can face for failure to comply with legal requirements.
9. Identify the issues regarding fire, health, and safety a risk management professional should consider when assessing an organization's life-safety loss exposures.
10. Identify causes of loss an organization should consider when promoting life safety.
11. Explain why a risk management professional should evaluate the effect of a potential risk control measure on both the loss frequency and the loss severity of the organization's loss exposures.
12. Describe the possible positive and negative externalities of a risk control measure.
13. Identify the factors insurance producers and underwriters commonly consider when examining loss exposures in commercial properties.
14. Which risk control techniques are commonly used to control liability loss exposures?
15. Describe loss prevention and loss reduction measures an organization might use to control work-related injury and illness.
16. Explain the purpose of business continuity management.

17. Identify potential situations that business continuity management might address to help achieve an organization's goal of survival and continuity of operations after a loss.
18. List the six steps in the business continuity process.
19. Identify guidelines for design of an effective business continuity plan.
20. List the content commonly contained in business continuity plans.

Application Questions

1. The Cooper Pharmaceutical Company manufactures and distributes both prescription drugs and medicines sold over the counter by pharmacies and other outlets. More than half of Cooper's annual expenses are for research and development of new products. About 50 percent of Cooper's revenues are derived from an ulcer remedy. The remedy's formula includes a chemical compound that is manufactured in only one chemical plant in the world. There are other similar ulcer remedies on the market, and management concedes that some of them are equally effective. However, Cooper's product was the first on the market and has acquired a large following among doctors, who usually prescribe it by Cooper's brand name. Management is concerned that any prolonged absence of their ulcer medicine from the market would cause doctors to prescribe another brand, and they might not return to Cooper's brand when it becomes available again.

   The testing process for some products is long and complex, sometimes involving several years of testing on dogs, primates, or other relatively long-lived animals, possibly followed by testing on human volunteers. Voluminous records accumulate during such tests and must be retained for many years for use in licensing applications, defense of products liability claims, and future research projects.

   Cooper stores its research records in fire-resistive filing cabinets in the records room of its research center. The center also houses research laboratories, offices for research personnel, and animals for research. The research center is located in a sprinklered, fire-resistive building adjacent to Cooper's factory. Personnel who handle the animals are thoroughly trained in animal care to ensure the safety of both the animals and employees. Although Cooper has more than 200 employees, its workers compensation claims have been well below the industry average over the last ten years.

   The factory building also is fire resistive and is sprinklered in all areas except the clean room. The clean room, used for manufacturing and packaging processes that require complete sterility, has its own air conditioning system with special filtering equipment to eliminate dust and other potential contaminants and other equipment to maintain the sterile atmosphere. Even very slight contamination of the clean room would require the discontinuation of production for several days until sterility

could be reestablished. All workers in the clean room must wear special sterile uniforms and surgical masks.

Identify the risk control measures used by Cooper for each of the following loss exposures: a. property loss exposures, b. personnel loss exposures, and c. net income loss exposures.

SUMMARY

Risk control is a conscious act or decision not to act that reduces the frequency and severity of losses or makes losses more predictable. Risk control techniques prevent losses, reduce the severity of losses, and speed recovery following a loss.

Risk control techniques can be categorized into one of six broad categories:

- Avoidance
- Loss prevention
- Loss reduction
- Separation
- Duplication
- Diversification

The goals of risk control are these:

- Implement effective and efficient risk control measures
- Comply with legal requirements
- Promote life safety
- Ensure business continuity

Insurance and risk management professionals need to examine all changes in loss frequency and loss severity of not only the targeted loss exposure, but also any loss exposure that may have its frequency or severity altered by the risk control measure under consideration, to ensure that the result of implementing a risk control measure is that the organization's overall expected losses are reduced.

The risk control techniques most applicable to property loss exposures vary based on the type of property as well as the cause of loss. Avoidance, loss prevention, and loss reduction are the risk control techniques most applicable to liability loss exposures. Most risk control measures for personnel loss exposures involve preventing and reducing workplace injury and illness. Net income exposures can be controlled by the measures that control the property, liability, or personnel losses that cause net income losses.

Business continuity management is a process that identifies potential threats to an organization and provides a methodology for ensuring an organization's continued business operations. The business continuity process assesses the threats to critical functions and develops a methodology for handling those

threats. It also provides organizations with the framework to develop a systematic response to a variety of risks that could potentially threaten the future viability of the organization.

ASSIGNMENT NOTE

1. Ron Coté, PE, and Gregory E. Harrington, PE, eds., *Life Safety Code® Handbook*, 9th ed. (Quincy, Mass.: National Fire Protection Association, 2003). Life Safety Code® is a registered trademark of the National Fire Protection Association, Quincy, Mass., 02169.

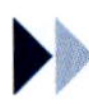

Direct Your Learning

6

Risk Management Alternatives—Loss Financing Techniques

Educational Objectives

After learning the content of this assignment, you should be able to:

- Explain how individuals or organizations can achieve their overall and risk management goals by fulfilling the following risk financing goals:
  - Pay for losses
  - Manage the cost of risk
  - Manage cash flow variability
  - Maintain an appropriate level of liquidity
  - Comply with legal requirements
- Describe the risk financing techniques of transfer and retention.
- Explain how the following can affect the selection of the appropriate risk financing measure:
  - Ability of a risk financing measure to meet risk financing goals
  - Loss exposure characteristics
  - Characteristics specific to an individual or organization
- Describe the types of contractual risk transfer for hazard risk.
- Describe the types of captive insurance plans available.

Outline

Risk Financing Goals

Risk Financing Techniques: Transfer and Retention

Selecting Appropriate Risk Financing Measures

Types of Contractual Risk Transfer

Types of Captive Insurance Plans

Summary

Risk Management Alternatives—Loss Financing Techniques

6

RISK FINANCING GOALS

Different risk control measures will help an individual or organization achieve its risk financing goals with varying degrees of effectiveness and efficiency. Therefore, when assisting others in selecting risk financing measures, insurance and risk management professionals seek to first understand the risk financing goals the individual or organization is trying to achieve.

Risk management program goals are designed to support an individual's or organization's overall goals. Because risk financing is an integral part of a risk management program, risk financing goals should support risk management program goals. See the exhibit "How Risk Financing Goals Support Risk Management Goals."

[DA02690]

Common risk financing goals include these:

- Pay for losses
- Manage the cost of risk
- Manage cash flow variability
- Maintain an appropriate level of liquidity
- Comply with legal requirements

Pay for Losses

Individuals and organizations need to ensure that funds are available to pay for losses when they occur. The availability of funds is particularly important in situations that disrupt normal activities, such as when an individual needs to replace an automobile used to commute to work or when an organization needs to replace damaged property necessary for continued operations. However, paying for losses is also important for other reasons, such as to promote public relations.

For example, an organization does not want to damage its reputation by not paying liability losses resulting from legitimate third-party claims (claims filed against the insured by a party who is not a party to the insurance contract). Similarly, it may want to launch an advertising campaign to demonstrate its commitment to resolving a product liability issue.

For many individuals or organizations, paying for losses does not only entail paying for the actual losses or portions of losses retained, it also covers transfer costs, which are costs paid in order to transfer responsibility for losses to another party.

For financial risks, transfer costs could be the price of buying options to hedge the costs associated with currency exchange rate risk. For hazard risks, transfer costs are often insurance premiums. In return for the premium, the insurer accepts the uncertainty of the cost of the insured's covered losses and agrees to reimburse the insured for covered losses or to pay covered losses on the insured's behalf. The premium would also need to cover expenses and profit margins for the insurer.

This section considers paying for losses and paying transaction costs separately. Paying for losses is one risk financing goal, whereas paying transaction costs is part of managing the cost of risk, a separate risk financing goal.

For example, an insurance premium would cover both paying for losses and the transaction costs associated with the insurance policy. These two separate goals are parallel to being effective and efficient. Risk financing measures should be effective (pay for losses that do occur) as well as efficient (pay for losses in the most economical way).

Manage the Cost of Risk

Risk financing seeks to manage an individual's or organization's cost of risk. These expenses form part of the cost of risk, regardless of whether losses are retained or transferred:

- Administrative expenses
- Risk control expenses
- Risk financing expenses

Administrative expenses include the cost of internal administration and the cost of purchased services, such as claim administration or risk management consulting. Although many of these expenses are unavoidable if a risk financing program is to be properly managed, an individual or organization may have an opportunity to save on some expenses by modifying procedures or eliminating unnecessary tasks. For example, an organization with a loss retention program might save expenses by outsourcing the claim administration function to a third party who can adjust the claims more cost effectively.

Risk control expenses are incurred to reduce frequency, reduce the severity of losses that do occur, or increase the predictability of future losses. An individual or organization can best analyze risk control expenses by conducting a cost-benefit analysis. Therefore, to ensure that risk control expenses promote an individual's or organization's long-term financial goals, resources should be devoted to risk control only if the benefit of a risk control measure exceeds its cost.

Risk financing expenses are incurred to manage the risk financing measures used to meet risk financing goals. Many of these risk financing measures involve transaction costs, including commissions paid to brokers, fees paid to banks or other investment institutions in order to establish accounts, and fees paid for trades on capital market transactions.

Depending on the transaction's size, these costs can be substantial, sometimes millions of dollars. Transaction costs vary based not only on the risk financing measure chosen but also on varying market conditions. For example, the commissions paid to brokers are often a percentage of the total insurance premium that the broker places with an insurer. If insurance prices increase, the commission paid will be higher.

If market conditions dictate lower insurance premiums, commissions will be lower as well. Managing the administrative expenses, risk control expenses, and risk financing expenses does not necessarily mean minimizing those costs in an attempt to operate economically or increase profitability. In fact, many of those costs are necessary to manage an effective risk management program. Individuals and organizations should be aware of the value of the risk financing measures used to ensure that they are receiving adequate service for the price that is being paid for them. In other words, an individual or organization should be wary of sacrificing effectiveness for efficiency.

Manage Cash Flow Variability

The level of cash flow variability that an individual or organization is able or willing to accept depends on the individual's or organization's tolerance for risk. Determining that level of tolerance can be difficult. Individuals or organizations can achieve their goals for managing cash flow variability by determining the maximum cash flow variability they are willing to tolerate and arranging their risk management programs within those parameters.

For an individual, risk tolerance often depends on financial strength, family obligations, and the individual's aversion to risk. For example, an individual with two young children may desire more stable income than an individual without children. Therefore, the individual with children may be more inclined to choose a career in which the majority of the compensation comes from salary rather than commissions.

For an organization, the maximum cash flow variability level depends on factors such as the organization's size, its financial strength, and management's own degree of risk tolerance. For example, if management is prepared to accept risk in order to gain a possible benefit, then the cash flow variability levels will be higher than if management prefers to avoid risk.

An organization's maximum cash flow variability level also depends on the degree to which the organization's other stakeholders, such as shareholders, suppliers, or customers, are willing to accept risk. For example, suppliers may be less willing to sell supplies on credit to organizations with high variability in their cash flows because of concern about the organization's ability to make its repayments.

Maintain an Appropriate Level of Liquidity

A certain level of cash liquidity (liquid assets) is required to pay for retained losses. A liquid asset is one that can easily be converted into cash. For example, marketable securities are liquid because they can readily be sold in the stock or bond markets. Assets such as real property and machinery are typically not liquid because they are difficult to sell quickly at prices close to their market values.

As an individual or organization's retention level increases, so does the level of liquidity required. Therefore, to meet risk financing goals, individuals or organizations must determine the appropriate level of liquidity for retained losses and consider both internal and external sources of capital to meet those needs. Internally, individuals or organizations can look to the liquidity of their assets and the strength of their cash flows.

Liquidity can be increased by selling assets or by retaining cash flow instead of using it to fund capital projects or to pay dividends. Externally, an organization can increase liquidity by borrowing, issuing a debt instrument (a bond),

or issuing stock (for a publicly traded organization). For an individual, borrowing is typically the only external option.

One problem with maintaining high levels of liquidity is that liquid assets do not typically offer the same return on investments as other, longer-term, less liquid investments. Individuals and organizations must consider the balance between desire for long-term returns in less liquid investments and the liquidity needs of retained losses.

Comply With Legal Requirements

Individuals and organizations need to consider the legal environment when making risk financing decisions. Ultimately, the goal of complying with legal requirements is a fundamental requirement of all risk financing goals. How individuals and organizations comply with these requirements depends on the individual requirements imposed by the applicable statutory or contractual obligations.

Sometimes laws and regulations will require specific risk financing measures. For example, most states require drivers to purchase auto liability insurance policies. Similarly, state workers compensation statutes require most employers to purchase workers compensation insurance or to qualify as self-insurers.

Alternatively, legal requirements will affect how risk financing measures are implemented. For example, an organization that intends to raise its liquidity by issuing bonds may be required by the bond purchasers to insure its property for a specific amount.

Similarly, contractual obligations, such as leases on automobiles or aircraft, may also require insurance coverage on the leased property.

RISK FINANCING TECHNIQUES: TRANSFER AND RETENTION

In examining the feasibility of risk management alternatives, the risk management professional will consider risk financing as well as risk control. **Risk financing** is a conscious act or decision not to act that generates the funds to pay for losses or offset the variability in cash flows that may occur. This section briefly discusses the fundamental risk financing techniques for accidental loss exposures. The exhibit shows the risk management techniques available for treating accidental loss exposures. See the exhibit "Risk Control and Risk Financing Techniques Applied to Business Risks."

Risk financing

A conscious act or decision not to act that generates the funds to pay for losses and risk control measures or to offset variability in cash flows.

Risk Control and Risk Financing Techniques Applied to Business Risks

As well as being used for hazard risks, both risk control and risk financing techniques have clear applications to business risks—that is, speculative losses that arise from business decisions, changes in technology, customer preferences, or shifting economic conditions. The following examples illustrate these applications:

- Business risk losses can be avoided by halting, or by never engaging in, a particular business activity that could lead to such losses.
- Business risk losses can be prevented (made less frequent) by using caution in selecting favorable circumstances for engaging in a particular business activity.
- Business risk losses can be reduced (made less severe) by limiting an organization's resources committed to a particularly risky project.
- Business risk losses can be diversified by participating in numerous projects, products, markets, or regions so that the organization's overall profitability or operating efficiency approaches the average profitability or efficiency of all of these diversified activities.
- Business risk losses can be transferred by subcontracting to another organization for a favorable fixed price an activity that an organization may or may not be able to perform profitably. An organization can use noninsurance contractual transfer to limit its potential business losses from that activity.
- Business risk losses can be retained by paying for (or absorbing as reduced profits or lowered surpluses) speculative business losses.
- Business risk losses can be financed by inserting provisions into business contracts with suppliers, customers, or joint venturers. This is, in effect, a noninsurance transfer for the benefit of the transferring organization that wants to avoid the financial burden of some business risks. The other contracting parties agree to reimburse the transferring organization for specified types of business losses if, for example, an inventory of merchandise does not prove as popular as expected or the price of a particular raw material changes.

Insurance, which is one of the most popular risk financing techniques for exposures to accidental losses, typically is not appropriate for protecting against losses from business risks. By definition, business risks have both a potential for gain as well as a potential for loss. If an organization was able to purchase insurance to remove the potential for loss, all that remains is the potential for gain. In financial terms, this is arbitrage, gaining reward without assuming risk. In properly functioning markets, arbitrage does not exist. That is, it is not possible for an organization to gain reward (profits) without assuming the potential losses associated with the business risk.

In insurance markets, the premium that an insurer would charge to guarantee an insured's profit on a business venture would actually be greater than the insured's expected profit (expected profit plus expenses and the insurer's profit margin), therefore removing any incentive to undertake the business venture.

To make a profit (or generate a surplus) an organization or individual must be willing to tolerate the accompanying potential losses by exposing itself to business risks.

[DA01673]

Risk financing techniques can be classified into two groups:

1. Transfer, which includes insurance and noninsurance techniques to shift the financial consequences of loss to another party
2. Retention, which involves absorbing the loss by generating funds within the organization to pay for the loss

Risk financing techniques are not necessarily used in isolation. Many techniques involve elements of both retention and transfer. For example, insurance with a deductible comprises retention of the deductible amount and transfer of losses above the deductible.

Transfer

Transfer involves the transfer of risk through insurance and noninsurance techniques to shift the financial consequences of loss to another party. Noninsurance techniques used to transfer risk include hold-harmless agreements and hedging.

Insurance

Insurance is a risk financing technique that transfers the potential financial consequences of certain specified loss exposures from the insured to the insurer. The insurance buyer substitutes a small certain financial cost, the insurance premium, for the possibility of a large uncertain financial loss, which would be paid by the insurer. Although insurance is only one approach to risk financing, it is a vital component of a risk management program.

Insurance

A risk management technique that transfers the potential financial consequences of certain specified loss exposures from the insured to the insurer.

Insurance is essentially a funded risk transfer. By accepting a premium, the insurer agrees to pay for all the organization's losses that are covered by the insurance contract. The insurer also agrees to provide necessary services, such as claim handling and defense of liability claims.

Noninsurance Risk Transfer

Noninsurance risk transfer is a risk financing technique that transfers all or part of the financial consequences of loss to another party, other than an insurer. Contracts that are not insurance contracts but that transfer loss exposures are therefore called noninsurance risk transfers.

Noninsurance risk transfer

A risk financing technique in which one party transfers the potential financial consequences of a particular loss exposure to another party that is not an insurer.

Some contracts deal solely with the responsibility for losses arising out of a particular relationship or activity. Under these contracts, which are known as hold-harmless agreements (also called indemnity agreements), one party (the indemnitor) agrees to assume the liability of a second party (the indemnitee). See the exhibit "Hold Harmless Agreement for Use in a Lease."

Hedging is also considered a noninsurance risk transfer technique. Hedging is a financial transaction in which one asset is held to offset the risk associated with another asset. Hedging often involves business risk rather than hazard

Hedging

A financial transaction in which one asset is held to offset the risk associated with another asset.

Hold Harmless Agreement for Use in a Lease

To the fullest extent permitted by law, the lessee shall indemnify, defend and hold harmless the lessor, agents and employees of the lessor, from and against all claims arising out of or resulting from the leased premises.

[DA01674]

risk. Hedging is practical when it is used to offset loss exposures to which one is naturally, voluntarily, or inevitably exposed. For example, a newspaper publisher faces the loss exposure of newsprint price variability. To offset this loss exposure, the publisher might enter into a futures contract with its paper supplier to purchase a fixed quantity of newsprint over the coming year at a pre-agreed price.

Futures contract
An exchange-traded agreement to buy or sell a commodity or security at a future date at a price that is fixed at the time of the agreement.

A **futures contract** is an agreement to buy or sell a commodity or security at a future date at a price that is fixed at the time of the agreement. If the market price of paper increases over the next year, the newspaper publisher will save money by buying paper below the prevailing price. If the market price drops, the newspaper publisher will pay more than the prevailing price for its paper. Either way, the newspaper publisher's loss exposure is reduced because the variability in the newsprint's cost is eliminated from the perspective of the newspaper publisher. The same can be said for the paper supplier. Whether the paper supplier would have made more money or less money depends on what the prevailing market price of paper turns out to be, but the paper supplier was able to reduce the variability by entering into the futures contract.

Retention

Retention
A risk financing technique by which losses are retained by generating funds within the organization to pay for the losses.

Retention is a risk financing technique that involves assumption of risk in which losses are retained by generating funds within the organization to pay for the losses. Because retention can be the most economic risk financing technique available, it is sometimes preferred even when insurance or non-insurance risk transfer is available. Retention can also be the risk financing technique of last resort; the financial burden of any losses that cannot be insured or otherwise transferred must be retained.

Retention can be planned or unplanned; complete or partial; or funded or unfunded.

- Planned retention is a deliberate assumption of a loss exposure (and any consequential losses) that has been identified and analyzed. Planned retention may be chosen because it is most cost-effective, because it is most convenient, or because no other alternatives are available.
- Unplanned retention is the inadvertent assumption of a loss exposure (and any consequential losses) because the loss exposure has not been identified or accurately analyzed. For example, many people inadvertently

retain flood losses because they do not anticipate that the rains associated with the remnants of hurricanes will endanger their property.

- Complete retention is the assumption of the full cost of any loss that is retained by the organization.
- Partial retention is the assumption of a portion of the cost of a loss by the organization and the transfer of the remaining portion.
- Funded retention is the pre-loss arrangement to ensure that funding is available post-loss to pay for losses that do occur.
- Unfunded retention is the lack of advance funding for losses that do occur.

Funding Retained Losses

Three general methods can be used to pay for (fund) retained losses:

- With **pre-loss funding**, the money to fund retained losses is set aside in advance. The principal advantage of pre-loss funding is that the money needed to fund losses can be saved over several budget periods. The principal disadvantage is that it ties up money that could otherwise be used by the organization and consequently has an opportunity cost for the organization. The reduction of available financial resources keeps pre-loss funding from being widely used except when an organization forms a captive insurer, which is a subsidiary formed to insure the loss exposures of its parents and affiliates.
- With **current-loss funding**, money to fund retained losses is provided at the time of the loss or immediately after it. Current-loss funding is the most popular and often the least expensive form of funding. Its main advantage is that it does not tie up funds before they are actually needed. Its principal disadvantage is that there may not be enough money in the current budget to cover the loss and satisfy other cash flow needs.
- With **post-loss funding**, the organization pays for its retained losses sometime after losses occur, using borrowing (or some other method of raising additional capital) in the meantime. For example, a building owner may have to take out a mortgage to fund the reconstruction of a damaged uninsured building. The mortgage would be the post-loss funding instrument.

There are advantages to using post-loss funding, including the opportunity to pay the cost of retained losses over several years instead of all at once, and only having to use the amount needed to pay for retained losses. However, post-loss funding also has several disadvantages. The organization using post-loss funding must pay interest on the borrowings. In addition, the loss event that produces the need to borrow may also reduce the organization's creditworthiness, therefore increasing the loan's cost. Although this disadvantage can be overcome by making pre-loss arrangements for a credit guarantee, that guarantee involves a fee. Also, guaranteeing post-loss credit may reduce the organization's capacity to borrow pre-loss funds that can be used for business operations.

Pre-loss funding
A funded retention arrangement under which money to fund losses is set aside in advance.

Current-loss funding
A funded retention arrangement under which money to fund retained losses is provided at the time of the loss or immediately after it.

Post-loss funding
A funded retention arrangement under which the organization pays for its retained losses sometime after losses occur, using borrowing (or some other method of raising additional capital) in the meantime.

SELECTING APPROPRIATE RISK FINANCING MEASURES

To select the appropriate risk financing measures to be used in a risk management program, an individual or organization needs to evaluate the relative advantages of all the available measures and consider the ability of each to meet the risk financing goals.

The major factors influencing the ability of a risk financing measure to meet an individual's or organization's risk financing goals are these:

- The mix of retention and transfer
- Loss exposure characteristics
- Individual- or organization-specific characteristics

Mix of Retention and Transfer

An organization's risk financing program needs to balance retention and transfer in light of the specific risk financing goals that the organization is trying to accomplish. This balance can be achieved through the appropriate mix of risk financing measures.

Some loss exposures may be fully retained, others mostly transferred, and the remainder addressed with risk financing measures that balance retention and transfer. See the exhibit "Ability of Retention and Transfer to Meet Risk Financing Goals."

Because retention can be the most economical risk financing measure, it enables an organization to meet its risk financing goal of managing the cost of risk. However, depending on the magnitude of the actual losses sustained, retention programs may have difficulty paying for losses.

The ability to pay for losses depends on the structure of the retention measure implemented and the relative strength of the individual's or organization's cash flows. For example, if a loss exposure suffers a substantial loss that was retained, the ability to pay for the loss depends on whether the retention measure was pre-funded (such as funded reserve) or post-funded (such as cash flows or borrowing), how large the loss is relative to what was expected when the retention decision was made, and how large the loss is relative to cash flows or assets of the individual or organization.

Retention also generates the highest level of cash flow variability and may threaten an organization's liquidity level. Often, how an organization structures and manages its retention determines how effective it is at achieving risk financing goals compared with transfer.

Risk transfer measures typically offer the greatest certainty regarding the ability to pay losses, offer the greatest cash flow certainty, and are useful in preventing liquidity problems, but they may be costly to arrange. Furthermore,

Ability of Retention and Transfer to Meet Risk Financing Goals

Risk Financing Goal	Retention	Transfer
Pay for Losses	Depends on magnitude of losses and structure and management of retention measure, as well as the relative strength of cash flows	Primary benefit of transfer measures
Manage the Cost of Risk	Primary benefit of retention	Rarely the most cost-effective option
Manage Cash Flow Variability	Typically exposes the individual or organization to more variability in cash flows	Important benefit of transfer measures
Maintain an Appropriate Level of Liquidity	Depends on magnitude of losses and structure and management of retention measure, as well as the relative strength of cash flows	Generally reduces the level of liquidity needed
Comply With Legal Requirements	Depends on structure and management of retention measure	Secondary benefit of transfer measures

[DA02604]

some organizations are required by statute or contractual obligation to transfer some risk.

For example, most mortgage lenders require that the property owner carry adequate limits of property insurance coverage. Similarly, many states require that motor vehicle owners, including organizations, have auto liability coverage. These requirements add to the overall cost of transfer and may therefore affect the benefit of transfer relative to retention.

Loss Exposure Characteristics

The frequency and severity of losses associated with each loss exposure are vital to determining whether a loss exposure should be fully retained or whether some form of transfer is appropriate. See the exhibit "The Effect of Frequency and Severity on the Retention or Transfer Decision."

The Effect of Frequency and Severity on the Retention or Transfer Decision

	Low Frequency	High Frequency
Low Severity	Retain	Retain
High Severity	Transfer	Avoid (if possible) Retain (last resort)

[DA02695]

Insurance products are often designed around these types of loss exposures.

The high-frequency, high-severity quadrant covers losses that occur frequently and are severe. These loss exposures should be avoided. Neither risk retention nor risk transfer is adequately designed to handle these types of loss exposures. If risk control measures can be applied to reduce the frequency or severity of the losses (or both), the loss exposure can be reclassified into the appropriate quadrant to be re-evaluated in terms of risk financing options.

The exhibit indicates that risk financing through retention is the appropriate technique for most loss exposures. It is only for loss exposures with low-frequency, high-severity losses that risk transfer measures are appropriate.

Individual- or Organization-Specific Characteristics

The optimal balance between retention and transfer varies for each individual or organization, depending on specific characteristics. Therefore, individuals and organizations will make different decisions in selecting the appropriate risk financing measures. Even if two organizations have the same set of loss exposures, differences between the organizations may result in vastly different selections. The individual- or organization-specific characteristics that can affect the selection of appropriate risk financing measures include these:

- Risk tolerance
- Financial condition
- Core operations
- Ability to diversify
- Ability to control losses
- Ability to administer the retention plan

Risk Tolerance

Individuals and organizations vary widely in their willingness to assume risk. A risk-averse organization may decide not to produce a certain type of prod-

uct because of the high instance of associated product liability claims, whereas another organization's primary source of revenue could be that same product.

The level of risk an organization is willing to assume directly affects its optimal balance between retention and transfer. All else being equal, the higher an individual's or organization's willingness to accept risk, the higher the likelihood that more risk will be retained.

Financial Condition

The financial condition of the individual or organization has a significant effect on ability to retain risk. The more financially secure an individual or organization is, the more loss exposures can be retained without causing liquidity or cash flow variability problems.

However, even financially secure individuals or organizations need to be careful. They may experience short-term liquidity problems if a significant loss has been retained and short-term cash flow or liquid assets are not sufficient to cover the loss.

Core Operations

An organization is often better able to retain the loss exposures directly related to its core operations because it has an information advantage regarding those operations. That is, the organization knows and understands its core operations and the loss exposures associated with them better than any outside party, including insurers. Because of this information advantage, an outside party would likely need higher compensation to enter into a transfer agreement.

Ability to Diversify

If an organization can diversify its loss exposures, similar to the way many individuals and organizations diversify their investment portfolios, it can gain the advantage of offsetting losses that occur to one loss exposure with the absence of losses associated with the other loss exposures. The organization is then better able to accurately forecast future losses. This increased level of loss accuracy would reduce uncertainty about losses and therefore allow the organization to retain more loss exposures.

Ability to Control Losses

Because risk control reduces loss frequency and/or loss severity, the more risk control an organization is able to undertake, the more loss exposures it is typically able to retain. All else being equal, the reductions in frequency and/or severity make it more likely that the organization will have the ability to fund the retention of that particular loss exposure.

Ability to Administer the Retention Plan

Risk retention requires more administration than risk transfer. Such administration may include claim administration, risk management consulting, or retention fund accounting. Organizations that have a better ability to fulfill these administrative requirements are able to use retention more efficiently.

Determining the optimal balance between risk transfer and risk retention measures keeps the risk financing program aligned with the individual's or organization's overall risk management goals. For the portion of those loss exposures that an individual or organization decides to transfer, a variety of risk financing measures are available.

TYPES OF CONTRACTUAL RISK TRANSFER

Insurance contracts allow an organization to transfer many of the financial consequences of accidental losses to an insurance company, which pools the risks of many insureds. Contract law allows contracting parties to transfer risks in ways that do not involve insurance. Several types of contractual (noninsurance) risk transfer are available for hazard risk.

Organizations use contractual (noninsurance) risk transfer to transfer many of the same types of hazard risks that are covered by insurance. For example, two parties may agree that one party will reimburse the other for its loss or that one party will undertake an activity (and with it, absorb the accompanying risks) that the other party normally would perform. Under another possible contractual arrangement, a party waives its rights to sue the other party for a tort (a wrongful act or omission, other than a crime or a breach of contract) related to the contracted-for activity.

The transferee in a contractual (noninsurance) risk transfer does not operate as an insurer. Consequently, it does not pool the risks of more than one transferor. However, like insurance, many contractual risk transfers deal with hazard risk; thus they transfer either risk control activities or the cost of recovering from a loss.

Types of Contractual Risk Transfer

Noninsurance risk control transfer
A noninsurance transfer in which the transferor transfers a loss exposure to the transferee, thereby eliminating the possibility that the transferor will suffer a loss from the transferred exposure.

A contractual risk transfer is an agreement in which one party (the transferee), not acting as an insurer, accepts another party's (the transferor's) exposure to loss or the financial consequences of the transferor's loss exposures as an incidental aspect of another business transaction. Contractual risk transfers fall into two categories:

- **Noninsurance risk control transfer**—When an organization contractually transfers risk control responsibilities to a party that is not an insurer, it essentially shifts the loss exposures associated with that risk to the

transferee. A noninsurance risk control transfer becomes effective only when the transferee performs the action that rids the transferor of risk.

- **Noninsurance risk financing transfer**—When an organization contractually transfers the financial burden of losses, the underlying loss exposures are not transferred between the parties. Noninsurance risk financing transfer provides the transferor with protection only after the funds to restore a loss have been paid. Until a loss occurs, the transferor cannot be certain that the transferee will pay. If the transferee fails to provide the expected funds, the financial burden of the risk was never truly transferred.

Noninsurance risk financing transfer
A noninsurance transfer in which the transferor transfers to the transferee the financial burden of losses by obligating the transferee to pay money to (or on behalf of) the transferor after the transferor or some third party suffers a loss.

Contractual risk transfers in both categories can assume a variety of forms, each designed to meet the specific needs of the parties involved. For both types of transfer, a contract is usually formed before any loss occurs.

A critical difference between a noninsurance risk control and a noninsurance risk financing transfer surfaces when a transferee becomes bankrupt or otherwise unable to fulfill the contractual transfer terms. In a noninsurance risk financing transfer, a bankrupt transferee provides no protection to the transferor, who must pay for its own accidental loss. In a noninsurance risk control transfer, a bankrupt or uncooperative transferee may continue to be responsible for losses it caused, preserving the transferor's protection.

Noninsurance Risk Control Transfer

Many risk management professionals are experienced in insurance or financial matters and are therefore accustomed to dealing with contracts that indemnify losses. However, many risk management departments do not handle contractual risk control transfer contracts. For example, some risk management professionals do not manage leases or other similar written contracts that transfer risk of possible loss as an incidental part of the overall transaction.

Examples of noninsurance risk control transfers include these:

- Incorporation
- Leasing
- Contracting for services
- Suretyship and guaranty agreements
- Waiver
- Limitation of liability
- Disclaimer of warranties

Incorporation

Incorporation statutes in many countries stipulate that a corporation is a legal entity distinct from its shareholders and solely responsible for its (or its

agents') own wrongs. Therefore, in the absence of fraud, other intentional wrongs, or statutory violation by its founding stockholders, a corporation can lose no more than the value of its assets as a result of a business venture, an accident, or a lawsuit. Incorporation statutes also typically limit any one stockholder's financial loss to the value of his or her own shares, thereby insulating stockholders' personal assets.

A businessowner can insulate the organization from potential losses by designating a separate corporation to conduct each of the organization's major activities. For example, one corporation may manufacture and sell products, while another installs and services them. This practice is known as **segregation**. With segregation, the "divisions" between an organization's exposure units constitute the legal boundaries of separate corporations, thereby limiting loss potentials that arise from business risks, property losses, liability losses, and net income losses.

Segregation
A risk control technique that separates or duplicates an organization's activities or property so that no single cause of loss can simultaneously affect all the organization's activities or property.

Stockholders can control the total value of the corporation's assets by contributing capital to or withdrawing it from the enterprise. The corporation thus serves as a transferee for risk that individual stockholders might otherwise face.

In some cases involving liability claims against corporations, courts have "pierced the corporate veil" by pursuing a major managing stockholder's personal assets. A court may take this approach, for example, when a corporation seeks bankruptcy protection after having apparently manipulated assets to frustrate creditors or when a predominant stockholder or corporate executive uses the corporation to hide personal wrongdoings. Courts in such cases may place greater importance on compensating individuals harmed by the corporation than on maintaining the usual separation between corporate liability and stockholders' personal assets.

Leasing

A **leasehold** right is asserted by a lessee. Before a leasehold is placed in effect and after it expires, the right to occupy or use the property remains with or returns to its owner.

Leasehold
The right to occupy or use real or personal property for a period of time.

Certain risks that attach to property ownership do not accompany its use or occupancy. These risks include loss from property destruction and liability to third parties for dangerous property conditions. A tenant (or lessee) does not normally take on these exposures when leasing the property unless the lease obligates the lessee to return the property to the lessor in the same condition in which it was received or unless the lessee alone has caused a dangerous condition that has harmed others.

Sale-and-lease-back (sale-and-lease-back arrangement)
A transaction through which an organization that owns property transfers its risk by selling the property while retaining the right to occupy or use it under a lease with the new owner.

An organization that leases property rather than owning it practices risk control by allowing the property owner to retain the risks related to property ownership. Under a **sale-and-lease-back arrangement**, a property owner transfers these risks—often to a corporation or another organization created or selected primarily for risk transferring, risk financing, or property manage-

ment purposes. If no fraud is involved, courts usually uphold such a transfer (except in cases in which dangerous property conditions were apparent before the property was sold and leased back). A sale-and-leasehold arrangement also allows the former property owner to convert its equity into cash.

Contracting for Services

An individual or organization that performs a particular activity is generally held primarily responsible for any losses caused by that activity. An organization that wants to avoid such risk can contract with another organization to perform the activity. This noninsurance risk control transfer method is called contracting for services or simply subcontracting; however, the transferor need not be an independent contractor, and the party that accepts the risk need not be a subcontractor. Any contract requiring another party to perform a service and, implicitly, to assume the risk associated with it, involves the act of subcontracting.

Generally, any property, net income, or personnel loss exposure associated with an activity can be transferred through subcontracting. The transfer agreement must meet the legal requirements for a fairly bargained transfer of both the loss exposures and the actual losses associated with the activity. In this case, both the loss exposure and the burden of financing recovery rest with the subcontractor.

Liability loss exposures associated with an activity are not easily transferred, especially those relating to harm to third parties. For example, if negligence by a high-rise building subcontractor's employees creates a hazard that injures a pedestrian, the employees and the subcontractor would be primarily liable. However, the injured pedestrian would probably sue the landowner as the party responsible for the land's general condition.

Because the courts seek to provide compensation to those who are injured, they favor restricting the general rule that exempts someone who hires an independent contractor from liability for that contractor's torts. As a result, these exceptions have been made to the rule:

- The party that hired the contractor is directly liable for any negligence in selecting the contractor, giving directions, or failing to stop any unnecessary dangerous practices of which the party was aware.
- The responsibility—created by statute, contract, or common law—that certain duties be performed safely cannot be delegated to another party. For example, the duty of common carriers to carry passengers safely is nondelegable.
- If the subcontracted work is inherently dangerous to others (such as blasting and excavating near a public highway), the party that hired the contractor retains liability for a third-party injury caused by the contractor's negligence.

Suretyship and Guaranty Agreements

Obligee
The party to a surety bond that receives the surety's guarantee that the principal will fulfill an obligation or perform as promised.

Surety
The party (usually an insurer) to a surety bond that guarantees to the obligee that the principal will fulfill an obligation or perform as required by the underlying contract, permit, or law.

Principal
The party to a surety bond whose obligation or performance the surety guarantees.

Surety agreements involve three parties—the **surety**; the **obligee**; and the **principal**, or obligor. The surety's contractual guarantee is to perform or hire someone to perform in the principal's place when the principal's failure or inability to perform becomes clear and the obligee demands performance from the surety. A surety agreement protects the obligee by providing a second source of performance. See the exhibit "Surety Agreements."

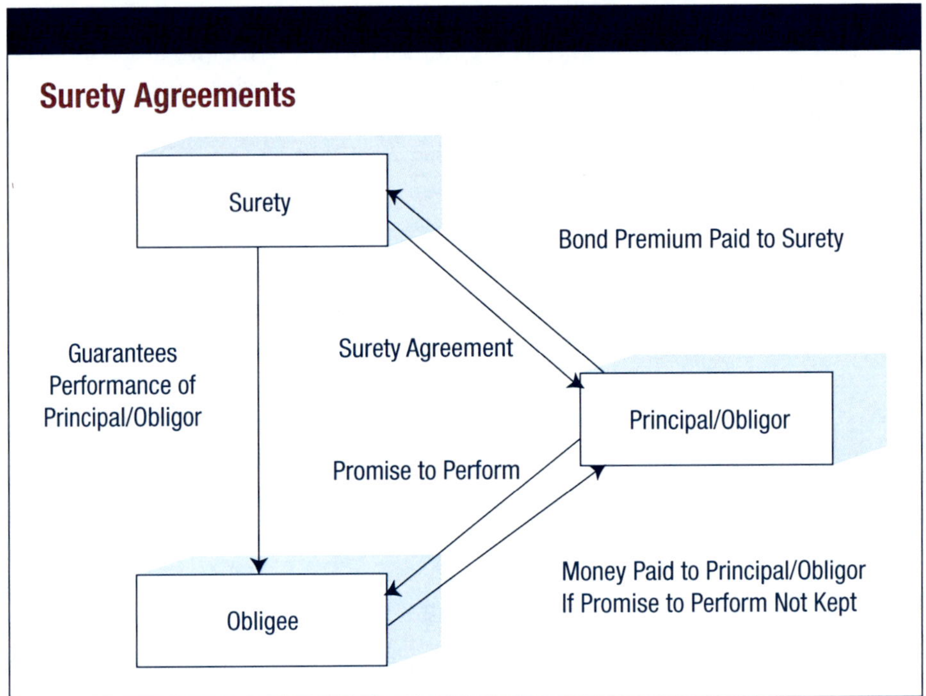

[DA01822]

Guarantor
A person or organization that has promised to perform a duty in the event the party whose duty it was initially (the principal) fails to perform it.

A guaranty agreement is similar to a surety agreement in that an obligee relies on another party—a **guarantor**—for performance. Unlike a surety, a guarantor is obligated to perform only after the obligee has made every reasonable and legal effort to compel the principal's performance.

Both suretyship and guaranty agreements allow the obligee to segregate loss exposures. If the principal does not perform, the obligee can rely on the surety or guarantor for performance. Suretyship law releases the surety from performance if the principal rightly refuses to perform for reasons such as fraud in securing the agreement or other contract defects. Whether a guarantor is released under similar circumstances depends on the wording of the guaranty agreement. See the exhibit "Fidelity Bond."

> **Fidelity Bond**
>
> Insurers that issue performance bonds promising performance of an obligation are acting as sureties, not as insurers. However, insurance written for employee dishonesty is often called a fidelity bond. A fidelity bond is a two-party contract between an employer and an insurer that pays the employer for loss resulting from theft by an employee. This arrangement is not a true bond because an insured's employees are not direct parties to the insurance contract.

[DA08641]

A surety has several rights that protect it against loss from the principal's misconduct or from collusion between the principal and the obligee:

- **Exoneration**—For example, assume that a principal has fallen behind its project schedule, and the obligee has failed to preserve its rights against the principal. In such a case, the surety is released from its liability to the extent that it can show that the obligee's inaction increased the loss of or otherwise harmed the surety.
- **Subrogation**—A subrogation clause in a surety agreement entitles the surety to the same payment the principal would have received. For example, if a surety completes the construction of a building after the default of the building-contractor principal, the building owner (the obligee) must pay the surety for the portion of the work completed on the same basis on which it would have paid the contractor.
- **Indemnity**—The surety can proceed directly against the principal to recover the fair value of its effort or any funds it has paid to the obligee as compensation for the principal's inaction. The principal must indemnify the surety for the costs of fulfilling the promise.

Exoneration
The removal of a duty.

Subrogation
In a surety agreement, the substitution of one party for another whose debt or performance the substituting party satisfies and that entitles the substituting party to the rights that belonged to the defaulting party.

Indemnity
In a surety agreement, the right of a surety to seek reimbursement from the principal for the resources the surety expended when it performed the principal's duty.

Because a surety's contractual commitment is the same as the principal's, any justification (or legal defense) for nonperformance that releases the principal from the underlying contract also releases the surety. The surety can also be legally released if the original contract is modified without the surety's consent.

Waiver

An individual or organization can relinquish its right to sue in contract or tort using a **waiver**. By allowing an organization to rid itself of the applicable liability loss exposures, waivers can function as effective risk control mechanisms.

An **exculpatory clause** is similar to a waiver. Both waivers and exculpatory clauses are intended to eliminate one party's liability loss exposure from another party. Many states use the terms "waive" and "exculpate" interchangeably.

Waiver
The intentional relinquishment of a known right.

Exculpatory clause (exculpatory agreement)
A contractual provision purporting to excuse a party from liability resulting from negligence or an otherwise wrongful act.

Real property leases often contain waivers or exculpatory clauses. For example, common law allows a real property lessee (tenant) to sue a lessor (landlord) for failing to maintain habitable premises. However, if a lessee waives the right to sue, the lessor no longer faces the liability loss exposure from the lessee. Here is a typical lease provision:

> Lessee, as a material part of the consideration to be rendered to the Lessor, hereby waives all claims against Lessor for damages to the goods, wares, and merchandise in, upon, or about said premises and for injuries to Lessee, his agents or invitees in or about said premises....

Unless improperly obtained or nullified by applicable state or local law, this lease provision lessens the landlord's concerns that the tenant will sue for damages to personal property or injuries to the tenant or others who are on the premises at the tenant's request. As worded, the provision is broad, apparently excusing the lessor from liability even for intentional harm to the lessee.

Although this lease provision limits the landlord's loss exposures to the lessee's lawsuits, it does not prevent others—such as the lessee's employees, guests, or other invitees—from suing the landlord. The provision also does not obligate the lessee to hold the lessor harmless from lawsuits—that is, to provide the lessor with a legal defense and to pay any verdicts or judgments levied against the lessor.

An effective waiver agreement is the result of fair bargaining, obtained without deceit or concealment, clear and unambiguous, and supported by legal consideration.

Waiver of subrogation
A special type of waiver that is a pre-loss voluntary relinquishment by an insurer of its right to seek reimbursement of its payment for damages that were caused by a party other than the insured.

Waivers are generally embodied in original contracts and are signed before the parties begin their contractual dealings or have suffered harm. However, a party may use a **waiver of subrogation** to waive its rights to sue after it has suffered harm. For example, a landlord's insurer may waive its right of subrogation against a tenant who negligently causes a fire that damages the landlord's insured property.

Limitation of Liability

When the transferor and transferee have equal bargaining power, the transferor may agree by contract to cap or limit the amount or type of its liability instead of waiving its liability entirely, as in this example of a contractual clause:

> In no event will (transferor) be liable to (transferee) or any third party for any incidental or consequential damages arising out of use or of inability to use (transferor's product which is being sold to transferee), or for any claim by any other party, even if (transferor) has been advised of the possibility of such damages. (Transferor's) total liability with respect to (transferor's product) shall not exceed the purchase price paid by the (transferee). (Transferee) acknowledges that these limitations permit (transferor) to provide this product at a lower cost than it otherwise could, and such limitations on liability are reasonable.

Disclaimer of Warranties

Sellers of property often assert disclaimers of warranties. A disclaimer in a sales contract may deny any express warranties made in conjunction with the property's sale. In addition, it may deny implied warranties, such as the implied warranty for a particular purpose—that the seller is aware of the particular purpose for which the buyer will use the property and that the property is suitable for that purpose—and the implied warranty of merchantability—that the property is suitable for the purpose for which most buyers use it.

This is an example of disclaimer language used in a software sales contract:

> (Seller's property) is provided "as is." To the maximum extent permitted by law, (seller) disclaims all warranties of any kind, either express or implied, including without limitation, implied warranties of fitness for a particular purpose and merchantability.

Noninsurance Risk Financing Transfer

In all forms of noninsurance risk financing transfers, the transferor's protection is only as reliable as the transferee's ability and willingness to pay money when needed to restore the loss. Despite this potential drawback, such transfers can provide dependable protection for a transferor under certain conditions, such as these:

- The transferor has a loss characteristic that places it beyond the scope of typical insurance contracts. For example, the cause of loss might not be covered in the only available or affordable insurance policy.
- The transferee is motivated, by the degree of its commitment to fulfilling the general business contract, to provide more complete indemnity because an insurer might question the indemnitee's right to payment.
- The transferee often has more direct and comprehensive knowledge of the risk it accepts than an insurer's underwriter would have, as is the case for maintenance agreements and guarantees for services.

Noninsurance risk financing contracts transfer the financial burden of losses. If the transferee fails to provide the compensation the contract requires, the financial burden of the loss remains with the transferor. Two prevalent noninsurance risk financing transfers are hold-harmless agreements and transfer of risk to the transferee's insurer.

Hold-Harmless Agreement

A hold-harmless agreement is a contract under which one party agrees to assume the liability of a second party. The parties to the indemnity clause of a hold-harmless agreement are the **indemnitor**—often referred to as the transferee—and the **indemnitee**—often referred to as the transferor. The indemnitor assumes liability for the legal claims that may be brought against the indemnitee because of the activities the contract covers.

Indemnitor
Party in a hold-harmless agreement who assumes the other party's liability.

Indemnitee
Party in a hold-harmless agreement whose legal liability is assumed by the indemnitor.

Hold-harmless agreements contain a broad array of indemnity clauses, which can provide a transferor with funds for restoring accidental losses to property, net income, liability claims, or the loss of the services of the transferor's key personnel. This is an example of a hold-harmless agreement:

> The (transferee) shall hold harmless and indemnify (the transferor) for any losses, claims, damages, awards, penalties, or injuries incurred by any third party, including reasonable attorney's fees, which arise from any alleged breach of such indemnifying party's representations and warranties made under this agreement, provided that the indemnifying party is promptly notified of any such claims. The indemnifying party shall have the sole right to defend such claims at its own expense. The other party shall provide, at the indemnifying party's expense, such assistance in investigating and defending such claims as the indemnifying party may request. This indemnity shall survive the termination of this agreement.

The effect of punitive damages and bankruptcy on hold-harmless and other indemnity agreements varies greatly among jurisdictions. In some jurisdictions, the transferee's payment of punitive damages is included automatically within a hold-harmless agreement. In others, punitive damages are included only if specified. In still others, contractual transfer of the obligation to pay punitive damages is illegal. Bankruptcy excuses a transferee/indemnitor in some jurisdictions, often depending on the nature of the harm the claimant suffered.

Because noninsurance risk financing transfers are largely unregulated, the provisions and practices of hold-harmless agreements are not standardized. Generally, such transfers are used when one party has the bargaining power to require another party to assume the risk and when such agreements are standard practice for a particular transaction or industry. Any such agreement must be in the form of a legally enforceable contract.

Transfer of Risk to the Transferee's Insurer

Insurance agreements can be modified to allow the transferee's insurer to treat a specified third party as an insured. This can be accomplished through two kinds of endorsements—additional insured and named insured—which obligate the transferee's insurer to pay (or pay on behalf of) the third party after it has suffered a loss.

Additional insured endorsement
An endorsement that adds coverage for one or more persons or organizations to the named insured's policy.

An **additional insured endorsement** offers a transferor several advantages:

- Rights under the policy that are independent of the enforceability of the general business contract between the transferor and the transferee
- Waiver by the transferee's insurer of its right to subrogate against the transferor
- Additional source of funds to pay for the transferor's losses
- The right to demand that the transferee's insurer pay the costs to defend the transferor for a covered liability loss
- Free coverage because the transferor often does not contribute funds toward payment of the transferee's insurance premium

Despite these clear advantages to the transferor, the transferee faces a disadvantage. A request to an insurer to add a transferor as an additional insured to a policy can change the transferee's acceptability to its insurer's underwriter. The underwriter usually has little information about the liability loss exposure presented by the additional insured. An underwriter who identifies correctable problems that present a liability loss exposure may be powerless to make the additional insured take corrective action. The underwriter may be forced to cancel or nonrenew the transferee's policy.

Another disadvantage is that the transferor must still control or finance through another mechanism any loss exposures that are excluded from the policy.

A **named insured endorsement**, by elevating the added insured to the status of a named insured, offers several advantages:

Named insured endorsement

An endorsement that, similar to an additional insured endorsement, adds coverage for one or more persons or organizations to the named insured's policy and elevates the new insured to the status of a named insured, giving it special rights and obligations.

- A transferor's agents, employees, officers, and directors are considered insureds and therefore are included in the transferee's coverage.
- The transferor, as the named insured, is likely entitled to receive notice if the transferee's policy is canceled or endorsed.

Several disadvantages also apply when a transferor is considered a named insured:

- The transferee's insurer may have a right to inspect the transferor's business and financial records.
- By entering the arrangement, the transferor may unknowingly agree to provide periodic reports to the insurer.
- The transferor may become involved in litigation unrelated to relevant insurance coverages.

Risk management professionals must weigh these advantages and disadvantages when considering these kinds of endorsements. Many risk management professionals prefer using the additional insured endorsement.

TYPES OF CAPTIVE INSURANCE PLANS

An organization's decision to use a captive insurance plan is the result of a process that considers the advantages and disadvantages of using such a plan relative to other risk financing alternatives.

Each type of captive insurance plan has unique features that address situations faced by an owner/insured(s). Captive insurance plan types include:

- Single-parent (or pure) captive
- Group captive
- Risk retention group
- Agency captive

- Rent-a-captive
- Protected cell company

Single-Parent (or Pure) Captive

Single-parent captive (pure captive)

A captive insurer owned by one company that insures all or part of the loss exposures of that company or its subsidiaries.

A **single-parent captive, or pure captive**, is a captive insurer owned by one company that insures all or part of the loss exposures of that company. Because a captive is an insurer, it requires an investment of capital by its parent(s), as well as expenditures to manage the company and to pay accounting, auditing, legal, and underwriting expenses.

For a captive insurer to be economically viable, it has to insure loss exposures that generate substantial premium revenues to cover these expenditures. Consequently, single-parent captive insurers generally require a minimum annual premium of $2 million.[1]

A single-parent captive is a hybrid risk financing plan because, from its parent's point of view, a single-parent captive usually combines elements of retention and transfer. Because a single-parent captive covers its parent's losses and is part of the same economic family as its parent, losses retained by the captive are, in effect, retained by its parent. For the same reasons, losses transferred by the captive insurer (for example, through reinsurance or some other means) are, in effect, transferred by its parent. Some single-parent captive insurers that do not purchase reinsurance retain all of their losses and therefore should not be considered a hybrid plan.

Group Captive

Group captive

A captive insurer owned by a group of companies, usually operating similar businesses, rather than a single parent.

Association captive

A group captive sponsored by an association.

A **group captive** is a captive insurer owned by a group of companies, usually operating similar businesses, rather than a single parent. A group captive is similar to a mutual insurer except that the insureds (owners) under a group captive exercise significantly more control over the management of the company than do the insureds under a typical commercial insurer.

An **association captive** is a group captive that is sponsored by an association. Many organizations consider the opportunity to obtain insurance through an association captive as one of the benefits of being a member of the association. For example, an association of paint manufacturers might sponsor a captive insurer for the benefit of its members.

A group captive (or an association captive) is considered a hybrid or a transfer plan, depending on its design. If each member (insured) of a group captive retains a portion of its own losses within the captive and shares the balance of its losses with other members, then the group captive is considered a hybrid plan. If each member shares all of its losses with the other members, then the group captive is considered a transfer plan.

Risk Retention Group

A **risk retention group** is a group captive formed under the requirements of the U.S. Liability Risk Retention Act of 1986 to provide liability coverage (except personal insurance, employers liability, and workers compensation). To form a risk retention group, all of its owners must be from the same industry and must be insured by the risk retention group. Conversely, all insureds must be owners.

Risk retention group

A group captive formed under the requirements of the Liability Risk Retention Act of 1986 to insure the parent organizations.

A major benefit of a risk retention group is that it needs to be licensed in only one state in order to provide liability coverage to group members anywhere in the United States. The act supersedes state law that requires an insurer to be licensed in every state in which it sells insurance, thereby saving the risk retention group the expense of complying with regulations in each of the fifty states.

Agency Captive

An **agency captive** is a type of group captive that is owned by insurance agents or brokers rather than by the organizations insured. Agency captives are often formed in response to hard markets to insure select accounts for which there is a limited or nonexistent market.

Agency captive

A type of group captive that is owned by insurance agents or brokers rather than by the organizations insured.

An agency may place a single line of insurance for heterogeneous businesses (such as workers compensation for all commercial insureds) in the captive or multiple lines for homogeneous businesses (such as businessowners policies for retail stores). An agency captive provides a way for agents or brokers to assume a portion of risk and, in turn, generate underwriting and investment income.

Rent-a-Captive

A **rent-a-captive** is an arrangement under which an organization rents capital from a captive insurer, to which it pays premium and receives reimbursement for its losses. The organization also receives credit for underwriting profits and investment income. Consequently, the organization benefits from using a captive insurer but is not required to invest its own capital. Each insured keeps its own premium and loss account, so no risk shifting or distribution occurs among the members of a rent-a-captive.

Rent-a-captive

An arrangement under which an organization rents capital from a captive, to which it pays premiums and receives reimbursement for its losses.

With some types of rent-a-captives, the insured organization must purchase nonvoting preferred stock and receives dividends on the stock equal to its underwriting profit and the investment income earned on its unearned premiums and loss reserves. If a plan does not involve the purchase of nonvoting preferred stock, then the rent-a-captive organization returns underwriting profit and investment income through some other means, such as policyholder dividends. The rent-a-captive organization charges a fee for its services. Rent-a-captives provide a means for an organization to form a captive insurer quickly without tying up capital.

Protected Cell Company

Protected cell company (PCC)

A corporate entity separated into cells so that each participating company owns an entire cell but only a portion of the overall company.

A **protected cell company (PCC)** is a group captive in which each participant pays premiums and receives reimbursement for its losses from, as well as credit for, underwriting profits and investment income, similar to a rent-a-captive. With a PCC, each participant is assured that other participants will not be able to access its capital and surplus in the event the other participants become insolvent. Each participant is also assured that third-party creditors cannot access its assets. This protection does not necessarily exist with a rent-a-captive structure, which involves the purchase of preferred stock by participants.

Review Questions

1. Describe the expenses that constitute an organization's cost of risk regardless of whether losses are retained or transferred.
2. Identify the factors that affect an organization's maximum cash flow variability level.
3. Describe internal and external methods an organization might use to increase cash liquidity.
4. Describe the following noninsurance risk transfer techniques and provide examples of each: a. hold-harmless agreement and b. hedging.
5. Describe the following general methods used to fund retained losses: a. pre-loss funding, b. current-loss funding, and c. post-loss funding.
6. Explain the basic distinction between transfer and retention as a means of risk financing.
7. Describe the respective abilities of using retention and transfer to meet an organization's risk financing goals.
8. Identify the loss exposure characteristics that help an organization determine which loss exposures to retain and which to transfer.
9. Explain how the following individual- or organization-specific characteristics affect retention levels: a. risk tolerance, b. financial condition, c. core operations, d. ability to diversify, e. ability to control losses, and f. ability to administer the retention plan.
10. Describe the two categories of contractual risk transfer.
11. Describe how segregation works to insulate a corporation from potential losses.
12. Describe how each of these types of transactions transfers risk exposures: a. leasing, b. suretyship agreements, c. waivers, and d. disclaimers of warranties.
13. Describe how each of these types of transactions transfers risk financing: a. hold-harmless agreement and b. insurance agreements.
14. Explain why a single parent captive is a hybrid refinancing plan.
15. Describe a major benefit of a risk retention group.
16. Describe a major benefit of a rent-a-captive.

Application Questions

1. A building owner contracts with a window cleaner for the cleaner to wash the exterior windows of the building each month. The contract contains a clause under which the window cleaner agrees to reimburse the building owner for any claims the building owner may have to pay because of damage or injury that the window cleaner's activities may cause to property or persons in the parking lot surrounding the building. Explain whether this agreement is an effective means of risk transfer.
2. Sports Gear Inc., manufactures sporting and exercise equipment. The equipment is assembled in health clubs and sports facilities by distributors. Sports Gear's risk management professional is looking for ways to reduce its products liability loss resulting from injuries caused by the machines. Recommend a contractual risk transfer option the risk management professional might consider.

SUMMARY

Risk financing goals include these:

- Pay for losses—both paying for the actual losses or portions of losses that an organization retains and paying transfer costs, which are the costs paid in order to transfer responsibility for losses to another party
- Manage the cost of risk—including administrative, risk control, and risk financing costs
- Manage cash flow variability—requires determining the organization's maximum tolerance levels and arranging the risk management program within those parameters
- Maintain an appropriate level of liquidity—preserving a level of cash liquidity that is sufficient to pay for retained losses
- Comply with legal requirements—adhering to laws and regulations that either mandate risk financing measures or affect how risk financing measures are implemented

Examining the feasibility of risk management techniques requires the risk management professional to systematically consider risk control and risk financing techniques used to treat loss exposures.

Risk financing techniques include:

- Insurance—A risk financing technique that transfers the potential financial consequences of certain specified loss exposures from the insured to the insurer.
- Noninsurance risk transfer—A risk financing technique that transfers all or part of the financial consequences of loss to another party, other than an insurer.
- Retention—A risk financing technique by which losses are retained by generating funds within the organization to pay for the losses.

When selecting appropriate risk financing methods, one must evaluate the relative advantages of the available measures and their ability to meet risk financing goals. The main factors to consider are these:

- The mix of retention and transfer needed to meet the goals
- Characteristics of the loss exposures
- Characteristics of the individual or organization

The two types of contractual (noninsurance) risk transfer are a noninsurance risk control transfer and a noninsurance risk financing transfer. A noninsured risk control transfer rids the transferor of most or all of the possibility of suffering a loss from the transferred exposure. A noninsured risk financing transfer creates the transferee's duty to pay money to (or on behalf of) transferors after the transferor has suffered a loss. Types of noninsurance risk control transfers include incorporation, leasing, contracting for services, suretyship and guaranty agreements, waiver, limitation of liability, and disclaimer of warranties. Types of risk financing transfers include hold-harmless agreements and transfer of risk to a transferee's insurer.

A variety of captive insurance plans exist, each of which is designed to address particular needs of its parent organization. Types of captive plans include single parent (or pure) captives, group captives, risk retention groups, agency captives, rent-a-captives, and protected cell companies.

ASSIGNMENT NOTE

1. International Risk Management Institute, Risk Financing: A Guide to Insurance Cash Flow (Dallas: International Risk Management Institute, Inc., 2000), 1st reprint, March 1997, p. IV.K.5.

Direct Your Learning

7

Decision Making Under Uncertainty—Risk Management Alternatives

Educational Objectives

After learning the content of this assignment, you should be able to:

- Describe the following steps that risk management professionals use to approach decision making in uncertain environments:
  - Construct a loss matrix: a structured approach to identifying outcomes
  - Describe precise risk management objectives
  - Explain how decision-making rules relate to each objective

Outline

Selecting the Proper Tools

Summary

Decision Making Under Uncertainty—Risk Management Alternatives

7

SELECTING THE PROPER TOOLS

Risk managers have greatly increased their awareness of, interest in, and use of more structured approaches than the insurance method to select the proper tools. Computers have also made the use of these techniques more feasible.[1]

The application of these approaches, however, is more limited than one might expect because (1) the data necessary to apply them (except in a modified form) are commonly missing or inadequate, and (2) many practicing risk managers have not been trained in their use. Even so, these approaches have immediate value, in that (1) even with inadequate data they can be useful in making some important risk management decisions, and (2) they make explicit the assumptions and decision rules that are implicit in less structured methods.

The approach that will be developed most completely in this assignment can be summarized as follows:

1. Construct a loss matrix or table that identifies the various after-tax expenses and accidental losses associated with (a) each possible decision and (b) each possible outcome.
2. Describe precisely the objective that the risk manager wishes to attain.
3. Design a decision-making rule that will attain this objective.

We will describe first several possible objectives and decision-making rules in the context of a highly simplified example.

The Loss Matrix: A Structured Approach to Identifying Outcomes

To illustrate the loss matrix concept, assume that a business is exposed to accidental property losses that are described by the following probability distribution:

Accidental losses	Probability
$ 0	.700
5,000	.160
50,000	.120
100,000	.018
500,000	.002

Further assume that the risk manager must decide among five courses of action:

1. Retain the possible accidental losses.
2. Retain the possible accidental losses, but introduce some loss-control measure that will change the probabilities in the first probability distribution as follows:

Accidental losses	Probability
$ 0	.800
5,000	.100
50,000	.090
100,000	.009
500,000	.001

3. Purchase an insurance policy that will cover accidental losses up to $50,000.
4. Purchase an insurance policy that will cover accidental losses up to $500,000.
5. Purchase an insurance policy that will cover accidental losses up to $500,000 but not the first $5,000.

Finally, assume that the firm's combined federal and state income tax rate is 40 percent[2] and that the accidental losses, the loss control cost, and the insurance premiums are all tax-deductible expenses.

In real life a risk manager must generally choose among many more courses of action and the firm will face many more than five possible accidental dollar losses. Recognizing more courses of action and possible losses, however, is not necessary to explain the methodology. To simplify the presentation we will also make some other assumptions that we will discuss further later:

1. We will ignore the additional losses the firm might incur if it retains the accidental losses, a large loss occurs, and the firm must borrow funds to make repairs. These additional costs might include interest costs on the loan plus higher interest charges on additional loans the firm might require later for other purposes.
2. We will ignore the opportunity cost to the firm of paying the premium before expenditures would have to be made under a retention program.
3. We will assume that the business places no value on the loss-control, loss-adjustment, and other services that the insurer would provide. Thus, if the firm decides to retain the losses it will not spend any money to replace those services.

The "After-Tax Tangible Loss Matrix" exhibit shows, for each of the five possible decisions in this example, the tangible after-tax losses (expenses plus accidental losses) the business will suffer under each of the five possible before-tax accidental losses. The matrix also shows for each possible accidental loss the probability that loss will occur (1) without loss control and (2) with loss control. See the exhibit "After-Tax Tangible Loss Matrix."

After-Tax Tangible Loss Matrix

		Possible before-tax accidental loss				
Amount		$ 0	$5,000	$50,000	$100,000	$500,000
Probability						
No loss control		.700	.160	.120	.018	.002
Loss control		.800	.100	.090	.009	.001
Decision:						
1 Retain	Accidental loss	$ 0	$ 3,000	$30,000	$ 60,000	$300,000
2 Retain, loss control ($2,500 cost)	Loss-control cost	$1,500	$ 1,500	$ 1,500	$ 1,500	$1,500
	Accidental loss	$0	$ 3,000	$30,000	$ 60,000	$300,000
	Total	$1,500	$ 4,500	$31,500	$ 61,500	$301,500
3 $50,000 insurance ($11,400 premium)	Premium	$6,840	$ 6,840	$ 6,840	$ 6,840	$6,840
	Accidental loss	$ 0	$ 0	$ 0	$ 30,000	$270,000
	Total	$6,840	$ 6,840	$ 6,840	$ 36,840	$276,840
4 $500,000 insurance ($14,000 premium)	Premium	$8,400	$ 8,400	$ 8,400	$ 8,400	$ 8,400
5 $500,000 insurance, $5,000 deductible ($11,800 premium)	Premium	$7,080	$ 7,080	$ 7,080	$ 7,080	$ 7,080
	Accidental loss	$ 0	$ 3,000	$ 3,000	$ 3,000	$ 3,000
	Total	$7,080	$10,000	$10,000	$ 10,080	$ 10,080

[DA08871]

If the business retains the potential accidental losses, the firm would incur no expenses and, if no accidents occur, would suffer no accidental loss. For each of the other four possible before-tax accidental losses the total loss would be the before-tax accidental loss less the 40 percent tax reduction, or 60 percent of the accidental loss. For example, if the before-tax accidental loss is $500,000, the after-tax tangible loss would be .60($500,000), or $300,000. If the business retains the possible accidental losses but also introduces the loss-control measure, the after-tax cost of the loss-control measure would be added to each of the after-tax accidental losses. In this example, the after-tax cost of the loss-control measure is .60($2,500), or $1,500. The probability distribution with loss control applies only to this decision.

If the business purchases a $50,000 insurance policy, it will make an after-tax premium expenditure of .60($11,400), or $6,840, plus, for each $100,000 and $500,000 possible accidental losses, 60 percent of the accidental loss less $50,000. For example, for the $500,000 loss outcome, the entry is the after-tax premium of $6,840 plus 60 percent of ($500,000 – $50,000), or $270,000. The total tangible loss, therefore, would be $276,840.

If the business purchases a $500,000 insurance policy, the tangible loss for all five of the possible accidental losses is the after-tax premium cost of .60($14,000), or $8,400.

Finally, if the business purchases a $500,000 insurance policy with a $5,000 deductible, in addition to paying an after-tax premium of .60($11,800), or $7,080, it will incur for each accidental loss except no accident, a .60($5,000), or $3,000, accidental loss.

Objectives and Decision Making Rules

It is impossible to consider each of the possible objectives that the risk manager might want to achieve in this case, but a few common objectives will suffice. The objectives will be divided into two major categories: (1) those objectives that assume the risk manager does not estimate the probability distribution of the accidental losses, and (2) those objectives that assume the risk manager does estimate this distribution.

Probabilities Not Estimated

Two objectives will be considered under the first category.

Case 1: Minimize the maximum potential loss during the period (minimax). The risk manager with this objective wants to be protected against the worst possible loss, regardless of the outcome. In those cases where for each decision the loss is at least as high for one possible accidental loss (in this case the $500,000 accidental loss) as for any of the other outcomes, a common situation in risk management problems, the decision rule is simple. Select the decision which for that outcome produces the smallest loss. In the "After-Tax Tangible Loss Matrix" exhibit, if there is a $500,000 loss, the smallest loss is associated with the decision to buy $500,000 insurance. Because this objective is unduly conservative in most instances and because insurance premiums are almost always a small fraction of the maximum insured loss, this decision rule would almost always lead to the purchase of insurance.

Case 2: Minimize the minimum potential loss during the policy period (minimin). This risk manager wants the lowest possible loss, no matter what outcome occurs. If, as is true in the present example, the losses for each decision are at least as low for one accidental loss (in this case no accident) as for any of the other outcomes, the decision rule is easy. Select the decision producing the minimum loss for that outcome. This optimistic risk manager will almost never select insurance.

Probabilities Estimated

The minimax and minimin objectives described above are of little value to risk managers. They will almost always lead the risk manager either to purchase insurance if the business is a "minimaxer," or not to purchase insurance if the firm is a "miniminer." They also ignore any information the risk manager may have concerning the probability distribution.

Case 3: Minimize the loss associated with the most probable outcome. Although not too useful, this objective deserves notice because some people may consider it reasonable. In most real-life situations involving one exposure unit such a person would favor retention because in such cases the probability of no losses is more than one-half. The consequences, however, could be drastic if the loss, though less likely, occurs. In our example, the risk manager would favor retention without any loss control. Even if some accidental loss is more likely than no accidental loss, the most probable outcome is usually much less than the maximum possible or the maximum probable loss.

Case 4: Minimize the expected tangible loss during the policy period. The risk manager who minimizes the expected tangible loss will, in the long run, have the smallest average tangible loss. "In the long run" can be interpreted in two ways. First, if the same situation is repeated many times, the average loss per year (or other budget period) will be minimized. Second, if the risk manager follows the same rule in making many decisions within a given year (or other budget period), the average loss per decision made will be minimized.

To attain this objective, the risk manager must first compute the expected tangible loss associated with each possible decision. The expected loss figure for a given decision is the sum of the products formed by multiplying each possible tangible loss associated with that decision by the probability that that loss will occur. The risk manager then selects the decision that yields the minimum expected tangible loss.

In the present case, we use the data in the "After-Tax Tangible Loss Matrix" exhibit to calculate the expected tangible loss for each decision as follows:

1. Retain the exposure.
   .700($0) + .160($3,000) + .120($30,000) + .018($60,000) + .002($300,000)
   = $0 + $480 + $3,600 + $1,080 + $600 = $5,760
2. Retain the exposure and introduce the loss-control measure.
   .800($1,500) + .100($4,500) + .090($31,500) + .009($61,500) + .001($301,500)
   = $1,200 + $450 + $2,835 + $553 + $302 = $5,340
3. Purchase a $50,000 insurance policy.
   .700($6,840) + .160($6,840) + .120($6,840) + .018($36,840) + .002($276,840)
   = $4,788 + $1,094 + $821 + $663 + $554 = $7,920
4. Purchase a $500,000 insurance policy.
   .700($8,400) + .160($8,400) + .120($840) + .018($8,400) + .002($8,400)
   = $8,400
5. Purchase a $500,000 insurance policy with a $5,000 deductible.
   .700($7,080) + .160($10,080) + .120($10,080) + .018($10,080) + .002($10,080)
   = $4,956 + $1,613 + $1,210 + $181 + $20 = $7,980

These calculations can be simplified if the losses that are common to all possible accidental losses (the cost of the loss-control measure and the insurance premiums) are treated separately. After calculating the expected value for all of the losses that depend upon which accidental loss occurs, the losses that are common to all possible accidental losses are added to this expected value. For example, for the $50,000 insurance policy, the insurance premium is $6,840. The expected value for the losses that depend upon which accidental loss occurs is .018($30,000) + .002($270,000), or $1,080. For this decision, therefore, the expected tangible dollar loss is $1,080 + $6,840, or $7,920.

Under this decision rule the risk manager should retain the exposure and introduce the loss-control measure. Because an insurance premium includes the insurer's estimate of the insured's expected (insured) loss plus an expense and profit loading, under the assumptions made in this example minimizing the expected tangible dollar losses would always favor retention over insurance. The retention-loss-control measure is favored over retention alone because the $1,500 after-tax cost of the loss-control measure is less than the $1,920 reduction in the expected after-tax accidental loss.

The expected tangible loss calculations are useful but the firm may also incur some important intangible losses in the form of worry and anxiety about the future outcome that, if recognized, would produce a much different optimum decision.

Case 5: Minimize the expected total loss during the period. This objective corrects the deficiency in the Case 4 objective. For each decision the expected total (tangible + intangible) loss is the expected tangible loss plus the dollar cost the risk manager assigns to the worry and anxiety he or she will experience because of uncertainty under that decision. In our example, the expected total losses are as follows:

1. Retain the exposure.
   $5,760 + worry, assuming retention
2. Retain the risk and introduce the loss-control measure.
   $5,340 + worry, assuming retention with loss control
3. Purchase $50,000 insurance.
   $7,920 + worry, assuming $50,000 insurance
4. Purchase $500,000 insurance.
   $8,400
5. Purchase $500,000 insurance with a $50,000 deductible.
   $7,980 + worry, assuming $500,000 insurance with a $5,000 deductible

Assigning a dollar value to the worry the manager will experience under each decision is difficult, but to ignore this cost would be misleading and could lead to some unwise decisions. The worry value is a highly subjective factor that depends upon the probability distribution (especially the severity of the possible losses and the risk), the risk manager's uncertainty about what will happen, the other risks faced by the firm,[3] and the firm's risk management objectives.

The risk management objectives should influence the worry factor because (1) they determine how much importance should be assigned to potential losses of various types and amounts, and (2) they reflect the risk attitudes of the business. To illustrate, a loss that would cause net earnings per share to drop 20 percent would be important if the firm's objective were to limit downside fluctuations to 10 percent, but would be of much less concern if the objective were mere survival. Similarly, if earnings stability were an objective, but the target were downside fluctuations of 30 percent or less, the 20 percent possibility would be less disturbing. A loss that would cause the firm to shut its doors for two months would bother a business that wants or needs to continue its operations more than it would a business desiring only stable earnings during the period of interruption. The strength of the desire for peace of mind, a "quiet night's sleep," or freedom from fear and worry reflects the business' attitudes toward risk. Other things being equal, some firms worry more than others about their ability to meet their post-loss objectives and the money value they would assign to this worry. A firm with a strong sense of social responsibility or a desire for a good public image may assign more importance to some potential losses than would be justified under the other post-loss objectives. It may also be more worried about the failure to achieve its objectives or the appearance of taking too many chances. Because its worry factor is higher, such a firm may lean toward more conservative decisions. The economy objective is implicit in the basic approach that seeks to minimize the average long-run cost. Once the cost of the tools selected is known, however, the firm may wish to reassess its other objectives, which might change the worry value. If the cost is too high, the post-loss objectives might become less ambitious or the desire for peace of mind or a good pre-loss image might be reduced. A post-loss growth objective may cause some potential losses to be rated more important than they otherwise would be, but a pre-loss growth objective may strengthen the desire for pre-loss economy. This would free more funds to finance pre-loss growth. Finally, externally imposed constraints can be viewed in most cases as dictating an extremely high worry value for all combinations of tools that do not satisfy the external constraint. For instance, to comply with a state statute, a small firm probably has to buy workers' compensation insurance; a firm that wants to get a mortgage on a building must purchase property insurance. In some cases, a firm might elect not to worry about meeting a particular external constraint, choosing instead to risk the consequences. For example, the penalty for noncompliance with a minor safety standard considered to have only nuisance value may be less than the extra cost of satisfying the constraint; however, such situations are unusual. Furthermore, ethical, social, and broader economic considerations may outweigh the more narrowly focused financial calculation.

For this example, assume for the present that the worry value for the retention decision is $4,000. The maximum possible after-tax tangible loss is $300,000, which causes the business some concern. For the decision to introduce a loss-control measure the worry cost is assumed to be somewhat less, say $3,500. The reason is that, although the maximum possible tangible loss is slightly

higher, the safety program is expected to reduce the chance that the business will incur each of the four possible accidental losses, thus reducing slightly the risk manager's anxiety.

For the decision to purchase a $50,000 insurance policy, the worry value, let us say, is $2,000. This worry value is less than the worry values for the two retention decisions because the worst possible after-tax accidental loss is reduced to $270,000 and the firm is insured completely against the $5,000 and $50,000 before-tax accidental loss possibilities.

For the $500,000 insurance decision, the worry value is zero. If a person purchases complete insurance (and has complete confidence in the insurer's ability to pay when an accidental loss occurs), the total loss is the insurance premium, regardless of the actual accidental loss. The business faces no uncertainty; the risk and the worry value are zero.

Finally, if the business decides to purchase a $500,000 policy with a $500 deductible, a $300 worry value is assumed. The worry value is not zero because some uncertainty remains; the value is small because the worst possible after-tax accidental loss is $3,000.

For these assumed worry values, in our example the expected total losses are as follows:

1. Retain the exposure.
   $5,760 + $4,000 = $9,760
2. Retain the exposure and introduce the loss-control measure.
   $5,340 + $3,500 = $8,840
3. Purchase $50,000 insurance.
   $7,920 + $2,000 = $9,920
4. Purchase $500,000 insurance.
   $8,400 + $0 = $8,400
5. Purchase $500,000 insurance with a $5,000 deductible.
   $7,980 + $300 = $8,280

In this situation the risk manager should purchase a $500,000 insurance policy with a $5,000 deductible because this decision should in the long run produce the lowest expected total losses. The risk manager will be proved right, however, only if his or her estimates of the probability distribution and the worry value are correct.

If the risk manager lacks confidence in these estimates, he or she should determine how sensitive the decision is to changes in these estimates. For example, suppose that the risk manager has some question about the probability of no losses and the probability of a $5,000 loss. He or she, however, is fairly confident that the probability of no losses lies between .680 and .720 with the corresponding probability of a $5,000 loss outcome lying between .180 and .140. The expected losses should be recalculated assuming these two sets of probability values.

If the decision to purchase insurance with a deductible is still preferred, as it is in this case (assuming no major changes in the worry factors), the risk manager should be more confident that this course of action is proper. If the preferred decision changes, the risk manager should recognize this sensitivity and reexamine the probability estimates. It is hoped that he or she can narrow these estimates to a range within which the preferred decision does not change. Otherwise, the method can only show the consequences of the various decisions over that range, which should better equip the risk manager to make the decision on some other basis.

The worry value can be reexamined in the same way. For example, assume that the risk manager prefers to specify a range of worry values for each decision instead of a single value. More specifically, assume that for the retention decision the risk manager specifies a range of $3,000 to $5,000. There is no need to test the effect of a $5,000 worry value because increasing the worry value above $4,000 will clearly make either insurance decision even more attractive. On the other hand, reducing the worry value below $4,000 would reduce the relative attractiveness of the insurance decisions. To test whether a $3,000 worry value would change the decision, the risk manager should recalculate the expected loss for retention assuming a $3,000 worry value. The answer is $8,760. Because $8,760 exceeds $8,280, the expected loss for the deductible insurance decision, deductible insurance is still the preferred alternative. Indeed, the worry value would have to be less than $2,520 before retention would become preferable to insurance. The reason is that until the worry value drops below $2,520, the expected loss is less for deductible insurance than for retention.

Specifying the worry value is extremely difficult. Fortunately, to select the proper tool one need not specify a single worry value. Instead, the risk manager has to state only whether the worry value exceeds a specified amount that depends upon the expected after-tax tangible loss calculations. This approach is best explained by continuing our example.

Given the expected tangible losses presented above for the five possible decisions, the decision rule to minimize the expected total loss can be rephrased as follows:

1. Purchase $500,000 insurance, the alternative for which the worry value is zero, if:
   a. The worry value assuming retention is greater than $8,400 (which is the premium for complete insurance) – $5,760 (the expected tangible loss under retention), or $2,640.
   b. The worry value assuming retention with loss control is greater than $8,400 – $5,340 (the expected tangible loss under retention with loss control), or $3,060.
   c. The worry value assuming $50,000 insurance is greater than $8,400 – $7,920 (the expected tangible loss under $50,000 insurance), or $480.
   d. The worry value assuming $500,000 insurance with a $55,000 deductible is $8,400 – $7,980 (the expected tangible loss under $500,000 insurance with a $5,000 deductible), or $420.
2. If all four worry values exceed the corresponding stated values, purchase $500,000 insurance.
3. If all but one of the four worry values exceed the corresponding stated value, make the decision whose worry value is smaller than the corresponding stated amount.
4. If two or more of the worry values do not exceed the corresponding stated amounts, drop the $500,000 insurance decision and any other decision whose worry value exceeds the corresponding stated amount. Compare the remaining options using a rule similar to step 1 except that, since each of the remaining options does pose some uncertainty, the test must be phrased in terms of the difference between the worry values for the two methods being compared. For example, assume that the two remaining decisions are retention with loss control and $500,000 insurance with a $50,000 deductible. The decision value would be as follows: Purchase the $500,000 insurance policy with a $50,000 deductible if the difference between the worry value for retention with loss control and the worry value for the deductible insurance is greater than $7,980 – $5,340, or $1,640. As was true in step 1, the general rule states that the alternative believed to pose the least uncertainty (the deductible insurance in this case) is to be selected if the difference between the worry values exceeds the difference between the expected tangible losses.
5. If step 4 does not eliminate all but one decision, the process must be continued.

Phrasing the decision rule in this way requires the risk manager to state for each paired comparison only whether the worry value (or the difference between two worry values if step 4 is required) would exceed a specified amount (the difference between the two expected tangible losses). The single values assumed in our example lead to the purchase of a $500,000 insurance policy with a $5,000 deductible because:

1a $4,000 > $2,640

1b $3,500 > $3,060

1c $2,000 > $480, and

1d $300 < $420

The worry values associated with retention, retention without loss control, and $50,000 insurance would have to be much less than the values we assumed before those decisions would be preferred to complete insurance, thus forcing additional comparisons.[4]

The Worry Method

Of the five decision rules presented, the fifth is clearly the most rational. Because of the important role the worry value plays in this method of making risk management decisions, we will call it the worry method.

The Worry Method and Why a Person Might Purchase Insurance

The worry method provides a useful vehicle for explaining why, assuming insurance is not compulsory, a person might purchase insurance instead of retaining the risk.

As stated earlier, in establishing the premium it will charge a prospective insured, an insurer first calculates the losses it expects to experience on the average on insureds with the same amount and quality of exposure. To this expected-loss estimate the insurer adds a loading for its expenses, profit, and contingencies. Consequently, before a person will purchase insurance, he or she must be willing to pay an insurer more than the insurer believes that person's insurable losses will average per year in the long run. Why might people be willing to do this?

1. Because they worry about fluctuations in accidental losses. For example, if the worst outcome happens the first year, the firm may have no opportunity to average losses in the long run. The reader should review the earlier discussion on the many factors that determine the worry value.[5]
2. Because they may experience some additional losses, if a loss occurs, as a result of retaining the insurable accidental losses that they would not incur if they were insured.
3. Because tax factors may favor the purchase of insurance.
4. Because they estimate their expected losses to be higher than does the insurer.
5. Because they value the services provided by the insurer, such as safety inspections and loss adjustments.

To illustrate, consider the example we have just discussed in which the risk manager selected $500,000 insurance with a $5,000 deductible. Of the five reasons noted above why the risk manager might have favored an insurance decision over retention, only the first was recognized. Both the $4,000 worry value for retention and the $3,600 worry value for retention with loss control were larger than the after-tax expense and profit loading ($8,400 - $5,760, or $2,640) included in the premium for $500,000 insurance. On the other hand, the $300 worry value for the deductible insurance was less than the $420 difference between the expense and profit loading included in the premium

for $500,000 insurance ($2,640, as calculated above) and the expense and profit loading included in the premium for the deductible insurance ($7,080 - $4,860, or $2,220).

The other four reasons noted above could have been recognized in our example, thus strengthening the case for some insurance. Instead, however, in our assumptions we stated that (1) we would ignore the additional losses (for example, interest charges on loans or less favorable credit terms in the future) the firm might incur if it decided to retain its potential accident losses and one occurred; (2) the same tax rate would be applied to retained losses as to insurance premiums; (3) the risk manager and the insurer agreed on the probability distribution of expected losses; and (4) the business placed no value on the loss-control, loss-adjustment, and other services that the insurer would provide.

On the other hand, we also ignored the opportunity cost to the firm of paying premiums before the money would be needed under a retention program to pay losses and expenses. Consequently, the tangible retention losses may be overstated. This deficiency can be corrected by substituting for the dollar losses in the tangible loss matrix the present value of those dollars. For example, if, in the "After-Tax Tangible Loss Matrix" exhibit under retention the $300,000 loss would actually be $100,000 at the end of each of the next three years, the present value, assuming a 5 percent interest rate, would be only $272,320. The after-tax loss would be $163,392. In many cases insurers have altered their pricing methods to permit interest-free installment payments of the premium or used other approaches that reduce the insured's opportunity cost.

Also, the firm may believe that its expected tangible losses under the retention decisions will be less than does the insurer and the worry values may be much less than we assumed.

The reader should compare this analysis with the factors affecting a retention decision.

The Worry Method and No Probability Information

The worry method was presented as a method to be used when the risk manager knows or can estimate the probability distribution. In an important class of decisions the worry method can be used when no such information is available, but the risk manager is willing to accept the information that can be derived from the premium he or she is quoted for insurance. For example, assume that a risk manager who must decide only between retention and complete insurance knows only that the worst possible loss is $500,000 and that the insurer typically uses about 70 percent of its premiums to pay losses. Assume that the insurance premium in this case would be $14,000. From this information the risk manager could find that the insurer believed his or her expected insurable losses to be about .70($14,000), or $9,800. The expense and profit loading, therefore, would be about $4,200. The question then

becomes: Is the risk manager willing to pay at least $2,520 more after taxes (assuming a 40 percent rate) than the after-tax expected losses of $5,880 to eliminate his or her worry? The answer will depend upon the risk manager's assessment of the impact of a $500,000 potential loss before taxes upon the firm and the risk attitudes of its management. If the answer is yes, insurance should be purchased. If the answer is no, the risk manager should ask whether his or her worry value is close enough to $2,520 that considering the additional costs that might be associated with retaining accidental losses and the loss of insurer services associated with retention would favor insurance. Considering the opportunity costs of purchasing insurance would increase the worry value required to favor an insurance decision.[6]

One final example will illustrate the use of the worry method in an insurance decision and the importance of the worry factor. Assume that a business has $10,000 to spend after tax on automobile insurance. With this $10,000, it can purchase either (1) complete physical damage insurance on its fleet of trucks, or (2) automobile liability insurance. The insurer involved uses 70 percent of its premiums to pay losses. According to this insurer, therefore, the firm's expected after-tax tangible loss for either type of insurance are .70($10,000) = $7,000. There are, let us assume, only three possible decisions: (1) Retain. (2) Purchase physical damage insurance. (3) Purchase liability insurance. Because the expected tangible losses are the same for physical damage insurance and liability insurance, the choice between them depends upon how the worry values for these two decisions compare. Because the potential liability losses are so much larger than the potential physical damage, most risk managers would probably be much more worried about the liability losses and would purchase liability insurance before physical damage insurance. Whether they would purchase liability insurance instead of retaining the liability risk would depend upon whether their worry value would exceed the after-tax loading of $3,000. For most businesses it probably would, even after considering the opportunity costs of insurance but ignoring the loss-control and loss-adjustment services of insurers.

Risk Management Tools and the Worry Value

In the case used in this assignment, worry values were established for one risk control tool, namely loss control, and two risk financing tools, retention and insurance. How would worry values be affected if some other major tools had been included in the analysis?

Because combination and separation reduce the risk inherent in the situation, they should reduce the worry. The less important the annual fluctuations in the loss experience become, the less the risk manager should worry. This helps to explain why a risk manager deciding whether to retain the risk or insure against losses on, say, 1,000 cars is more likely to retain the risk than a risk manager with one car.

Noninsurance transfers, like insurance, should reduce the worry value to zero unless the protection is incomplete or some concern exists over the ability of the transferee to pay if the occasion arises.

Whose Worry Value?

Up to this point in the discussion, it has been assumed that in applying the worry method the risk manager establishes a worry value consistent with top management's worry value. In order to make this assessment, the risk manager must be thoroughly acquainted with the firm's operations and the philosophy of its top managers. Top management typically gives the risk manager considerable leeway in establishing the worry value, but the risk manager must remember that he or she is managing the firm's affairs, not his or her own. A risk manager who disagrees with the attitudes of top management toward pure risks should attempt to persuade them to his or her point of view. Top management, in turn, should recognize that the risk manager needs to be aware of their risk preferences. They should also recognize that, in practice, the personal preferences of risk managers are bound to affect the decisions made. Consequently, top management should hire risk managers whose attitudes are consistent with their own.

In establishing worry values, risk managers may be tempted to consider the impact on their own jobs of various outcomes. For example, they may reason that if a fire occurs after they have recommended retention, they may lose their jobs. Consequently, they may recommend insurance in this situation even though they believe the firm would be well advised to retain the risk. Top management can encourage better decision making by judging risk managers on how they make decisions, not on short-run results.

The Worry Method and the Insurance Method

The worry method is consistent with the insurance method in the sense that one would expect the worry value to be the highest for losses covered by insurance in the essential category and lowest for losses covered by insurance in the available category.

The Capital Asset Pricing Model and the Worry Factor

According to the capital asset pricing model (CAPM), in a perfect capital market stockholders with widely diversified portfolios face little or no uncertainty with respect to the pure loss exposures of the businesses whose stock they own.[7] The total risk associated with each firm's stock can be divided into systematic risk and unsystematic risk. Systematic risk is caused by factors that affect all securities simultaneously, but in varying degrees. The systematic risk of a security is measured by ß. If ß equals, say, 2, on the average the rate of return on that security will rise or fall twice as much as the entire market's rate of return. If ß equals, say, 0.5, on the average the rate of return on that security will rise or fall only half as much as the market rate of return.

Unsystematic risk is caused by factors such as marketing mistakes, explosions, or theft, which tend to be peculiar to a firm or industry.[8] A stockholder can reduce the unsystematic risk associated with his or her portfolio by including in the portfolio a large number of stocks, i.e., by relying on the law of large numbers. According to this model, therefore, the worry value of stockholders would be too small to explain why the corporations they own buy or should buy insurance.

Many persons have questioned the validity of CAPM,[9] but it continues to command considerable support among finance theorists. Although CAPM theorists downgrade the worry factor of stockholders with diversified portfolios, they have suggested other reasons why businesses might buy insurance.

Review Questions

1. Identify the disadvantages of using the loss matrix approach to risk management decision making.
2. Identify the advantage of applying the risk management tools discussed in the assignment to risk management decision making.
3. Identify the risk management technique a risk manager usually selects when his or her goal is to minimize the maximum potential loss during a period.
4. Identify the factors on which a worry factor depends.
5. Identify the assumption that underlies the capital asset pricing model.

SUMMARY

Risk management professionals can use these steps to approach decision making in uncertain environments:

- Construct a loss matrix: a structured approach to identifying outcomes
- Describe precise risk management objectives
- Design decision-making rules related to each objective

The worry method may also be used when the risk management professional knows or can estimate the probability distribution.

ASSIGNMENT NOTES

1. This assignment is based on Chapter 13 of "Risk Management and Insurance," sixth edition, by C. Arthur Williams Jr. and Richard M. Heins (New York: McGraw-Hill Book Company, 1989), pp. 269-283. Used with permission.
2. A 40 percent rate was used here to simplify the arithmetic.
3. The importance of considering all the risks faced by the firm is discussed later in this assignment in the section on "The Capital Asset Pricing Model and the Worry Factor."

4. One way to determine the worry value for each decision, given the expected tangible loss for that decision, is as follows: The worry value is the maximum amount the risk manager would be willing to pay in addition to the expected tangible loss to eliminate the annual fluctuations in his or her experience. Such a value can be estimated by starting with $1 and increasing this amount until the risk manager believes the appropriate value has been reached. To illustrate, for the retention decision without loss control, the expected tangible loss is $5,760. If the business experienced a $5,760 loss each year, the expected loss would also be $5,760, but there would be no fluctuations, no uncertainty, and no worry. In this instance, however, the tangible loss next year could range between $0 and $500,000 ($300,000 after taxes). The risk manager has indicated, through the $4,000 worry value, that to achieve certainty, he or she would be willing to pay as much as $4,000 in addition to the $5,760 expected tangible loss instead of facing a possible after-tax tangible loss as high as $300,000. In other words, the risk manager finds no difference between accepting the certainty of losing $9,760 each year and facing each year the possibility of losing amounts ranging between $0 and $300,000.
5. See also the discussion later in this assignment under "The Capital Asset Pricing Model and the Worry Factor."
6. Note that this example resembles the one discussed in detail except that only two of the five possible decisions are considered. The worry value necessary to favor complete insurance over retention is slightly lower here because the insurer in the earlier example used slightly less than 60 percent of its premium to pay losses.
7. For more details, see David Mayers and Clifford W. Smith, Jr., "On the Corporate Demand for Insurance," The Journal of Business, LV, no. 2 (April 1982), pp. 281-296. The following discussion relies heavily on this article. See also Richard L. Meyer and Fred B. Power, "The Investment Values of Corporate Insurance," The Journal of Risk and Insurance, L, no. 1 (March 1983), pp. 151-156, and Neil Doherty, Corporate Risk Management: A Financial Exposition (New York: McGraw-Hill Book Company, 1985).
8. Some pure risks may also involve some systemic risk. For example, fire and theft losses vary to some extent with the state of the economy. See Meyer and Power, op cit., pp. 154-155. See also Doherty, op. cit.
9. See, for example, Bruce D. Fielitz, "Modern Portfolio Theory: Where Do We Stand?" The Wall Street Transcript, Oct. 30, 1978, pp. 52, 299.

Direct Your Learning

8

Definition and Characteristics of Insurance

Educational Objectives

After learning the content of this assignment, you should be able to:

- Explain how insurance reduces risk through pooling.
- Describe the principle of indemnity.
- Explain how insurance benefits individuals, organizations, and society.

Outline

How Insurance Reduces Risk

Contract of Indemnity

Benefits of Insurance

Summary

Definition and Characteristics of Insurance

8

HOW INSURANCE REDUCES RISK

Pooling is a fundamental risk management concept that is essential to the operation of insurance. Understanding how insurance reduces risk through pooling helps risk management and insurance professionals evaluate the effectiveness of insurance relative to other risk management techniques.

In the context of risk financing, a pool is a financial arrangement that combines the loss exposures and financial resources of individuals or organizations within the group to share the losses experienced by members of the group. Although insurance is primarily a risk transfer technique, insurers use, and benefit from, pooling when they insure large numbers of loss exposures.

Pooling

Pooling is an arrangement that facilitates the grouping of loss exposures and the resources to pay for any losses that may occur. Pooling arrangements function best (reduce the most risk to the group) when the loss exposures being pooled are independent of (uncorrelated with) one another. Losses are independent when a loss at one loss exposure has no effect on the probability of a loss at another loss exposure.

For example, two warehouse properties, one in Hawaii and the other in Pennsylvania, would be independent loss exposures in terms of the possibility of loss by fire. A fire at one warehouse would not affect the frequency or severity of a fire at the other. However, two warehouses in Miami would not be independent loss exposures with respect to the windstorm cause of loss, because one hurricane could cause damage to both locations.

Loss exposures do not necessarily have to be independent to benefit from pooling. Correlated loss exposures (exposures that are not independent) can still benefit from pooling arrangements, provided that the loss exposures are not perfectly positively correlated (that is, if a loss happens to one exposure, it definitely happens to the other). However, although pooling correlated loss exposures can reduce risk to the pool members, the risk is not as effectively reduced as when the exposures are independent.

How Pooling Reduces Risk

To understand how pooling reduces risk (uncertainty), consider this example. Rachel owns a $100,000 home that is exposed to the possibility of loss in the coming year. Assume that a loss distribution for houses in Rachel's area is used to determine that, without any pooling arrangements, the expected loss for Rachel's house is $744, and the standard deviation of the loss is $9,121.

Suppose that Rachel agrees to enter a pooling arrangement with Keith, who owns the same type of house and faces the same loss distribution as Rachel. Also assume that the two houses are independent of one another and that Rachel and Keith agree to evenly split any losses that the two might incur. That is, they are pooling both their loss exposures and their resources to pay for any losses to those exposures.

The "Loss Distribution for Pools" exhibit shows that when there are two pool members (in this case, Rachel and Keith), the expected losses of the pool are twice the expected losses of one member (2 × $744 = $1,488). However, although the standard deviation of the pool has increased ($12,899 compared with $9,121), it has not doubled. The standard deviation of the pool is calculated using a formula that is beyond the scope of the educational objective.

The standard deviation of the pool will increase as the number of members increases. However, the standard deviation increases at a decreasing rate, which means that the standard deviation of losses on a per member basis actually decreases. See the exhibit "Loss Distribution for Pools."

Loss Distribution for Pools

Number of Members in Pool (*n*)	Expected Loss		Standard Deviation	
	Pool	Per Member	Pool	Per Member
1	$ 744	$744	$ 9,121	$ 9,121
2	$ 1,488	$744	$ 12,899	$ 6,450
10	$ 7,440	$744	$ 28,843	$ 2,884
100	$ 74,400	$744	$ 91,210	$ 912
1,000	$ 744,000	$744	$ 288,431	$ 288

[DA02743]

As shown in the exhibit, as the number of members in the pool increases, the expected losses and standard deviation of the pool both increase. However, on a per member basis, the expected value remains unchanged and the standard deviation decreases. This occurs because the extreme outcomes become less likely at the pool level.

For example, because Rachel's losses are independent of Keith's losses, the probability that neither individual will have a loss is simply the probability that Rachel does not have a loss multiplied by the probability that Keith does

not have a loss. Assuming that the probability of each person's having no loss is .855, then the probability of neither one's having a loss is .855 × .855 = .731, or 73.1 percent.

Similarly, if the probability of each person's having a $100,000 loss is .005, then the probability of both of them having a total loss is .005 × .005 = .000025, or 0.0025 percent. Before the pooling arrangement, the chance of Rachel's not having any loss (and not having to pay anything) was 85.5 percent. With the pooling arrangement, the chance of Rachel's not having to pay anything has been reduced to 73.1 percent because Rachel has agreed to pay a part of Keith's losses as well as part of her own.

As far as losses are concerned, without the pooling arrangement Rachel had a 0.5 percent chance of having to pay $100,000 in losses. With the pooling arrangement, Rachel will have to pay $100,000 in losses only if both she and Keith suffer total losses, which will happen only 0.0025 percent of the time.

As this example demonstrates, the pooling arrangement does not change the frequency or severity of the individual loss exposures. It does change the probability distribution of losses facing each person simply because the sources of the loss exposures and resources to pay for losses have been combined. The expected value remains the same, but the uncertainty around that expected value (as measured by standard deviation) has decreased. Therefore, both Rachel's and Keith's risks are reduced by pooling.

The exhibit also shows that as the number of members of the pool increases, the standard deviation per member continues to decrease. This is a social benefit of pooling; it helps to reduce risk in society. As more members are added to the pool, it becomes more likely that the pool members will have to pay closer to the expected loss rather than an amount at the extremes of the original loss distribution.

In summary, the pooling arrangement does not change either person's expected cost, but it makes the actual cost more consistent and less variable, thereby reducing risk in society. Although pooling arrangements do not prevent losses or transfer risk, they reduce each individual's risk or uncertainty through sharing of losses and resources. See the exhibit "Pooling Arrangements With Correlated Losses."

How Insurance Uses Pooling

Insurers benefit from pooling, and, in fact, most insurers act as large, well-financed pools. However, although an insurer resembles a formal pooling mechanism, there are two key differences between pooling and insurance.

First, pooling is a risk-sharing mechanism, whereas insurance is primarily a risk transfer mechanism. With insurance, the insurance contract transfers the risk from the insured to the insurer in exchange for premiums. If premiums are not adequate to cover insureds' losses in a given year, the insurer cannot collect more from the insureds, as would happen in a pooling arrangement.

Pooling Arrangements With Correlated Losses

Pooling arrangements work best with loss exposures that are independent. However, most loss exposures are not independent. The occurrence of a loss is often the result of events that are common to many people or organizations. Catastrophes, such as hurricanes, tornadoes, wildfires, and earthquakes, cause property losses to many individuals at the same time. Consequently, property losses in certain geographic regions during a given period are positively correlated. Pooling arrangements still work when loss exposures are correlated, provided they are not perfectly positively correlated. With independent loss exposures, there is a high probability that one person's large losses will be offset by other participants' small losses. Therefore, the average loss becomes more predictable. When losses are positively correlated, similar losses are incurred by more participants; therefore, one person's large losses are less likely to be offset by other participants' small losses.

From the "Loss Distribution for Pools" exhibit, if Rachel and Keith's houses were close together, their loss exposures would be positively correlated. Their proximity would determine how highly correlated. Therefore, although the expected loss would remain unchanged ($1,488 for the two of them), the standard deviation for the two of them would be higher. For example, the standard deviation for the two of them may be $15,000 rather than $12,899 if they were on the same street, or $17,000 if they were next-door neighbors. Therefore, although pooling would still reduce the risk to both Rachel and Keith if they were next-door neighbors, and the standard deviation would drop from $9,121 per member to $8,500 ($17,000 ÷ 2), it would not reduce as much risk as it would have had their loss exposures been uncorrelated.

[DA02744]

Even with insurance products that are loss sensitive, such as retrospective rating plans, the risk sharing occurs between the insurer and the insured, not the insured and other insureds. In a retrospective rating plan, if the insured's losses were higher than expected, the insurer can adjust the premium amount. However, the insurer would not adjust all insureds' premiums because one insured's losses were higher. The insurer simply has to pay the additional losses from its policyholders' surplus.

With a pool, losses are shared among all pool members, not transferred to the pool. If the losses of the pool were greater than expected, each member of the pool would have to commit additional resources to pay for losses. Because there is no cost certainty, pools are risk-sharing mechanisms rather than risk transfer mechanisms.

Second, the insurer has additional financial resources that enable it to provide a stronger guarantee that sufficient funds will be available in the event of a loss, further reducing risk. Such additional financial resources are primarily derived from these sources:

- Initial capital from investors—The initial capital is the money that investors provide to establish an insurer. The minimum amount of initial capitalization is established by law in the state where the insurer is chartered. This startup fund might be provided by stockholders, who expect

a return on their investment, or by insureds, who want to establish an insurer that will provide a market for their particular insurance needs.

- Retained earnings—Retained earnings are derived from premiums in excess of amounts used to pay claims and expenses, and from earnings on invested money. Each premium should be sufficient to cover that insured's fair share of claims and expenses—and to provide a profit for the insurer. The premium might also include an amount to cover contingencies (known as a risk loading) to pay claims when aggregate loss experience is worse than expected without impairing the insurer's solvency.

Because the premiums charged are greater than the expected average loss costs and expenses, and because the insurer begins with an initial capitalization, the insurer can be comfortable agreeing to accept the transfer of risks from its insureds—provided the risks it accepts are within its capacity.

The "Pooling and Capital Requirements" exhibit demonstrates the limitations on the financial resources of an insurer. The loss distribution is the same as that shown in the "Loss Distribution for Pools" exhibit. In the "Pooling and Capital Requirements" exhibit, assume the insurer has been funded by investors with $1 million in initial capital. If the insurer sells one policy to Rachel, the insurer assumes the risk that loss amounts will be greater than the premium it charged. See the exhibit "Pooling and Capital Requirements."

Pooling and Capital Requirements

Insurer's initial capital = $1,000,000.

Number in Pool	Expected Loss		Standard Deviation		Resources Needed to Pay Losses Two Standard Deviations From the Expected	Additional Resources per Policy
	Pool	Per Member	Pool	Per Member		
1	$ 744	$744	$ 9,121	$9,121	$ 18,986	$ 0
10	$ 7,440	$744	$ 28,843	$2,884	$ 65,126	$ 0
1,000	$744,000	$744	$288,431	$ 288	$1,320,862	$321

[DA02746]

Suppose that the insurer wants to ensure that it can pay losses that are two standard deviations above the expected loss. In this case, that means the insurer must have at least $18,986 to pay for losses to Rachel's policy (calculated as $744 + [2 × $9,121]). With $1 million in initial capital and only one policy sold, the insurer has more than enough capacity to pay any loss that Rachel may suffer. Therefore, the insurer does not need any significant additional resources beyond the premium on the policy.

If the insurer sells ten identical policies to ten independent insureds, the resources needed to pay losses that are two standard deviations above the expected loss of $7,440 are $65,126 (calculated as $7,440 + [2 × $28,843]). With ten policies, the initial capital still provides more than enough capacity. However, if the insurer sold 1,000 policies, it would need $1,320,862 (same calculation method) to be able to pay losses two standard deviations above the expected losses of $744,000. In this case, the initial investment of $1 million does not provide enough capacity. Therefore, the insurer would need to charge an extra $321 per policy to cover its desired contingencies.

Every insurer's capacity is limited by its financial resources, and its ability to fulfill its obligations is based on remaining solvent. Just as insurance buyers transfer risks that they are unwilling to retain to insurers, insurers can transfer risks that they are unwilling to retain to reinsurers. Through reinsurance, primary insurers pool or transfer risks, thereby staying within capacity constraints and helping to ensure their solvency. Reinsurance helps to reduce risk for insurers that accept risks transferred by insurance buyers. Therefore, reinsurance also contributes to the social function of insurance by assisting insurers in reducing risk for society.

CONTRACT OF INDEMNITY

The purpose of insurance is to indemnify an insured who suffers a loss.

To indemnify is to restore a party who has had a loss to the same financial position that party held before the loss occurred. Most property and liability insurance policies are **contracts of indemnity**.

Contract of indemnity
A contract in which the insurer agrees, in the event of a covered loss, to pay an amount directly related to the amount of the loss.

Property insurance generally pays the amount necessary to repair covered property that has been damaged or to replace it with similar property. The policy specifies the method for determining the amount of the loss.

For example, most auto policies, both personal and commercial, specify that vehicles are to be valued at their actual cash value (ACV) at the time of a loss. If a covered accident occurs that causes a covered vehicle to be a total loss, the insurer will normally pay the ACV of the vehicle, less any applicable deductible.

Liability insurance generally pays to a third-party claimant, on behalf of the insured, any amounts (up to the policy limit) that the insured becomes legally obligated to pay as damages because of a covered liability claim, as well as the legal costs associated with that claim. For example, if an insured with a liability limit of $300,000 is ordered by a court to pay $100,000 for bodily injury incurred by the claimant in a covered accident, the insurer will pay $100,000 to the claimant and will also pay the cost to defend the insured in court.

A contract of indemnity does not necessarily pay the full amount necessary to restore an insured who has suffered a covered loss to the same financial position. However, the amount the insurer pays is directly related to the amount

of the insured's loss. Most policies contain a policy limit that specifies the maximum amount the insurer will pay for a single claim. Many policies also contain limitations and other provisions that could reduce the amount of recovery.

For example, a homeowners policy is not designed to cover large amounts of cash. Therefore, most homeowners policies contain a special limit, such as $200, for any covered loss to money owned by the insured. If a covered fire destroys $1,000 in cash belonging to the insured, the homeowners insurer will pay only $200 for the money that was destroyed.

Principle of Indemnity

According to the **principle of indemnity**, the insured should not profit from a covered loss. That is, insurance should provide a benefit no greater than the loss suffered by the insured. Insurance policies usually include certain provisions that reinforce the principle of indemnity.

Principle of indemnity
The principle that insurance policies should provide a benefit no greater than the loss suffered by an insured.

Insurance contracts usually protect the insurer's subrogation rights. Other insurance provisions and subrogation provisions clarify that the insured cannot collect more than the amount of the loss. For example, following an auto accident in which the insurer compensates its insured when the other driver is at fault, the subrogation provision stipulates that the insured's right to recover damages from the responsible party is transferred (subrogated) to the insurer. The insured cannot collect from both the insurer and the responsible party.

Another factor enforcing the principle of indemnity is that a person usually cannot buy insurance unless that person is in a position to suffer a financial loss. In other words, the insured must have an insurable interest in the subject of the insurance. For example, property insurance contracts cover losses only to the extent of the insured's insurable interest in the property. This restriction prevents an insured from collecting more from the insurance than the amount of the loss he or she suffered. A person cannot buy life insurance on the life of a stranger, hoping to gain if the stranger dies. Insurers normally sell life insurance when there is a reasonable expectation of a financial loss from the death of the insured person, such as the loss of an insured's future income that the insured's dependents would face. Insurable interest is not an issue in liability insurance because a liability claim against an insured results in a financial loss if the insured is legally responsible. Even if the insured is not responsible, the insured could incur defense costs.

Valued Policy

Valued policy
A policy in which the insurer pays a stated amount in the event of a specified loss (usually a total loss), regardless of the actual value of the loss.

Some insurance contracts are not contracts of indemnity but **valued policies**. For example, a fine arts policy may specify that it will pay $250,000 for loss of a particular painting or sculpture. The actual market value of the painting or sculpture may be much smaller or much greater than $250,000, but the policy

will pay $250,000 in either case. In most valued policies, the insurer and the insured agree on a limit that approximates the current market value of the insured property.

BENEFITS OF INSURANCE

Insurance is a prominent risk management technique, and several risk financing measures involve the use of insurance to some degree. It is therefore important for risk management and insurance professionals to consider the benefits of insurance when selecting the most appropriate techniques for meeting risk management goals.

When used as a risk financing measure, insurance can help an individual or organization achieve risk financing goals such as paying for losses, managing cash flow uncertainty, and complying with legal requirements. Insurance also provides benefits to individuals, organizations, and society as a whole by promoting insureds' loss control activities, enabling insureds to use resources efficiently, providing support for insureds' credit, providing insurers with a source of investment funds, and reducing social burdens.

Paying for Losses

The primary role of insurance is to indemnify individuals and organizations for covered losses. This benefit is consistent with the risk financing goal of paying for losses. Provided that the loss is to a covered loss exposure and a covered cause of loss, insurance will indemnify the insured, subject to any applicable deductibles and policy limits.

Managing Cash Flow Uncertainty

Insurance also enables an individual or organization to meet the risk financing goal of managing cash flow uncertainty. Insurance provides the insured with some degree of financial security and stability. The insured can be confident that as long as a loss is covered, the financial effect on the insured's cash flow is reduced to any deductible payments and any loss amounts that exceed the policy limits. The remainder of the loss will be paid by the insurer, reducing the variation in the insured's cash flows.

Meeting Legal Requirements

The final risk financing goal that insurance meets is the goal of meeting legal requirements. Insurance is often used or required to satisfy both statutory requirements and contractual requirements that arise from business relationships.

For example, all states have laws that require employers to pay for the job-related injuries or illnesses of their employees. Employers generally purchase

workers compensation insurance to meet this financial obligation. In addition, certain business relationships require proof of insurance. For example, building contractors are usually required to provide evidence of liability insurance before a construction contract is granted.

Promoting Risk Control

A major benefit of insurance is the promotion of risk control. Insurance often provides the insured with the incentive to undertake cost-effective risk control measures. Insurers provide this incentive through risk-sharing mechanisms such as deductibles, premium credit incentives, and contractual requirements.

Because these incentives can lead to a reduction in losses paid by the insurer and therefore lower premiums, they benefit not only the individual insured but also all other insureds. Furthermore, risk control measures can save not only financial resources but also the lives of individuals or employees. Therefore, society as a whole benefits.

Enabling Efficient Use of Resources

People and businesses that face an uncertain future often set aside funds to pay for future losses. However, insurance makes it unnecessary to set aside a large amount of money to pay for the financial consequences of loss exposures that can be insured. In exchange for a relatively small premium, individuals and organizations can free up additional funds. As a result, the money that would otherwise be set aside to pay for possible losses can be used to improve an individual's quality of life or to contribute to the growth of an organization.

Providing Support for Insured's Credit

Insurance can also provide support for an insured's credit. Before making a loan, a lender wants assurance that the money will be repaid. For example, when loaning money to a borrower to purchase property, the lender usually acquires a legal interest in that property. This legal interest enables the lender to take actions such as repossessing a car or foreclosing a home mortgage if the loan is not repaid. Without this ability to recover the loan amount, the lender would be less likely to make the loan. Insurance facilitates loans to individuals and organizations by guaranteeing that the lender will be paid if the collateral for the loan (such as a house or a commercial building) is destroyed or damaged by an insured event, thereby reducing the lender's uncertainty.

Providing Source of Investment Funds

Insurance provides a source of investment funds for both insureds and insurers:

- Insureds are not required to set aside large retention funds to pay for losses that are covered by insurance.
- The premiums collected by insurers are invested until needed to pay claims. Such investments can provide money for projects such as new construction, research, and technology advancements.

Insurers also invest in social projects, such as cultural events, education, and economic development projects. Investment funds promote economic growth and job creation that, in turn, benefit individuals, organizations, and society. Also, because investment brings additional funding to insurers in the form of interest, this additional income helps keep insurance premiums at a reasonable level.

Reducing Social Burdens

Finally, insurance can help reduce social burdens. For example, the social costs of natural disasters, such as Hurricanes Katrina and Rita in 2005, are increased by uninsured losses suffered by individuals and organizations that can amount to billions of dollars. Without other assistance, the victims of natural disasters would rely on the state or federal government. Insurance helps to reduce this burden by providing compensation to the affected parties.

Compulsory auto insurance is another example, because it provides compensation to auto accident victims who might otherwise be unable to afford proper medical care or who might be unable to work because of the accident. Without insurance, victims of job-related or auto accidents might become a burden to society and need some form of state welfare. See the exhibit "Benefits of Insurance."

Review Questions

1. Describe the traits of an independent, or uncorrelated, loss exposure.
2. Describe the likelihood of extreme outcomes when using a pooling arrangement.
3. Describe the effect of pooling on the frequency of loss, severity of loss, and the probability distribution of losses.
4. Explain how the following types of insurance act as contracts of indemnity: a. property insurance and b. liability insurance.
5. Identify two factors enforcing the principle of indemnity.
6. A liability insurance policy promises to pay any covered claims against the insured up to a limit of $100,000. Is this a valued policy or a contract of indemnity? Explain.

Benefits of Insurance

Benefit	Explanation
Pay for losses	The primary role of insurance is to indemnify (restore to pre-loss status) individuals and organizations for covered losses.
Manage cash flow uncertainty	Insurance provides financial compensation when covered losses occur. Therefore, insurance greatly reduces the uncertainty created by many loss exposures.
Comply with legal requirements	Insurance can be used both to meet the statutory and contractual requirements of insurance coverage and to provide evidence of financial resources.
Promote risk control activity	Insurance policies may provide insureds with incentives to undertake risk control activities as a result of policy requirements or premium savings incentives.
Efficient use of insured's resources	Insurance makes it unnecessary to set aside a large amount of money to pay for the financial consequences of loss exposures that can be insured. This allows that money to be used more efficiently.
Support for insured's credit	Insurance facilitates loans to individuals and organizations by guaranteeing that the lender will be paid if the collateral for the loan (such as a house or a commercial building) is destroyed or damaged by an insured event, thereby reducing the lender's uncertainty.
Source of investment funds	The timing of insurer's cash flows, premiums collected up front, and claims paid at a later date enable insurers to invest funds in a variety of investment vehicles.
Reduce social burden	Insurance helps to reduce the burden to society of uncompensated accident victims.

[DA02722]

7. List the ways insurance benefits individuals, organizations, and society.
8. Explain how an organization can achieve risk financing goals through the use of insurance.
9. List risk-sharing mechanisms an insurer may use to promote risk control.

Application Questions

1. The Atwell Bus Corporation is a publicly held corporation providing school bus transportation to public and private schools in Midland County. Atwell owns 200 school buses, garaged in three different cities within the county. Its major competitors are two larger bus companies that operate in the same area. School districts and private schools generally award contracts to the lowest bidder from among the bus companies, but they also consider overall performance and level of service in their

evaluations. a. Give one example of a correlated loss exposure faced by Atwell. b. Give one example of an uncorrelated loss exposure faced by Atwell. c. Suppose Atwell were to enter into a formal arrangement with the Green Bus Company, a similar company that operates in another state, to pool the losses suffered by both companies. How would this arrangement affect Atwell's risks with respect to each of the loss exposures you identified above? Explain. d. Suppose, instead, Atwell were to participate in a formal pool with fifteen other school bus companies. How, if at all, would this arrangement change your answer to b., above? Explain.

2. A fire in Evelyn's apartment burned her five-year-old sofa. Evelyn received a check from her insurer for $1,000, which was the cost of a new sofa ($1,500) minus the depreciation on the sofa because it was five years old ($300) and minus her deductible ($200). Evelyn was angry because she had a nice sofa and was not able to replace it with the $1,000 that she received. Explain whether the principle of indemnity has been satisfied in this transaction.

SUMMARY

Pooling is an arrangement that facilitates the grouping of loss exposures and resources. Insurance works as a pooling mechanism to reduce risk (uncertainty) for individuals, organizations, and ultimately society.

According to the principle of indemnity, the insured should not profit from a covered loss. Insurance policies usually include certain provisions that reinforce the principle of indemnity.

The benefits of insurance include paying for losses, managing cash flow uncertainty, complying with the law, promoting risk control, allowing efficient use of the insured's resources, providing support for the insured's credit, providing a source of investment funds, and reducing social burdens.

Direct Your Learning

9

Characteristics of an Insurable Risk

Educational Objectives

After learning the content of this assignment, you should be able to:

- Explain the dynamics of supply and demand in establishing product prices and the factors that affect the supply and demand for insurance.
- Describe the following economic issues related to insurance pricing:
  - Adverse selection
  - Moral and morale hazard
  - Actuarial compared with social equity
  - Timing
- Explain why each of the six characteristics of an ideally insurable loss exposure is important to the insurance mechanism.
- Explain how the six characteristics of an ideally insurable loss exposure apply to commercial loss exposures.
- Explain how the six characteristics of an ideally insurable loss exposure apply to personal loss exposures.
- Explain how state and federal governments are involved in the insurance market and the rationale for, and level of, their involvement.
- Describe reinsurance and its principal functions.

Outline

Economic View of Insurance

Economic Issues Related to Insurance Pricing

Characteristics of an Ideally Insurable Loss Exposure

Insurability of Commercial Loss Exposures

Insurability of Personal Loss Exposures

Government Insurance Programs

Reinsurance and Its Functions

Summary

Characteristics of an Insurable Risk

9

ECONOMIC VIEW OF INSURANCE

There is supply and demand for insurance products just as there is supply and demand for other products, such as automobiles, tax preparation services, theater tickets, or video game consoles. Therefore, the fundamental supply-and-demand dynamics that apply to other products and services in the economy also apply to insurance policies. Although the remainder of this section describes supply and demand in terms of products, the dynamics affecting supply and demand of products apply equally to services.

The dynamics of supply and demand are such that the seller (supplier) will not offer a product at a price lower than the minimum possible price. Below this minimum possible price, the supplier prefers to keep the product rather than sell it. See the exhibit "Supply and Demand in the Video Game Console Market."

Similarly, the buyer will not pay more than the buyer's maximum possible price. Above this maximum possible price, the buyer would rather not have the product. If the seller's minimum possible price is lower than the buyer's maximum possible price, then a price exists between these two boundaries at which the transaction can occur such that both the seller and buyer are satisfied. The seller is paid an amount that is higher than the minimum the seller is willing to accept, and the buyer pays an amount lower than maximum the buyer is willing to pay. See the exhibit "Price Agreement Between Buyers and Sellers."

In insurance, the transaction can occur only when the premium charged by the insurer is higher than the minimum premium the insurer is willing to accept and lower than the maximum premium the insurance buyer is willing to pay. Provided the premium is higher than the minimum premium the insurer will accept, the insurer can make a profit. See the exhibit "Shopping for Insurance."

Examining how supply and demand interact in the insurance market provides useful insights about how insurers contribute to social wellbeing (buying insurance is financially advantageous to insureds), even when insurers are making profits.

Supply and Demand in the Video Game Console Market

Ellen wants to buy a new video game console and is considering a new Game Tower 500. Not many video game consoles of this model are available. Video Games, Inc. (Video), a nearby dealer, does have the Game Tower 500 in stock.

Supply

Video wants to maximize its profits. It wants to sell as many video game consoles as possible for as high a price as possible and to minimize the costs of keeping video game consoles in inventory. Conversely, video game console buyers want a low price; the lower the price, the more video game consoles will be purchased. Video seeks a price that maximizes sales revenue at its lowest cost for the number of units sold.

Demand

Ellen can only afford to spend a certain amount of money for a video game console. If she believes the price Video is charging is reasonable, Ellen may buy the video game console. If she thinks the price is too high, she will shop elsewhere, delay her purchase until the price is reduced, or consider a different brand of video game console. Each buyer determines what cost is within his or her price range.

Combining Supply and Demand

What price is appropriate for selling or buying a Game Tower 500? If Video's minimum price (for example, $500) is lower than Ellen's maximum price (for example, $600), the parties will probably be able to negotiate a price that is acceptable to both of them. If Video's price (for example, $550) is higher than Ellen is willing or can afford to pay (for example, $450), Ellen will delay her purchase or shop elsewhere.

Competition

Competition has a bearing on the supply and demand for a particular product or service. If a satisfactory substitute is available, a buyer can always decide to purchase the substitute. The presence of competition reduces the amount that buyers like Ellen are willing to pay for a Game Tower 500 (that is, it reduces the demand). As a result, sellers like Video are forced to lower their prices. Competition among suppliers tends to keep prices down.

[DA02730]

Supply and Demand

For any product, demand is inversely proportional to its price: the higher the price, the smaller the quantity that consumers are willing to purchase. Alternatively, the smaller the quantity that can be purchased, the higher the price that consumers are willing to pay.

The opposite is true for supply: the higher the price of a product, the greater the quantity that sellers are willing to offer, and vice versa. See the exhibit "Supply and Demand Curves."

Combining the supply and demand curves on one graph, reveals that there is a point at which the two curves intersect. At this point, referred to in economics as market equilibrium, demand and supply are equal. Market equi-

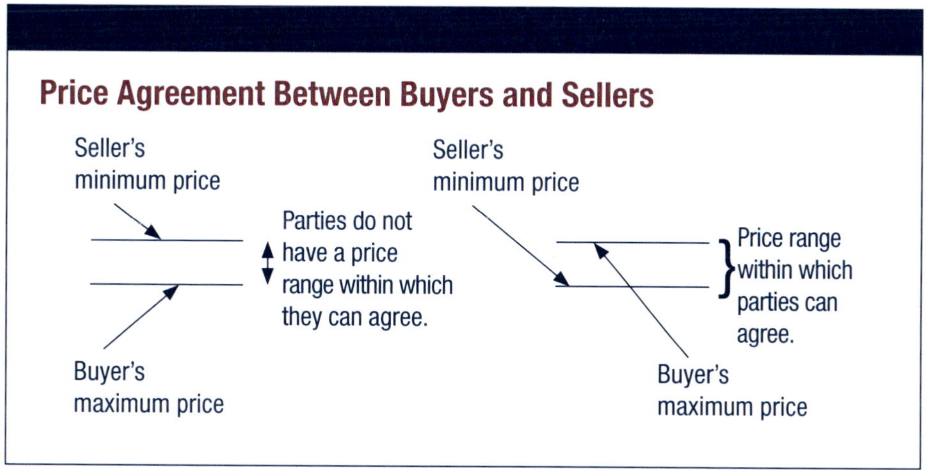

[DA02725]

Shopping for Insurance

Bridget is shopping for auto insurance. The most Bridget is willing to spend on auto insurance is $2,000 per year. She shops on XYZ Insurance Company's website, which states that XYZ is willing to sell her an auto insurance policy for $2,500 per year. The minimum price that XYZ is willing to accept, $2,500, is higher than the maximum premium that Bridget is willing to pay, $2,000. Therefore, Bridget and XYZ will not enter into an insurance contract.

Bridget then contacts her local insurance agent, who informs her that he has quotes from three different auto insurers with premiums that range from $1,500 to $1,800 per year. As all three premiums are below the maximum Bridget is willing to pay for auto insurance and above the minimum that the insurers are willing to accept, Bridget will be able to choose auto insurance from one of these three insurers based on not only the price, but also other factors that differentiate their products.

[DA02726]

librium is reached at equilibrium price (P*) and equilibrium quantity (Q*). See the exhibit "Market Equilibrium."

Market equilibrium can be attained in a free market (a free market being one without constraints such as limits on price or quantity). In market equilibrium, all sales transactions occur at the equilibrium price (P*). Any price that is higher than the equilibrium price would generate a supply greater than demand and would result in an over-abundance of the product. With an over-abundance of a product, the price declines back toward P*.

Similarly, any price lower than the equilibrium price would generate a shortage, because demand would be greater than supply. With a shortage, the price rises back toward P*. Eventually, the price of the product will return to P*, and the amount supplied will return to Q*.

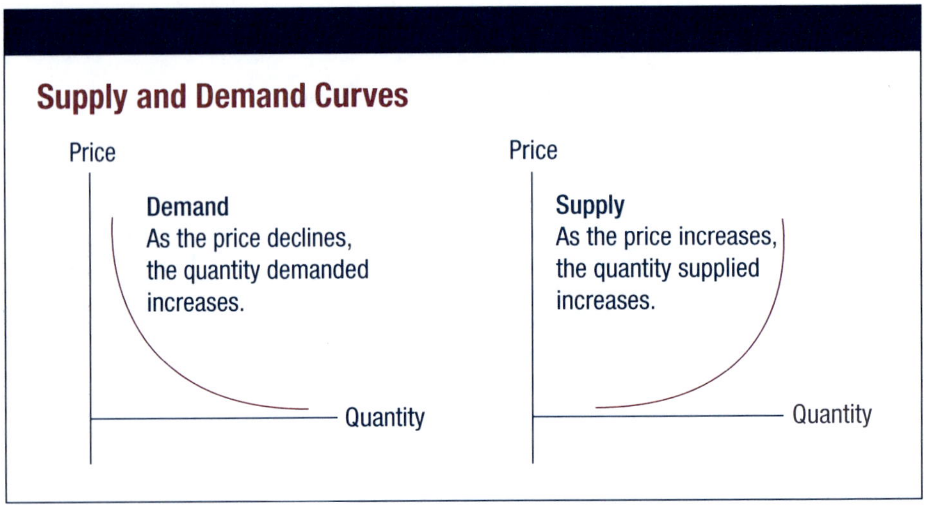

Supply and Demand Curves
Price
Demand
As the price declines, the quantity demanded increases.
Quantity
Price
Supply
As the price increases, the quantity supplied increases.
Quantity

[DA02727]

Market Equilibrium
Price
Supply
Demand
Market equilibrium
P*
Quantity
Q*

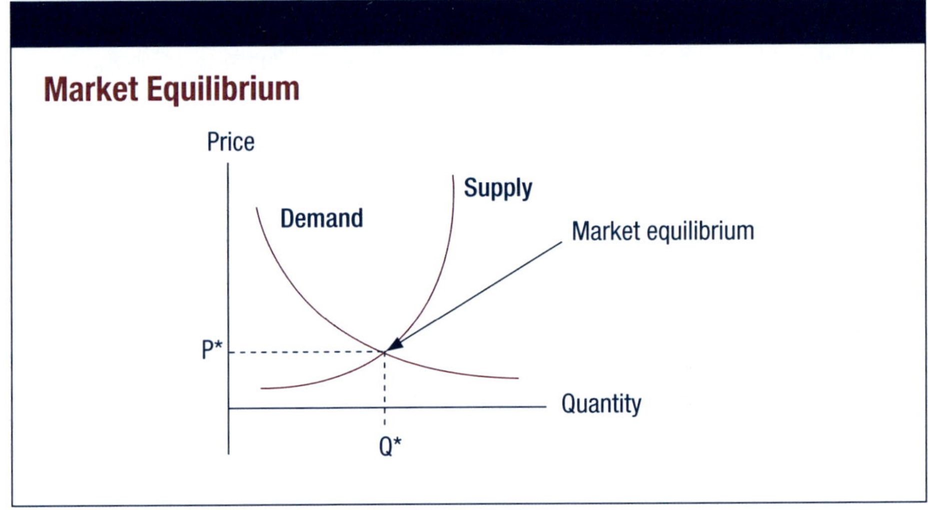

[DA02729]

The supply of, and the demand for, insurance is influenced by many factors that depend not only on consumers and insurers, but also on the economic and regulatory environment. See the exhibit "Insurance Supply and Demand Factors."

Insurance Supply

The supply of a manufactured product depends on many factors, such as the cost of the raw materials, administrative costs, manufacturing costs, and the total compensation of the workers. Similarly, for insurance products, the supply depends on factors such as how much the insurers must pay for rent, marketing services, and salaries. The premiums an insurer collects must cover these costs plus any losses that the insurer has to cover.

Insurance Supply and Demand Factors

Supply (Insurers)	Demand (Consumers)
• Capacity to assume new business	• Insurance mandates and regulation
• Investment opportunities	• Risk tolerance
• Production costs	• Financial status
• Regulatory environment	• Real services rendered
	• Tax incentives

[DA02731]

One difference between an organization that sells insurance and a manufacturer or retailer is that an insurer sells a promise of a service that may be needed in the future, whereas a manufacturer or retailer sells a product that the consumer usually brings home (or consumes) immediately after the payment is made. At the time of sale, a manufacturer knows the exact production cost of each unit because these costs are incurred before the product is sold. The manufacturer can therefore price the product accordingly.

The same is not true for an insurer. Some of the production costs of an insurance policy are known. For example, the insurer knows its marketing and underwriting costs. However, the major component of the production cost of an insurance policy, the losses and loss adjustment expenses, are not known at the time the premium is set. The fixed premium, combined with the unknown cost of the promise to pay losses, distinguishes insurance from most other products or services sold in the economy.

If the price an insurer could charge were unrestricted, it would seem that the supply of insurance could be virtually limitless. The more policies sold, the greater the premium income, which means more money to invest and thus greater investment income, as well as greater diversification of risk and better predictability of losses. However, insurers do not have an unlimited capacity to sell policies. Because an insurer sells a promise of a future payment in the event of a covered loss, an insurer could make too many promises and ultimately be unable to fulfill them. An insurer must eventually have enough resources to compensate all the policyholders who make a claim. Insurance regulators monitor insurers to help ensure that they have the financial resources to ultimately pay their claims.

The supply of insurance is therefore determined by these important factors:

- Capacity to assume new business
- Investment opportunities

- Production costs
- Regulatory environment

Capacity to Assume New Business

An insurer's capacity to assume new business is limited by the risk that it will be unable to fulfill the payment promises that it has made. In other words, an insurer's capacity for new business is greatly affected by its **insolvency risk**. Insolvency risk limits the supply of insurance provided by insurers.

Insolvency risk
The risk of an insurer being unable to meet its financial obligations.

For most insurers, the probability of not being able to pay claims is low. For example, an insurer may want to keep its insolvency risk below 1 percent, meaning that there is only a 1 percent probability that the insurer will not have enough capital to pay all the claims that it must pay in the coming year.

The two major variables that affect an insurer's claims-paying ability are (1) the number and the size of the policies sold (its liabilities) and (2) the funds available to pay for the promises made under those policies (its assets).

The first variable, liabilities, is usually measured by the insurer's total **written premiums**. A better measure would be the size of future claims that the insurer expects to pay, but accurately predicting those claims is difficult. Therefore, total written premiums is typically used as an approximation of the liability that the insurer is expected to face in the future.

Written premiums
The total premium on all policies written (put into effect) during a particular period.

The second variable is measured by assets—such as stocks, bonds, real estate, and other investments—that can be liquidated to pay for claims. **Policyholders' surplus** is a measure of how much capital the insurer has to pay claims that are greater than expected.

Policyholders' surplus
Under statutory accounting principles (SAP), an insurer's total admitted assets minus its total liabilities.

Premium-to-Surplus Ratio

Insurance regulators closely monitor the relationship between an insurer's premiums and its policyholders' surplus. This relationship is measured by the **premium-to-surplus ratio** (also called the capacity ratio).

Premium-to-surplus ratio, or capacity ratio
A capacity ratio that indicates an insurer's financial strength by relating net written premiums to policyholders' surplus.

The premium-to-surplus ratio indicates the extent to which insurers can issue new policies, because it provides a rough measurement of how adequate available funds (measured by the policyholders' surplus) are to pay unexpected claims (measured by the total written premiums). Financial capacity constraints limit an insurer's ability to grow rapidly, because a rapid growth in new business increases an insurer's obligations faster than it increases policyholders' surplus.

The premium-to-surplus ratio formula is calculated as this:

Premium-to-surplus ratio = Written premiums ÷ Policyholders' surplus

The policyholders' surplus represents the insurer's financial cushion for absorbing unexpected claims. If losses and expenses exceed written premiums,

an insurer must draw on its policyholders' surplus to meet its obligations. Therefore, an insurer's new written premiums should not become too large relative to the policyholders' surplus.

Insurance regulators use the premium-to-surplus ratio as a benchmark to determine whether an insurer might be facing financial difficulty. A premium-to-surplus ratio above 3-to-1 is often considered a sign of financial weakness, and many consider a ratio above 2-to-1 to be too high.

However, although this ratio is important, it is not the only measure of ability to absorb unexpected claims and is not the only indicator that should be used to evaluate an insurer's financial condition. More sophisticated measures recognize factors such as the lines of business written, the adequacy of the loss reserves, the quality of assets, and the amount of reinsurance. See the exhibit "Insurer Capacity and Reinsurance."

Insurer Capacity and Reinsurance

An insurer (primary insurer) can use a reinsurance arrangement to transfer some of its claim liability to another insurer in the reinsurance market. By using reinsurance, a primary insurer increases its capacity because it increases its ability to pay future claims by sharing the premium it collected and any future losses claimed with a reinsurer. This increase in the primary insurer's ability to indemnify losses is, however, not infinite. Just as the supply of primary insurance is limited, the supply of reinsurance is also limited. The factors that limit the supply of reinsurance are similar to those that limit the supply of primary insurance, such as investment opportunities, production cost, and financial capacity.

[DA02732]

Investment Opportunities

When a consumer purchases an insurance policy, he or she purchases the right to claim an amount of money from the insurer at a future time, conditional on an event or a set of events occurring. Until the event occurs and the claim is made, the insurer has the opportunity to invest the premium it collected at the start of the policy.

The amount of investment income generated by the insurer reduces the premium the insurer has to collect to cover future losses. The premiums the insurer collects must be adequate to pay expenses plus the present value of future losses. The greater the income the insurer can earn on its investments, the lower its present value of future losses. An increase in the expected return on the insurer's investments increases the supply of insurance because although capacity may limit the total amount of premium an insurer can write, the insurer can charge a lower premium for coverage and therefore provide more coverage for the same total amount of premium written.

Production Costs

In addition to the actual losses that an insurer must pay, the production of insurance policies involves a variety of expenses that limit the supply of insurance policies that an insurer can provide. These expenses can be associated with two of the insurer's primary assets: physical assets and human assets.

Insurers, similar to manufacturers, need physical assets to produce insurance products and services. Although an insurer's office and equipment needs may not be as extensive as a manufacturer's, an insurer still has physical asset requirements. For example, an insurer needs an efficient information system to track information such as the premiums paid by the insureds, the payments made to claimants, investments, and regulatory filings. Information systems can also be used to assess applicants in order to determine the appropriate underwriting decisions.

Other physical assets an insurer needs include office space and company vehicles for claim representatives who are adjusting claims in the field. The more expensive it is for the insurer to acquire and maintain its physical assets, the more costly it is for the insurer to produce insurance policies.

Human assets are also vital to the supply of insurance policies that an insurer can produce. The cost associated with the insurer's human assets influences the supply of insurance policies in the same way as the cost of the physical assets. The more the insurer expends on human assets, the fewer insurance policies it can supply.

Employees who possess the appropriate knowledge and skills can help the insurer to accurately price policies, efficiently pay claims, and provide other services that are important to consumers, such as loss control. Salaries paid to claim representatives; producer commissions; and compensation paid to underwriters, actuaries, investment analysts, and other employees are the human asset costs for an insurer.

Regulatory Environment

Even if a particular loss exposure would be deemed acceptable by the underwriting department, an insurer may still be unable to sell an insurance policy for that loss exposure because of externally imposed regulatory constraints. The two main types of regulatory constraints on the supply of insurance are business practices regulation and price regulation.

When regulation limits the price of insurance, some consumers pay less for coverage than before, but other consumers cannot find any coverage at any price. Insurers often limit the amount of insurance they are willing to sell if price regulation prevents them from charging a premium that is necessary to cover losses and expenses and to generate profits. If the coverage is mandatory, some consumers might have to purchase insurance through the state's residual markets, in which losses are often shared among all of the insurers selling insurance in the state.

Many business practices related to the supply of insurance policies, such as licensing, policy language, minimum financial requirements, and participation in residual markets, are regulated at the state level. State regulations also prescribe the minimum financial requirements (capital and policyholders' surplus requirements) that an insurer must have to transact business in that state.

Some financial requirements may be high enough that an insurer decides not to sell that line of business in that state. State regulation on marketing practices and other insurer activities may also involve substantial administrative requirements, making it relatively unattractive for an insurer to offer certain insurance products and services. Because regulatory approval is often a slow process, it may constrain an insurer's ability to quickly provide new products and services.

The second regulatory constraint that insurers face is price regulation. State regulators have the power to limit prices by regulating insurance rate increases and the underwriting factors used in setting premiums for many lines of business. For example, insurers may be prohibited from using a driver's gender to determine auto insurance premiums.

Regulators have used these powers primarily in automobile liability and in workers' compensation insurance lines, although other lines have also been affected on occasion, such as homeowners' insurance in areas susceptible to natural disasters (such as earthquakes and hurricanes) and title insurance. See the exhibit "Examples of Internal and External Obstacles to Supplying New Insurance Products."

Examples of Internal and External Obstacles to Supplying New Insurance Products

In addition to regulatory constraints on new product development, insurers often face other obstacles to the supply of new products. Some of these obstacles include the following:

- Personnel—The insurer may want to enter a certain line of business but concludes that its present staff is not capable of profitably writing and servicing this new line. Hiring additional personnel may not be feasible or might not generate sufficient volume to justify the cost.
- Reinsurance—The insurer's interest in writing a new line of business may depend on whether it can obtain reinsurance for large losses or catastrophes.
- Custom and tradition—Some insurers may hesitate to pioneer in areas that other insurers have not successfully tested.
- New business—A new line of insurance, in which losses are indeterminable, might lead to variable underwriting results, making it difficult to determine prices and leaving the insurer's assets exposed to catastrophic losses.

[DA02734]

Insurance Demand

Several factors affect the demand for insurance. These factors relate to both the market and the characteristics of the typical insureds. See the exhibit "Hurricane Andrew and the Supply of Property Insurance."

Hurricane Andrew and the Supply of Property Insurance

After Hurricane Andrew struck in 1992, inflicting $15½ billion in insured damage, many Florida residents found it almost impossible to purchase property insurance. The supply of property insurance was dramatically reduced, even though demand increased as people became more aware of the extent of their loss exposure (subjective risk) to severe windstorms. These changes in supply and demand occurred despite the fact that the objective risk (the probability of windstorm damage to property) was essentially unchanged. Insurers and consumers, however, became much more aware of the risk of future windstorm damage.

The following three factors dramatically affected the supply of insurance:

- A change occurred in the assessment of the risk of bankruptcy to insurers. Although the probability of a hurricane did not change, the size of the losses and the correlation across the individual losses changed, so that insurers acquired more information about their exposure to catastrophic losses. In other words, insurers became better informed about the consequences of natural catastrophes. Many insurers that had been aggressively marketing property insurance in Florida decided they were no longer interested in expanding their market share, and most wanted to reduce their exposure in that market.
- Because most property insurers had to use their policyholders' surplus to pay the claims from Hurricane Andrew, the catastrophe reduced insurers' financial capacity to write new business because less capital was available after the storm.
- The supply of reinsurance decreased dramatically because reinsurers also suffered significant losses. A catastrophe like Hurricane Andrew has a major effect on insurers writing property reinsurance. Consequently, a decrease in reinsurance market capacity reduces the capacity of primary insurers.

[DA05060]

Insurance Mandates and Regulation

Demand for insurance products and services does not necessarily have to be voluntary. There are insurance mandates in many common lines of insurance (including auto insurance and workers' compensation) that increase demand for those insurance products.

For example, states impose financial responsibility requirements on auto owners or operators. These requirements are typically satisfied by purchasing auto liability insurance. In this case, the question is not whether to buy insurance, but from whom. Although self-insurance is usually permitted, it is not a common practice among most consumers.

In self-insurance, a person or an organization with sufficient financial resources might post a bond, demonstrating to the state that adequate financial resources exist to pay for any losses resulting from an auto accident. Insurance mandates are often violated. For example, some motorists with limited financial resources weigh the risks of being caught and choose to go without insurance.

Most employers are required to provide the workers' compensation benefits prescribed by law. Although self-insurance alternatives are permitted for large employers, small employers with limited financial resources often have no choice about purchasing insurance.

In addition to regulatory mandates, some contracts that organizations and consumers enter into require insurance purchases. For example, most home purchases are financed by a mortgage, and the mortgage lender invariably requires insurance to protect its interest in the property and its ability to recover the loan amount.

Creditors also require insurance on business property of many types when it is used as loan collateral. Similarly, many business contracts require one or more contractual parties to purchase liability insurance. All of these mandates and contractual requirements to purchase insurance increase the demand for insurance.

Risk Tolerance

The demand for insurance is strongly influenced by the insurance buyer's attitude toward risk. All else being equal, the greater the individual's risk tolerance, the less insurance that consumer will purchase. Although an insurance policy reduces the uncertainty of losses, this reduction comes at the expense of paying an insurance premium.

The cost-benefit analysis (comparing the benefit of the reduced uncertainty with the premium cost of the insurance policy) determines who purchases insurance and who does not. A consumer who has a greater risk tolerance is less likely to purchase an insurance policy, because the cost of the premium outweighs the benefits of the reduced uncertainty.

A consumer's risk tolerance may change with age, with economic or social conditions, or with a significant loss event like a hurricane. For instance, an individual may feel more risk tolerant when younger.

Alternatively, a change in economic conditions may increase the cost of retaining risk so that risk tolerance is reduced. For example, a wealthy individual who is suffering losses in an investment portfolio may no longer be willing to assume significant property loss exposures and therefore may choose to purchase a homeowners insurance policy.

Ultimately, consumers' risk tolerance can increase or decrease the demand for insurance.

Financial Status

For individuals or organizations with severely limited financial resources, insurance purchases are often a luxury that cannot be afforded. Only individuals or organizations whose income exceeds a certain level are likely to purchase insurance. The higher an individual's (or an organization's) income, wealth, or asset level is, the more likely it is that an insurance policy will be purchased.

However, as levels of income or wealth increase, the demand for some forms of insurance actually diminishes because individuals or organizations have the financial resources sufficient to retain losses as current expenses or to use various forms of retention, such as captive insurers.

Real Services Rendered

One of the factors that individuals and organizations consider when purchasing insurance is the services offered with the insurance policy. This can be the deciding factor for those that can afford to retain the risk but choose to insure it. Furthermore, insurers can achieve product differentiation by offering services that are valued by the consumers, such as fast claims service, loss control services, or a personable sales force.

The real services an insurer chooses to offer often depend on the type of customer they are trying to attract and the lines of business that the insurer offers. For example, individuals often develop close business relationships with their insurance agent. Therefore, insurers operating in personal lines may want to ensure that they offer a personable sales force. Similarly, they may want to ensure fast claims service, which is another factor that individual consumers value. Alternatively, insurers that are active in commercial lines may focus on offering more extensive loss control services that are valuable to organizations.

Another way to increase demand, both for individual insurer's products and in the aggregate, is to introduce new insurance products, such as extended warranty products for automobiles, warranties for home buyers, and insurance against financial losses resulting from identity theft.

An insurer who recognizes the consumer's need for a new insurance product (such as terrorism insurance) or for an old product in a new region, offers a valuable service for which consumers are willing to pay more. By distinguishing its insurance products and services from those of its competitors through new product development or additional services on existing products, an insurer can increase the demand for its insurance policies.

Tax Incentives

Tax incentives affect demand by encouraging people to purchase certain lines of insurance in which the premium is tax-deductible. For example, the cost of employer-provided group life and health insurance is not considered taxable

income to an employee (subject to limitations), and it is a tax-deductible expense for the employer. A tax deduction has the same effect as a discount because it lowers the net cost of insurance to purchasers, thereby increasing demand. The difference between a tax deduction and a discount is that the deduction is provided by the government, not the insurance provider.

Tax considerations affecting the purchase of property or liability insurance policies are often more subtle. For example, an individual's or a family's casualty losses (as defined by the tax code) can be income-tax-deductible insome cases, but property-liability insurance premiums are not tax-deductible. The tax deduction helps subsidize the cost of uninsured losses. Recognizing this, wealthy individuals in a high tax bracket might decide to forgo the purchase of property insurance or to purchase insurance with a high deductible.

Alternatively, a business's casualty losses (as defined by the tax code) are tax-deductible at the time they are paid, not during the year when they are incurred. A long delay often exists between the date of an occurrence and the date the loss is paid. Some losses, such as those involving a serious disability,are paid over a period of many years. In contrast, insurance premiums are tax-deductible as a business expense when they are paid. In many cases, the annual cost of insurance is much more consistent from year to year than the amounts that would otherwise be paid as retained losses. This is a powerful argument for the purchase of insurance when earnings stability is a risk management program goal.

ECONOMIC ISSUES RELATED TO INSURANCE PRICING

In a free market (one that is free of any external constraints), the structure of supply and demand dictates that an insurance transaction will occur at a price that is satisfactory to both the insurer and the consumer. Insurers supply insurance at a price that is greater than the expected value of the losses they cover (plus expenses and profits), and consumers purchase insurance when the premium is less than the cost to them of assuming the risk. For some individuals, the cost of retention can be substantially higher than the expected loss. Therefore, they will purchase insurance even if the premium is greater than the expected loss they face.

When selling insurance to a group of insurance buyers, an insurer's goal is to collect premiums that in the aggregate are adequate to generate an operating profit from the group. This goal is accomplished when the insurance premium for each policy reflects the loss exposures the policy covers, with an allowance for the insurer's expenses, profits, contingencies, and (perhaps) an adjustment for investment income. Insurers refer to this as a premium that is commensurate with the loss exposure.

Actuaries develop insurance rating systems for many different types of coverage that match premiums with loss exposures, and underwriters ensure that the specific loss exposures being insured are properly classified within the rating system. Provided the actuaries have developed the proper rating system and the underwriters have accurately classified the individual loss exposures, the loss exposures should be adequately priced and the insurance markets should function properly.

Four key issues affect how insurance markets function with regard to pricing: adverse selection, moral hazard, actuarial compared with social equity, and timing. Any of these issues can affect the proper functioning of insurance markets and, in the extreme case, cause market failure. Market failure occurs when supply and demand do not intersect at a sustainable price and quantity. An example of a market failure was the general liability crisis in the mid-1980s, in which many organizations were unable to obtain liability insurance coverage at any price.

Adverse Selection

Appropriate insurance pricing requires that the insurer be able to gather sufficient information about the applicant to adequately assess and price a particular policy. This information gathering is typically handled by the underwriter and insurance producer. Although much information about an applicant is available from the application and other sources, it can be expensive for insurers to collect.

After taking into account all of the information that can be collected cost-effectively, a portion of the information about the applicant remains unknown to the insurer. In economic terms, this is called information asymmetry and it occurs when one party has information that is relevant to the transaction that the other party does not have. Although this information is important to insurers, and would enable them to appropriately price their insurance products, the benefits to the insurer of appropriate pricing do not outweigh the costs of obtaining the additional information.

For example, Tamika lives in Savannah and wants to purchase auto insurance on her new minivan. For a relatively minor cost, the auto insurers that Tamika calls can obtain information from various statistical organizations on the number of auto accidents that occur in the Savannah area, the types of vehicles involved, the ages of the drivers, and the cost of claim settlements.

In fact, if the insurers that Tamika calls sell a significant amount of auto insurance in the area, they will already have this information. Furthermore, those insurers can get a copy of Tamika's driving record to determine if she has been involved in any recent traffic violations or auto accidents. However, this information does not completely inform the insurers about what type of driver Tamika is.

Assume that Tamika has not had any moving violations or been involved in any accidents. This could mean that Tamika is a very good driver (low risk) or it could mean that she is a very bad driver (high risk) who has just been lucky to avoid accidents and moving violations. The insurers could spend a considerable amount of money to attempt to verify which of the alternatives is correct.

In theory, insurers could require a driving test, hire an investigator to follow Tamika and report on her driving habits, or, with Tamika's permission, install a tracking device in her minivan to track her movements to determine her driving habits. However, the additional information may not be worth the expense.

Instead of obtaining this additional information, an insurer could charge Tamika an average rate (the same rate they would charge all drivers with the same characteristics as Tamika) and hope that she is a good driver (a low risk). If the insurer sells enough insurance policies to people with characteristics similar to Tamika, the insurer hopes that any poor drivers in the pool are more than offset by all of the good drivers in the pool so that the average rate is sufficient to cover losses and expenses of the group and also to generate profits.

When an insurer charges an average rate because it cannot differentiate between a high risk and a low risk, high-risk individuals have an incentive to buy the insurance policy because the premium is too low relative to their individual risk level.

Conversely, low-risk individuals do not want to buy the insurance because the premium is too high. This results in adverse selection. Adverse selection is the process by which consumers with the greatest probability of loss are those most likely to purchase insurance.

In the example, if the insurer were to offer the average rate to all the drivers, then the high-risk drivers in the group would buy the insurance and the low-risk drivers would not. Therefore, despite offering the average rate, the group of people the insurer has insured is not an average group—it is worse than average because of adverse selection. This group of insureds would tend to have more accidents and higher claims than the average group, because they are poor drivers.

There are significant ethical, social, and legal issues regarding the information insurers need to develop appropriate insurance prices. The continued advances in data collection and dissemination have given insurers the ability to access and analyze an increasing amount of information.

However, this access to information has raised privacy concerns about what information is relevant to accurate pricing and how much information is too much. Avoiding adverse selection is one of the main functions of underwriting and is the major information issue faced by insurers. Another key issue concerns moral and morale hazard.

Moral and Morale Hazard

Just as adverse selection can be thought of as an information problem, moral hazard and morale hazard can be thought of as behavior problems. A moral hazard is a condition that increases the frequency and/or severity of a loss resulting from a person acting dishonestly. A morale hazard is a condition that increases the frequency and/or severity of loss resulting from careless or indifferent behavior.

Both moral and morale hazard are behavior problems that often arise in risk transfer measures, especially insurance. Individuals and organizations do not behave in the same way when they are insured as when they are uninsured because they will not bear the entire cost of the loss as they would with retention. Some of the loss costs are assumed by the insurer and, therefore, the insureds are less careful.

Moral and morale hazard problems are common in automobile insurance and are also present in products liability and general liability insurance. Insurers need to be aware of the existence of moral and morale hazards, the two main behavior problems that affect insurance markets, when providing insurance to individuals and organizations. The most common method of reducing moral and morale hazard behavior issues is to ensure that the insured participates in the loss by including a risk-sharing mechanism (such as a deductible) in the insurance policy. See the exhibit "Examples of Moral and Morale Hazard."

Examples of Moral and Morale Hazard

Vince has workers compensation insurance and healthcare coverage through his employer. Doctors' visits covered by workers compensation do not have a co-pay, although Vince's healthcare coverage does require him to pay a $25 co-pay per doctor's visit. Vince injures his knee skiing on a Sunday. To avoid having to pay the co-pay for a doctor's visit, he reports to his superior on the following Monday that the injury occurred at work early on Monday morning. Vince's situation is a moral hazard problem; he has intentionally caused a loss to the workers compensation insurer who has to pay for the cost of treatment.

Abigail owns a two-and-a half-year-old car that she drives to work every day. The car is fully paid for and has a market value of $20,000. Abigail purchased a comprehensive automobile insurance policy that guarantees that if her car is stolen within the first three years of the policy, she receives a brand new car. This policy is a replacement-cost new insurance policy (similar clauses exist for homeowners insurance and commercial buildings). If Abigail purchased the same new car today, she would need $30,000. Because she has purchased the insurance policy, Abigail does not bear the cost of a new car if her car is stolen. Even if she does not want to have her car stolen, Abigail will not invest as much time, effort, and energy in preventing her car from being stolen as she would if she was uninsured. Abigail's situation is a morale hazard problem; she is indifferent to loss because she will not bear any of the cost if a loss occurs.

These are two classic cases of moral and morale hazard. The behaviors of Abigail and Vince are different when they are insured compared with when they were uninsured.

[DA02735]

Actuarial Equity Compared With Social Equity

Ideally, the premiums charged to insureds should vary in direct proportion to the insureds' loss exposures and expected losses. Fair discrimination, which charges an equitable premium to each insured, is an essential element of insurance pricing. State insurance laws generally prohibit insurance rates that are unfairly discriminatory. At issue is that equity has a different meaning for different people, and opinions often vary about whether insurance pricing should achieve actuarial equity or social equity.

Insurers generally want to achieve actuarial equity, in which each insured pays a premium directly proportional to the loss exposures that are transferred to the insurer. The concept of actuarial equity is founded in cost-based pricing. The goal of cost-based pricing is to identify every variable that will signal the differences between otherwise identical loss exposures. Actuarial equity has been the traditional test applied by regulatory authorities to distinguish between fair and unfair discrimination, but there has been an increasing trend towards consideration of another test—social equity.

Neither the states nor the courts have specifically defined social equity, but it generally involves two concepts. The first of those concepts is that insurers should relate the amount each person should pay for insurance to his or her ability to pay rather than to the person's loss exposure or expense factor.

The second concept is that insurers should not increase an insured's insurance premium because of criteria that are beyond that individual's control. To help achieve social equity, legislators and the public have identified certain insurance rating variables that are socially unacceptable—including, in virtually every state, the use of race, religion, and national origin.

Even if loss experience differs based on these variables, they cannot be reflected in rating plans. This can affect underwriters' decisions. For example, in some jurisdictions, sex has been eliminated as a rating factor for auto insurance—although insurers have gathered historical loss information that indicates that youthful male operators have more losses relative to youthful female operators. In those jurisdictions where sex has been eliminated as a rating factor, youthful males and youthful females with similar characteristics are required to pay the same rates.

When rules and regulation prevent insurers from using easily accessible information (such as age, sex, and race), they need to find costlier and less-efficient mechanisms to gather that information. In the case of age, for example, insurers may want to look at the type of automobile, income source, and any other variable that correlates with the age of an individual. If insurers can find variables that correlate to the characteristics they are forbidden to use, then insurers will often use these less-efficient characteristics in their risk classification schemes.

Timing

One final important issue in insurance pricing is timing.

For some types of losses, especially large losses arising from liability exposures, a substantial delay can occur between the date of an occurrence, the date the loss is discovered, and the date the loss is paid. During this period, which can span several years, the insurer invests the premium paid for the coverage and generates investment income.

The investment income partially offsets the cost of the insurer's expected losses. This partial offset is often reflected in the insurer's pricing. In other words, the insurer considers not the expected loss amount, but the present value of the expected loss amount, when determining the appropriate premiums. As the present value of the expected loss is lower than the expected loss amount, the effect is to reduce premiums.

As well as determining the timing of a loss, an insurer has to assess the value of future losses. In binary insurance policies (policies, such as life insurance policies, under which a lump sum of money is paid if a particular event occurs) this is not an issue because the insurer knows exactly what amount will be paid. The only thing the insurer needs to forecast is when the claim will be paid.

However, for most property and liability insurance policies, the claim size is as much an unknown as is the time when the claim will be made. This means that insurers need to forecast the size of the payment that it will eventually disburse to the insured. The longer the time before the amount is paid, the harder it is for the insurer to forecast the size of payment.

For example, it is more difficult for an insurer to predict the severity of claims ten years in the future than it is to predict the severity of claims six months in the future. Because the level of uncertainty is much greater for certain liability lines of insurance (long-tail lines) than for other liability lines and for property lines of insurance (short-tail lines), the risk of mispricing the insurance policy is greater. Consequently, everything else being equal, insurers generally price long-tail line insurance policies higher than short-tail lines. See the exhibit "What Is an Ideally Insurable Risk?."

What Is an Ideally Insurable Risk?

Insurance is not appropriate for all risks. To determine whether a risk is insurable, insurers analyze it against these six characteristics of an ideally insurable risk:

- A sufficiently large quantity of similar people or objects may be subject to a loss.
- Loss would be fortuitous (accidental) and is not controlled by the insured.
- Loss would not affect a large number of insureds simultaneously (be catastrophic).
- Time, location, and extent of a loss can be determined.
- The amount of an expected loss can be predicted.
- The amount of an expected loss is economically feasible for the insurer to absorb relative to what it charges for coverage of the risk.

No risk meets all of these criteria. However, an insurer generally will only insure a risk that meets most of them.

[OV08855]

CHARACTERISTICS OF AN IDEALLY INSURABLE LOSS EXPOSURE

Private insurers insure some, but not all, loss exposures. Insurable loss exposures ideally have certain characteristics. Although most insured loss exposures do not completely meet all of these criteria, the criteria can be useful to an insurer when deciding whether to offer new coverages or whether to continue offering existing coverages.

The six characteristics of an ideally insurable loss exposure are summarized in the exhibit. See the exhibit "Six Characteristics of an Ideally Insurable Loss Exposure."

Six Characteristics of an Ideally Insurable Loss Exposure

1. Pure risk—involves pure risk, not speculative risk
2. Fortuitous losses—subject to fortuitous loss from the insured's standpoint
3. Definite and measurable—subject to losses that are definite in time, cause, and location and that are measurable
4. Large number of similar exposure units—one of a large number of similar exposure units
5. Independent and not catastrophic—not subject to a loss that would simultaneously affect many other similar loss exposures; not catastrophic
6. Affordable—premiums are economically feasible

[DA02747]

Pure Risk

The first ideal characteristic of an insurable loss exposure is that the loss exposure should be associated with pure risk, not speculative risk. Unlike many other risk financing measures, such as hedging, insurance is not designed to finance speculative risks. See the exhibit "Industry Language: Private."

Industry Language: Private

Insurance organizations that are not owned or operated by federal or state governments are generally referred to as private insurers. The insurance products they sell are sold in the private insurance market. The term "private" may be confusing because some insurers are publicly traded stock organizations (owned by the public), not privately owned. Furthermore, the markets they compete in are open to all consumers, not restricted to certain parties. When federal or state governments compete with private insurers, they compete in the private insurance market. When federal or state governments are the only source of an insurance product, then no private market exists.

[DA02748]

One purpose of insurance is to indemnify the insured for the loss, not to enable the insured to profit from the loss. Indemnification is the process of restoring an individual or organization to a pre-loss financial condition. If the loss exposure has the possibility of gain, the insurance premium the insurer would need to charge would offset the potential gain. See the exhibit "Industry Language: Insurability."

Industry Language: Insurability

Although a particular loss exposure has the characteristics of a commercially insurable loss exposure, an insurer still may prefer not to sell an insurance policy for it. This may be the result of externally or internally imposed constraints placed on the insurer or simply because the insurer prefers not to cover those types of exposures. Internal constraints may be a lack of expertise or resources to offer insurance coverages in that particular line of business. External constraints include state regulation.

State laws regulate the types of insurance that can be written in each state and prescribe the minimum capital and surplus an admitted insurer must have to transact business. Some financial requirements are so high that an insurer might forgo writing a type of business it would otherwise prefer to include in its portfolio. In addition, state insurance departments regulate forms and rates for some types of coverage, which could involve substantial paperwork, making it relatively unattractive for an insurer to offer those coverages. Finally, regulatory approval is often a slow process that constrains insurers' ability to provide new products and services because various marketing practices are also regulated, and some activities are prohibited.

[DA02749]

For example, assume a gambling opportunity involves a roulette wheel that has only red and black numbers (50 percent red and 50 percent black; no green), a mandatory $5 bet, and an insurer that is willing to insure a red number outcome. Consider two scenarios:

- The insurer does not charge a premium—If a roulette player can place a bet on black, knowing that if the result is black, he or she will win $5.00, and if the result is red, an insurer will refund the bet, the player can gain without any risk of loss. This is arbitrage (or risk-free) profits. The roulette player would win $5 with a black number and $0 with a red number (the $5 bet is refunded by the insurer). In the long run, the roulette player can expect to win $2.50 ([$5 × .50] + [$0 × .50] = $2.50) every spin of the roulette wheel, without ever losing.
- The insurer charges an appropriate premium—The insurer can expect to lose $2.50 every spin of the roulette wheel. If the outcome is a black number (which happens 50 percent of the time), the insurer loses nothing and if the outcome is a red number, the insurer loses $5.00. This gives an expected value of a loss of $2.50 ([$5 × .50] + [$0 × .50] = $2.50). If the insurer has no expenses, makes no profit, and has no risk charges, then the premium it would charge would be $2.50 per spin (the expected loss). Therefore, the minimum premium an insurer would have to charge offsets any potential gain the insured could have earned from the speculative risk.

Although this example is not realistic, it demonstrates that to insure the downside in a speculative risk, an insurer would have to charge a premium that removed all the expected profits for the insured. In addition, to cover an insurer's expenses, risk charges, and profitability, the minimum premium an insurer would have to charge more than offsets any expected profits. This in turn removes the incentive for the insured to buy the insurance.

Furthermore, limiting insurance coverage only to pure risks helps reduce the complexity of the loss exposures insured by the policy and therefore reduces the difficulty in analyzing the loss exposures during the underwriting process. Insuring speculative risks would require the underwriter to calculate all the possible bad outcomes that would involve the claims against the insurer in order to accurately price the insurance policy. The additional work required in the underwriting process would add to the cost of insurance for all policyholders.

Fortuitous

The second characteristic of an ideally insurable loss exposure is that the loss associated with the loss exposure should be a **fortuitous loss** from the insured's standpoint.

Fortuitous loss

A loss that is accidental and unexpected.

Some causes of loss may be fortuitous only from one point of view. For example, vandalism and theft are intentional (and therefore not fortuitous) acts

from the perspective of the individual or organization committing the acts. However, they are fortuitous (and insurable) from the victim's standpoint because they were not intended or expected by the victim.

Other causes of loss are fortuitous regardless of the perspective from which they are examined. For example, naturally occurring events such as windstorms, hail, or lightning are fortuitous events whether one is the insurer, the insured, or any third party associated with the loss exposure.

If the insured has some control over whether or when a loss will occur, the insurer is at a disadvantage because the insured might have an incentive to cause a loss (moral hazard). Also, if losses are not fortuitous, the insurer cannot calculate an appropriate premium because the chance of loss could increase as soon as the policy is issued.

Ideally, private insurance is suitable for situations in which there is reasonable uncertainty about the probability or timing of a loss without the threat of a moral or morale hazard. If policyholders were compensated for losses they cause, they may be encouraged to generate losses for property they no longer wish to own. This could undermine the pricing structure for insurance and increase insurance premiums for all policyholders.

Definite and Measurable

The third characteristic of an ideally insurable loss exposure is that the loss exposure is subject to losses that are definite in time, cause, and location and that are measurable.

Definite

For a loss exposure to be definite in time, cause, and location, the insurer must be able to determine the event (or series of events) that led up to the loss, when that event or series of events occurred, and where it occurred.

All insurance policies have a policy period that specifies the precise dates and times of coverage. A typical property-casualty policy has a policy period ranging from six months to one year. Although other periods may be specified, shorter or longer policy periods are not as common. As an example, the policy period for a homeowners policy is shown in the exhibit. In this policy, the policy period appears in the declarations. See the exhibit "Homeowners Policy Declarations."

The insurer usually needs to be able to determine that the event occurred during the policy period. For some events, this may be a difficult process; insurers are reluctant to insure such events. For example, suppose an insurer was considering insuring a gas station against environmental pollution. A definite loss would be a fire that ruptured an underground gas tank if the gasoline that was in the tank leaked into the surrounding soil and caused a large environmental pollution loss.

Homeowners Policy Declarations

Homeowners Policy Declarations

POLICYHOLDER: (Named Insured)	David M. and Joan G. Smith 216 Brookside Drive Anytown, USA 40000	**POLICY NUMBER:**	296 H 578661
POLICY PERIOD:	**Inception:** March 30, 20X1 **Expiration:** March 30, 20X2	**Policy period begins 12:01 A.M. standard time at the residence premises.**	

A less definite loss might be an inspector's discovery of a high concentration of gasoline in the soil of an adjacent property that has been caused by a leaking underground gas tank. It is impossible to pinpoint the exact date or the cause of the leak. The leak could have been occurring for months or even years. Therefore, it may be impossible to determine a precise cause of loss or whether the event occurred during the policy period. Because they are not definite, these types of loss exposures are not ideally insurable.

Measurable

As well as being definite, the loss needs to be measurable in order to be ideally insurable. Insurers cannot determine an appropriate premium if they cannot measure the frequency or severity of the potential losses. As discussed, when evaluating a loss exposure, an insurance professional needs to be able to quantify both the frequency and severity of potential losses to determine what future losses may be.

The fact that the future losses may be immeasurable creates a substantial amount of uncertainty for the insured and the insurer. Insurers are reluctant to insure losses that are highly uncertain without receiving substantial compensation (high premiums) from the insured. In summary, if a loss cannot be defined in time or measured, it would be extremely difficult for an insurer to write a policy that specifies what claims to pay and how much to pay for them.

If multiple insurance policies issued by different insurers were issued to cover the loss exposure at various renewals, it would be difficult to determine which policy applied and which insurer was responsible for the loss. At a minimum, the costs of adjusting losses would increase and the likelihood of litigation would be greatly increased.

Large Number of Similar Exposure Units

The fourth characteristic of an ideally insurable loss exposure is that the loss exposure is one of a large number of similar exposure units. Some common loss exposures that satisfy this requirement include homes, offices, and automobiles. There are two risk transfer functions that insurance can provide—cross-sectional and intertemporal risk transfer. See the exhibit "Industry Language: Loss Exposure, Exposure Units, Exposures."

Industry Language: Loss Exposure, Exposure Units, Exposures

The term "loss exposure" can be defined as any condition or situation that presents a possibility of loss, whether or not an actual loss occurs. An exposure unit is defined as a fundamental measure of the loss exposure assumed by an insurer. The terms "exposure" and "exposure unit" are often used interchangeably by insurance professionals. However, this practice can lead to confusion as to whether the individual is referring to loss exposures or exposure units.

A loss exposure may be made up of multiple exposure units. For example, Henry may own a $300,000 house (a property loss exposure). Similarly, Alison may own a $500,000 house (also a property loss exposure). From each insured's point of view, these are single loss exposures. To the insurer, they are not identical exposure units, because one house is more valuable than the other. The insurer may use $100,000 as a single exposure unit. Therefore, Henry's house is equivalent to three exposure units, and Alison's house is equivalent to five exposure units. The three exposure units that Henry's house comprises are not independent exposure units, but those three exposure units are independent of the five exposure units that Alison's house comprises. The insurer can increase the number of independent exposure units ($100,000 units) it insures by increasing the number of independent loss exposures (houses) it insures.

[DA02751]

Cross-Sectional Risk Transfer

The most common risk transfer function that insurance provides is the spreading of risk across a large number of similar exposure units within the same period. This is commonly referred to as cross-sectional risk transfer, and it requires a large number of similar loss exposures. Cross-sectional risk transfer is achieved through pooling, which takes advantage of the law of large numbers. The law of large numbers has three criteria:

- The events have occurred in the past under substantially identical conditions and have resulted from unchanging, basic causal forces.
- The events can be expected to occur in the future under the same unchanging conditions.
- The events have been, and will continue to be, independent and sufficiently numerous.

The third criterion ensures that the loss exposures are numerous enough for the insurer to pool a large number of exposure units. This large pool enables the insurer to more accurately project losses and determine appropriate premiums because loss statistics can be maintained over time and losses for similar exposure units can be projected with a higher degree of accuracy.

Intertemporal Risk Transfer

Another risk transfer function insurance can provide is the spreading of risk through time, known as intertemporal risk transfer. This function does not require a large number of similar exposure units; therefore, insurers are willing to insure unique loss exposures where there is little or no pooling of similar exposure units.

Independent and Not Catastrophic

The fifth characteristic of an ideally insurable loss exposure is that the loss exposure is not subject to a loss that would simultaneously affect many other similar loss exposures (that is, the loss exposure would be independent) and that the loss exposure would not be catastrophic to the insurer. This characteristic is similar to the characteristic of a large number of similar exposure units in that they are both tied to the third criterion of the law of large numbers. The difference is that this characteristic focuses on the independence of the loss exposures, not their number and similarity.

Independent

For insurers to utilize pooling most effectively, the insured exposure units need to be independent. Although pooling will work to some degree if the exposure units are correlated (not independent), it will not be as effective. An example of correlated loss exposures would be two adjacent houses. Given the proximity of the houses to each other, certain causes of loss, such as a tornado, hurricane, or fire, could affect both houses at the same time. The fact that one of the houses is on fire does not mean the other house will catch fire, but the probability of the second house catching fire is much higher. Therefore, these two loss exposures are correlated.

Not Catastrophic

Insurance operates economically because many insureds pay premiums that are small relative to the cost of the potential losses they could each incur. The cost can stay relatively small because insurers project that they will incur far fewer losses than they have loss exposures. However, if a large number of insureds who are covered for the same type of loss were to incur losses at the same time, the insurance mechanism would not operate economically and losses to the insurer could be catastrophic.

Following Hurricane Andrew in 1992 (and reinforced by Hurricane Katrina in 2005), property-casualty insurers are much more aware of the catastrophic risk that a correlated portfolio of insured loss exposures presents. Geographic diversification, line of business diversification, and reinsurance can help insurers both to improve the independence of their insured loss exposures and to minimize their catastrophic exposure.

In addition to correlated losses, single events or a series of events can also present catastrophic risk to an insurer. Consequently, an insurer should not insure any single loss exposure that would pose a serious financial hardship if a loss occurred.

For example, a small insurer should not insure a multimillion dollar property, such as an oil refinery. Although the loss exposure may be independent of the other properties the insurer has chosen to insure, a loss at such a single location may cause the insurer severe financial difficulty.

Economically Feasible Premium

The final characteristic of an ideally insurable loss exposure is that the insurer is able to charge an economically feasible premium—one that the insured can afford to pay. Of all the characteristics of an ideally insurable loss exposure, this is probably the most important. Supply and demand of insurance demonstrate that if an insurer cannot provide the insurance product at a reasonable premium, there will be no demand. The first five characteristics are designed to ensure that the insurer can provide insurance at a reasonable premium.

Loss exposures involving only small losses, as well as those involving a high probability of loss, are generally considered uninsurable. Providing insurance to cover small losses may not make economic sense when its expense exceeds the amount of potential losses. It also may not make economic sense to insure losses that are almost certain to occur. The expense of providing insurance increases with the frequency of claims because insurers incur some of their largest expenses settling insured claims. In such a situation, the premium would probably be as high as or higher than the potential loss. To maintain the balance of supply and demand, it is important that the insurance mechanism establish a pricing structure that adequately supports the expenses for providing coverage at a price (premium) appropriate for the purchaser when compared with the potential loss.

INSURABILITY OF COMMERCIAL LOSS EXPOSURES

Evaluating a sampling of commercial loss exposures against the six characteristics of an ideally insurable loss exposure demonstrates why insurers may choose to insure some loss exposures and not others. The same method of analyzing insurability can be applied to any other loss exposures.

The commercial loss exposures examined are property (caused by fire, windstorm, and flood), liability (caused by premises and operations liability and products liability), personnel (caused by death and retirement), and net income (caused by property and liability losses).

Property

All organizations have property loss exposures related to their business operations. Some organizations may rely more on real property and others may rely more on personal property, but all rely on property to some extent. This section focuses on a real property loss exposure—the building that houses an organization's main operations—and on three different causes of loss: fire, windstorm, and flood.

A review of how and why the property loss exposure generally meets the ideally insurable criteria reveals that this widely insured loss exposure may not always meet these criteria. The exhibit summarizes whether the building that houses an organization's main operations meets the six ideally insurable characteristics for fire, windstorm, and flood. See the exhibit "Ideally Insurable Characteristics: Commercial Property Loss Exposures."

Ideally Insurable Characteristics: Commercial Property Loss Exposures

	Fire	Windstorm	Flood
Pure risk	Yes (except for arson-for-profit)	Yes	Yes
Fortuitous	Yes (except for arson-for-profit)	Yes	Yes
Definite and measurable	Yes	Yes	Yes
Large number of similar exposure units	Depends on property location, property type, and use	Depends on property location, property type, and use	Depends on property location, property type, and use
Independent and not catastrophic	Yes	Can be catastrophic	Can be catastrophic
Premiums are economically feasible	Yes	Depends on location	Depends on location

[DA02753]

Fire

For most property loss exposures, the main underwriting criteria focus on the threat of loss by fire. As shown in the exhibit, commercial property loss exposures associated with fire generally meet all six characteristics.

Fire loss to a building is a pure risk rather than a speculative risk because it generally involves only the possibility of loss and no possibility of gain. An exception would be arson-for-profit. For example, an organization might own an obsolete, run-down building in a prime location whose land is worth more without the building.

In an arson-for-profit, the organization would deliberately burn down the building, both to claim on the insurance and to increase the value of the land. Insurance underwriters guard against knowingly providing insurance for such obviously potential moral hazards. Moreover, insurers use claim investigation techniques to detect arson-for-profit claims so that such claims can be lawfully denied. Insurance policies can be modified to limit losses for these exceptions.

An accidental fire loss would be fortuitous from the perspective of both parties. However, not all fires are accidents. Again, arson committed by the insured (arson-for-profit) is the exception because it is intentional.

Similarly, other intentional fires may not be started by the insured, such as fires resulting from riots or civil commotion. As long as the intentional fire is not started by the insured, it is fortuitous from the perspective of both the insurer and insured.

An insurer can project aggregate claims from fortuitous fire losses with reasonable confidence, based on past experience. However, it is not as easy to project the number and extent of claims that are not fortuitous. So although fires generally meet the fortuitous criteria, the fact that they can be deliberately set detracts from their being considered an ideally insurable loss exposure.

Property fires are typically definite and measurable. Occasionally, pinpointing the time of an unobserved property fire is difficult, such as when the fire that destroys an office building occurs over a weekend. Because fire insurance is usually written for a one-year policy period, loss timing becomes critical only if the loss occurs near the policy's expiration date and a question exists about whether the loss occurred during the policy period. In some cases, continuous coverage exists (such as a renewal policy), but the question remains as to which policy was in force at the time of the loss.

Knowing the value of a building or its contents is critical in measuring the amount of a fire loss. Such value can be measured in different ways. It is often necessary to specify—before a loss occurs—whether the insured loss will be the amount necessary to repair or replace the loss with like kind and quality, or whether the insured loss will be a depreciated actual cash value.

Some insurance provides coverage for additional living expenses, fair rental value, or other financial losses resulting from a building that cannot be used.

These losses are somewhat more difficult to measure because they depend on an estimate of what an insured's financial position would have been had the event not occurred.

Therefore, with respect to being definite and measurable, fire loss exposures are usually ideally insurable because a fire's occurrence typically is obvious. However, uncertainty about the timing of a fire's occurrence or the value of the property at the time of the loss may make insuring such a fire loss less than ideal.

Many properties present a large number of similar loss exposures for an insurer. For example, many retail organizations are located in malls, which tend to be rather homogenous. However, many organizations have unique locations, or perform a unique function at their locations, making pooling by the insurer very difficult. Whether a specific commercial property location meets this ideally insurable criterion depends on the location, type, and usage of the property.

The characteristic of being independent and not catastrophic applies to the insurer's perspective, based on its portfolio of insurance policies. The insurer needs to consider whether a loss exposure under consideration for insurance coverage could be subject to a loss that would simultaneously affect many other similar insured loss exposures.

For example, a retail shop in an enclosed mall would not be an independent loss exposure if its insurer covered other retail shops in the same mall. A large fire at the mall could simultaneously affect all of the shops, which could be catastrophic if a single insurer had insured most or all of the shops. If an insurer is insuring only one retail shop in the mall, the loss exposure would be independent of the other loss exposures it has chosen to insure and a fire loss would not be catastrophic.

Fires at an organization's main location tend to be low-frequency, high-severity (from the insured's perspective) events that insureds could not usually recover from financially without insurance. Although the frequency of fire loss to any one specific building is usually too small for insurers to project with confidence, aggregate fire losses generate credible statistical information on which insurance rates can be based. Because fires tend to be low-frequency events, and because a fire loss exposure typically exhibits most or all of the first five ideally insurable characteristics, this cause of loss is usually economically feasible to insure.

Windstorm

As shown in the previous exhibit, many of the ideally insurable characteristics that are met by fire are also met by windstorm. Windstorm damage to commercial property loss exposures is generally a pure risk subject to fortuitous losses that are definite and measurable. However, it may not meet the last three ideally insurable characteristics. This drastically changes how some insurers view the insurability of windstorm loss.

As with fire, windstorm can be insured on many similar buildings. However, identical buildings at different locations can face substantially different windstorm exposure. With fire, property type and use are significant factors in determining if there are a large number of similar exposure units. With windstorm, those factors are still important, but not as important as location.

Hurricanes and tornadoes, the most common windstorms, are geographically concentrated, making pooling a large number of similar, yet independent loss exposures more difficult. The exhibit shows the geographic regions of the United States that have the highest exposure to hurricane activity. See the exhibit "Hurricane Risk Map."

Hurricane Risk Map

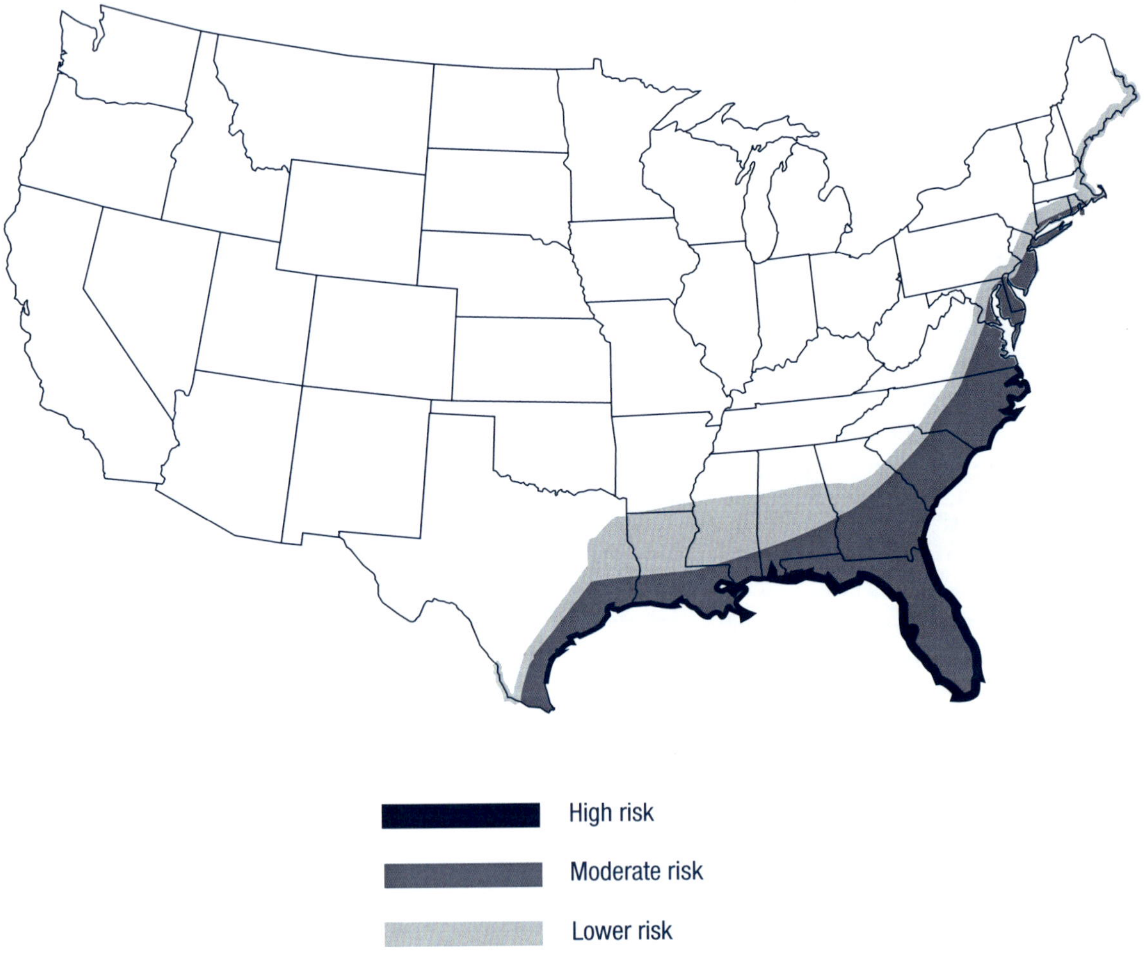

High risk

Moderate risk

Lower risk

[DA02754]

Different buildings in the same geographic area are not independently exposed to windstorm loss. Unlike fire, a single windstorm is likely to damage many buildings; for example, hurricanes generally affect a widespread geographic area. Although tornadoes are more concentrated, they can still cause catastrophic damage to all property in a limited area, sometimes wiping out an entire community.

For small insurers in geographic locations that are exposed to hurricane or tornado activity, windstorm can therefore be catastrophic. Adverse selection (when high-risk individuals or organizations are more likely to demand insurance than low-risk individuals or organizations) is present because property owners in windstorm-prone areas are more likely to demand insurance.

The catastrophic nature of some windstorms—notably hurricanes—makes windstorm insurance difficult to underwrite, especially for insurers with a high volume of business in a limited geographic area. Appropriate rating is complicated by the fact that premium and loss calculations are performed in one-year periods, whereas weather cycles are much longer.

Advances in catastrophe modeling have increased the accuracy of predicting storm damage. These models indicate that, in high-risk areas, higher premiums are typically necessary to offset the insurer's predicted losses.

As catastrophe modeling improves, it may lead to economically infeasible premiums for some insureds. Windstorm does not meet as many of the ideal characteristics of an insurable loss exposure as does fire. Although common commercial property insurance policies have previously tended to cover windstorm, this has been changing in states where the probability of hurricane activity is highest. For example, insurers in some coastal states such as Florida, Texas, and South Carolina are able to sell homeowners insurance policies in the highest-risk coastal regions that do not cover windstorm damage. Homeowners can obtain coverage for windstorm damage through state-run windstorm pools.

Flood

Flood damage to property at fixed locations has traditionally been considered uninsurable by private insurers, even for property that was insured against fire and windstorm losses. In contrast, flood insurance is readily available for autos and other personal property that can easily be moved in order to avoid damage.

Similar to windstorm, flood generally involves pure risk and losses that are fortuitous, definite, and measurable. Whether property is part of a large number of similar loss exposures suitable for pooling depends on the location, property type, and use.

The main issue is that the flood cause of loss is geographically concentrated, so loss exposures tend not to be independent, and losses could be catastrophic from the insurer's perspective. As a result of the potentially catastrophic losses

resulting from floods, flood loss premiums are high and flood can be economically unfeasible to insure for some organizations.

Although some uncertainty exists about whether a flood will occur at a particular location in a particular year, in many areas the long-term probability of flood can be forecast. Property located within a 10-year, 20-year, or 100-year flood plain is almost certainly exposed to loss. Although that does not mean a flood occurs at specified intervals (a 100-year flood could occur in two consecutive years), on average, a flood can be expected with certain regularity.

Premiums in these flood zones would be too high for most insureds to pay without government assistance. Flood insurance is now available under the National Flood Insurance Program (NFIP). The federal government has also devoted engineering resources to evaluating flood zones, and these evaluations have facilitated underwriting flood insurance by private insurers. Some private insurers are willing to insure commercial properties against flood loss if they are located outside flood-prone areas as determined by the federal government. See the exhibit "Hurricane Damage: Windstorm or Flood?."

Hurricane Damage: Windstorm or Flood?

For commercial properties with windstorm coverage, distinguishing between covered windstorm damage and not-covered flood damage can be difficult because a storm may produce both causes of loss. For example, hurricanes produce a phenomenon known as storm surge, in which ocean waves are larger and ocean levels rise. Flooding caused by storm surge is not covered by property insurance policies that exclude flood coverage. Damage caused by flood must then be covered by separate policies sold by the National Flood Insurance Program. Ongoing litigation in those states severely affected by Hurricane Katrina in 2005 is challenging the validity of the flood exclusion in many property policies where it has been difficult to discern the cause of loss because of the extent of the damage. For example, consider the properties for which all that remained of a structure was a concrete slab. Was it wind or flood that caused the complete destruction of the building and contents?

[DA02755]

Liability

The second category of loss exposures is liability loss exposures. The frequency and severity of liability losses associated with these exposures vary widely, depending on factors such as the organizations' operations and product lines and on the legal environment in which the organizations operate. This section focuses on commercial liability loss exposures stemming from two sources of risk faced by many organizations—premises and operations liability and products liability. The exhibit summarizes how well these two categories of liability loss exposures meet the six characteristics of an ideally insurable loss exposure. See the exhibit "Ideally Insurable Characteristics: Commercial Liability Loss Exposures."

Ideally Insurable Characteristics: Commercial Liability Loss Exposures

	Premises and Operations Liability	Products Liability
Pure risk	Yes	Yes
Fortuitous	Yes	Yes
Definite and measurable	Yes	Depends on product
Large number of similar exposure units	Yes	Depends on product
Independent and not catastrophic	Yes	Can be catastrophic
Premiums are economically feasible	Yes	Depends on product

[DA02757]

Premises and Operations Liability

The premises and operations liability loss exposure is the possibility that an organization will be held liable because of injury or damage from either of two causes:

- An accident occurring on premises owned or rented by the organization
- An accident occurring away from such premises, but only if it arises out of the organization's ongoing operations

Examples of accidents that would be classified as premises or operations liability loss exposures include these:

- A customer's bodily injury resulting from a slip-and-fall in ice, snow, or wet conditions at the insured's premises
- A visitor's bodily injury or property damage resulting from the insured's failure to provide sufficient premises security

Premises and operations liability loss exposures often exhibit all the characteristics of an ideally insurable loss exposure. The loss exposures involve pure risk and generate fortuitous losses that are definite in time, cause, and location and are measurable. Some organizations are more exposed to premises and operations liability loss exposures than others.

For example, retail stores have a large volume of customers visiting their premises relative to other types of organizations, such as manufacturers. Therefore, retail stores are more likely to see a higher frequency of liability claims from customers.

Given the large number of retail stores in the U.S., the premises and operations liability loss exposure is one of a large number of similar exposures. Each loss would be independent and not catastrophic, and premiums should be economically feasible because all the other five characteristics are met.

Products Liability

Products liability loss exposures arise out of injury or damage that results from defective or inherently dangerous products. Unlike premises and operations liability loss exposures, not all products liability loss exposures exhibit all the characteristics of an ideally insurable loss exposure. Although they involve pure risk and fortuitous losses, the losses are not necessarily definite in cause.

For example, the cause of a person's injury is not always definite. There could be several potential causes, only one of which is the insured's product. The loss may also not be measurable. For example, it may be difficult to measure the monetary value of an injury. If the product has been widely distributed, then the loss may simultaneously affect many individuals or organizations. Therefore, the loss could be catastrophic in terms of the number of claims. As a result, some products may not be economically feasible to insure.

Personnel

The third category of loss exposures is personnel loss exposures. A personnel loss exposure is a condition that presents the possibility of loss caused by a key person's death, disability, retirement, or resignation that deprives an organization of that person's special skill or knowledge that cannot be readily replaced. The frequency and severity of personnel losses vary widely by organization and industry. In general, personnel losses are fairly infrequent, but their severity will depend on the personnel involved.

The more valuable the key person is to the organization, the more severe the loss. Unlike property, liability, and net income loss exposures, personnel loss exposures are generally not insured through property-casualty insurers. Personnel loss exposures resulting from the death of a key person can be insured by employer-owned life insurance policies, but the remaining causes of loss are often uninsurable. This section focuses on two causes of personnel losses—death and retirement. The exhibit summarizes how well personnel loss exposures associated with these two causes of loss meet the six characteristics of an ideally insurable loss exposure. See the exhibit "Ideally Insurable Characteristics: Commercial Personnel Loss Exposures."

Death

Unless a disaster occurs, an organization's losses from death are of low frequency, with the loss severity depending on the employee's value to the organization. Because of the low frequency of employee deaths in many organizations, it is difficult to predict their number over a given period with much accuracy.

Ideally Insurable Characteristics: Commercial Personnel Loss Exposures

	Death	Retirement
Pure risk	Yes	Yes
Fortuitous	Yes	Depends on circumstances and personnel involved
Definite and measurable	Depends on personnel involved	Depends on personnel involved
Large number of similar exposure units	Depends on personnel involved	Depends on personnel involved
Independent and not catastrophic	Yes	Yes
Premiums are economically feasible	Yes	N/A

[DA02758]

Personnel loss exposures associated with death generally exhibit the six characteristics of an ideally insurable loss exposure. The loss exposure involves pure risk that is fortuitous, independent, and not catastrophic, and that is usually economically feasible to insure. The two characteristics that death may not meet are that losses are definite and measurable and that they are among a large number of similar exposure units. Although the death of a key employee is typically definite in time, cause, and location, it may be difficult to measure the actual loss to the organization.

Personnel losses are often difficult to quantify because a single employee's value to an organization may be incalculable. Many organizations have hundreds or thousands of employees. This can make it difficult to quantify their number of key employees. In some industries, qualified employees are difficult to find and replace. For example, very few individuals in the world are experts in oil location and extraction. In these cases, there are not a large number of similar exposure units to create an ideally insurable loss exposure.

Retirement

Although death often occurs suddenly, retirement is usually planned. Therefore, most personnel losses resulting from retirement can be handled with proper planning by the organization. However, sudden retirements can cause severe personnel losses. The personnel loss exposures associated with retirement involve pure risk; are definite in time, cause, and location (although they may be hard to measure); may not be one of a large number of similar loss exposures; and are generally independent and not catastrophic.

The characteristics that retirement does not meet are that the loss may not be fortuitous and it may not be economically feasible to insure.

Organizations can influence key employees' retirement decisions through a variety of methods. For example, benefits such as early retirement packages may induce key employees to retire. Alternatively, organizations may lose key employees to retirement because of poor work conditions or poor compensation packages. Therefore, a personnel loss resulting from a key employee's retirement may not be fortuitous, from the organization's perspective.

Because it is not possible to purchase retirement insurance on key employees to compensate the organization if they retire, it is impossible to determine whether premiums are economically feasible. Given that a loss may not be fortuitous, premiums for such a product would have to account for the moral hazard and adverse selection that would exist in the market, making premiums less likely to be affordable.

Net Income

The fourth category of loss exposures is net income loss exposures. Net income is the difference between an organization's total revenues and its total expenses (including taxes). In a broad sense, a net income loss could involve any decrease in net income an organization incurs, for whatever reason. Net income can be higher or lower than expected as a result of either the business environment or fortuitous events (such as property, liability, or personnel losses).

Net income losses caused by the business environment clearly do not meet the first characteristic of the loss exposure involving pure risk. The remainder of this section therefore focuses on net income loss exposures associated with two causes of loss that are pure risks—property losses and liability losses. The exhibit summarizes how well net income loss exposures associated with property and liability causes of loss exhibit the six characteristics of an ideally insurable loss exposure. See the exhibit "Ideally Insurable Characteristics: Commercial Net Income Loss Exposures."

Net Income Loss Associated With Property Losses

Net income losses stemming from property losses result from physical damage to property (either property the organization owns or property of others on which the organization depends) that either prevents the organization from operating or that reduces its capacity to operate. Net income losses associated with property losses are insured by a variety of business income insurance coverages.

Net income loss exposures associated with property losses exhibit almost all the characteristics of an ideally insurable loss exposure. The net income loss exposure associated with the property cause of loss involves pure risk, with

Ideally Insurable Characteristics: Commercial Net Income Loss Exposures

	Net income loss associated with property losses	Net income loss associated with liability losses
Pure risk	Yes	Yes
Fortuitous	Yes	Yes
Definite and measurable	Yes	May not be definite
Large number of similar exposure units	Yes	Yes
Independent and not catastrophic	May be catastrophic	Yes
Premiums are economically feasible	Yes	N/A

[DA02759]

losses that are fortuitous, definite and measurable, one of a large number of similar exposure units, and economically feasible to insure.

Net income losses may not be independent and can be catastrophic if the property losses they are associated with were caused by catastrophic causes of loss such as a windstorm. A substantial portion of insured losses following hurricanes, such as Hurricane Katrina in 2005, are business income losses stemming from the property damage done to businesses in the affected areas.

Net Income Loss Associated With Liability Losses

Unlike the net income losses associated with property losses, there are no standardized insurance products that provide first-party coverage for net income losses stemming from liability losses.[1] The major difference between net income losses stemming from property losses and those stemming from liability losses involves the determination of the time of the loss. For net income losses associated with property losses, insurance coverage is provided until the property has been restored or should have been restored (plus some additional time to return to normal operations). The restoration of the property provides a definite end to the payment of benefits by the insurance policy.

There is no similar end point for net income losses that are associated with liability losses. For example, a restaurant could suffer a net income loss because customers stop frequenting it after it is found liable in a food poisoning case. There is no definite end point in such a case, because there is no definite time when customers will return.

INSURABILITY OF PERSONAL LOSS EXPOSURES

Evaluating a sampling of personal loss exposures against the six characteristics of an ideally insurable loss exposure demonstrates why insurers may choose to insure some loss exposures and decline to insure others.

In general, many of the loss exposures faced by organizations are also faced by individuals. For individuals, these loss exposures can be divided into property, liability, and net income loss exposures. Although individuals do not typically have personnel loss exposures, they do have life, health, and retirement loss exposures that organizations do not face.

Property

An individual's key property loss exposure is typically a residence. Therefore, this section focuses on how the fire, windstorm, and flood causes of loss affect the insurability of that residence. Although all homes are different, they generally can be grouped into classes that face essentially the same loss potential. Individual homes are easier to group together than commercial property exposures, mainly because individual homes all serve the same function. See the exhibit "Ideally Insurable Characteristics: Personal Property Loss Exposures."

Ideally Insurable Characteristics: Personal Property Loss Exposures

	Fire	Windstorm	Flood
Pure risk	Yes (except for arson-for-profit)	Yes	Yes
Fortuitous	Yes (except for arson-for-profit)	Yes	Yes
Definite and measurable	Yes	Yes	Yes
Large number of similar exposure units	Yes	Yes	Yes
Independent and not catastrophic	Yes	Can be catastrophic	Can be catastrophic
Premiums are economically feasible	Yes	Depends on location	Depends on location

[DA02760]

Insurers still must identify buildings with higher-than-normal hazards, guard against arson-for-profit, avoid excessive concentration of loss exposure, ensure adequate diversification of exposures, and carefully establish the insurable value of property subject to loss. The exhibit summarizes whether an individual's residence meets the six ideally insurable characteristics for fire, windstorm, and flood.

The property loss exposures associated with fire are ideally suited to insurability because the loss exposure involves a pure risk, a large number of similar, yet independent exposure units, and losses that are fortuitous, definite, measurable, and not catastrophic. These characteristics make premiums economically feasible. However, windstorm and flood losses can be catastrophic and, depending on the location of the residence, may not be economically feasible to insure.

Liability

The exhibit titled "Ideally Insurable Characteristics: Personal Liability Loss Exposures" focuses on liability loss exposures stemming from two common sources of risk faced by many individuals: real property ownership (premises) liability loss exposures and automobile liability loss exposures. The exhibit summarizes how well these two categories of liability loss exposures meet the six characteristics of an ideally insurable loss exposure. See the exhibit "Ideally Insurable Characteristics: Personal Liability Loss Exposures."

Ideally Insurable Characteristics: Personal Liability Loss Exposures

	Premises liability	Automobile liability
Pure risk	Yes	Yes
Fortuitous	Yes	Yes
Definite and measurable	Yes	Yes
Large number of similar exposure units	Yes	Yes
Independent and not catastrophic	Yes	Yes
Premiums are economically feasible	Yes	Yes

[DA02761]

The exhibit shows that both premises and automobile liability loss exposures display all six of the characteristics of an ideally insurable loss exposure. Premises liability loss exposures are generally covered by the variety of homeowners insurance policies available, and the automobile liability loss exposures are covered by a personal auto policy.

Net Income

A net income loss could involve any decrease in net income, regardless of the reason. Revenues (such as salary) and expenses (such as housing) can be higher or lower than expected as a result of either the economic environment or fortuitous events such as a property or liability loss.

Net income losses caused by the economic environment clearly do not meet the first characteristic of the loss exposure involving pure risk. For example, rising gas and oil prices would cause an individual's expenses to increase, resulting in a net income loss. However, falling gas and oil prices would result in a net income gain.

Net income losses caused by fortuitous events, such as a fire to an individual's residence, would involve pure risk because there is no potential for the individual to gain.

Life, Health, and Retirement

In addition to the property, liability, and net income loss exposures, individuals and families can face financial difficulty resulting from life, health, and retirement loss exposures. These loss exposures are generally managed through life and health insurance products and also through government programs. See the exhibit "Ideally Insurable Characteristics: Personal Life, Health, and Retirement Loss Exposures."

Ideally Insurable Characteristics: Personal Life, Health, and Retirement Loss Exposures

	Life loss exposures	Health loss exposures	Retirement loss exposures
Pure risk	Yes	Yes	Yes
Fortuitous	Yes (except for suicide)	Depends on cause of loss	Not usually, but may be forced retirement
Definite and measurable	Yes	Depends on cause of loss	Yes
Large number of similar exposure units	Yes	Yes	Yes
Independent and not catastrophic	Yes	Yes	Yes
Premiums are economically feasible	Usually	Usually	N/A

[DA02763]

A variety of causes of loss contribute to the life, health, and retirement personal loss exposures. Although some of these causes of loss are fortuitous, others are under the control of the person involved and therefore make life,

health, and retirement causes of loss subject to moral and morale hazards. The exhibit shows how life, health, and retirement causes of loss meet the characteristics of an ideally insurable loss exposure.

Life Loss Exposures

Although life is not generally considered a loss exposure, the loss of life to premature death is. Premature death is a term used to refer to the death of a person with outstanding financial obligations. These financial obligations, such as children to support or mortgage payments, can result in financial difficulty for the family that depended on the deceased's earnings if they are unable to generate replacement income from other sources.

There are individual circumstances, such as health conditions or hazardous occupations, that may prevent insurers from offering an economically feasible premium. However, for most individuals, life loss exposures satisfy all six of the ideally insurable characteristics.

Health Loss Exposures

Poor health is another personal loss exposure that can create serious financial problems for individuals and families. First, an individual might incur significant medical bills. Without health insurance or significant personal savings, these expenses can cause financial distress or bankruptcy. Second, if a person is unable to work because of poor health or disability, earnings can also be lost, again resulting in financial difficulties.

Similar to the life loss exposures, widely available health insurance appears to indicate that health loss exposures have the ideally insurable characteristics. However, health insurance is subject to adverse selection as well as moral and morale hazard.

Unlike life loss exposures, for which most causes of loss are fortuitous, many causes of loss to health are under some control of the individual involved. Smoking and obesity are examples of health-related causes of loss over which an individual may have some control. These factors have contributed to some of the issues in the health insurance market. The two major issues are availability and affordability of health insurance.

Whereas most Americans obtain health insurance through their employer, those who need to purchase coverage individually often have difficulty obtaining coverage, or obtaining coverage at an economically feasible premium. Furthermore, pre-existing health conditions exacerbate the problem for those shopping for coverage individually. The affordability issue exists for employers as well. Rising healthcare costs are a major concern for both small and large organizations.

Retirement Loss Exposure

The possibility of insufficient income during retirement is another important loss exposure faced by individuals. Although workers are not typically forced to retire, most retire by age sixty-five. If the replacement income generated by Social Security, private retirement plans, and personal savings is not sufficient to cover expenses, financial hardship may result. This situation is compounded by increasing life expectancy, which lengthens the retirement period. If the individual has underestimated the number of years that could be spent in retirement, his or her savings may not be adequate.

Retirement does not usually exhibit the fortuitous characteristic of ideally insurable loss exposures because the individual has control over savings and choice of retirement dates. Consequently, individuals are not able to purchase retirement insurance.

GOVERNMENT INSURANCE PROGRAMS

In some cases, property-casualty insurance for certain loss exposures can be obtained only through government insurance programs. It is therefore important for insurance and risk management professionals to know why government insurance programs exist, how they are structured, and why some are run at the state level while others are federal programs.

Government insurance programs exist to fill unmet needs in the private insurance market, to facilitate compulsory insurance purchases, to provide efficiency in the marketplace, and to accomplish social goals. Government can participate in such programs as an exclusive insurer, as a partner with private insurers, or as a competitor to private insurers. Whether a program involves federal or state government is often a politically motivated decision, but other motivating factors can exist.

Rationale for Government Involvement

The United States, like most developed countries, has a mature private property-casualty insurance market that provides a mechanism for consumers and insurers to interact in the demand and supply of insurance products. Although much of the market is heavily regulated and behaves in a somewhat cyclical manner, in general it functions properly. That is, consumers are able to purchase insurance products they desire for a price determined by the market, and insurers can earn an appropriate rate of return on their capital. In a perfectly functioning market, there is no need for state or federal governments to supply insurance products.

However, private insurance markets do not always function perfectly. Occasionally, insurers are unable or unwilling to supply an insurance product

to consumers at a mutually acceptable price. In addition to market failures, other reasons for government involvement in insurance include these:

- To fill insurance needs unmet by private insurers
- To compel people to buy a particular type of insurance
- To obtain greater efficiency and/or provide convenience to insurance buyers
- To achieve collateral social purposes

Fill Unmet Needs

When private insurers are unable or unwilling to satisfy certain insurance needs, government programs can provide insurance to meet legitimate public demands. By doing this, the government provides protection against loss that would otherwise not be provided.

An example of a government insurance program formed to fulfill an unmet need in the private insurance market is the Terrorism Risk Insurance Program (TRIP), formed by the Terrorism Risk Insurance Act of 2002 (TRIA). The program was intended as a temporary provider of reinsurance for losses caused by terrorism and was designed to run until the end of 2005, when it was assumed that the private insurance market would have developed its own terrorism insurance products.

In December 2005, Congress extended TRIP for two more years, and in December 2007, Congress extended it for seven more years. Although the private market role was increased and the federal share of compensation for losses insured under TRIP was decreased, the private market for terrorism insurance and reinsurance has not been deemed adequate to let TRIA expire as originally anticipated.

Compel Insurance Purchase

Another reason federal and state governments are involved in insurance is to facilitate compulsory insurance purchases. For example, workers compensation insurance has proven to efficiently manage workplace injuries. However, it is possible that some employers would not purchase workers compensation insurance if they were not required to do so.

Because states require employers to purchase this insurance (or provide proof of self-insurance), they must have a mechanism to ensure that workers compensation insurance is available at a reasonable cost. Another example is personal automobile liability insurance. As auto liability coverage is required in almost all states, each state has some type of mechanism in place to provide insurance for those drivers who cannot obtain coverage at a reasonable price in the private market. In the workers compensation and auto liability insurance markets, most consumers obtain coverage through private insurers.

Government programs are necessary to fulfill the needs of those who cannot obtain the required coverage in the private market; they are not required to insure all consumers.

Obtain Efficiency and Provide Convenience

Two related rationales for government involvement in insurance are providing efficiency in the market and convenience to insureds. In economic terms, these two rationales are essentially the same. Providing convenience to insureds, by reducing either the time or the resources they need to expend to obtain the desired insurance coverage, adds to the efficiency of the market.

Legislators often find it is more straightforward to establish government insurance plans for particular purposes than to invite and analyze bids from private insurers and then supervise and regulate the resulting plans. When insurance provided by the government is compulsory, spending money on marketing or paying sales commissions (two large expenses for insurers) is unnecessary. Governments sometimes try to avoid sales costs by setting up their own distribution channels. Alternatively, as is the case with the National Flood Insurance Program (NFIP), they market through established insurance producers who also market other insurance.

Achieve Collateral Social Purpose

The government may participate in insurance to accomplish social goals because insurance is often seen as a social good. By making use of the pooling mechanism, insurance can reduce risk to society. This is beneficial both to society and to the overall economy. In economic terms, these benefits are often referred to as positive externalities.

An issue arises when individuals do not have an incentive to purchase insurance, even though it would benefit society. Individuals and organizations make decisions that are in their best interest. If, for example, an organization conducted a cost-benefit analysis and determined that workers compensation insurance was too expensive, it would not want to purchase the insurance.

However, workers compensation laws encourage injury prevention and injured workers' rehabilitation, a positive externality. Therefore, it falls to the government to provide incentives for the purchase of insurance. It does this through a combination of regulation and provision of insurance at a reasonable price.

Organizations respond to these measures by purchasing insurance, which, as well as benefiting the organization, benefits society. Similarly, the NFIP provides strong incentives to amend and enforce building codes and otherwise reduce the loss exposure of new construction to floods. Without the involvement of the federal government in providing flood insurance, these incentives would be lacking.

Level of Government Involvement

The level of government involvement varies widely and depends on many factors, such as the rationale for government involvement, the availability and willingness of private insurers to partner with the government program, and the level of competition in the market. There are three levels at which the government can participate:

- Exclusive insurer
- Partner with private insurers
- Competitor to private insurers

Exclusive Insurer

The government can be an exclusive insurer either because of law or because no private insurer offers a competing plan. A federal or state government can function as a primary insurer by collecting premiums, providing coverage, and paying all claims and expenses (with the backing of government funds if necessary).

Examples include some state government-run workers compensation programs. Alternatively, the government can function as a reinsurer, either by providing 100 percent reinsurance to private insurers writing a particular coverage (an exclusive reinsurer), or by reinsuring part of the risk in excess of the private insurer's retention. If the government is reinsuring only part of the risk, the program is essentially a partnership with private insurers.

Partner With Private Insurers

Government partnerships with private insurers can develop when private insurers are no longer able to adequately provide coverages they had typically offered previously. Two examples of such partnerships are TRIP and NFIP.

TRIP is an example of a partnership under which the government operates a reinsurance plan, providing reinsurance on specific loss exposures for which private insurers retain only part of the loss. The NFIP is an example of a partnership under which the federal government underwrites the insurance policy but private insurers and insurance producers deliver the policies to consumers. The private insurers take a percentage of the premium as a sales commission and pass the remainder of the premium on to the NFIP.

Both terrorism and flood coverage had previously been offered by private insurers, but the nature of the loss exposures indicated that the insurance industry was not well suited to providing coverage alone. In addition to the TRIP and NFIP partnership structures, other partnerships use a wide variety of structures.

Competitor to Private Insurers

Government involvement may also take the form of operating an insurance plan in direct competition with private insurers. This type of involvement often evolves when the private insurance market has not failed, but is not operating as efficiently as regulators would like. In these instances, the government performs essentially the same marketing, underwriting, actuarial, and claim functions as a private insurer. Examples include the competitive workers compensation funds offered in some states.

Federal Compared With State Programs

The final distinction among government property-casualty insurance programs is whether a state government or the federal government is involved with the program. Because federal government involvement in these types of issues is often a politically motivated decision, predicting what factors will influence federal government involvement is difficult. One motivating factor may be that if the rationale for government involvement extends beyond state boundaries or would affect interstate commerce, the federal government should be running the insurance program. See the exhibit "Examples of Property-Casualty Insurance Offered by the Federal Government."

Examples of Property-Casualty Insurance Offered by the Federal Government

Plan	Characteristics of Government Plan	Relationship to Private Insurance
National Flood Insurance Program	• Meets previously unmet needs for flood insurance. • Serves the social purposes of amending and enforcing building codes and reducing new construction in flood zones.	• Federal government can act as primary insurer. • Federal government can partner with private insurers. Private insurers sell the insurance and pay claims; government reimburses insurers for losses not covered by premiums and investment income.
Terrorism Risk Insurance Program	• Designed to temporarily meet the unmet needs for a backstop to insured terrorism losses. • Serves the social purpose of preventing economic disruptions that market failures in terrorism coverage could have caused.	• Private insurers act as the primary insurer for terrorism coverages. • Federal government temporarily acts as reinsurer for terrorism coverage.
Federal Crop Insurance	• Provides crop insurance at affordable rates to reduce losses that result from unavoidable crop failures. • Covers most crops for perils such as drought, disease, insects, excess rain, and hail.	• Federal government subsidizes and reinsures private insurers; private insurers sell and service the federal crop insurance. • Private insurers also independently offer crop insurance for certain perils.

[DA02764]

This may explain why the federal government is involved with the NFIP and Federal Crop Insurance. However, it would not explain why windstorm and

beach plans are state government-run insurance programs. Hurricanes often cause damage in multiple states. Although hurricane risk is regional, the same can be said for flood risk. In fact, when taking into account storm surge, hurricane risk and flood risk often go together. The first exhibit contains examples of property-casualty insurance plans that involve the federal government, and the second exhibit contains examples of property-casualty insurance plans that involve state governments. See the exhibit "Examples of Property-Casualty Insurance Offered by State Governments."

Examples of Property-Casualty Insurance Offered by State Governments

Plan	Characteristics of Government Plan	Relationship to Private Insurance
Fair Access to Insurance Requirements (FAIR) Plans	Make basic property insurance available to property owners who are otherwise unable to obtain insurance because of their property's location or any other reason.	• Organization varies by state. Typically it is an insurance pool through which private insurers collectively address an unmet need for property insurance on urban properties. • Does not replace normal channels of insurance; is only for consumers who could not obtain coverage in the private market.
Workers Compensation Insurance	Helps employers meet their obligations under state statutes to injured workers.	• Private insurers provide workers compensation insurance. • State government can operate as an exclusive insurer, as a competitor to private insurers, or as a residual market.
Beach and Windstorm Plans	Make property insurance against the windstorm cause of loss available to property owners who are otherwise unable to obtain insurance because of their property's location.	• Organization varies by state: some states are insurance pools of private insurers; other states are ultimately guaranteed with taxpayer funds. • Does not replace normal channels of insurance; is only for consumers who could not obtain coverage in the private market.
Residual Auto Plans	Make compulsory automobile liability coverage available to high-risk drivers who have difficulty purchasing coverage at a reasonable rate in the private market.	• Organization varies by state. Typically it is an insurance pool through which private insurers collectively address an unmet need for compulsory auto liability coverage. • Does not replace normal channels of insurance; is only for consumers who could not obtain coverage in the private market.

[DA02765]

Primary insurer
In reinsurance, the insurer that transfers or cedes all or part of the insurance risk it has assumed to another insurer in a contractual arrangement.

Reinsurer
The insurer that assumes some or all of the potential costs of insured loss exposures of the primary insurer in a reinsurance contractual agreement.

REINSURANCE AND ITS FUNCTIONS

Just as insurance buyers transfer risks that they are unwilling to retain to insurers, insurers can transfer risks that they are unwilling to retain to reinsurers.

Reinsurance, commonly referred to as "insurance for insurers," is the transfer from one insurer (the **primary insurer**) to another (the **reinsurer**) of some or all of the financial consequences of certain loss exposures covered by the primary insurer's policies. The loss exposures transferred, or ceded, by the primary insurer could be associated with a single subject of insurance (such as a building), a single policy, or a group of policies. Additionally, reinsurers perform certain functions.

Reinsurance Basics

An insurer that transfers liability for loss exposures by ceding them to a reinsurer can be referred to as the reinsured, the ceding company, the cedent, the direct insurer, or the primary insurer. Although all these terms are acceptable, "primary insurer" is used to denote the party that cedes loss exposures to a reinsurer.

Reinsurance agreement
Contract between the primary insurer and reinsurer that stipulates the form of reinsurance and the type of accounts to be reinsured.

Reinsurance is transacted through a **reinsurance agreement**, which specifies the terms under which the reinsurance is provided. For example, it may state that the reinsurer must pay a percentage of all the primary insurer's losses for loss exposures subject to the agreement or must reimburse the primary insurer for losses that exceed a specified amount. Additionally, the reinsurance agreement identifies the policy, group of policies, or other categories of insurance that are included in it.

Insurance risk
Uncertainty about the adequacy of insurance premiums to pay losses.

The reinsurer typically does not assume all of the primary insurer's **insurance risk**. The reinsurance agreement usually requires the primary insurer to retain part of its original liability. This retention can be expressed as a percentage of the original amount of insurance or as a dollar amount of loss. The reinsurance agreement does not alter the terms of the underlying (original) insurance policies or the primary insurer's obligations to honor them. See the exhibit "Risk."

Risk

Although "risk" is often defined as uncertainty about the occurrence of a loss, risk has several other meanings that are useful in understanding reinsurance practices. In reinsurance, the term risk often refers to the subject of insurance, such as a building, a policy, a group of policies, or a class of business. Reinsurance practitioners use the term risk in this way and include it in common reinsurance clauses.

[DA05756]

The primary insurer pays a **reinsurance premium** for the protection provided, just as any insured pays a premium for insurance coverage, but because the primary insurer incurs the expenses of issuing the underlying policy, the reinsurer might pay a **ceding commission** to the primary insurer. These expenses consist primarily of commissions paid to producers, premium taxes, and underwriting expenses (such as policy processing and servicing costs, and risk control reports).

Reinsurers may transfer part of the liability they have accepted in reinsurance agreements to other reinsurers. Such an agreement is called a **retrocession**. Under a retrocession, one reinsurer, the **retrocedent**, transfers all or part of the reinsurance risk that it has assumed or will assume to another reinsurer, the **retrocessionaire**. Retrocession is similar to reinsurance except for the parties involved in the agreement. The discussion of reinsurance in the context of a primary insurer-reinsurer relationship also applies to retrocessions.[2]

Reinsurance premium

The consideration paid by the primary insurer to the reinsurer for assuming some or all of the primary insurer's insurance risk.

Ceding commission

An amount paid by the reinsurer to the primary insurer to cover part or all of the primary insurer's policy acquisition expenses.

Retrocession

A reinsurance agreement whereby one reinsurer (the retrocedent) transfers all or part of the reinsurance risk it has assumed or will assume to another reinsurer (the retrocessionaire).

Retrocedent

The reinsurer that transfers or cedes all or part of the insurance risk it has assumed to another reinsurer.

Retrocessionaire

The reinsurer that assumes all or part of the reinsurance risk accepted by another reinsurer.

Reinsurance Functions

Reinsurance helps an insurer achieve several practical business goals, such as insuring large exposures, protecting policyholders' surplus from adverse loss experience, and financing the insurer's growth. The reinsurance that an insurer obtains depends mainly on the constraints or problems the insurer must address to reach its goals. Although some of its uses overlap, reinsurance is a valuable tool that can perform several functions for primary insurers.

For example, a single insurer that sells a $100 million commercial property policy and a $100 million commercial umbrella liability policy to the owners of a high-rise office building may appear to be jeopardizing its financial stability. Insurers who provide billions of dollars of property insurance in wind-prone Florida and earthquake-prone California may seem similarly imperiled. However, such transactions are possible when insurers use reinsurance as a tool to expand their capacity.

No insurer intentionally places itself in a situation in which a catastrophic event could destroy its net worth. Additionally, insurance regulators attempt to prevent insurers from being left in such a position. Reinsurance is one way insurers protect themselves from the financial consequences of insuring others.

Through reinsurance, primary insurers pool or transfer risks, thereby staying within capacity constraints and helping to ensure their solvency. Reinsurance helps to reduce risk for insurers that accept risks transferred by insurance buyers. Therefore, reinsurance also contributes to the social function of insurance by assisting insurers in reducing risk for society.

Review Questions

1. Identify the factors that determine the supply of insurance.
2. Describe two variables that affect an insurer's claim-paying ability (and therefore its capacity to assume new business) and the measurement method used for each.
3. Describe how the following measures indicate an insurer's capacity to assume new business: a. policyholders' surplus and b. premium-to-surplus ratio.
4. Describe two main types of state regulatory constraints that affect the supply of insurance.
5. List the factors that affect the demand for insurance.
6. List three examples of insurance that is commonly required by mandate or statute, resulting in an increased demand for insurance.
7. Identify factors that affect an individual's risk tolerance.
8. Describe how an insurer can increase the demand for its insurance products.
9. Describe the pricing goal of an insurance transaction and how to determine when that goal is accomplished.
10. Describe four key issues that affect the proper functioning of insurance market pricing.
11. Identify two social equity concepts that apply to insurance pricing.
12. Identify the six characteristics of an ideally insurable loss exposure.
13. Explain why insurance is designed to cover pure, not speculative, risk.
14. Identify the factors an insurer must be able to determine for a loss exposure to be definite in time, cause, and location.
15. Describe the types of losses an insurer might consider uninsurable because the premium charged would not be economically feasible.
16. Explain whether the building that houses an organization's main operations would meet the six ideally insurable characteristics for the following causes of loss: a. fire, b. windstorm, and c. flood.
17. Describe two common sources of liability risk faced by many commercial organizations.
18. Compare the insurability of personnel losses caused by an employee's death and those caused by an employee's retirement.
19. Identify common sources of liability risk faced by individuals.
20. For purposes of life insurance, identify individual circumstances that may prevent insurers from offering an economically feasible premium.
21. Explain why retirement does not usually exhibit the fortuitous characteristics of ideally insurable loss exposures.
22. Identify reasons for government involvement in insurance.
23. Explain how the government provides incentives for the purchase of insurance.

24. Identify three levels of governmental participation in governmental insurance programs.
25. Explain how state or federal governmental involvement in insurance programs is determined.
26. Describe the basic purpose of reinsurance.
27. Explain the two ways in which a primary insurer's retention may be expressed.
28. Identify examples of practical business goals that reinsurance allows an insurer to achieve.

Application Questions

1. The terrorist attacks of September 11, 2001, Hurricanes Rita and Katrina, and subsequent events have all had a substantial effect on the economics of the insurance business. a. What do higher prices tell us about the supply of insurance? b. How, if at all, has public attitude toward risk affected the demand for insurance? c. What effect does the combination of a decrease in supply and an increase in demand have on the market equilibrium for insurance?
2. Kathleen, the chief actuary at Sommer Insurance Company, has determined that eye color is a predictor of the frequency of auto accidents. By analyzing thousands of auto accidents, Kathleen has discovered that individuals with light eye color (green or blue) are twice as likely to have an auto accident as individuals with a dark eye color (brown). She wants to use this information in setting Sommer's auto insurance rates. Describe any social equity issues a regulator may raise if Sommer does decide to charge individuals with light-colored eyes higher auto rates.
3. Shore Point Mall is a mall of sixty retail stores located along the Outer Banks of North Carolina's shoreline. Outer Banks Insurance Company, a small local property insurer that insures more than 40 percent of properties in the Outer Banks area, is considering selling a commercial property policy to Shore Point Mall that includes coverage for windstorm damage. Determine whether Shore Point Mall exhibits all six characteristics of an ideally insurable loss exposure for windstorm damage.
4. The Pennsylvania state insurance commissioner is concerned that the state's workers compensation insurance market is not competitive. Only a few insurers are selling workers compensation in Pennsylvania, and rates are high relative to many other comparable states. Describe some of the considerations the insurance commissioner should take into account before recommending that the state become involved in providing workers compensation insurance to employers in Pennsylvania.

SUMMARY

The dynamics of supply and demand are such that the seller (supplier) will not offer a product at a price lower than the minimum possible price. Similarly, the buyer will not pay more than the buyer's maximum possible price. If the seller's minimum possible price is lower than the buyer's maximum possible price, then a price exists between these two boundaries at which the transaction can occur such that both the seller and buyer are satisfied.

The supply of insurance is influenced by capacity to assume new business, investment opportunities, production costs, and the regulatory environment. The demand for insurance is influenced by insurance mandates and regulation, risk tolerance, financial status, real services rendered, and tax incentives. Insurers supply insurance at a price that is greater than the expected value of the losses they cover, and consumers purchase insurance when the premium is less than the cost to them of assuming the risk.

Economic issues affecting insurance pricing include adverse selection, moral and morale hazard, actuarial compared with social equity, and timing.

The six characteristics of an ideally insurable loss exposure include these:

1. Pure risk—Involves pure risk, not speculative risk.
2. Fortuitous losses—Subject to fortuitous loss from the insured's standpoint.
3. Definite and measurable—Subject to losses that are definite in time, cause, and location, and that are measurable.
4. Large number of similar exposure units—One of a large number of similar exposure units.
5. Independent and not catastrophic—Not subject to a loss that would simultaneously affect many other similar loss exposures; loss would not be catastrophic.
6. Affordable—Premiums are economically feasible.

Applying the six characteristics of an ideally insurable loss exposure can help an insurer to decide whether to insure commercial loss exposures that are under consideration.

Applying the six characteristics of an ideally insurable loss exposure can help an insurer to decide whether to insure personal loss exposures that are under consideration.

Government insurance programs may provide insurance coverage when insurers are unwilling or unable to insure loss exposures that do not exhibit ideally insurable characteristics. These government programs vary based on their purpose or rationale, the level of government involvement, and whether the program is run at the state or federal level.

Reinsurance (insurance for insurers) is the transfer of insurance risk from one insurer to another through a contractual agreement under which the reinsurer

agrees, in return for a premium, to indemnify the primary insurer for some or all of the financial consequences of the loss exposures covered by the reinsurance contract. Reinsurance helps an insurer achieve several goals, such as insuring large exposures, protecting policyholders' surplus from adverse loss experience, and financing the insurer's growth.

ASSIGNMENT NOTES

1. Various liability policies cover their insureds against third-party claims for property damage, including resulting loss of use, which encompasses net income loss caused by damage to tangible property.
2. Many of the definitions of terms in this section were adapted from the Reinsurance Association of America's (RAA) Glossary of Terms. The RAA's website is at www.reinsurance.org (accessed March 31, 2010).

Direct Your Learning

10

Legal Principles Supporting the Insurance Mechanism

Educational Objectives

After learning the content of this assignment, you should be able to:

- Describe how the following concepts support the principle of indemnity:
  - Actual cash value
  - Insurable interest
  - Utmost good faith
  - Subrogation

Outline

Principle of Indemnity

Summary

Legal Principles Supporting the Insurance Mechanism

10

PRINCIPLE OF INDEMNITY

Indemnity is an overarching legal principle that supports the insurance mechanism. The duty to indemnify another party is typically detailed in a contract and involves one party agreeing to compensate another party for a loss sustained.

Insurance enables parties covered under an insurance contract to be financially restored to the positions they were in immediately before a covered loss. Stated differently, because of the principle of indemnity, a covered individual should be left in a financial position neither worse nor better off than if the loss had not occurred. An insurance contract is based on the principle of indemnity, which prevents an insured from benefiting, or profiting, from the existence of insurance. An insurance contract indemnifies (compensates) an insured for a loss, subject to any deductions described in the policy.

These crucial insurance concepts support the principle of indemnity and its role in the insurance mechanism:

- Actual cash value
- Insurable interest
- Utmost good faith
- Subrogation

How Actual Cash Value Supports the Principle of Indemnity

In property insurance, recovery is usually limited by the policy to the **actual cash value (ACV)** of the property, subject to the stated dollar amount of insurance on the Declarations page.

An insurer determines the ACV of personal and real property by taking the **replacement cost** of the property and subtracting **depreciation**; therefore, ACV supports the principle of indemnity by limiting recovery to the value of the property at the time of loss. Because the insured's loss payment based on ACV does not provide adequate funds to replace depreciated property with new property, the insured does not profit under ACV provisions.

For example, Mark purchased a television for $500, which is covered under his homeowners policy based on ACV. One year later, the television was

Actual cash value (ACV)
Cost to replace property with new property of like kind and quality less depreciation.

Replacement cost
The cost to repair or replace property using new materials of like kind and quality with no deduction for depreciation.

Depreciation
The reduction in value caused by the physical wear and tear or technological or economic obsolescence of property.

destroyed by a covered cause of loss. Over that year, the replacement value of the specific television model had declined because of advances in technology, so the new cost for the same television at the time of the loss is $400. With depreciation of the television based on a standard depreciation rate of $100 per year, the insurer determines the ACV of the television to be $300 ($400 replacement cost minus $100 depreciation), the price at which Mark may be able to purchase a one-year-old television of the same make and model (like kind and quality) in the standard market. As provided under the principle of indemnity, the ACV does not allow the insured enough funds to purchase a new, late-model television—so the insured does not gain any value, or profit, from his television loss. This result would have remained the same even if technological improvements did not affect the price of new property. If that had occurred, the value of the television would still have declined by $100 based on the depreciation deduction used to determine ACV.

Because the principle of indemnity is not well-understood, many people wonder why their insurer does not pay the cost to purchase a new car if theirs is destroyed in an accident. As the party who pays the insurance premium, the insured may reason that a fair loss payment would enable him or her to purchase a new vehicle similar to the one destroyed. What such an insured is not considering, however, is that providing a new vehicle to replace the older vehicle would allow him or her to benefit from the loss, violating the principle of indemnity.

How Insurable Interest Supports the Principle of Indemnity

Insurable interest

An interest in the subject of an insurance policy that is not unduly remote and that would cause the interested party to suffer financial loss if an insured event occurred.

A person has an **insurable interest** if the occurrence of an event to be insured would cause financial loss or injury to that person. Therefore, a person's legally insurable interests depend on the relationship between that person and the property, life, or event in question. If the relationship exposes the person to financial loss, it is sufficient to support an insurable interest. Relationships that can expose a person to financial loss—requiring insurable interest in property and liability insurance—include ownership, secured creditor rights, and certain contractual rights (such as auto leases, real estate leases, and home or commercial mortgages). Under property or liability insurance, an insured must have an insurable interest to obtain both a legally enforceable contract —and the right to purchase insurance to protect property rights in goods or legal interests.

For a loss to be paid, the insured must have an insurable interest at the time of the loss. Consequently, insurable interest supports the principle of indemnity by returning the insured to his or her financial position, based on the insurable interest, which would have existed had the loss not occurred. Courts will not enforce an indemnity contract (insurance policy) and rule in favor of an insured who did not have an insurable interest at the time of the loss; doing so would unjustly enrich a person who did not suffer a financial loss, which, in turn, would violate not only the principle of indemnity, but also public policy.

How Utmost Good Faith Supports the Principle of Indemnity

The two parties to an insurance contract, the insured and the insurer, must trust each other to fulfill certain obligations, disclose relevant information, and respond to requests promptly in a contract in which the principle of indemnity is supported by **utmost good faith**.

Utmost good faith

An obligation to act in complete honesty and to disclose all relevant facts.

Utmost good faith requires the insured to reveal all material facts to the insurer and to notify the insurer of any material change in a property or liability exposure that is insured. For example, if Amy, an insured, sells her car and replaces it with a newer, more valuable car, she must notify the insurer within a specified time period described in the policy; otherwise, her auto coverage might be jeopardized. Honest, timely disclosures support the principle of indemnity because they enable the insurer to charge appropriate premiums for the insured's property or liability exposures.

In Amy's case, if she failed to disclose her car replacement to the insurer within the specified time period, the insurer would collect a lesser premium based on the value of the older car. If the new car were subsequently damaged by a covered cause of loss, the insurer could deny Amy's claim for breach of contract or limit payment for this loss to the value of her older car. The doctrine of utmost good faith and the principle of indemnity would support the insurer's decision and would prevent Amy from enrichment by her underinsured loss.

In some cases, the insured may also be required to warrant that certain conditions exist. If these conditions do not exist, the insurer may deny coverage based on breach of warranty. For example, upon purchasing commercial property insurance, a building owner deceptively warrants that the building has a functioning sprinkler system to obtain a premium discount for that system. When a fire loss occurs and the sprinkler system does not work, the insurer may deny coverage for the subsequent, substantial loss on the grounds that the insured knew or should have known that the sprinkler system was defective. Utmost good faith demands that any warranted condition exists, and the principle of indemnity prevents the insured from the unjust enrichment of the premium discount allowed for the sprinkler system. Together, these principles support a claim denial based on a breached warranty.

The insurer is required to act in utmost good faith in investigating losses, paying claims, and defending the insured against claims. Should the insurer fail to perform these obligations reasonably, and in accordance with the principle of indemnity, it can be penalized under the state-specific Unfair Claims Settlement Practices Act. Utmost good faith, as provided in each state, requires the insurer to return the insured to his or her financial position that would have existed had the loss not occurred, in accordance with the principle of indemnity.

How Subrogation Supports the Principle of Indemnity

Subrogation

The process by which an insurer can, after it has paid a loss under the policy, recover the amount paid from any party (other than the insured) who caused the loss or is otherwise legally liable for the loss.

Subrogation provides that if an insurer has paid a covered insurance loss, the insured's right of recovery from a responsible third party is transferred to the insurer.

Specifically, the insurer claims the right of subrogation, having paid the debt that the responsible third party had a legal obligation to pay. The insurer paid the third party's debt to the insured because the insurance policy is a contract that specifies that the insurer will pay the insured's loss —the insurer did not voluntarily pay the third party's debt. The insurer is only secondarily liable for the third party's debt (through the insurance contract), and the third party is primarily liable because the third party was responsible for the insured's **damages**. No harm will come to any party by allowing the insurer to exercise the right of subrogation against the responsible third party.

Damages

Money claimed by, or a monetary award to, a party who has suffered bodily injury or property damage for which another party is legally responsible.

For example, if Jane is negligent in causing an auto accident that damages Hank's auto, Hank's insurer may pay the expense of repairing Hank's auto, minus his deductible. However, after Hank's insurer has paid him for the loss, the insurer is "subrogated" to Hank's rights of recovery against Jane. Based on this right, Hank's insurer will attempt to recover the damages from Jane or her insurer, as well as any deductible amount that Hank paid out of his pocket and any expenses the insurer incurred in collecting the subrogation. When Jane's legal obligation to pay the damages is paid in full, Hank's insurer will pay Hank the amount recovered for his deductible.

Subrogation of rights to the insurer supports the principle of indemnity by preventing the insured from being paid twice (by the third party as well as the insurer); an at-fault third party from being unjustly enriched by the existence of the insured's coverage (the insurer seeks reimbursement of damages from the at-fault third party); and an insurer or insured from benefiting, while allowing each to be reimbursed for expenses incurred, such as claim expenses to collect the debt or the amount of the insured's deductible.

Review Questions

1. Explain how actual cash value (ACV) supports the principle of indemnity.
2. Explain how the requirement that an insured has an insurable interest in property at the time of a loss supports the principle of indemnity.
3. Explain how utmost good faith supports the principle of indemnity as it applies to the insured and the insurer.
4. Explain how subrogation supports the principle of indemnity with regard to the insured, the responsible third party, and the insurer.

Application Questions

1. Madison purchased a homeowners insurance policy from Arkwright Insurance for a home that she inherited from her parents' estate, based on the actual cash value (ACV) of the home. When completing the insurance application, Madison dishonestly claimed that she occupied the home as her primary residence, when, in fact, the home was vacant. Near the end of the one-year policy term, vandals set fire to the vacant home, which burned to the ground. While investigating the loss, Arkwright's personnel discovered that the home had been vacant since Madison took possession of it and throughout the time it was insured. Explain which crucial insurance concepts exist in this case, and explain whether they support the principle of indemnity.

SUMMARY

The principle of indemnity directs the insurer to put an insured in a financial position that would have existed had a loss not occurred. ACV, insurable interest, utmost good faith, and subrogation are crucial insurance concepts that support the principle of indemnity by ensuring that no party is unjustly enriched by a loss.

Direct Your Learning

11

Insurance Policy Provisions

Educational Objectives

After learning the content of this assignment, you should be able to:

- Describe the three types of other-insurance provisions.
- Explain why insurance to value is important to the insured and to the insurer in property insurance, what problems are associated with maintaining insurance to value, and what can be done to minimize these problems.
- Analyze the function of coinsurance.

Outline

Other-Insurance Provisions

Insurance to Value

Coinsurance

Summary

Insurance Policy Provisions

11

OTHER-INSURANCE PROVISIONS

If there are multiple insurance policies covering the same loss exposure, the relationship between the insurance policies is governed by the "other-insurance" provisions in either a property or liability insurance policy.

In general, other-insurance provisions include all policy provisions, regardless of their title, that attempt to specify in advance of a loss how an insurer's obligations (amounts payable) will be affected by other insurance applying to the same loss. Significant characteristics of other-insurance provisions include:

- Other-insurance provisions are not necessarily labeled "other insurance" within the policy document. An excess clause or a subrogation provision, among others, may address other insurance situations.
- Other-insurance provisions, regardless of their title, are usually found in the Conditions section of an insurance policy.
- Policies with more than one distinct coverage section often contain more than one other-insurance provision.
- A single other-insurance clause often includes more than one other-insurance provision. For example, the clause may address several possible types of other insurance situations.
- Two other-insurance provisions of the same general type are not necessarily consistent with one another.
- Group medical insurance policies include a coordination of benefits provision that addresses other-insurance situations.

Using these characteristics, a subrogation provision often qualifies as an other-insurance provision. So do provisions labeled "other insurance."

Most other-insurance provisions that appear in property and liability insurance policies are one of three broad types, based on how the provision allows for the sharing of the claim payments

- Primary/excess provisions
- Proportional provisions
- Escape clauses

Overall, these provisions resolve insurers' responsibilities when more than one policy may provide coverage for the same loss. This relieves each insurer from having to prove its responsibility when there is conflicting language in multiple policies.

Primary/Excess Provisions

Primary coverage provision
An other-insurance provision that specifies that the policy pays the loss amount before other applicable policies until its own limits have been exhausted.

Excess coverage provision
An other-insurance provision that specifies that the policy pays any remaining loss amount, up to its policy limits, after the primary policy's coverage limits have been exhausted.

A policy's other-insurance provisions may specifically indicate that the policy provides either primary coverage or excess coverage. A **primary coverage provision** is an other-insurance provision that specifies that the policy pays the loss amount before other applicable policies until its own limits have been exhausted. An **excess coverage provision** is an other-insurance provision that specifies that the policy pays any remaining loss amount, up to its policy limits, after the primary policy's coverage limits have been exhausted.

To illustrate, assume Sue owns property insured under two policies:

- Policy A with a $6,000 limit states that it is primary coverage.
- Policy B with a $10,000 limit states that it is excess coverage.

Further assume that Sue has an $8,000 loss covered by both policies. The insurer with Policy A pays its $6,000 limit of coverage. The insurer with Policy B then pays an additional $2,000.

An excess other-insurance provision should not be confused with an excess insurance policy. An excess insurance policy covers losses over either underlying primary insurance or a large self-insured retention amount. An excess other-insurance provision is usually found in a primary insurance policy that provides payment only after the coverage of other primary policies is exhausted.

Proportional Provisions

Proportional other-insurance provision
A policy provision that limits the insurer's obligations to a portion of the overall loss.

Proportional other-insurance provisions are policy provisions that limit the insurer's obligations to a portion of the overall loss. Insurers typically share the loss amount proportionally when two policies both state that they are primary, when both state that they are excess, or when no statement of primary/excess coverage is indicated.

Proportional provisions may be perceived as prescribing an equitable way for two or more insurers to share in a loss. Equitable loss-sharing is the result only when every applicable policy has the same type of other-insurance provision. The purpose of any proportional provision is to limit the obligations of the insurer issuing that policy.

Two points are crucial to understanding proportional other-insurance provisions:

- An other-insurance provision affects only the policy in which it appears. One insurer's policy cannot specify the coverage that will be provided by another insurer.
- A proportional provision limits an insurer's amount payable, but it does not reduce coverage. If losses exceed the total policy limits available, each insurer pays its full policy limit, barring indications to the contrary elsewhere in the policy.

Losses are typically proportioned between insurers either by equal shares or by pro rata sharing based on policy limits. **Contribution by equal shares** is a method of paying losses in which both policies pay the loss equally until the limits under one policy have been exhausted; thereafter, the other policy alone pays. To illustrate, assume that two policies, Policy A and Policy B, specify contribution by equal shares. Policy A's limit is $90,000 and Policy B's limit is $10,000. In the event of a $40,000 loss, Policies A and B would pay equal shares until Policy B has paid its $10,000 limit. At that point, each policy has paid $10,000, so $20,000 of the loss would remain. Policy A would pay the remaining $20,000. Therefore, Policy A would pay a total of $30,000 ($10,000 + $20,000), and Policy B would pay $10,000.

Contribution by equal shares
Method of sharing loss when two or more policies apply in which each insurer pays an equal amount until the claim is fully paid or until one insurer exhausts its limit, in which case the other insurer pays the remainder of the claim (up to its limit).

Contribution by equal shares is often used in liability insurance policies in which each insurer's premium is not directly proportional to policy limits. In other words, the first $100,000 layer of liability insurance generally costs much more than the next $100,000 layer of insurance, and so forth. Under these circumstances, contribution by equal shares tends to distribute losses among insurers in proportion to the premium they collected for the risk.

Pro rata sharing based on policy limits restricts the insurer's maximum amount payable to the proportion of the loss that the insurer's policy limit bears to the sum of all applicable policy limits. This example of pro rata sharing based on policy limits specified in an other insurance policy provision is from the American Association of Insurance Services (AAIS) Building and Personal Property Coverage Part:

> 6. **Insurance Under More than One Policy** – **You** may have another policy subject to the same plan, **terms**, conditions, and provisions as this policy. If **you** do, **we** pay **our** share of the covered loss. **Our** share is the proportion that the applicable limit under this policy bears to the **limit** of all policies covering on the same basis.

Pro rata sharing can be expressed by this formula:

$$\text{Policy A's maximum amount payable} = \frac{\text{Policy A's limit}}{(\text{Policy A's limit} + \text{Policy B's limit} + \ldots + \text{Policy N's limit})} \times \text{Loss}$$

For example, suppose two insurers have insured the same property and that both insurance policies (Policy A and Policy B) specify that any loss will be shared on a pro rata basis based on policy limits. Policy A's limit is $90,000, Policy B's limit is $10,000, and a $40,000 loss occurs. The maximum amount payable under Policy A can be calculated as:

$$\text{Policy A's maximum amount payable} = \frac{\text{Policy A's limit}}{(\text{Policy A's limit} + \text{Policy B's limit})} \times \text{Loss}$$

$$= \frac{\$90{,}000}{(\$90{,}000 + \$10{,}000)} \times \$40.000$$

$$= 0.90 \times \$40.000$$

$$= \$36{,}000$$

If B's policy has a similar proration by policy limits provision, Policy B's maximum amount payable can be calculated as:

$$\text{Policy B's maximum amount payable} = \frac{\text{Policy B's limit}}{(\text{Policy B's limit} + \text{Policy A's limit})} \times \text{Loss}$$

$$= \frac{\$10{,}000}{(\$10{,}000 + \$90{,}000)} \times \$40.000$$

$$= 0.10 \times \$40.000$$

$$= \$4{,}000$$

Even if Policy B did not contain a pro rata other-insurance provision, the amount payable under Policy A is still limited to $36,000 because the insured also had coverage under Policy B. Policy A cannot dictate the amount payable by Policy B.

If a loss of $100,000 or more occurred, then Policy A would pay $90,000. If Policy B had a similar pro rata policy limits provision, then Policy B would pay $10,000. These amounts would not change if the loss were greater than $100,000 because an insurer is not obligated to pay more than its policies' limits.

Pro rata sharing based on policy limits is commonly used in property insurance policies. It provides an equitable way of allocating losses in situations in which each insurer's premium is directly proportional to policy limits. Pro rata sharing is not as prevalent in liability insurance policies; it is much more common to see contribution by equal shares.

Escape Clauses

Escape clause

An other-insurance provision that relieves the insurer of any obligation to pay a claim for which other insurance applies.

The third type of other-insurance provision in insurance policies is the escape clause. An **escape clause** is an other-insurance provision that relieves the insurer of any obligation to pay a claim for which other insurance applies. Escape clauses generally function in one of four ways:

- Prohibitions—forbidding other insurance
- Exclusions—excluding property or activities covered by other insurance
- Disclaimers—denying responsibility if other insurance applies
- Offsets—reducing the coverage limit by the amount of other insurance

Prohibitions

Prohibition escape clauses forbid the purchase of other insurance. An insurer may deny coverage to any insured who fails to comply with a policy provision that prohibits other insurance.

For example, the ISO Personal Auto Policy contains an escape clause based on a prohibition. The automatic termination provision begins by stating that the policy ceases to provide further coverage at the end of the policy period if the insured does not accept the insurer's renewal offer. This statement is followed by this escape clause: [1]

> **C. Automatic Termination**
>
> ...If you obtain other insurance on "your covered auto", any similar insurance provided by this policy will terminate as to that auto on the effective date of the other insurance.

People usually do not buy extra auto insurance deliberately. In most cases, this provision reflects the intent of the insured who decided to replace one policy with another. The provision also addresses the rare insurance fraud situation in which duplicate claims are filed with two or more insurers. However, the provision is effective only when the insurer knows a duplicate claim has been filed with another insurer.

Exclusions

Exclusion escape clauses negate coverage only if other insurance applies. These function as other-insurance provisions even if they appear in a policy's exclusions section. For example, the personal property coverage of an ISO HO-3 policy specifically excludes items insured elsewhere, as follows:[2]

> **4. Property Not Covered**
>
> We do not cover:
>
> a. Articles separately described and specifically insured, *regardless of the limit for which they are insured*, in this or other insurance; [emphasis added]

The italicized phrase in the wording of exclusions was added in the 2000 policy edition to make it clear that this is an exclusion, not an offset. Coverage is completely excluded for items covered elsewhere in the homeowners policy, an endorsement to the homeowners policy, or a separate policy such as a personal articles floater. For example, suppose a firearms collection worth $10,000 is destroyed in a house fire and the collection has $5,000 of scheduled coverage under a Scheduled Personal Property Endorsement. Without the endorsement, the homeowners policy would provide $10,000 coverage on the collection (assuming its value could be proven).

However, the endorsement provides only $5,000 of coverage. The homeowners policy does not pay the difference. This exclusion and others like it shift all responsibility for the loss to the policy that has generated a premium coverage on that valuable item, and it also encourages insurance to value on scheduled items. Exclusions in some policies reinstate coverage to the extent that other insurance is inadequate. These exclusions are properly categorized as excess provisions.

Because of the differences in the way they determine amounts payable, insurance professionals should be able to differentiate between an exclusion and an exclusion escape clause. Exclusions are not escape clauses because they apply even when the other insurance does not exist. For example, the liability coverage of homeowners policies excludes coverage for most auto-related losses. The exclusion applies even if a particular homeowner does not have an auto policy. In contrast, exclusion escape clauses apply only if the other insurance coverage is in effect.

Disclaimers

Disclaimer escape clauses provide coverage only if no other insurance applies. Disclaimers usually apply only to fringe or supplemental coverages rather than the whole policy. For example, a state's no-fault law might prohibit stacking of coverages and prescribe the order in which insurance applies. To illustrate, insurance "on the car" might be the first to pay for injuries to any occupant, but if there is no insurance "on the car," a guest passenger's own personal injury protection would apply.

Offsets

Offset escape clauses apply when available policy limits are reduced by policy limits of other insurance that applies to the same loss. If Policy A contains an offset, the following two scenarios are possible:

- If the other insurance's policy limits equal or exceed the limit of Policy A, which has an offset escape provision, then the insurer pays nothing under Policy A. The offset essentially becomes an exclusion.
- If Policy A's limits are higher than the other insurance's policy limits, the insurer with Policy A pays no more than the difference in policy limits.

This example, part of the other-insurance provision under the uninsured motorists coverage of the ISO Personal Auto Policy, functions as an offset escape clause:[3]

> OTHER INSURANCE
>
> If there is other applicable insurance available under one or more policies or provisions of coverage that is similar to the insurance provided under this Part of the policy:
>
> 1. Any recovery for damages under all such policies or provisions of coverage may equal but not exceed the highest applicable limit for any one vehicle under any insurance providing coverage on either a primary or excess basis.

INSURANCE TO VALUE

Every insurance policy must indicate how an insurer determines the amount payable for a covered loss. Under a property insurance policy, the amount payable depends on the policy's valuation methods, policy limits, deductibles, and the coinsurance or other insurance-to-value provisions. Each of these features must be evaluated to accurately determine the amount of payment an insured should receive from the insurer for a claim.

Insurance to value is the choice of a limit in property insurance that approximates the maximum potential loss. Therefore, a building with an insurable value of $100,000 that is covered by $100,000 of insurance is insured to value. Insurance buyers and sellers usually attempt to closely align the insurable value of property with the amount of insurance that covers it.

Insurance to value
Insurance written for an amount approximating the full value of the asset(s) insured.

Loss Frequency and Loss Severity

Insurance to value is best understood by first examining loss frequency and loss severity.

During the risk management process, loss exposures are assessed to determine potential loss frequency and loss severity. For property loss exposures, the severity loss distribution is often skewed. That is, most of the losses that occur to property loss exposures, especially real property, are small losses (low severity), with a total loss being a rare occurrence. See the exhibit "Probability Distribution of Loss Severity of Residential Property Losses."

Probability Distribution of Loss Severity of Residential Property Losses

Size Category of Losses (bins)	Probability of Loss	Cumulative Probability of Loss	Average Bin Value	Expected Value of Loss	Expected Value Truncated
$0–$1,000	.700	.700	$ 500	$ 350	$ 350
$1001–$5,000	.200	.900	3,000	600	600
$5,001–$10,000	.050	.950	7,500	375	375
$10,001–$15,000	.020	.970	12,500	250	250
$15,001–$25,000	.015	.985	20,000	300	300
$25,001–$50,000	.0075	.993	37,500	281	
$50,001–$100,000	.005	.998	75,000	375	
$100,001–$150,000	.0025	1.000	125,000	313	
Total	1.000			$2,844	$1,875

Probability of Loss × Average Bin Value

Expected Value of Insured Losses: $25,000 Policy Limit

Expected Value of Insured Losses: Insured to Value

[DA03229]

The severity distribution shown in the exhibit shows that if a loss occurs, 90 percent of the time that loss is less than \$5,000 (because the cumulative probability is 90 percent). Because the cumulative probability of a loss less than \$25,000 is 98.5 percent, then only 1.5 percent of the time is the loss greater than \$25,000. The maximum possible loss for the property is \$150,000, which would occur only if the property were totally destroyed.

To calculate the insurance rate and premium to insure the property, an insurer would combine the severity distribution shown in the exhibit with a frequency distribution. For example, the severity distribution in the exhibit has an expected value of approximately \$2,844. If an insurer were to assume a simple frequency distribution that has only two possibilities—80 percent of the time no loss would occur and 20 percent of the time one loss would occur—then the insurer would be able to calculate an expected loss of approximately \$569 [(0.8 × \$0) + (0.2 × \$2,844) = \$569]. If the insurer had a 40 percent expense ratio, the premium it would charge would be \$948 [\$569 ÷ (1 – .40) = \$948].

The importance to the insurer of insurance to value can be illustrated by showing how the lack of insurance to value affects premium adequacy. For example, suppose that an insurer provides a property insurance policy with a policy limit of \$150,000 and that the premium is based on an insurance rate per \$100 of coverage. Dividing \$150,000 by \$100 yields 1,500 units of coverage that the insurer is providing.

The insurer, charging a premium of \$948 for a policy with a limit of \$150,000 (the value of the property), is using an insurance rate of approximately \$0.63 per unit of coverage (\$948 ÷ 1,500 = \$0.63). Further, suppose that the insured evaluated the severity distribution and chose to retain the 1.5 percent probability that losses would be above \$25,000 by buying a policy with a limit of only \$25,000.

The insurer would lose money on the \$25,000-limit policy (250 units of coverage) if it charged the same rate (\$0.63 per unit of coverage) as for the policy with the \$150,000 limit, because it would result in a premium of only \$158 (250 units × \$0.63 = \$158). This lower premium would not be enough to cover the expected losses under the policy.

If the severity distribution that the insurer faces stops at \$25,000, the expected value of that distribution is now \$1,875. With the same frequency distribution as previously, the expected loss is now \$375 [(0.8 × \$0) + (0.2 × \$1,875) = \$375], and assuming the same expense loading, the premium would be \$625 [\$375 ÷ (1 – 0.4) = \$625]. For a policy limit of \$25,000, the insurer is offering 250 units of coverage with a rate of \$2.50 per unit of coverage, which is substantially higher than the \$0.63 per unit rate that was calculated when the property insurance limit was equal to the property's total value.

The insurer is then faced with a decision to either charge a higher rate for property insurance when the policy limit is less than the property's value or require insureds to choose policy limits that are close to the full value of the property. The second choice is what is referred to as insurance to value.

The Importance of Insurance to Value

The insurable value of property is partly determined by the valuation provision in the applicable insurance policy. The insurance amount depends on the applicable policy limits. Insuring to value is typically beneficial for both the insurer and the insured. The insurer benefits in two ways. First, the premium is adequate to cover potential losses.

Second, it simplifies the underwriting process by reducing the need to determine exact values during underwriting. The determination of underinsurance (not insuring to value) is made at the time of loss; therefore, the underwriter does not need to determine whether the property is being underinsured. The insured benefits because sufficient funds are available in the event of a total loss and the uncertainty associated with large retained losses is reduced. See the exhibit "Industry Language—Insurance to Value, Coinsurance, and Insurance-to-Value."

Industry Language—Insurance to Value, Coinsurance, and Insurance-to-Value

The property policy limit chosen should be close to the value of the insured property. Many insurance professionals call this fully insuring the property, but it is also called insurance to value. The term insurance to value is often confused with provisions in homeowners and businessowners insurance policies called insurance-to-value provisions. The distinction is important. Insurance to value (without the hyphens) refers to the relationship between the policy limit and the insured property's value. Insurance-to-value (with hyphens) refers to the provisions in specific property insurance policies that determine the amounts payable by the policy based on the relationship between the policy limit and the insured property's value. Insurance-to-value provisions are similar to coinsurance provisions in commercial property insurance policies. They both are based on the relationship between policy limits and the insured property's value. However, they determine the amounts payable using different formulas, described subsequently in this assignment.

This text refers to the relationship between policy limits and the insured property's value as insurance to value.

[DA03230]

Problems Associated With Insurance to Value

Maintaining insurance to value is important to avoid coinsurance penalties and other insurance-to-value provision penalties that might reduce the amount payable in the event of a loss. Underinsurance penalties are not a concern for those who maintain property insurance limits that meet or exceed coinsurance requirements or the insurance-to-value requirement. However, maintaining such limits is difficult, for at least these reasons:

- The amount of insurance necessary to meet coinsurance requirements is based on the insured property's value at the time of the loss, but the policy limit is selected when the policy is purchased.
- When selecting insurance limits, an insurance buyer typically estimates property values based on an informed guess.
- The insurable value at the time of the loss often cannot be precisely measured until the property is actually rebuilt or replaced.
- Values change over time.

Minimizing Insurance to Value Problems

Insurance professionals can help property insurance buyers minimize problems associated with valuation by recommending that they take these steps:

- Hire a qualified appraiser to establish the property's current replacement cost value. The property owner should adjust the appraisal using indexes and/or a record of additions and deletions each year and should reappraise the property every few years.
- Purchase an inflation guard coverage option. Inflation guard coverage is designed to ensure that policy limits rise as the property values increase as a result of inflation.
- Purchase a peak season endorsement if a business's personal property values fluctuate in a cyclical pattern. A peak season endorsement automatically increases the policy limits during the specified peak season of the organization.
- Review and revise limits periodically to ensure that the policy limits are adequate to cover potential losses.

In order to ascertain whether a property is being insured at or near its value, and to determine the amount payable under a policy, an insurance professional needs to understand the various valuation methods available and the differences that can result from taking alternate valuation approaches.

COINSURANCE

Coinsurance provides an incentive for insureds to purchase adequate insurance. If the coinsurance requirement is not met and a loss occurs, the insurer will pay for only a portion of the loss. In such an instance, the insured must also pay a portion of the loss and effectively becomes a coinsurer.

The coinsurance clause in a property insurance policy provides the conditions under which a loss will be fully covered by the insurer and the means to calculate a partial payment if those conditions are not met. If an insured does not have the required amount of insurance at the time of a loss, an insurer uses a coinsurance formula to calculate its reduced payment for the loss. The coinsurance formula is used only if the coinsurance requirement is not met, and the insurer never pays more than the loss amount or the applicable policy limits.

Coinsurance Overview

Coinsurance clauses serve a dual purpose, both rewarding those who have insured to value and penalizing those who have not. Coinsurance is a requirement in most property insurance policies that makes the insured responsible for part of a loss if the property is underinsured below some specified percentage of the property's insurable value. The concept of coinsurance may be described as a penalty the insurer imposes on the insured for not buying enough insurance. However, coinsurance is also effectively a reward for insuring property to value. If the insured insures property to value, then the insurer agrees to waive the insured's participation in the loss, except to the extent of the deductible. See the exhibit "Coinsurance in Property Insurance and in Health Insurance."

Coinsurance in Property Insurance and in Health Insurance

Coinsurance means something different in the context of property insurance than it does in the context of health insurance.

- A coinsurance clause in a property insurance policy provides that the insurer pays losses in full (subject to other policy provisions) for any insured who carries an amount of insurance that equals or exceeds some stated percentage of the covered property's insurable value. For example, in a property policy with an 80 percent coinsurance clause, an insured who carries $80,000 or more of property insurance on a building with an insurable value of $100,000 recovers in full for a covered loss (subject to any applicable deductible and the policy limit). Only a policyholder who does not insure to value shares the loss with the insurer, thereby becoming a coinsurer.
- A coinsurance clause in a health insurance policy is, in effect, a percentage deductible in which the insured and the insurer each agree to pay a stated percentage of covered losses. For example, in a health insurance policy with an 80 percent coinsurance clause, the insurer pays 80 percent of every covered claim, and the insured pays 20 percent. In a claim for $1,000 of covered medical expenses, the insurer pays $800, and the insured pays $200 (subject to other applicable policy provisions). Every policyholder shares the loss with the insurer and is therefore a coinsurer.

[DA08863]

Coinsurance Clause

A coinsurance clause in a property insurance policy requires the insured to carry an amount of insurance equal to or greater than the stated coinsurance percentage of the covered property's insurable value in order to pay a lower rate per unit of coverage and avoid a partial recovery for a covered loss. Common coinsurance percentages for buildings and personal property are 80, 90, and 100. The insurable value is the actual cash value (ACV), the replacement cost value, or whatever other value is determined according to the policy's valuation clause.

The more insurance a consumer agrees to buy—in other words, the more closely the amount of insurance purchased reflects the covered property's full insurable value—the lower the rate for insurance that consumer will pay. Insurers charge a lower rate per $100 of coverage to those who agree to meet the 80 percent coinsurance requirement. This rate is reduced by another 5 percent for those who purchase a policy with a 90 percent coinsurance percentage, and a further 5 percent for those who opt for 100 percent coinsurance. Insureds buy more insurance (higher limits), but each unit of insurance costs less. Insurance professionals usually call this the "coinsurance requirement," although it is not literally required. Failure to meet a coinsurance requirement does not void coverage. If the requirement is not met, the policy remains in effect, but the insured will receive only a partial recovery when a covered loss occurs.

Given the coinsurance requirement, it might seem to be most cost-effective for property insurance buyers to choose a 100 percent coinsurance clause and insure to full value. This approach essentially provides full coverage at the lowest rate per $100 of insurance. However, 80 percent coinsurance is the most common for several reasons:

- It is traditional practice. For many years, 80 percent coinsurance has been viewed as the standard approach.
- Few property losses are total losses. Insurance to 80 percent of the full insurable value provides adequate insurance limits to cover the majority of losses.
- Eighty percent coinsurance allows some margin for error in predicting the full insurable value of property at the time of the loss.
- The total premium for insurance to 80 percent of value with an 80 percent coinsurance clause is less than the total premium for insurance to 100 percent of value with a 100 percent coinsurance clause. However, when property insurance rates are low, this is not a significant factor.

Some property insurance buyers use a conservative approach, insuring to approximately 100 percent of the estimated full insurable value, subject to an 80 percent coinsurance clause. If the estimated value is accurate, this approach provides insurance limits adequate to offer indemnity for a total loss. It further provides a margin of error that usually prevents a coinsurance penalty if the property is underinsured at the time of the loss. Coinsurance penalties can also be avoided by using agreed value coverage. See the exhibit "Coinsurance Clause in the ISO BPP Coverage Form."

Coinsurance Clause in the ISO BPP Coverage Form

F. Additional Conditions

1. Coinsurance

If a Coinsurance percentage is shown in the Declarations, the following condition applies.

a. We will not pay the full amount of any loss if the value of Covered Property at the time of loss times the Coinsurance percentage shown for it in the Declarations is greater than the Limit of Insurance for the property.

Instead, we will determine the most we will pay using the following steps:

(1) Multiply the value of Covered Property at the time of loss by the Coinsurance percentage;

(2) Divide the Limit of Insurance of the property by the figure determined in Step **(1)**;

(3) Multiply the total amount of loss, before the application of any deductible, by the figure determined in Step **(2)**; and

(4) Subtract the deductible from the figure determined in Step **(3)**.

We will pay the amount determined in Step **(4)** or the limit of insurance, whichever is less. For the remainder, you will either have to rely on other insurance or absorb the loss yourself.

Coinsurance Formula

The coinsurance formula explains how the amount payable is determined if the coinsurance requirement has not been met:

$$\text{Amount payable} = \frac{\text{Limit of insurance}}{\text{Value of covered property (at time of loss)} \times \text{Coinsurance percentage}} \times \text{Total amount of covered loss}$$

Insurance students often remember this formula as "did over should times loss," which can be written as this:

$$\text{Amount payable} = \frac{\text{Did}}{\text{Should}} \times \text{Loss},$$

where

"Did" = The amount of insurance carried (the policy limit), and

"Should" = The minimum amount that should have been carried to meet the coinsurance requirement based on the insurable value at the time of the loss.

Three points are crucial in applying the coinsurance formula:

- Applying the coinsurance formula is necessary only when the coinsurance requirement is not met, because the policy limits are less than the insurable value multiplied by the coinsurance percentage. In other words, the coinsurance penalty applies only when the "did" is less than the "should." If the coinsurance requirement is met ("did" is greater than or equal to "should"), the amount payable is the full loss amount, subject to the deductible, applicable policy limits, and other relevant policy provisions.
- The insurer never pays more than the loss amount. If the amount of insurance carried is greater than the minimum policy limit required ("did" is greater than "should"), the coinsurance formula would indicate that the insurer should pay more than the loss amount.
- The insurer never pays more than the applicable policy limits, even though the formula might indicate otherwise if the loss amount is greater than the minimum policy limits required by the coinsurance clause ("loss" is greater than "should").

Coinsurance can be critical in the event of a major partial loss and substantial underinsurance. To impose a coinsurance penalty, an insurer must accurately appraise the full insurable value of all covered property at the time of the loss, subject to the applicable policy limits. This process alone can be time-consuming and costly and can lead to disputes over the appraisal estimate's accuracy. If the appraised value of the property results in a value high enough to invoke the coinsurance penalty, it can even lead to litigation. For these and other practical reasons, many property claims are settled without any attempt to determine precisely whether a coinsurance requirement has been met. Coinsurance calculations usually are invoked only when both clear evidence of substantial underinsurance and a sizable loss exist.

Coinsurance clauses apply in policies covering direct damage to buildings and personal property. The coinsurance requirement in these policies is based on the building's full insurable value, normally the ACV or replacement cost. Coinsurance clauses are also used in business income policies for indirect losses. In those policies, the coinsurance formula requires an amount of insurance based on net income and operating expenses that, if no loss had occurred, would have been earned or incurred during the current policy period. See the exhibit "Coinsurance Example."

Review Questions

1. Describe the three types of other-insurance provisions.
2. Describe situations in which insurers share loss amounts proportionally.
3. Describe the two crucial points to understanding proportional other-insurance provisions.
4. Describe the four types of escape clauses.
5. Describe two benefits to the insurer of insuring property policies to value.

Coinsurance Example

Barbara and Carlos own a building with a replacement cost value of $300,000. They insure the building for $200,000 with a property insurance policy providing replacement cost coverage subject to a 100 percent coinsurance clause. A covered peril causes $60,000 of damage to the building. How much will the property insurer pay Barbara and Carlos for the damage to the building?

Insured value = $300,000

Coinsurance percentage = 100%

Loss amount = $60,000

Policy limit = $200,000

Alternatively:

Did = Policy limit = $200,000

Should = Insured value × Coinsurance percentage = $300,000 × 100% = $300,000.

Is "did" greater than or equal to "should"?

If yes, the policy pays the loss amount subject to policy limits and deductible.

If no, the policy pays [(Did ÷ Should) × Loss amount].

In this case, the answer was no. Therefore, Barbara and Carlos did not meet the coinsurance requirement, and the policy pays the following:

$$\text{Policy payout} = \frac{\text{Did}}{\text{Should}} \times \text{Loss amount}$$

$$= \frac{\$200{,}000}{\$300{,}000} \times \$60{,}000$$

$$= \$40{,}000$$

Because Barbara and Carlos did not meet the coinsurance clause, even though the loss was well below the policy limits, the amount payable under the property insurance policy was reduced.

[DA08865]

6. Explain how the insured benefits from insuring property to value.
7. Explain why it is difficult to maintain property insurance limits that meet or exceed policy coinsurance or insurance-to-value requirements.
8. Compare the role of coinsurance as both a penalty and a reward.
9. Explain how an insured becomes a coinsurer in a health insurance claim.
10. List three common coinsurance percentages for building and personal property.

11. Describe the relationship between the amount of insurance purchased and the rate charged by insurers.
12. State the coinsurance formula.
13. Identify the only time the coinsurance formula needs to be applied when determining the loss payment.

SUMMARY

Most other-insurance provisions that appear in property and liability insurance policies are of three broad types: primary/excess provisions, proportional provisions, and escape clauses. A primary coverage provision is an other-insurance provision that specifies that the policy pays the loss amount before other applicable policies until its own limits have been exhausted. An excess coverage provision is an other-insurance provision that specifies that the policy pays any remaining loss amount, up to its policy limits, after the primary policy's coverage limits have been exhausted.

Proportional other-insurance provisions limit the insurer's obligations to a portion of the overall loss. Insurers typically share the loss amount proportionally when two policies both state that they are primary, when both state that they are excess, or when no statement of primary/excess coverage is indicated. Losses are typically proportioned between insurers either by equal shares or by prorated sharing based on policy limits.

An escape clause is an other-insurance provision that relieves the insurer of any obligation to pay a claim for which other insurance applies. Escape clauses generally function as either prohibitions (forbidding other insurance), exclusions (excluding property or activities covered by other insurance), disclaimers (denying responsibility if other insurance applies), or offsets (reducing the coverage limit by the amount of other insurance).

Insurance to value is the choice of a limit in property insurance to approximate the maximum potential loss. The insurable value of property is partly determined by the policy's valuation provision and the insurance amount depends on the policy limits. The insurer benefits from insuring to value because the premium is adequate to cover potential losses. The insured benefits because sufficient funds are available in the event of a total loss and the uncertainty of large retained losses is reduced.

The coinsurance requirement provides an incentive for insureds to maintain adequate insurance. When an insured carries property insurance at the stated coinsurance percentage of insurable value, the insurer waives the insured's participation in the loss payment except for the deductible. When an insured does not carry the required amount of insurance, the insurer's reduced loss payment is calculated by using the coinsurance formula, and the insured effectively pays a portion of the total loss.

ASSIGNMENT NOTES

1. Includes copyrighted material of Insurance Services Office, Inc., with its permission. Copyright, ISO Properties, Inc., 1997.
2. Includes copyrighted material of Insurance Services Office, Inc., with its permission. Copyright, ISO Properties, Inc., 1999.
3. Includes copyrighted material of Insurance Services Office, Inc., with its permission. Copyright, ISO Properties, Inc., 1997.

Direct Your Learning

12

Introduction to Employer-Provided Benefits

Educational Objectives

After learning the content of this assignment, you should be able to:

- Describe the types of employer-funded employee benefits.
- Describe the rationale for employer-provided employee benefits.
- Describe these characteristics of employee benefits plans:
  - Eligibility and participation
  - Financing issues
  - Group structure versus individual structure
- Describe the tax treatment of employer-provided benefits.
- Describe the advantages and disadvantages of employer-funded benefits and group insurance.

Outline

Employer-Funded Employee Benefits

Rationale for Employer-Provided Benefits

Characteristics of Employee Benefits Plans

Tax Treatment of Employer-Provided Benefits

Advantages and Disadvantages of Group Insurance

Summary

Introduction to Employer-Provided Benefits

12

EMPLOYER-FUNDED EMPLOYEE BENEFITS

An employer may contribute substantial funding to provide various benefits to its employees in addition to paying their wages or salaries.

Some **employee benefits** are required by law, while employers offer other benefits voluntarily. Common offerings include health expense benefits, retirement benefits, death benefits, disability benefits, and unemployment benefits.

Employee benefits

A form of compensation that workers may receive from their employers in addition to their salaries or wages.

Health Expense Benefits

The costs associated with a single illness or injury can be financially devastating to an individual or a family without health insurance. However, purchasing an individual health insurance policy directly from an insurer can be unaffordable for many families.

As a means of addressing this situation, the federal government extends tax advantages to employers that offer health benefits to their employees. In addition to these tax incentives, employers offer such programs to be competitive in attracting and retaining workers and because a healthy workforce contributes to productivity.

Employers commonly offer health expense benefits under group health plans for employees and their family members. Such plans pay for all or part of the costs of services provided by doctors, other healthcare professionals, and hospitals to prevent, diagnose, and treat illness and injury. Both the employer and the employee usually pay a share of the premium.

Retirement Benefits

A worker who retires no longer earns a salary. Many retired workers face the possibility that they will outlive their retirement savings or benefits, particularly if they become ill or unable to care for themselves. Most workers are eligible to receive federal Social Security benefits, which provide a minimum level of retirement income but rarely enough to live on exclusively. Both employers and workers pay Social Security taxes to support the federal program.

Employer-sponsored retirement plans can provide additional income for workers when they retire—ideally, enough for the remainder of their lives.

Employers offer retirement benefits in various forms. Some pension plans are funded entirely by employer contributions. Other pensions and retirement savings plans are funded by a combination of employer and employee contributions.

Death Benefits

When a worker dies, his or her family members may be faced with unforeseen expenses, including funeral costs, and are also deprived of the worker's income. Death benefits (or survivor benefits) replace part of a deceased worker's income and may also pay funeral expenses up to a set amount.

Death benefits come from several sources, including employer-sponsored life insurance and retirement plans, Social Security, and workers compensation. Life insurance policies pay a specified amount upon the worker's death. All states have workers compensation laws that require employers to pay benefits to workers who have a job-related injury or disease and to surviving dependents of workers who die from a job-related accident or disease.

Disability Benefits

A serious injury or an illness can cause disability that interferes with an employee's ability to work for a time or even permanently. The resulting loss of income can cause severe hardship for the worker and his or her family. The employer, in turn, loses a worker and may have to find and train a temporary or permanent replacement.

Disability benefits typically pay a portion of a disabled worker's salary during the period of disability. Benefits may cover short-term disability (typically less than six months), long-term disability (typically lasting from six months to life), or both.

Some states sponsor disability benefits programs—usually short term and with low benefit rates. Employers in states that do not sponsor these programs may voluntarily offer such insurance, and employers in states that do offer them may choose to offer additional coverage. Disability benefits are also available under employers' workers compensation programs (but only for disabilities resulting from work-related injury or illness) and Social Security.

Unemployment Benefits

Workers who lose their jobs through no fault of their own may suddenly find themselves without an income. Unemployment compensation provides income for jobless workers for a specific time or until those workers find new jobs. To qualify, a jobless worker must have been employed by the organization for a designated period (based on state law) and must be available and looking for work.

Unemployment benefits are required by federal law and provided by state programs. State laws determine eligibility, benefit amounts, and duration of payments. Employers with payroll over a certain amount must pay a state unemployment tax and are also charged for any benefits paid to their former employees.

Social Insurance Provided Through Employers

Some employee benefits were initiated by the United States government to alleviate social problems that arose from industrialization and the Great Depression in the early part of the twentieth century. Before this government intervention, families who were impoverished because of the unemployment or disability of a wage earner often had no recourse, and elderly people who could no longer work often became destitute.

Government-mandated programs such as unemployment insurance, workers compensation, and Social Security continue to address their original social objectives. Employers are required by state law to purchase or implement unemployment insurance and workers compensation insurance. Federal law requires employers to participate in Social Security by paying a tax and withholding and remitting a tax from their employees' salaries. See the exhibit "Types of Employer-Funded Employee Benefits."

Types of Employer-Funded Employee Benefits

Required by Law

Social Security
- Retirement benefits
- Disability benefits
- Survivors benefits

Workers compensation
- Occupational disability
- Death benefits

Disability insurance (in some states)

Unemployment insurance

Consolidated Omnibus Budget Reconciliation Act (COBRA)—temporary continuation of healthcare coverage after job termination

Family and medical leave

Minimum wage

Overtime

Voluntary

Health insurance
- Indemnity plans
- Managed-care plans
  - Health maintenance organizations (HMOs)
  - Preferred provider organizations (PPOs)
  - Point-of-service (POS) plans
- Consumer-driven health plans
  - Personal health savings accounts (HSAs)
  - Health reimbursement accounts (HRAs)
  - Flexible spending accounts (FSAs)
- Specialty plans
  - Dental insurance
  - Vision insurance
  - Prescription drug insurance
  - Long-term care insurance

Retirement benefits
- Defined benefit plans
- Defined contribution plans
- 401(k) and 403(b) plans
- Cash-balance plans

Death benefits
- Group term life insurance
- Survivor benefits under retirement plans

Disability benefits
- Sick leave
- Short-term disability insurance
- Long-term disability insurance

Unemployment benefits, such as a severance package

Paid vacation days and holidays

[DA09038]

RATIONALE FOR EMPLOYER-PROVIDED BENEFITS

Providing benefits for employees also benefits employers.

Although providing employee benefits can be costly, employers do benefit from such programs. Tax advantages and group insurance rates can offset costs. A sound employee benefits package can attract new employees, encourage current employees to stay with the organization, and increase productivity.

Tax Advantages

Many of an employer's contributions to an employee benefits plan are tax-deductible. For example, an employer can deduct as business expense its contributions to employee group health plans and retirement plans. Health

plan costs are also deductible. Each deduction reduces an organization's taxable income, and, in turn, the amount of taxes it must pay.

Employees also receive tax advantages when they contribute pretax earnings to benefits programs such as healthcare coverage or retirement plans. Lower taxes based on reduced taxable income can increase employees' after-tax earnings. In addition, they do not pay taxes on the value of the employer's contribution to their benefits. The employer indirectly benefits from this because each nontaxable dollar it contributes to an employee benefit goes further than a dollar of taxable employee compensation.[1]

Healthcare plan benefits are tax free to employees. Without healthcare coverage, employees would have to either buy private insurance or go without, exposing themselves to high medical costs for any serious injury or illness, and they would typically pay medical bills with after-tax dollars. (Medical expenses are deductible to those taxpayers who itemize, but the IRS has a steep threshold that eliminates the deduction for all but a relatively few.)

Attract and Retain Employees

Attracting and retaining employees is becoming increasingly important in many industries, as baby boomers enter retirement and, because of lower birthrates starting in the late 1960s, fewer job applicants are available in the employee pipeline to replace them.[2] A generous employee benefits package can make an employer more attractive to job applicants. As a result, employers may try to match or exceed the types and levels of benefits offered by their competitors.

A generous benefits plan can also encourage current employees to stay with their employers rather than seek more attractive jobs with competitors. Retention saves money, because constantly having to replace and train employees can be costly.

Access to Group Pricing

Insurers incur lower costs when they sell and underwrite group insurance compared with individual insurance, and those savings are passed on to insurance purchasers. By providing group health, life, and disability insurance, employers offer affordable and attainable options for employees who would otherwise have to either buy more costly individual policies or go uninsured.

Increase Employee Productivity

Employee benefits plans provide solutions that are difficult for employees to find elsewhere. Group health insurance is an example. Without it, many employees would be burdened with worries about the health of family members and the financial hardships associated with illness, injury, long-term treatments, or high personal insurance premiums. A worried employee may

find it hard to concentrate on the job, reducing productivity and ultimately compromising his or her employer's success.

By alleviating this worry, group health insurance can increase productivity. Similarly, life, disability, and retirement plans impart a sense of security to employees and their families by giving them the means to plan and prepare for crises and life events, thus also improving morale and productivity.

Finally, benefits can represent how much an organization values its employees. Employees who feel valued are likely to be productive—and organizations with productive, satisfied employees are more likely to succeed.

CHARACTERISTICS OF EMPLOYEE BENEFITS PLANS

Many employee benefits are offered under group insurance plans that define who can or must participate and how the benefits are financed.

For employee benefits to be offered in a manageable way, employers must be able to offer them on a group basis, providing the benefits (or coverage) and services under a single policy (often called a master policy) at a reduced cost per employee. Reduced costs are often available because group plans have so many participants, because insurers often treat group insurance more favorably than individual insurance from an underwriting perspective, and because insurance benefits can be tailored to the employer's preferences. For example, under group plans, limitations may be placed on dependent care coverage, vision care, or choice of treatment type available.

Group benefits plans may place restrictions not only on who can participate but also on who pays for the plan. The structure of group insurance differs from individual insurance by the very nature of both types (a single employer master policy versus many individual policies based on the employer's number of employees); consequently, a factor such as ease of administration is a consideration in an employer's decision-making process.

Eligibility and Participation

A group health insurance policy is purchased and owned by the employer. Coverage is offered to eligible employees of the company and often to employees' family members. Ultimately, the employer and the insurer's policy provisions determine eligibility for participation in a plan. For example, some group insurance plans cover all of an employer's full-time employees (and their dependents) but exclude part-time or temporary employees. Some plans allow new employees to participate only after a waiting, or probationary, period, such as one month after employment begins.

Placing limits on eligibility can reduce the employer's administration costs and, at the same time, discourage people with high potential losses from

seeking employment at an organization solely for the insurance benefits. For example, a person with a serious, chronic medical condition might seek employment specifically to obtain affordable healthcare coverage. Without a waiting period, an employer's group insurance plan might attract more participants with frequent and costly healthcare needs, significantly raising the costs of coverage—a result known as **adverse selection**.

Adverse selection
In general, the tendency for people with the greatest probability of loss to be the ones most likely to purchase insurance.

Financing Issues

Group health insurance plans can be contributory or noncontributory. Employees pay some or all of the costs of a contributory plan. For example, employees might pay a percentage of their health insurance premiums, and the employer might pay all other plan costs as well as the remainder of each employee's premium. With noncontributory plans, the employer pays the entire amount.

Noncontributory group insurance plans usually require the participation of every employee (once eligibility requirements are met). Because employees participate at no cost, adverse selection is of little concern, and both the insurer's and the employer's costs are lower than for contributory plans because administrative processes are uniform for all employees.

Contributory plans are more likely to invite adverse selection because employees with low risk may choose not to spend part of their earnings to participate. Although state laws typically prohibit requiring 100 percent participation in a contributory plan, some states permit insurers to reduce the likelihood of adverse selection by requiring a certain percentage of employee participation, such as 75 percent.

Group Insurance Structure Versus Individual Insurance Structure

An examination of the differences between how group insurance is structured and how individual insurance is structured can demonstrate why group plans are more readily included as part of employee benefits packages.

An individual insurance plan covers an individual and his or her family members or dependents. An employer-sponsored group plan typically covers employees, their dependents, and, in some cases, former employees.

With group insurance, employees may be added to and removed from the employer's master policy at any time, typically based on employment. The master policy alone has a fixed renewal date and a single group premium; employees are simply issued evidence of coverage, typically through group insurance cards or certificates. With individual insurance, each insured must address a separate renewal date, including a possible policy review, and premium due.

Premiums for individual policies are based on the characteristics and claim experiences of the covered individuals. For this reason, unlike persons covered under group plans, purchasers of individual health policies are often required to submit evidence of insurability—such as, for health insurance, a report of a medical exam indicating that they have no serious medical conditions. Under the Affordable Care Act of 2010 (ACA), a person or family who has been denied health insurance because of a preexisting medical condition may qualify at the federal and state levels for coverage under special preexisting-condition insurance plans. These plans will be available until 2014, when, under the ACA, insurers will be prohibited from denying coverage or charging higher rates because of preexisting conditions.

Under a group plan, individual characteristics such as a serious illness are not considered; therefore, evidence of insurability is rarely required of group plan participants. Instead, premiums are based on the broad characteristics of the group (employees and their family members and dependents), such as age distribution, occupation, gender mix, and levels of past claims. As a result, premiums are uniform per exposure: all employees with the same number of family members and/or dependents and who choose the same level of coverage pay the same premium, regardless of their personal health status.

The parties to an individual insurance contract are the insurer and the policyholder—the latter of which, along with dependents and family members, is covered under the policy. The parties to a group insurance contract are the insurer and the policyholder (the employer for employee benefit plans). Those covered under the policy (employees) are not parties to the contract but are considered third-party beneficiaries.

Coverage under an individual insurance policy begins when the insurance contract is entered into and ends when it is terminated. Coverage of an employee under a group plan is not based on duration of the insurance contract, as long as it remains in force, but on company eligibility requirements and participants' employment or personal circumstances. For example, an employee who gets married may opt out of the employer group plan in favor of coverage under the spouse's group policy. See the exhibit "Comparison of Group Insurance Plans and Individual Insurance Plans."

Comparison of Group Insurance Plans and Individual Insurance Plans

	Group Insurance	Individual Insurance
Parties to contract	Insurer and policyholder (employer), but not participants (employees).	Insurer and policyholder (individual), who is also covered by policy.
Covered parties	Participants and their family members and dependents.	Policyholder, family members, and dependents.
Duration of coverage	Not specifically related to term of insurance contract.	From contract inception to termination.
Underwriting	Based on entire group's general characteristics and level of past claims. Evidence of insurability is not required.	Based on characteristics and claim experience of individual policyholder and other covered parties. Applicant may be evaluated, or evidence of insurability may be required, to determine acceptability and price of coverage. (At the federal level, preexisting condition exclusions will be fully prohibited and medical underwriting significantly limited beginning January 1, 2014, because of the Affordable Care Act.)

[DA09042]

TAX TREATMENT OF EMPLOYER-PROVIDED BENEFITS

Employer-provided benefits plans offer tax advantages for both employers and employees.

An employer can reduce its tax bill significantly by offering employee benefits such as group healthcare insurance and retirement savings plans. To encourage employers to offer employee benefits, United States tax regulations allow employers to deduct the costs of providing such programs, and the amount they contribute as benefits, from their taxable income as business expenses. Other tax credits may also be available. For example, the Affordable Care Act, passed by Congress in 2010, extends a tax credit to employers that provide health insurance for their employees.

Employees also receive tax advantages from these programs. Unlike employee earnings (wages or salary for work performed), the value employees receive from employer-provided health insurance, retirement savings plans, and other benefits is not subject to taxes (such as income, Social Security, Medicare, and federal unemployment taxes). Any employee contributions made to such benefits with pretax earnings are also nontaxable. Because of these preferential tax treatments, a benefits plan—and the funds the employer spends on it—can provide an employee greater value, dollar for dollar, than the equivalent amount of taxable compensation.

Tax advantages vary according to types of plans, benefits offered, and methods of financing. An examination of two common employee benefits—group term life insurance and disability income insurance—demonstrates how various factors can affect tax treatment.

Tax Treatment of Group Term Life Insurance

A group term life insurance plan covers a group of employees under a single employer-owned policy. Just as with health and retirement plans, an employer's contributions to a group term life insurance plan are deductible from income as a business expense and are not taxable income for employees.

To qualify for preferential tax treatment, a group term life insurance plan must be nondiscriminatory—that is, it must treat all employees in the same age bracket the same. Employer plans that include special coverages for key employees do not qualify for preferential tax treatment.

In addition, favorable tax treatment of group term life insurance plans applies only to coverages of up to $50,000 per employee. The cost of any additional coverage per employee is taxed, whether it is provided by the employer or purchased by employees with their own funds. Some employer-provided plans include life insurance for employees' spouses or dependents. For such plans, the cost of coverage amounts up to $2,000 are nontaxable.

The beneficiary of the employee's group life insurance policy also receives favorable tax treatment: the death benefit from a group insurance policy (for example, a full $50,000 limit) is typically not subject to federal or state income tax, regardless of who paid the premium for the coverage.

Tax Treatment of Disability Income insurance

If an employee becomes disabled, disability income insurance replaces a percentage of the employee's salary with regular benefit payments. Tax treatment of these payments depends on who pays the insurance premium and whether the payments are made with pretax or taxable dollars.

The general rule is that disability benefits payments are taxable if coverage premiums have been paid with nontaxable funds; disability benefits payments are not taxable if premiums have been paid with after-tax funds. Application of this rule depends on these circumstances:

- If the employer pays the entire disability premium and the employee does not pay taxes on that amount, disability benefits are taxable.
- If the employee pays the entire premium with pretax dollars from his or her own compensation (typically withheld from the employee's paycheck before taxes are deducted), disability benefits are taxable.
- If the employee pays the entire premium with after-tax dollars (typically withheld from the employee's paycheck after taxes have been deducted), the disability benefits are tax free.
- If both the employer and the employee pay a share of the premium, the benefits are taxable in the same proportion that the premium is tax free to the employee; only that portion of the benefits attributable to employee premium payments made with after-tax dollars would be tax free.

Employees can save money by using pretax dollars to pay for their share (if any) of the disability premium. However, this savings could be negated if an employee becomes disabled, because the benefits paid for with tax-free dollars would become taxable. Because benefits payments normally exceed the amount paid in premiums, taxes paid on the benefits received would likely exceed the tax savings on the pretax premium payments.

ADVANTAGES AND DISADVANTAGES OF GROUP INSURANCE

While group insurance provides savings for both employers and employees, as well as needed coverages for employees without requiring evidence of insurability, it is not without limitations.

Group insurance can generally be purchased less expensively than individual insurance policies. Tax incentives encourage employers to offer group insurance as an employee benefit, giving employees access to group-plan savings that might otherwise be unavailable to them. Employers may pay all or part of the costs of group insurance with tax-deductible dollars, making group insurance even more affordable to employees. In addition, because insurers base the price of group insurance on the characteristics of a covered group rather than individual risk, participants are not required to provide evidence of insurability.

Despite their advantages, group insurance plans can pose disadvantages for employees through their inflexibility. For example, the savings afforded by group insurance is firmly tied to employment; loss of group coverage can significantly increase the financial hardships a family faces after a wage earner's job loss. Group plans also typically offer limited choices for participants with varying needs. This can be disadvantageous for employers as well, because

plans perceived as limited in value can erode the morale and productivity-boosting effects of a good employee benefits package.

The United States Congress has addressed some of the limitations of employer-provided group insurance by passing laws that require employers to provide safety nets and that authorize alternative types of benefit plans.

Less Expensive

When underwriting a group policy, an insurer considers the characteristics of the group rather than the insurability of each individual; therefore, underwriting costs are lower. Selling group insurance is also less costly per insured because a single group policy covers many individuals, while individual policies must be sold separately. Group policy administrative costs are less for the same reason, and insurers can further reduce such costs because group policyholders take on many of the administrative tasks.

These insurer savings make group policies affordable to employers, whereas purchasing multiple individual insurance policies to cover employees might be prohibitively costly. Employers' costs are further reduced by favorable tax treatment of their expenditures for and contributions to group insurance plans.

Tied to Employment

Employer-funded group insurance plans typically cover employees and their dependents. Therefore, loss of a job may eventually lead to loss of insurance coverage (for example, if the employee is unable to obtain another job with benefits, or if the employee remains unemployed and is unable to retain coverage such as COBRA or obtain other replacement coverage). An employee could also become ineligible for coverage by reducing hours from full time to part time work, and an employee's death or divorce can leave a family or a spouse without coverage.

When financial security is compromised by loss of or reduced earnings, loss of group coverage can present individuals and their families with additional hardship because of the necessity of finding coverage elsewhere—either through other employment or a more costly individual insurance policy. Sometimes a family's only option is to go without coverage.

Conversion From Group Insurance to Individual Insurance

Because insurers base the price of group insurance on the characteristics of a covered group rather than individual risk, participants are not required to provide evidence of insurability. In contrast, some types of individual insurance coverages—for example life insurance and health insurance—currently require such proof. However, starting in 2014, insurers will be prohibited by

the Affordable Care Act (ACA) from denying health insurance coverage or charging higher premiums because of preexisting medical conditions.

Currently, individual health insurance policies may require the insured to submit proof of good health, such as results of a medical exam. Under a group plan, a single employee with a serious chronic medical condition pays the same amount as single healthy employee in the same age group. Both employees, on termination, might consider converting to an individual health insurance policy, and both might be required to submit the results of a medical exam. As a result, until 2014, the employee with the medical condition might be denied coverage, eligible only for restricted coverage, or charged a much higher premium than the healthy employee.

Continuation of Health Care Coverage Under COBRA

Congress addressed the issues relating job termination to loss of group insurance eligibility by passing the Consolidated Omnibus Budget Reconciliation Act (COBRA) in 1985. COBRA provides a safety net for employees and their dependents by giving them the right to temporarily continue group coverage following loss of employment or full-time status, divorce, or employee death. The continuation period can range from eighteen to thirty-six months from the date of the change in eligibility status.

COBRA requires that the group benefits be continued without any evidence of insurability requirements. Employers must offer continuation coverage that is identical to the coverage offered in the group plan, although the recipient may choose to drop any dental or vision coverage provided. The employee has sixty days from the date of receiving notification that continuation coverage is available to decide to continue coverage and must pay the necessary premiums. Typically, coverage provided under COBRA costs more than the same group coverage but less than individual coverage.

Inflexible Group Insurance Benefits

Most group insurance plans offer all employees the same benefits. However, people have varying needs, and some employees may find that the inflexible structure does not adequately meet their needs or that their share of the premium goes for unneeded coverages. For example, an employee with a chronic medical condition and a large family may appreciate the coverage that group health insurance offers, but a single employee who enjoys excellent health and makes an effort to maintain it may resent the fact that his pretax dollars go to an insurer he had no role in selecting for coverage he rarely uses.

Some group health plans offer employees options to pay lower premiums in exchange for higher deductibles or copayments or to pay higher premiums for a greater selection of healthcare providers. However, employees still have little choice about how benefit dollars are spent.

In response to these issues, programs have evolved that allow employees more flexibility in how they use their pretax contributions to a benefit plan.

Flexible Spending Accounts (FSAs)

Flexible spending accounts (FSAs) allow employees to designate an amount of pretax dollars to fund accounts for two primary types of expenses not covered by group insurance, medical and dependent care. Employees estimate the amounts for each account at the beginning of the year, and salary or payroll deductions are determined accordingly.

Medical FSAs (also referred to as health care FSAs) can be used to pay for out-of-pocket medical (including drug and health insurance co-pays), dental, and vision care expenses. If an employee does not use all funds in the medical FSA by year's end (or after a wind-down period), they revert back to the employer. No IRS maximum limits exist for medical FSAs, but employers typically limit annual employee contributions to avoid the risks associated with prefunding miscalculations and forfeiture of funds.

Dependent care FSAs can be used to pay for out-of-pocket dependent care expenses, such as child care, including day care, with pretax dollars. There is a prefunding limit on dependent care FSAs, currently set at $5,000 per year. As with a medical FSA, any unused dependent care funds in the employee's account at year's end (or after a wind-down period) revert to the employer.

Cafeteria Plans

Cafeteria plans provide an even wider range of employee choices. Under these plans, employees use a dollar amount specified by the employer to purchase from a list of available options. Employees who want additional benefits can pay for them with their own funds through payroll deductions.

Cafeteria plans allow employees to choose among different types of benefits, both taxable and nontaxable. A cafeteria plan typically includes group health insurance and may also include such nontaxable benefits as group term life insurance, 401(k) retirement savings plans, and FSAs. Taxable benefits included in cafeteria plans may include discounted group auto or homeowners insurance, vacation days, or cash.

Cafeteria plans also help control benefits costs for employers. For example, to make their cafeteria plan dollars go further, employees may choose higher-deductible health coverages that cost employers less. In addition, as benefits costs rise, employers can pass along some of the expense to employees—and an increase in the cafeteria plan amount allotted to each employee can be less than the employer's cost increase.

Review Questions

1. Identify three sources of employee death benefits.
2. Explain why an employer that has workers compensation insurance, which includes disability coverage for employees, might also offer a discretionary disability insurance benefit for its employees.
3. Identify five employee benefits that are required by law.
4. Describe the indirect benefit an employer receives from employee contributions to an employer-sponsored retirement plan that are made from pre-tax earnings.
5. Describe how an employer can use an employee benefits package to attract and retain employees.
6. Explain how employee benefits plans contribute to employee productivity.
7. Give an example of eligibility and participation requirements in an employer-sponsored group health insurance plan.
8. Contrast contributory group insurance plans and noncontributory group insurance plans.
9. Contrast how premiums are determined under individual insurance plans and group insurance plans.
10. Describe, in general terms, the tax advantages employers and employees receive from employee benefits plans.
11. Describe how a group term life insurance plan qualifies for preferential tax treatment.
12. Describe how the taxation of disability benefits payments is affected by whether premium payments are made with pretax or taxable dollars.
13. Describe two advantages of group insurance over individual insurance.
14. Describe two disadvantages of group insurance relative to individual insurance.
15. Describe three measures that address the disadvantages of group insurance.

Application Questions

1. Under a group term life insurance policy sponsored by his employer, Michael is entitled to $65,000 in coverage for himself and $5,000 in coverage for his wife, Charlotte. Michael's employer pays 100 percent of the premium for this coverage. Determine the amount of this life insurance coverage benefit that would be considered taxable income for Michael.

SUMMARY

Employee benefits are forms of compensation that workers may receive from their employers in addition to their salaries or wages. Some employee benefits are required by law; others are voluntary. Common offerings include health expense benefits, retirement benefits, death benefits, disability benefits, and unemployment benefits.

Employers receive tax advantages for paying for and contributing to benefits plans and have access to group rates for insurance coverage that, if purchased by individual employees, would cost substantially more. Competitive benefits plans can help an employer attract new employees and retain current ones. By offering solutions not available elsewhere, employee benefit plans give employees peace of mind and a sense of security that can enhance productivity.

Employee group insurance plans insure many individuals under a single policy purchased by the employer. Group insurance plans are often restricted to full-time employees and may require a probationary period before a new employee is eligible to participate. A group plan may be financed solely by the employer (noncontributory) or by a combination of employer and employee financing (contributory). A primary difference between group insurance plans and individual insurance plans relates to how premiums are determined. Group premiums are based on the broad characteristics and claim experience of the group; individual premiums are based on the characteristics and claim experience of the individuals covered.

Employers can deduct the costs of providing many employee benefits from their taxable income as business expenses. Employees also receive tax advantages from employer-provided benefits because the value they receive from such plans may not be subject to taxes and because contributions they make to such programs may be from pretax earnings.

Compared with individual insurance policies, group insurance plans are less expensive to sell, underwrite, and administer. Employers that purchase group policies benefit from these savings, as well as from tax incentives. Employees have access to group-plan savings that might otherwise be unavailable to them, and they also receive tax advantages. In addition, because insurers base the price of group insurance on the characteristics of a covered group rather than individual risk, participants are not required to provide evidence of insurability. However, because group insurance is tied to employment, loss of a job can leave an employee and dependents without coverage, and the inflexibility of group plans may not meet all employees' needs. COBRA provides temporary continuation coverage for employees who lose their eligibility for group coverage, and some employers offer FSAs and cafeteria plans that present more flexibility for employees.

ASSIGNMENT NOTES

1. Stephen Leimberg and John McFadden,Tools and Techniques of Employee Benefit and Retirement Planning, 9th ed., (Erlanger, KY: The National Underwriter Company, 2005), p. 293.
2. "The Looming U.S. Labor Shortage," Market Watch, March 14, 2012, http://articles.marketwatch.com/2012-03-14/commentary/31160294_1_baby-boomer-skilled-workers-labor-shortage (accessed September 18, 2012).

Direct Your Learning

13

Health Risks and Employee Benefits Plans

Educational Objectives

After learning the content of this assignment, you should be able to:

- Describe the basic issues facing healthcare as well as the parties to a healthcare transaction.
- Describe the characteristics of the following nongovernment programs for providing healthcare benefits:
  - Traditional health insurance plans
  - Managed-care plans
  - Consumer-directed health plans
- Describe each of the following government programs for providing healthcare benefits:
  - Original Medicare
  - Medicare Advantage
  - Medicare Supplement Insurance
  - Medicare Part D Prescription Drug Coverage
  - Medicaid

Outline

The Healthcare Fee-for-Service Indemnity System

Health Insurance Plans

Government-Provided Health Insurance Plans

Summary

Health Risks and Employee Benefits Plans

13

THE HEALTHCARE FEE-FOR-SERVICE INDEMNITY SYSTEM

The United States has the highest healthcare costs in the world. Many experts attribute this to the fee-for-service model for delivering healthcare goods and services as well as to an overall lack of cost controls.

Rising healthcare costs have resulted in some employers ceasing to provide healthcare coverage for their employees and in other employers charging more to employees for the coverage. The rise in costs has also made health insurance unavailable to or unaffordable for many people who do not have healthcare coverage through their employers and who are ineligible for government programs.

Basic Issues Facing Healthcare

These are the two basic issues facing healthcare in the U.S.:

- High cost of healthcare goods and services
- High number of uninsured individuals

Although some people believe the U.S. has the highest healthcare costs because it has the best healthcare, statistics do not support this conclusion. In 2011, the U.S. ranked 27th in life expectancy. Also, the U.S. is not ranked at the top of global destinations for medical treatment.

Instead, the model of healthcare delivery in the U.S. is often cited as the cause of the high cost. The U.S. has a fee-for-service model in which healthcare providers charge a fee every time they deliver a good or perform a service, despite no guarantee of outcomes. U.S. citizens also use more specialists, who charge higher fees, than do people in other countries.[1]

In 2010, 50 million people in the U.S., or approximately 17 percent of the population, did not have health insurance. This number declined by 1.4 million people in 2011, the first decline in a long trend of increasing numbers of the uninsured.[2] The high number of uninsured individuals is likely a factor in the lower life expectancy in the U.S. compared with nations that have universal healthcare coverage.

The primary purpose of the Patient Protection and Affordable Care Act of 2010 was to provide near-universal healthcare coverage. A central tenet of the act was the prohibition of preexisting condition provisions in all insurance policies by 2014. Also effective in 2014 is the requirement for Americans who are not covered by an employer-sponsored healthcare plan, or other public or eligible health insurance, to purchase health insurance or pay a penalty. If affordable coverage is not available or if the individuals' income levels are below a certain level, a waiver can be applied.

Parties to a Healthcare Transaction

There are three parties to a healthcare transaction:

- The seller of healthcare goods and services—a hospital, a doctor, or another provider
- The buyer of healthcare goods and services—a patient, an injured person, or a family member of an insured employee
- The entity responsible for paying for healthcare goods and services—an insurer, an employer, or the government (Medicare or Medicaid)

Most payments for healthcare goods and services in the U.S. are made by third parties—typically, insurers, third-party administrators for self-insured employers, or government programs such as Medicare. Because of this three-party system, individuals and their employers who provide more than 50 percent of healthcare coverage have little control over cost. Issues such as waste, duplication of services and billing, and outright fraud by some medical providers contribute to the problem of rising healthcare costs.

Most patients have little understanding of complex medical services. They cannot compare different providers' services and costs for healthcare the way they could comparison shop for an electronic product. One surgeon whose fee is higher may be more successful than one with a lower fee. The better surgeon, although charging more up front, may generally experience fewer complications and perform fewer corrective surgeries than a less-experienced or -skilled surgeon. An expensive diagnostic test may prevent a severe and more expensive problem in the future. Even patients with high levels of education do not have access to the data necessary to make informed decisions. Although large employers may have the resources to make some of these decisions, employee privacy and other concerns, such as access to provider networks, typically require them to use third-party administrators to make payments for healthcare services.

Reality Check

The Uninsured Party in Healthcare Transactions

The uninsured individual, a special type of buyer of healthcare goods and services, has a significant effect on the healthcare delivery system in the United States.

Some individuals, a small minority, are uninsured by choice, preferring to pay out-of-pocket for healthcare services as needed. A more common scenario is that of uninsured individuals who have little access to healthcare except for hospital emergency rooms. Few physicians in private practice will agree to take on the care of anyone who is uninsured. Other physicians, frustrated with the entire insurance reimbursement system, accept cash only, fee-for-service, or even charge based on minutes per appointment.

For the majority of the uninsured who resort to hospital emergency rooms when ill, delivery of health services in emergency rooms is the least cost-effective and efficient method of delivery for anything other than a true medical emergency. The use of emergency rooms for nonemergency medical conditions by the uninsured increases hospital costs, which are often passed on to other payers in the form of higher fees. This usage of emergency rooms can also result in delayed care and worse outcomes for individuals with true medical emergencies.

Hospitals either access limited federal funding for the uninsured or pass costs along to other payers for services for low-income individuals. However, in the case of uninsured middle-class individuals who may have assets, such as a home, hospitals charge their highest rates without applying the discounts and fee schedules that are available to government programs and insurers. One hospital admission can cost more than $50,000 and result in bankruptcy or a lifetime of payments for an individual or family without health insurance.

[DA09043]

HEALTH INSURANCE PLANS

Various types of group and individual (nongroup) healthcare plans are available in the private, nongovernmental market. Some employers offer self-insured plans for their employees.

Most American healthcare consumers participate in group healthcare plans (as opposed to individual plans). In addition to employer self-insured plans, three broad types of healthcare plans provide the majority of private healthcare resources for Americans:

- Traditional health insurance plans
- Managed-care plans
- Consumer-directed health plans (CDHPs)

These plans vary in terms of premiums, fees, benefits, out-of-pocket requirements, healthcare delivery, eligibility requirements, and regulatory authority. See the exhibit "Self-Insurance Plans."

Self-Insurance Plans

In addition to the availability of commercial health insurance and Blue Cross and Blue Shield plans, many employers self-insure part or all of the health insurance benefits they provide to their employees. Self-insurance, also called self-funding, means that the employer funds and pays part or all of an employee's medical expenses. Employers that self-insure either perform their own claim processing or contract with third-party administrators to manage the plans, including enrolling employees and processing claims.

[DA05661]

Traditional Health Insurance Plans

Indemnity plan
A type of healthcare plan that allows patients to choose their own healthcare provider and reimburses the patient or provider at a certain percentage (usually after a deductible is paid) for services provided.

Traditional health insurance plans insure many individuals and families through the use of "fee for service" or **indemnity plan** coverage. Providers of traditional health insurance plans include commercial insurers and Blue Cross and Blue Shield plans.

Major life and health insurers, and some property-casualty insurers, offer commercial, or private, health insurance (any nongovernmental health coverage) to the public. Commercial health insurance offers many benefits packages and premium variations, often tailored to specific needs of large or small groups, or of individuals.

Individual plan consumers include workers of all ages with no employer-sponsored health insurance coverage, young unemployed adults, and business owners with no group coverage. Purchasers of non-group policies for family coverage tend to be over age thirty-five.

Basic medical expense coverage
Coverage for medical expenses, such as hospital and surgical expenses, physicians' visits, and miscellaneous medical services.

Major medical insurance
Insurance that covers medical expenses resulting from illness or injury that are not covered by a basic medical expense plan.

Blue Cross and Blue Shield plans historically were not-for-profit plans, although they are now often administered by for-profit organizations. Because of this not-for-profit history, Blue Cross and Blue Shield providers usually are not described as "commercial insurers" and typically are regulated by state laws separate from those regulating other insurers. Blue Cross and Blue Shield plans provide **basic medical expense coverage** and **major medical insurance** on either an individual or a group basis. Blue Cross and Blue Shield plans also sponsor managed-care plans.

Blue Cross plans usually contract with hospitals and pay them directly, rather than paying insureds (also called 'subscribers'), and Blue Shield plans often pay physicians directly. Basic medical expense coverage pays for routine healthcare expenses. Major medical insurance plans provide broader coverage for medical expenses, as well as catastrophic coverage for more costly treat-

ment. Major medical insurance plans usually have deductibles, which insureds must pay out of pocket. See the exhibit "Example Benefits of Basic and Major Medical Insurance Coverage."

Example Benefits of Basic and Major Medical Insurance Coverage

Basic Medical Insurance Coverage	Major Medical Insurance Coverage
• Hospital expenses	• Hospital room and board
• Surgical expenses	• Hospital services and supplies
• Physician visits	• X-rays
• Additional medical services, such as ambulance and mental health services	• Diagnostic tests
	• Physician and surgeon services
	• Prescription drugs
	• Home healthcare services
	• Durable medical equipment
	• Additional services, such as convalescent nursing-home care and dental services

[DA07792]

Managed-Care Plans

Managed-care plans manage the quality of their members' care and control healthcare costs. Managed-care plans often involve the same insurers that administer traditional plans; however, managed care involves an insurer negotiating benefits and fees with a network of healthcare providers. The customer receives significant premium savings and reduced out-of-pocket costs as a result, but often with reduced flexibility. Most managed-care plans cover a standard array of services including hospital care, physicians' and surgeons' services, laboratory and x-ray services, and outpatient and maternity care, among other services. Some plans provide emergency care, while others do not or only provide emergency services at a higher cost to the member.

Managed care plan

A type of healthcare plan providing members with comprehensive services and incentives to use providers belonging to the plan.

These are the most prevalent forms of managed-care plans:

- **Health maintenance organization (HMO)**—An HMO contracts with healthcare providers to provide comprehensive services to its members for a low, fixed, prepaid fee, with small co-payments for routine visits. A "gatekeeper physician" usually must pre-approve specialists' visits. HMOs control costs by requiring preapproval for specified physicians' treatments and specialists' services, along with oversight of diagnostic tests and treatments. Members save costs through lower premiums and out-of-pocket

Health maintenance organization (HMO)

An organization that provides all the care needed by its members in exchange for a fixed fee.

expenses. For example, Courtney's HMO family plan may provide routine care for her family with small co-payments per visit, while covered visits to an emergency room—or to a specialist referred by her primary care physician—would be more than the primary care copayment.

Preferred provider organization (PPO)

An administrative organization that meets the common needs of healthcare providers and clients and that identifies networks of providers and contracts for their medical services at discounted rates.

- **Preferred provider organization (PPO)**—PPO members may choose any provider, but preferred providers offer decreased medical service costs and lower deductibles. No primary care physician is required and any physician may make specialist referrals. Some Blue Cross-Blue Shield plans are PPOs. PPOs are one of the more expensive forms of managed-care plans, but they are popular because they blend the advantages of both traditional indemnity plans and HMOs. For example, Jacob and his family, with school-age children, may benefit from a PPO family plan. It would enable his wife to see her out-of-network OB-GYN (though her copayment would be more than if the OB-GYN were in-network). Their routine care with in-network providers would require minimal copayments, while the copayments would double for network specialists. Hospital and emergency care would require a somewhat larger copayment.
- Exclusive provider organization (EPO)—EPOs contract with insurers to provide healthcare to plan members at a much lower premium than healthcare provided by other plans. The EPO charges insurers an access fee for use of the network, negotiates with healthcare providers to set fee schedules for guaranteed service levels, and helps resolve issues between insurers and healthcare providers. Except for emergencies, plan members must exclusively use EPO network healthcare providers. For example, Tabitha and her husband obtain healthcare strictly from EPO providers with small copayments per visit. Out-of-network emergency care would be covered, but the copayment would be relatively large. An EPO is similar to an HMO plan in many ways, such as the very limited out-of-network coverage. The differences between an EMO and HMO are more evident to the providers. Providers in an HMO receive payments from the insurer on a monthly basis. Providers in an EPO receive payment only for services they provide. Plus, EPO premiums are frequently lower than those for an HMO.

Point-of-service (POS) plan

Managed care plan that combines the characteristics of an HMO and a PPO; has a network of preferred providers who, if used by the member, charge little or nothing for services; heathcare received out of the network is covered, but members must pay substantially higher coinsurance charges and a deductible.

- **Point-of-service (POS) plan**—A POS has characteristics of both HMOs and PPOs, but more closely resembles an HMO. A POS plan controls medical costs, but the member must choose a primary care physician from within the POS network. This physician becomes the member's "point of service" and can refer a member inside or outside the network. Some services are provided by non-network providers with reduced POS payments. The POS handles all paperwork and billings for network care, whereas the member handles paperwork, bills, and record-keeping for out-of-network care. For example, Kaleb's POS family plan provides routine care from a selected primary care physician with small copayments. If Kaleb's primary care physician referred him to a specialist outside of the POS network, Kaleb's insurer would pay for a reduced portion of his covered medical

care. Kaleb would be required to pay the specialist's medical bills up front and then file an insurance claim and await reimbursement.

Some private insurers extend managed-care benefits to Medicare recipients. Medicare Advantage (MA) plans, often called Medicare Part C, offer options similar to other managed-care plans. In addition to the basic benefits provided by Medicare under Part A and Part B, beneficiaries may be eligible for managed-care services and supplemental benefits and health services. Some supplemental benefits are mandatory for enrollees, and others are optional.[3] MA plans may offer these managed-care options:

- HMO
- Provider-sponsored organizations
- PPO
- Medical savings accounts (MSAs), which combine the use of a health savings account (HSA) with a high-deductible catastrophic health plan
- Private fee-for-service (PFFS) plans, which give beneficiaries more choices through the ability to obtain services from any Medicare-approved provider accepting the plan's payment
- Special needs plans (SNPs), which enroll one or more types of individuals with special needs as defined by law, including those who have been institutionalized, who are eligible for both Medicare and Medicaid, and who have severe or disabling chronic conditions

Consumer-Directed Health Plans

Consumer-directed health plans (CDHPs) provide consumers with access to high-quality care without requiring deductibles for preventive care. CDHPs can provide healthcare benefits to those who might otherwise be uninsured. CDHPs usually include three major components:

- A health savings account (HSA) or a health reimbursement arrangement (HRA)
- High-deductible medical coverage, with preventive care not charged against the deductible
- Access to informational tools for making informed healthcare decisions

People covered by CDHPs pay lower premiums for their health coverage because the deductibles are high. Using either an HSA or HRA, they set aside money that can be used to help satisfy the deductible. HSAs are funded by enrollees themselves, and the money in the HSA can be rolled over for future use at year's end. No taxes are withheld from the funds contributed to an HSA. The money in an HRA is contributed by the employer and is not included in the employees' income for tax purposes. The employer's distributions to the employee are tax deductible, and unused funds in HRA accounts can be rolled over from year to year for future use.

Participants set aside HSA and HRA funds at the start of a year for medical expenses before the participant begins to pay out-of-pocket costs. For example, if a consumer has an annual deductible of $2,000 and a $1,000 HSA or HRA fund, the consumer's first $1,000 of medical expenses are paid from that fund. The consumer then pays the remaining expenses out-of-pocket, up to $2,000, when major medical coverage applies. See the exhibit "Basic Provisions of the Affordable Care Act of 2010."

Basic Provisions of the Affordable Care Act of 2010

The Patient Protection and Affordable Care Act (PPACA) of 2010, often called the Affordable Care Act, was intended to reform the private health insurance industry and help curb rising medical care costs. Provisions of the act make health insurance available to more individuals and provide improved coverage provisions. These benefits are or will be evident under the new laws:

- Insurers cannot decline insurance for children (under age nineteen) with pre-existing medical conditions; this protection will extend to individuals of all ages as of 2014.
- Adult children (up to age twenty-six) can join or remain covered under a parent's healthcare plan.
- Insurers cannot rescind benefits (retroactively cancel coverage) because an insured or the employer made an honest mistake or omission on the insurance application.
- Insurers cannot place lifetime dollar limits on essential benefits; annual dollar limits are being phased out and will not be allowed after 2014.
- Insurers may be required to pay for certain preventative services (such as screenings, flu and pneumonia vaccines, well-baby and well-child visits) without applying co-payments, coinsurance, or deductibles.
- Individuals can choose primary care physicians from within a plan's provider network, can obtain services from an OB-GYN without a referral from a physician, and can seek emergency care at a hospital outside of the plan's network without prior approval.
- Insurers are required to spend set percentages of premiums received on direct medical care or improvements to the quality of care provided, and must meet annual federal reporting requirements; insurers must provide rebates to participants if the percentages are not met.

U.S. Department of Health & Human Services, "Understanding the Affordable Care Act: Provisions," December 1, 2010, www.healthcare.gov/law/provisions/index.html (accessed June 17, 2011). [DA07793]

Apply Your Knowledge

Bonita has a ten-year-old son, Ray, who has a number of medical conditions and prefers to see certain specialists for his treatments. Bonita changed jobs and her new employer offers two managed care options, a PPO plan and an EPO plan. While Bonita would prefer a flexible plan with low deductibles and

co-payments and minimal paperwork, Ray would like to continue treatments with his preferred specialists.

Which one of these options would best meet Bonita's and Ray's healthcare needs?

a. Her employer's PPO plan
b. Her employer's EPO plan
c. Private healthcare insurance

Feedback: a. A PPO plan offered by her new employer would best meet their healthcare needs because it would provide greater flexibility to enable Ray and Bonita to seek medical care from the physicians and specialists with whom they have been treated previously. If one of their providers is out-of-network, they could still see that provider, but they would pay higher costs, co-payments, and deductibles for such treatments.

GOVERNMENT-PROVIDED HEALTH INSURANCE PLANS

Medicare and Medicaid provide the cornerstone of America's healthcare services.

People age sixty-five or older, under sixty-five with certain disabilities, or of all ages with specified medical conditions can qualify to receive federal Medicare health benefits. Medicare provides benefits under four programs:

- Original Medicare
- Medicare Advantage (Part C)
- Medicare Supplement Insurance (Medigap)
- Medicare Part D Prescription Drug Coverage

In addition to the original Medicare Part A and Part B, the Medicare Advantage (MA) program (called Part C) became available in 1997. Some private insurers offer Medicare Supplement Insurance (Medigap) to cover costs that are not paid by Medicare. The Medicare Prescription Drug, Improvement, and Modernization Act of 2003 provided Medicare beneficiaries with assistance in paying for prescription drugs (Medicare Part D).

Medicaid, a federal-state government healthcare plan, provides a public assistance (welfare) healthcare plan for low-income persons.

Original Medicare

Medicare

Social insurance program that covers the medical expenses of most individuals age sixty-five and older.

Medicare is part of the federal Old Age and Survivors Disability Health Insurance (OASDHI) program. It is a social insurance program that covers the medical expenses of most individuals age sixty-five and older, providing them with an affordable healthcare option.

Under the original Medicare program, beneficiaries have two basic coverages: Part A (hospital insurance) and Part B (medical insurance). Beneficiaries have options when deciding how to receive Medicare-covered services. The options available can vary depending on where the beneficiary lives. Most beneficiaries are placed in the original Medicare program, but they can then review their health and prescription needs annually and switch to different plans during certain periods toward the end of each year.

Medicare Part A is largely financed through payroll taxes paid by employees and employers. Medicare Part B is largely financed through a monthly premium paid by beneficiaries and the federal government's general revenues. The premiums are adjusted each year based on plan experience.

Medicare Part A helps pay for in-hospital services and Medicare Part B pays for medically necessary non-hospital services. See the exhibit "Medicare Benefits."

Generally, people are eligible for Medicare if they or their spouses worked for at least ten years in Medicare-covered employment, are age sixty-five or older, and are a citizen or permanent resident of the United States. People who are not yet sixty-five may also qualify for coverage if they have a disability or end-stage renal disease (permanent kidney failure requiring dialysis or transplant).

Most people receive Part A coverage automatically when they reach sixty-five years of age. Enrolling in Part B is optional. A beneficiary can enroll in Part B any time during a seven-month period that begins three months before turning sixty-five. The premium is usually taken out of monthly Social Security, Railroad Retirement, or Civil Service Retirement payments, and beneficiaries who do not receive those payments must pay the Part B premium every three months. Requirements for premium-free or premium-based coverage can vary in some circumstances. People who have limited income and resources may qualify for state assistance to pay for Part A and Part B.

Medicare Advantage (Part C)

Medicare Advantage plans

Health insurance plan options that provide benefits in addition to basic Medicare; offered by private insurers that contract with Medicare and available to beneficiaries currently enrolled in Medicare Part A and Part B.

Beneficiaries who need more services than Medicare covers can choose private health insurance (Medicare approved) plans called **Medicare Advantage (MA) plans** or Part C plans. Part C plans cover medically necessary care offered by nearly any hospital or doctor in the country, but they do not cover all healthcare costs. The benefits offered by MA plans must at least equal Medicare Part A and B benefits, but they do not have to cover every benefit in the same manner. For example, plans that pay less than Medicare for some

Medicare Benefits

Medicare Hospital Insurance (Part A)	Medicare Medical Insurance (Part B)
• Inpatient care in hospitals • Critical access hospitals (rural, small facilities that offer limited outpatient and inpatient services) • Skilled nursing facilities (not custodial or long-term care) • Hospice care • Some home healthcare	• Doctors' services • Outpatient hospital care • Some other medical services that Part A does not cover, such as physical and occupational therapy, and some home healthcare
Medicare Advantage (Part C) Plans	**Medicare Supplement Insurance (Medigap)**
• Benefits consistent with Medicare Part A and B • Medically necessary care offered by nearly any United States hospital or physician • Choices of Medicare-managed care plans, private fee-for-service (PFFS) plans, and special needs plans (SNP), if applicable • Supplemental benefits could include lower out-of-pocket costs, dental, vision, hearing, and/or health and wellness programs • Some offer replacement prescription drug program for Part D	• Medicare exclusions and limitations • Medicare cost-sharing provisions • Medicare out-of-pocket charges (deductibles, coinsurance, co-payments, and emergency healthcare out of the U.S.)
Medicare Prescription Drug Coverage (Part D)	
• Subsidizes costs of prescription drugs underwritten through private insurance carriers • Provides coverage for beneficiaries having high or unexpected prescription drug bills	

[DA07794]

benefits, like skilled nursing facility care, can balance their benefits package by offering lower co-payments for doctor visits.

The plans, services, and fees of MA plans vary by location. People participating in an MA plan may pay a monthly premium in addition to the Medicare Part B premium and generally pay a fixed co-payment (such as $20) for each doctor visit. Medicare pays the MA plan a set monthly amount for each beneficiary who participates.

MA plans can use excess Medicare subsidies to offer supplemental benefits to members. For example, some plans limit members' annual out-of-pocket spending to protect against catastrophic medical costs or to provide benefits not available through Medicare.

A Medicare beneficiary can choose between different types of MA plans:

- Medicare-managed care plans, such as health maintenance organizations (HMOs), preferred provider organization (PPO) plans, and others—Also called coordinated care, these plans may require the beneficiary to pay fixed fees and co-payments for services obtained from preferred providers. These plans may also offer prescription drug plans which replace the Medicare prescription drug program (Medicare Part D).
- Private fee-for-service (PFFS) plans—A type of Medicare Advantage plan in which a beneficiary may go to any Medicare-approved doctor or hospital that accepts the plan's payment. Medicare pays the PFFS plan a portion of the premium, and the beneficiary must pay the difference to the provider, although Medicare has strict limits on what patients can be charged. The PFFS plan provides all Medicare and additional benefits to the beneficiary.
- Special needs plans (SNP)—A special plan providing more-focused healthcare for specific groups of people, such as those who have both Medicare and Medicaid, who reside in a nursing home, or who have certain chronic medical conditions. SNP providers coordinate the services and medical care providers to meet beneficiaries' unique needs. Except in emergencies, SNP beneficiaries may be required to use services available within the plan network. SNPs are required to provide Medicare prescription drug coverage (Part D).

Medicare Supplement Insurance (Medigap)

Medicare Supplement Insurance policies (also called Medigap policies) are sold by private insurers to fill the gaps in original Medicare Parts A and B coverage. Premiums for Medigap policies can be costly, but they provide coverage for a number of benefits and fill the gaps left within Medicare provisions. However, the benefits provided by Medigap policies do not include paying the costs for Medicare Parts C and D. Additionally, a person who has purchased an MA plan does not require a Medigap policy because the benefits covered are typically the same.

Medicare Prescription Drug Coverage (Part D)

Medicare Part D is a voluntary program through which the government subsidizes the costs of beneficiaries' prescription drugs underwritten through private insurance carriers. It provides coverage for beneficiaries who have very high or unexpected prescription drug bills. All Medicare beneficiaries are eligible for this coverage, except when it is provided separately under MA plans.

Beneficiaries may sign up for Part D upon first becoming eligible for Medicare (three months before the month they reach sixty-five years of age until three months after they turn sixty-five). If they receive Medicare coverage as a result of a disability, they can sign up from three months before to three months after their twenty-fifth month of receiving cash disability payments.

Medicare beneficiaries generally pay monthly premiums for Part D, which vary by plan, and a yearly deductible. They also pay a part of the prescription costs, including a deductible (co-payment) or **coinsurance**. Some plans offer more coverage and cover additional drugs for higher monthly premiums. Beneficiaries with limited income and resources may qualify for extra governmental assistance and may not have to pay a premium or deductible.

Coinsurance
An insurance-to-value provision in many property insurance policies providing that if the property is underinsured, the amount that an insurer will pay for a covered loss is reduced.

Medicaid

Medicaid is a means-tested federal-state welfare program that covers the medical expenses of low-income persons, including those who are aged, blind, or disabled; members of families with dependent children; and pregnant women and certain children. Low-income Medicare beneficiaries requiring nursing home coverage are also eligible. An investigative process determines eligibility.

Benefits and eligibility for Medicaid can vary by state because states help fund the program. The federal government pays almost 60 percent of all Medicaid expenses, so while each state administers its own program, the federal Centers for Medicare and Medicaid Services (CMS) set requirements for quality, funding, and eligibility. To receive matching funds and grants, each state must conform to federal guidelines. Each state's poverty level determines the federal matching formula. The wealthiest states receive a federal match of 50 percent, while poorer states receive a greater percentage of funding. Medicaid's costs average 22 percent of each state's budget.

The largest group of Medicaid recipients is children, comprising almost half the number of total recipients. A limited income is one of the primary eligibility requirements for Medicaid, but poverty alone does not qualify applicants to receive Medicaid benefits. See the exhibit "Medicaid Provisions."

Medicaid sends benefit payments directly to healthcare providers. In some states, Medicaid beneficiaries must pay a small fee (co-payment) for medical services. While Medicaid eligibility is based on income and assets, specific requirements can vary. In some situations, any category of applicant may be denied coverage.

Special rules apply to applicants who are disabled children living at home, are living with HIV/AIDS, or are residents of a nursing home. Disabled children may be covered under Medicaid if they are U.S. citizens or permanent residents. They may be eligible even if their parents are not, or if they live with people other than their parents.

Additionally, Medicaid provides the largest portion of federal money spent on healthcare for people living with HIV/AIDS, who usually must progress from an HIV-positive diagnosis to AIDS before qualifying under the "disabled" category. More than half of Americans who have AIDS receive Medicaid payments.

Medicaid Provisions

Persons Eligible for Benefits	Eligibility Requirements	State-Dependent Benefits
Low Income: • Children • Pregnant women • Parents of eligible children • People with disabilities • Eligible people who have little or no medical insurance	Criteria include: • Age • Pregnancy • Disability • Blindness • Income and resources • Status as a U.S. citizen or a lawfully admitted immigrant	May provide: • Inpatient and outpatient hospital services • Physician services • Medical and surgical dental services • Some in-home care • Custodial nursing home care • Personal care • Some prescriptions

[DA07795]

While a living Medicaid recipient does not pay for services, once that recipient dies, Medicaid may recover costs paid for healthcare from the recipient's property, if any. Eligibility guidelines, for example, may allow a recipient to own one home, one car, and $2,000 in assets (such as savings accounts or retirement plans), but recipients' financial records are reviewed up to five years prior to an application for benefits to determine eligibility.

Retirees and other people facing high nursing home costs are subject to special Medicaid eligibility standards that attempt to prevent them from disposing of substantial assets before applying for Medicaid. As a result, any asset or financial transfers without fair market value (usually gifts) that take place during the five years preceding the Medicaid application can be subject to penalties.

Apply Your Knowledge

Harold retired at age sixty-five after working thirty-five years at a job that contributed to Medicare. Harold's retirement income and investments allow him to afford some healthcare coverage. Harold has ongoing treatments for normal hearing and vision loss. Harold believes participation in a wellness program improves his quality of life and reduces his medical costs. Harold prefers to save on premiums by paying some of his medical costs out of pocket.

Which one of these Medicare benefits would be most appropriate for Harold's preferences and needs?

a. Medicare Part A and Part B
b. Medicare Advantage (MA) (Part C) plan
c. Medicare Supplement Insurance (Medigap)
d. Medicare prescription drug coverage (Part D)

Feedback: b. A Medicare Advantage (MA) (Part C) plan would be most appropriate because it would pay benefits equal to Medicare Part A and Part B but could provide additional benefits that would meet Harold's preferences and needs. For example, such a plan might provide hearing and/or vision coverage and might provide a wellness program. An MA plan might also include limitations on high-cost medical treatments. Medicare Part A and Part B (a.) would not be needed with an MA plan, and, because Harold prefers to pay some out-of-pocket costs, neither Medicare Supplement Insurance (c.) nor Medicare prescription drug coverage (d.) would meet his needs.

Review Questions

1. Identify where the United States ranks in healthcare costs compared with other countries.
2. Describe the two basic issues facing healthcare in the U.S.
3. List the three parties to a healthcare transaction.
4. Name the types of insurers that offer traditional health plans to the public.
5. Name the most prevalent forms of managed-care plans.
6. Explain the operation of consumer-directed health plans (CDHPs).
7. Name the groups of people Medicare covers.
8. Explain whether the federal government provides Medicare Part D coverage for all Medicare beneficiaries.
9. List the eligibility requirement criteria an applicant must meet to qualify for Medicaid.

Application Questions

1. Brian's employer offers two healthcare plan options: a health maintenance organization (HMO) and a preferred provider organization (PPO). Brian and his wife, Deb, are both recent high school graduates and currently have no known health issues. They would prefer a plan with low premiums and out-of-pocket expenses. The couple are new to the area, and they are not familiar with area physicians or other medical care providers. Which one of the two healthcare plan options would best meet the couple's current needs? Explain your answer.
2. Spouses Bridget and Don have both worked in Medicare-covered employment for over fifteen years and are U.S. citizens. At age forty-five, Bridget is diagnosed with cancer and is forced to leave work because of the disability. Don has to reduce his employment to a part-time basis, and, as a result of their reduced income, the couple falls below the poverty level of their state and is left with little discretionary income. Bridget's medical treatments and prescription medicines are costly, and her doctor advises that she will need hospice care within the next four months. Explain

why Bridget would qualify for Medicare and may qualify for Medicaid. Assuming Bridget did not qualify for Medicaid, explain the likelihood and reasons why these parts of Medicare would or would not meet the couple's needs: Medicare Part A, Medicare Part B, and Medicare Prescription Drug Coverage (Part D).

SUMMARY

The two basic issues facing healthcare in the U.S. are high costs and high numbers of uninsured individuals. Many experts believe that both can be attributed, directly and indirectly, to the delivery model for healthcare, which is based on a three-party fee-for-service transaction.

Healthcare plans can be categorized into three types of plans. The most common providers of traditional health insurance plans are commercial insurers, Blue Cross and Blue Shield plans, and employer self-insured plans. The most common managed-care plans are health maintenance organizations, preferred provider organizations, exclusive provider organizations, and point-of-service plans. Medicare Advantage plans offer managed care for Medicare beneficiaries. Consumer-directed health plans combine health savings accounts or health reimbursement arrangements with high-deductible medical coverage.

People age sixty-five or older, under sixty-five with certain disabilities, and of all ages with certain medical conditions can qualify to receive federal Medicare health benefits, which include Part A (hospital insurance), Part B (medical insurance), and Part D (prescription drug coverage). Medicare beneficiaries can choose Medicare Advantage plans (Medicare Part C) for benefit levels in addition to those provided by Medicare. Medicare Supplement Insurance (Medigap) helps cover any gaps.

Low-income people can receive healthcare benefits under the state-federal Medicaid program, a public assistance plan for low-income persons, including people with certain disabilities and low-income Medicare beneficiaries requiring nursing home coverage.

ASSIGNMENT NOTES

1. Julie Mack, "So Why DOES U.S. Healthcare Cost So Much? A Look at the Myths and Realities," www.mlive.com/news/kalamazoo/index.ssf/2012/07/so_why_does_us_health_care_cos.html (accessed September 13, 2012).
2. Jerry Geisel, "Number of Uninsured U.S. Residents Declined in 2011: Census Bureau," Business Insurance, September 12, 2012, www.businessinsurance.com/article/20120912/NEWS03/120919958?tags=|62|63|307|74|278# (accessed September 13, 2012).
3. Health Insurance Online, "Merritt Personal Lines Manual: Mechanics of Medicare Managed Care," 2011, www.online-health-insurance.com/health-insurance-resources/MPLM/content/mechanics-of-medicare-managed-care.htm (accessed June 17, 2011).

Direct Your Learning

14

Retirement Risks and Employee Benefits Plans

Educational Objectives

After learning the content of this assignment, you should be able to:

- Describe the financial impact of the retirement personal loss exposure on individuals and families.
- Describe (a) the evolution of retirement funding, (b) retirement funding categories, and (c) tax advantages available for funding retirement.
- Explain how employer-sponsored retirement plans are categorized.
- In terms of operation, eligibility, and advantages and disadvantages, compare these types of employer-sponsored retirement plans:
  - Qualified defined benefit plans
  - Qualified defined contribution plans
  - Nonqualified plans
- Describe the retirement income choices for an individual or a family.
- Describe the requirements for employer-provided retirement plans specified by ERISA.
- Describe pension funding and the potential for underfunded pension plans.

Outline

The Financial Impact of Retirement

Introduction to Retirement Funding

Categories of Employer-Sponsored Retirement Plans

Comparing Employer-Sponsored Retirement Plans

Retirement Income Choices

Eligibility Requirements for Retirement Benefits

Pension Funding

Summary

Retirement Risks and Employee Benefits Plans

14

THE FINANCIAL IMPACT OF RETIREMENT

Individuals and families face the loss exposure of outliving their financial resources in retirement.

When individuals and families plan for retirement, they should determine the financial resources required for future expenses that will arise after income from full-time employment ends. Such planning should account for the effects of inflation and the future value of the dollar on retirement savings.

Retirement Loss Exposures

Many individuals look forward to retiring from the active workforce and enjoying time off for relaxation, pursuing a hobby, or traveling to exotic places. Leaving the workforce, however, means that regular earnings cease while living expenses continue. The resulting financial consequences form the basis of the retirement loss exposure. Actual retirement funding losses are influenced by these factors:

- Planning effectively
- Accumulating sufficient retirement funds
- Aging population
- Inflation

Planning Effectively

One of the most significant determinants of financial security in retirement is effective planning. This planning involves estimating the living expenses that will arise after income from full-time employment ceases and the anticipated length of retirement. Some individuals erroneously assume that expenses will decrease in retirement. Although housing expenses may be lower if a mortgage is paid in full, healthcare costs usually increase as people age. Planning should also consider the potential costs of long-term care and the expenses related to spending more time on a hobby, recreational activity, or travel. Failure to accurately plan for retirement needs such as these can result in a lower standard of living in retirement or the need to continue working past a planned retirement age.

Accumulating Sufficient Retirement Funds

The objective of effective retirement planning is to accumulate sufficient funds to meet expenses and to maintain an acceptable standard of living. Social Security is one source of retirement income. However, individuals must supplement the minimal income Social Security provides with additional sources of retirement income, such as retirement and pension plans.

In recent years, employers have moved away from defined benefit pension plans in favor of defined contribution plans. As a result of this trend, individuals must assume responsibility for establishing and/or contributing to their own retirement plans. Some employer plans are funded exclusively by employees, while others are funded by employees and employers.

For example, William contributes 9 percent of his salary annually to a defined contribution plan, a tax-deferred 401 (k) plan. His employer matches up to 4 percent of all contributions; therefore William's annual defined contribution is 13 percent. Under this plan, William is responsible for making decisions on allocating funds among different investment options. Unlike a defined benefit plan, William's actual payout at retirement is not predetermined and will depend on how long the plan is funded, the investment returns earned, and the age at which William decides to retire.

In addition to Social Security benefits and qualified employer-based retirement plans, individuals may use personal savings and investments, annuities, individual retirement accounts (IRAs), and cash value from life insurance policies to supplement their retirement savings.

Aging Population

As the baby boom generation (those born between 1946 and 1964) continues to age, the proportion of the United States population over age sixty-five is expected to increase from 12.4 percent in 2000 to 19.6 percent in 2030.[1] This growth in the number of older individuals threatens to place a strain on the Social Security and healthcare systems. Furthermore, members of this generation are expected to live longer than previous generations and, therefore, spend more years in retirement. See the exhibit "U.S. Population Projection."

Members of the baby boom generation face several obstacles to adequately funding their retirement expenses. Because Social Security benefits will provide only a minimum level of income and their retirement funds must sustain them longer than previous generations, they must use other methods to accumulate the savings required to meet retirement expense needs. This may mean working full-time beyond a planned retirement age of sixty-two or sixty-five or considering part-time employment in retirement.

The financial situation of many baby boomers whose retirement plans included investments in equities changed dramatically as a result of global financial crisis starting in 2008. This crisis caused a substantial decline in the value of retirement accounts. Baby boomers were most affected, as they had

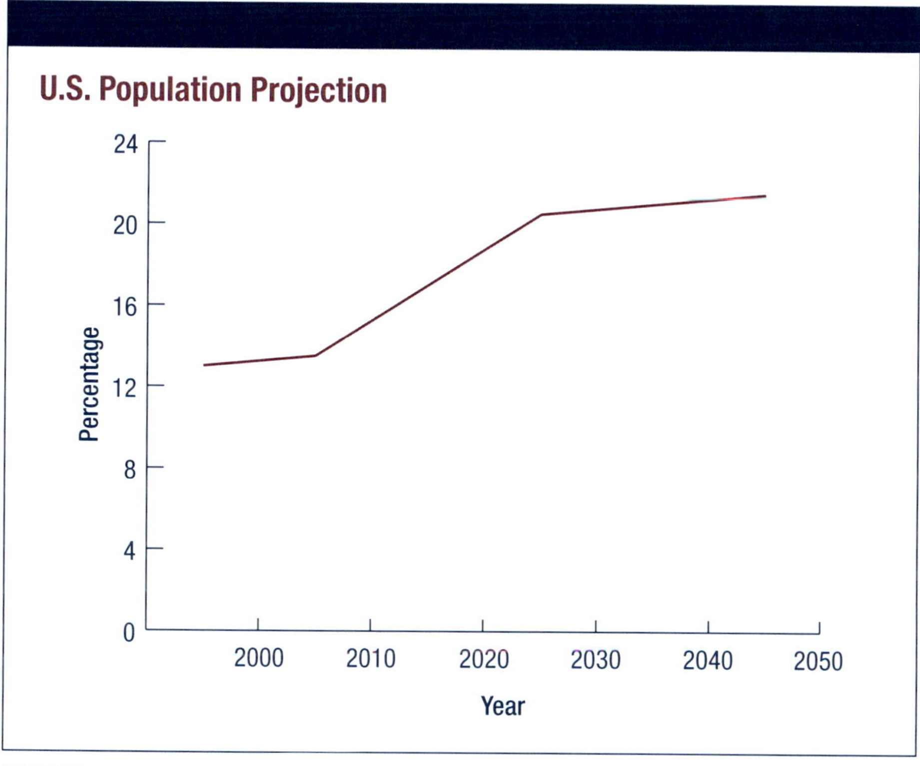

[DA05287]

been contributing to funds for a longer period of time than younger generations. The downturn also caused a decline in housing values, which represent a large portion of many baby boomers' financial assets. Baby boomers over age fifty-five were most affected by these market conditions and have less time to recover lost savings prior to retirement.[2]

The ability of baby boomers to increase their retirement savings is also affected by what is sometimes referred to as the "sandwich generation"[3] effect. Many baby boomers have expenses related to the care of elderly parents and must also support or pay college tuitions for adult children. This effect further constrains individuals from increasing contributions to retirement plans or personal savings.

The Effect of Inflation

It is important to consider the effect of inflation in planning for retirement and estimating future expenses. The inflation rate is a reflection of the increase in pricing levels for goods and services. Rising prices are especially problematic for retirees whose income is fixed. Also, goods and services such as healthcare, assisted living, long-term care, and prescription drugs are especially sensitive to higher inflation rates. Furthermore, during inflationary periods, interest rates tend to rise, which can negatively affect the overall economy. The effect of inflation on the future value of the dollar must be considered from the current planning period through the retirement age period.

For example, at age forty-five, Dana assumes that she will require an annual income of $60,000 in current dollars in retirement starting at age sixty-five. Assuming an inflation rate of 3 percent, her projected income need at retirement is over $108,000 (the future value of $60,000). If inflation rates were actually 5 percent rather than the 3 percent estimate, there would be a $51,000 income gap, as her income need would grow to over $159,000.

INTRODUCTION TO RETIREMENT FUNDING

The burgeoning population over age sixty-five offers important opportunities to insurance and financial services professionals. Those opportunities include assisting clients in establishing various types of retirement plans.

In 2000, 12.4 percent of Americans were sixty-five or older, the ages many Americans consider their retirement years. By 2010, the number of Americans sixty-five and older had grown by more than 5 million, increasing the percentage of that age group to 13 percent of the United States population.[4]

The increased growth rate of this demographic is not a new phenomenon. In fact, the rate has increased with each census. By 2030, it is anticipated that 20 percent of the U.S. population—one of every five people—will be sixty-five or older.

This growth, in turn, increases the need for financial services professionals who can provide expert advice about retirement planning and funding. At the foundation of this expertise is an understanding of the evolution, funding categories, and tax advantages of retirement funding.

Evolution of Retirement Funding

Defined benefit plan

A pension plan that is based on the monthly retirement benefit rather than on the contribution rate.

The first private pension plan—a type of plan that came to be known as a **defined benefit plan**—was established in 1875. It represented an early attempt by an employer to develop a stable and career-oriented workforce.[5] By the 1920s, pension plans had largely become a staple of employment benefits.

The stock market crash of 1929 and the ensuing Great Depression contributed to the growth of private pension plans. As a result of the federal government's dramatic increase in individual income tax rates at that time, corporations contributing to pension plans received enhanced tax benefits. The top income tax brackets continued to be 70 percent or greater until 1982.

Section 401(k) plan

A qualified retirement plan that meets the rules set forth in Section 401(k) of the IRC; participants may choose to contribute to the plan with before-tax dollars.

The business environment of the early 1980s was characterized by soaring interest rates and declining marginal tax rates. During that time, the Internal Revenue Service (IRS) issued proposed **Section 401(k) plan** regulations sanctioning the use of employee salary reductions to fund 401(k) plans.

These influences had a profound effect on traditional defined benefit pension plans. They enabled businesses to transfer the burden of funding employees' retirement incomes from themselves to their employees. Armed with these

new IRS regulations, many firms froze their defined benefit pension plans and offered new employees a 401(k) plan as their primary retirement plan.

Unlike traditional defined benefit pension plans that were funded entirely by employer contributions, 401(k) plans maintained by employers require employees to bear some or all the retirement funding burden.

Retirement Funding Categories

Retirement plan funding generally falls into three categories: employer-sponsored plans, government-sponsored plans, and individual plans.

Employer-Sponsored Retirement Plans

Employer-sponsored retirement plans are of two types: qualified plans and nonqualified plans. The two types differ based on tax treatment.

Although **qualified retirement plans**, which offer tax advantages, may differ substantially from each other, all qualified plans share several characteristics:

Qualified retirement plan
A retirement plan that meets the requirements established by the Internal Revenue Code for favorable tax treatment.

- The deferral of employee compensation
- The allocation of contributions to a trust, an insurance contract, or an individual retirement arrangement
- The investment of funds for employees' use in the future
- Distribution of contributions and plan earnings to employees at a later time

Qualified plans include pension plans, profit-sharing plans, thrift plans, 401(k) plans, employee stock ownership plans (ESOPs), simplified employee pensions (SEPs), and savings incentive match plans for employees (SIMPLE plans).

In contrast to qualified plans, **nonqualified retirement plans**, while not offering tax advantages, give an employer significantly greater flexibility in developing a plan to meet business requirements. Nonqualified retirement plans are primarily selective deferred compensation plans usually designed to cover only one or more executives.

Nonqualified retirement plan
A retirement plan that does not meet requirements established by the Internal Revenue Code for favorable tax treatment.

Government-Sponsored Retirement Plans

Two important government-sponsored retirement plans—Social Security (administered by the Social Security Administration) and Railroad Retirement (administered by the Railroad Retirement Board)—provide substantial retirement benefits.

The Social Security Act, providing a social safety net for millions of retired and disabled persons, was passed in 1935 at the height of the Great Depression. At the time, it was estimated that more than one-half of the elderly in America could not support themselves. State-administered welfare plans were largely nonexistent. Plans that did exist were deemed inadequate

and ineffective, serving an estimated 3 percent of the elderly population and providing an average benefit of about $0.65 per day. The maximum monthly Social Security retirement benefit for a worker retiring at sixty-six in 2011 was $2,366.[6]

The Railroad Retirement Acts were signed into law in 1934, 1935, and 1937. They established a railroad retirement system separate from the Social Security program. Although the two government-sponsored retirement plans remain separate, they are closely coordinated. While the Railroad Retirement System is much smaller than Social Security, it paid an average monthly retirement benefit to its retirees of $2,216.[7]

Retirement benefits provided under Social Security and Railroad Retirement are jointly funded by the individual and employer.

Individual Retirement Plans

Individual retirement account (IRA)

A retirement savings plan by which an individual can use tax-deductible and tax-deferred methods for accumulating funds.

Individual retirement accounts (IRAs) can be categorized into those plans that provide tax advantages and those that do not, a contrast similar to the difference between employer-sponsored qualified plans and employer-sponsored nonqualified plans.

The individual retirement plans that provide tax advantages are known as individual retirement accounts (IRAs). Annual contributions may generally be made up to the lesser of $5,000 or the individual's annual compensation. Individuals fifty or older may make an additional catch-up contribution of up to $1,000 each year.

All IRAs offer deferral of the tax on the increase in value of the underlying securities; however, IRAs may be further classified in terms of their additional tax benefits as traditional IRAs and Roth IRAs. Traditional IRAs generally offer individuals the opportunity to receive a tax deduction for contributions made; traditional IRA distributions, however, are fully taxable as ordinary income. Roth IRAs, in contrast, offer no tax deduction for contributions; qualified distributions from Roth IRAs, however, are entirely tax free.

Individual retirement plans that do not qualify for the tax advantages characteristic of IRAs include deferred annuities and other savings and investment assets.

Tax Advantages for Retirement Funding

As noted, the federal government provides tax incentives to encourage employers, employees, and individuals to actively fund retirement. The tax benefits vary somewhat depending on whether the retirement plan is an employer-sponsored retirement plan or an IRA.

The tax benefits available in funding an employer-sponsored retirement plan are these:

- Employer contributions are deductible in the year made and are not included in the employee's current income.
- Employee elective deferrals are made with before-tax funds unless directed to an employer's designated Roth account.
- Plan income is tax deferred until distributed.
- Tax deferral can be continued by rolling over the account.
- Qualified distributions from a designated Roth account are entirely tax free.

The tax benefits available in funding an IRA depend on whether it is a traditional IRA or a Roth IRA. Traditional IRA tax benefits are these:

- Contributions are tax-deductible unless the individual is an active participant in an employer-sponsored retirement plan and adjusted gross income exceeds certain limits.
- Contributions and income on plan assets are tax deferred until distributed.

Distributions received from a traditional IRA are taxable as ordinary income in the year received.

Roth IRA tax benefits are these:

- Income on plan assets is tax deferred until distributed.
- Contributions may be withdrawn from a Roth IRA tax free on a first-in, first-out (FIFO) basis.
- Qualified distributions from a Roth IRA are entirely tax free.

Contributions made to a Roth IRA are made with after-tax funds. No tax deduction for Roth IRA contributions is permitted.

Apply Your Knowledge

Your client, Arthur, has heard about a Roth IRA that offers tax-free distributions and thinks he may be interested in contributing to it because he is eager to avoid taxes. He is currently ten years away from retirement and at the peak of his earnings. When he retires, he expects his income will decline significantly and that he will need less income. What is your recommendation concerning an IRA for Arthur?

Feedback: Because Arthur is interested in tax savings and he is likely to be in a lower tax bracket in retirement, the suitable IRA recommendation would be for a traditional IRA rather than a Roth IRA. A traditional IRA offers Arthur current tax-deductible contributions at a time when his tax bracket is highest and taxable distributions in retirement when his tax bracket is likely to be at

its lowest. Because of that dynamic, a traditional IRA will offer him greater tax benefits than a Roth IRA.

A Roth IRA provides tax deferral of gain during accumulation and tax-free qualified distributions. For many clients, it offers significant tax benefits, even though contributions are made with after-tax funds. In Arthur's case, because his motivation is principally tax benefits, it is likely to be the wrong recommendation.

Common Retirement Income Funding Sources

Employer-Sponsored Plans

Qualified plans:

a. Defined contribution plans
- Money purchase pension plan
- Target benefit plan
- Profit-sharing plan
- Thrift plan
- 401(k) plan
- Stock bonus plan
- Employee stock ownership plan (ESOP)
- Simplified employee pension (SEP)
- Savings incentive match plan for employees (SIMPLE)

b. Defined benefit plans
- Traditional pension plan
- Flat benefit plan
- Unit benefit plan
- Cash balance plan

Nonqualified plans:
- Supplemental Executive Retirement Plan (SERP)
- Salary reduction plan

Government-Sponsored Plans

Social Security

Railroad Retirement

Individual Plans

Tax-advantaged plans:

a. Traditional IRA

b. Roth IRA

Non-tax-advantaged plans:

a. Deferred annuity

b. Various investments
- Mutual funds
- Individual stocks
- Individual bonds

c. Savings vehicles:
- Certificate of deposit
- Passbook savings

[DA08254]

CATEGORIES OF EMPLOYER-SPONSORED RETIREMENT PLANS

A corporation with 10,000 employees wants to establish an employer-sponsored retirement plan. A five-person plumbing company also wants to start a retirement plan. Although the objectives that the two firms hope to accomplish by sponsoring retirement plans are likely to differ considerably, the firms have a range of qualified and nonqualified employer-sponsored plans to choose from to meet their business and personal needs.

There are three categories of employer-sponsored retirement plans:

- Qualified or nonqualified plans
- Defined contribution or defined benefit plans
- Pension or profit-sharing plans

The categories may overlap; that is, defined contribution and defined benefit plans could be qualified plans, and profit-sharing plans are a type of defined contribution plan. See the exhibit "Employer-Sponsored Retirement Plan Characteristics."

Qualified or Nonqualified Plans

An employer-sponsored retirement plan may also be categorized based on whether it is a qualified retirement plan or a nonqualified retirement plan. Although the terminology might imply that a nonqualified plan is somehow inferior to a qualified plan, such a conclusion would be erroneous. They are simply different approaches to meeting specific employer objectives.

Section 401 of the Internal Revenue Code (IRC) is central to an employer-sponsored retirement plan qualifying for tax advantages. It provides a list of requirements for a retirement plan to be considered a qualified plan and confers favorable tax treatment on the plans that meet those requirements. Section 401 does not apply to nonqualified plans.

To be considered a qualified plan, an employer-sponsored retirement plan must include these elements:

- A requirement that it must be established to benefit employees or their beneficiaries
- A prohibition on the use of plan assets for purposes other than the exclusive benefit of the employees or their beneficiaries
- Minimum age and service standards and minimum coverage requirements
- Nondiscriminatory contributions or benefits within specified limits
- Minimum **vesting** standards
- Provisions related to benefit commencement and required minimum distributions that meet IRC requirements

Vesting
A retirement plan participant's nonforfeitable right to his or her accrued plan benefit.

Employer-Sponsored Retirement Plan Characteristics

Qualified or Nonqualified Plans	
Qualified Plans	**Nonqualified Plans**
• Must meet various Internal Revenue Code (IRC) Section 401 requirements to obtain tax advantages.	• Do not meet IRC Section 401 requirements.
• Receive favorable tax treatment.	• Do not receive favorable tax treatment.
• Generally less flexible due to the need to meet coverage, vesting, and other requirements.	• Flexible as to benefits and coverage (may cover as few as one participant).
Defined Contribution or Defined Benefit Plans	
Defined Contribution Plans	**Defined Benefit Plans**
• Individual participant accounts.	• No individual participant accounts.
• Annual employer contributions may be mandatory or discretionary, depending on plan type.	• Annual contribution required and determined by actuary.
• Contributions may come from employer or employees.	• Employer generally makes all contributions.
• No promised retirement benefit. Retirement benefits based on contributions, gains, losses, and expenses.	• Definitely determinable retirement benefit.
• Participant bears investment risk.	• Employer bears investment risk.
• Contribution levels easier for employer to manage.	• Annual contribution levels more volatile and affected by plan asset performance.
• Generally less costly for employer to maintain.	• Generally more costly to maintain.
• Wide range of plan types.	• Plan types limited to defined benefit pension and cash balance plans.
• Not insured by the Pension Benefit Guaranty Corporation (PBGC).	• Insured by PBGC.
Pension or Profit-Sharing Plans	
Pension Plans	**Profit-Sharing Plans**
• Mandatory annual contributions.	• Contributions flexible and may be discretionary.
• Contributions or benefits guaranteed.	• Neither contributions nor benefits guaranteed.
• Object is to provide retirement income.	• Object is to share tax-deferred profits with employees.
• Distributions not available until retirement or termination.	• In-service distributions may be permitted.
• Limit of 10 percent employer stock investment.	• No limits as to investments in employer stock.

[DA08286]

- Automatic survivor benefits as appropriate
- Certain provisions related to top-heavy plans
- Prohibition of assignment of benefits
- Various other requirements related to permanence, early retirement, Social Security offset, and maximum considered compensation

An employer-sponsored retirement plan that meets IRC requirements for qualified plans enjoys certain tax advantages related to contribution deductibility and tax deferral, among others.

Nonqualified employer-sponsored retirement plans do not enjoy as many tax advantages as qualified plans. However, they offer other benefits designed to help employers meet specific business needs.

Nonqualified plans have these common characteristics (although some may vary depending on the language of a particular nonqualified retirement plan document):

- Tax deferral for employees on funds allocated to the plan
- Deferral of an employer's deduction until benefits are paid to the employee
- Employer's ability to recover some or all benefits costs through life insurance
- In some cases, tax deferral of accumulated earnings, depending on the investment used to informally fund the benefit
- Employer's ability to reduce retirement costs by discriminating in favor of selected employees
- Minimal and inexpensive administration, reporting, and disclosure requirements

Because employers are allowed under nonqualified plans to discriminate in favor of selected employees, offering such a plan can be an effective method to attract, retain, and motivate selected workers.

Defined Contribution or Defined Benefit Plans

Qualified plans generally fit into one of two categories: defined contribution plans or defined benefit plans. A qualified plan's status as a defined contribution plan or a defined benefit plan has significant implications for sponsoring employers and participating employees.

A **defined contribution plan** is often referred to as an individual account plan. It offers these features:

Defined contribution plan
A retirement plan in which employer and employee contributions are allocated to participants' accounts and participant benefits are based on the account balance.

- An individual account for each plan participant
- Benefits based solely on the amount contributed to each participant's account and the income, expenses, gains and losses, and any forfeitures credited to the account

In a qualified retirement plan that is categorized as a defined contribution plan, annual contributions are generally determined by formula—3 percent of annual compensation, for example—rather than by actuarial requirements. Earnings and losses are allocated to each participant's individual account and do not affect the employer's retirement plan costs. Thus, regardless of whether plan investment returns are good or bad, the employer's contribution

is unaffected. Plan benefits are not insured by the Pension Benefit Guaranty Corporation (PBGC).

Types of defined contribution plans include money pension plans, profit-sharing plans, and 401(k) plans, among others.

Defined benefit plan
A retirement plan that specifies definitely determinable participant benefits payable at retirement.

Technically, a **defined benefit plan** is a qualified retirement plan other than an individual account plan. It is generally referred to as a traditional pension plan.

Unlike a defined contribution plan, whose benefit is unknown until retirement, a defined benefit plan's retirement benefit must be definitely determinable. In other words, an employee who is still twenty years away from retirement can determine what his or her pension benefit will be. Although defined benefit plan formulas may vary considerably, a typical formula may set a participant's monthly pension payable for life at 35 percent of monthly compensation.

A key difference in a defined benefit plan is that it must pay the promised benefit at retirement, regardless of the investment performance of the plan assets. Consequently, a defined benefit plan's poor investment performance may require the employer to increase its contribution to the plan; however, poor investment performance will not reduce the participant's retirement benefit. The employer bears the investment risk.

Defined benefit plans are normally funded entirely through employer contributions. Annual employer contributions must be sufficient to pay the promised benefits when due. This requirement has important implications for sponsoring employers:

- The cost of funding the plan is determined actuarially, based on assumptions as to interest, mortality, employee turnover, and salary scale. The requirement for actuarial determination generally increases the employer's cost to administer a defined benefit plan.
- Required annual contributions may vary substantially from one year to another. If plan investment performance falls short of assumptions, the employer must increase contributions; if investment performance exceeds assumptions, the employer generally must reduce its annual contribution.

Defined benefit plans include pension plans that offer flat benefit plan formulas or unit benefit plan formulas, as well as cash balance plans.

Pension or Profit-Sharing Plans

Profit-sharing plan
A defined contribution plan in which the employer's contributions are based on the employer's profits.

Qualified retirement plans can also be categorized as pension plans or **profit-sharing plans**. Pension plans and profit-sharing plans differ from one another with respect to these characteristics:

- The employer's financial commitment
- Plan guarantees
- Primary objective

- Timing of permitted distributions
- Investment flexibility

The employer's financial commitment to a pension plan is different from its commitment to a profit-sharing plan. Pension plans require annual employer contributions, while profit-sharing plans do not. Employers are, however, obligated to make only "substantial and recurring" contributions to profit-sharing plans.

The participant guarantees provided by pension plans are more significant than those under profit-sharing plans. Pension plan guarantees apply to either the contributions that will be made (money purchase pension plans) or the benefits that will be provided (defined benefit pension plans). In contrast, profit-sharing plans provide no guarantee that the sponsoring employer will make a contribution in any specific year or that a particular benefit will be provided.

Instead, a profit-sharing plan simply provides that if the employer makes a contribution in any year, the contribution will be credited to participating employee accounts based on a particular allocation. The allocation of contributions normally considers the employee's salary and, in some cases, the employee's age (age-based profit-sharing plan) and/or status (new comparability profit-sharing plan).

Pension plans and profit-sharing plans also have different primary objectives. A pension plan provides a retirement benefit. A profit-sharing plan, however, allows an employer to share profits with participants on a tax-deferred basis. Profit-sharing plans do not necessarily provide retirement benefits.

The permitted distributions under pension plans and profit-sharing plans are consistent with their differing objectives. Because the objective of a pension plan is to provide a retirement income, pension plan distributions generally cannot begin until the plan participant has terminated employment or reached normal retirement age.

In contrast, profit-sharing plans may provide for in-service distributions—that is, distributions while the participant is still employed by the plan sponsor. For example, a profit-sharing plan may distribute a plan participant's account value at these times:

- Upon attainment of a stated age
- After a fixed number of years
- Upon the occurrence of a specified event, such as financial hardship, illness or disability, retirement, death, or severance of employment

Pension plans and profit-sharing plans also differ as to the permitted investment of plan assets. Pension plans are generally limited to investing not more than 10 percent in the sponsoring company's stock; profit-sharing plans have no limit. However, the Pension Protection Act of 2006 requires that plans investing in sponsoring-employer stock allow plan participants to diversify their investments.

COMPARING EMPLOYER-SPONSORED RETIREMENT PLANS

A large, publicly owned business may seek to provide meaningful retirement benefits to its workforce by installing a qualified retirement plan and, in so doing, try to overcome union organizing efforts. In contrast, a small high-tech company may look to its retirement plan as a way to attract and retain key executives by promising additional selective retirement income benefits based on length of service or productivity. To meet their respective needs, these organizations can choose from among a wide range of employer-sponsored retirement plans with various features, advantages, and disadvantages.

The characteristics, operation, advantages and disadvantages of an employer-sponsored retirement plan may vary significantly from those of a different employer-sponsored retirement plan, depending on the categories in which the plans fall. This section examines the characteristics, advantages, and disadvantages of these categories of employer-sponsored retirement plans:

- Qualified defined benefit retirement plans
- Qualified defined contribution retirement plans
- Nonqualified retirement plans

Qualified Defined Benefit Retirement Plans

Cash balance plan

A defined benefit plan that uses hypothetical participant accounts to look like a defined contribution plan.

A qualified defined benefit retirement plan may be a defined benefit pension plan or a **cash balance plan**. When an employer installs a defined benefit pension plan or cash balance plan, the initial plan contribution is determined by an actuary, based on the promised benefits, the age and incomes of plan participants, and various assumptions about the future. The contribution is made to a trust, and plan trustees invest the assets.

Each year, the plan actuary determines the employer's contribution based on the current value of the plan assets and on assumptions about interest, mortality, employee turnover, and salary scale. If the actuary's assumptions are realized exactly, the contribution will be sufficient to pay the promised benefits. If the investment performance of the plan assets is better than assumed, the employer's subsequent contribution will be reduced. However, if the investment performance is poorer than assumed, the employer's contribution will increase.

For an employer-sponsored retirement plan to be a qualified plan, it must meet various federal law requirements, including a minimum age and service requirement for coverage. Pursuant to that requirement, qualified plans may require the completion of no more than one year of service or an age limit of no more than twenty-one, whichever occurs later, before employees can participate. They may have more liberal age and service requirements but may not have greater limitations.

The advantages of a defined benefit retirement plan generally include these:

- Older participants receive adequate benefits.
- Older business owners make higher contributions.
- Internal Revenue Service contribution limits do not apply.
- Benefits are unaffected by investment performance.
- Future benefits can be accurately estimated.
- Benefits are funded entirely by the employer.
- Funds are guaranteed by the Pension Benefit Guaranty Corporation (PBGC).

The disadvantages of a defined benefit retirement plan include these:

- Maintenance costs are higher.
- Contributions are inflexible.
- The employer bears the investment risk.
- Contribution levels are volatile.
- Communication of benefits is generally difficult.
- The plan is generally less attractive to employees.
- In-service distributions are not available.

Defined Benefit Pension Plans

A defined benefit pension plan is often referred to as a traditional pension plan. Benefits promised under a defined benefit pension plan are stated in terms of a life income payable beginning at normal retirement age. The life income promised may be provided under various formulas, the most common of which are flat benefit and unit benefit formulas.

Under a flat benefit formula, the life income payable at retirement is based solely on the participant's salary. A typical flat benefit formula presented in the plan document might provide a monthly pension benefit equal to 45 percent of the participant's final average monthly salary. Under a unit benefit formula, both income and years of service are taken into consideration. The plan document for a defined benefit plan with a unit benefit formula might provide a benefit equal to 1.5 percent of final average monthly salary multiplied by years of service not exceeding thirty years.

Cash Balance Plans

A cash balance plan is a defined benefit plan whose benefit is defined more like that of a defined contribution plan. Rather than defining the benefit in terms of an income to be received by the participant, a cash balance plan defines it in terms of a specified account balance. As with any defined benefit plan, the employer is required to make an actuarially determined annual contribution sufficient to pay the promised benefit.

Under a cash balance plan, every plan participant has a hypothetical account. Each year, the account statement is published showing a benefit credit and an interest credit to the account. Such benefit credits may be a fixed percentage of earnings for all participants or a percentage of earnings that varies based on age, length of service, or earnings.

Qualified Defined Contribution Plans

Under qualified defined contribution plans, each participant has an individual account to which contributions are allocated. Each participant's account balance is affected by investment experience and expenses. Such plans provide no guarantee of the benefit amount at retirement. Thus, plan participants bear the plan asset investment risk.

Contributions made to a defined contribution plan are determined by the type of plan and the formula contained in the plan document. Defined contribution plans include profit-sharing plans, 401(k) plans, and employee stock ownership plans (ESOPs). Although not technically meeting all the requirements of a qualified plan, 403(b) tax-sheltered annuity plans, simplified employee pension (SEP) plans, and savings incentive match plan for employees (SIMPLE) plans are also defined contribution plans.

Profit-Sharing Plans

Profit-sharing plans provide a mechanism for employers to share tax-deferred profits with employees. Depending on plan provisions, contributions may be required based on profits earned by the employer or may be entirely discretionary. Unlike pension plans, which require annual contributions, contributions to a profit-sharing plan need only be substantial and recurring.

A profit-sharing plan must specify a formula for allocating contributions and plan earnings to the plan participants' accounts. Three approaches to contribution allocation may be used:

- Each participant receives the same percentage of the contribution as the participant's compensation bears to the plan participants' total compensation under a traditional profit-sharing plan.
- Each participant receives a percentage of the contribution based on the participants' age and length of service under an age-weighted profit-sharing plan.
- Each participant receives a percentage of the contribution based on the category of the participant under a new comparability profit-sharing plan.

401(k) Plans

A Section 401(k) plan is a qualified retirement plan that meets the rules set forth in Section 401(k) of the Internal Revenue Code; participants may choose to contribute to the plan with before-tax dollars. An employer profit-

sharing plan, a 401(k) includes a cash or deferred arrangement (CODA). Under a CODA, the employee may elect to receive compensation in cash or defer it to the plan through an elective deferral. Participant contributions are always nonforfeitable.

Elective deferrals are normally excluded from the employee's income for the year. Employers may make matching contributions. A typical employer contribution would match 50 percent of the employees' elective deferrals up to the first 6 percent of the employees' compensation.

Under 401(k) plans that provide for it, a plan participant may allocate some or all elective deferrals to a **designated Roth 401(k) account**. Such elective deferrals are not excluded from income, but qualified distributions from such designated Roth accounts are entirely tax free. The maximum amount that may be deferred under a 401(k) plan is subject to change to reflect inflation.

Designated Roth 401(k) account
A feature that combines the advantages of a Roth IRA with the convenience of a 401(k) plan.

403(b) Plans

A 403(b) plan, also known as a tax-sheltered annuity, is a retirement plan that provides employer and employee benefits similar to a 401(k) plan. The organizations eligible to offer employees tax-sheltered annuity plans are public schools and tax-exempt organizations.

A 403(b) plan participant may also defer compensation under an elective deferral arrangement. The maximum amount of the deferral for 2011 is $16,500; an additional catch-up contribution of no more than $5,500 may be made by participants age fifty or older. Contributions may also be made to the plan by the participant's employer.

A 403(b) plan may make a designated Roth account available, similar to a designated Roth 401(k) account. Contributions to a 403(b) plan may be directed to an annuity contract or to a custodial account for the purchase of mutual fund shares.

Employee Stock Ownership Plans

An employee stock ownership plan (ESOP) is a defined contribution plan whose funds must be invested primarily in employer securities. It has characteristics similar to profit-sharing plans and other characteristics that differ from such plans.

Employer contributions to an ESOP are flexible and discretionary. Additionally, ESOPs must permit distributions to be made in employer stock, which can increase participant tax benefits.

Although ESOPs provide retirement benefits for participants, they also offer employers and participants other advantages, including a market for company stock, a method for financing company growth, and an estate planning tool for closely held corporation owners.

Simplified Employee Pension Plans

Simplified employee pension (SEP) plan
A retirement plan that closely resembles an IRA but that has higher annual contribution limits and is sponsored by employers.

Simplified employee pensions (SEPs) permit employers to make discretionary contributions for employees up to the greater of 25 percent of compensation or the defined contribution limits. They offer employers a much simpler alternative to qualified retirement plans and are generally far less costly to install and administer than qualified plans.

SIMPLE Plans

Savings incentive match plan for employees (SIMPLE)
A plan that a small business with fewer than 100 employees can establish to allow its sole proprietors, partners, and employees to save for retirement on a tax-deferred basis.

Employers that have no other retirement plan and who have 100 employees or fewer earning $5,000 or more may establish and maintain a **savings incentive match plan for employees (SIMPLE) plan**. Similar to an SEP, a SIMPLE plan permits an employer to avoid the costly setup and administrative costs characteristic of qualified retirement plans while still offering employees a plan to which elective deferrals and employer contributions may be made. All participant contributions are nonforfeitable.

Mandatory employer contributions may be matching contributions at least equal to the lesser of the amount deferred by the participant or 3 percent of the participant's compensation or nonelective contributions (nonmatching, in other words). If an employer matches contributions, employer contributions need to be made only for those employees making elective deferrals. An employer choosing not to match employee contributions must make nonelective contributions equal to 2 percent of compensation for every eligible employee.

Nonqualified Retirement Plans

Nonqualified plans do not meet the qualified-plan requirements or qualify for tax advantages; however, they do provide a flexible method for employers to attract, retain, and reward executives. Nonqualified plans may permit participants to avoid taxation on amounts deferred until paid. If taxation is deferred, the employer's deduction is also deferred until employee benefits are paid.

An employer may choose to include only one executive or several executives in a nonqualified plan. The executives chosen obtain the benefits of the nonqualified plan in addition to any qualified plan sponsored by the employer.

Supplemental executive retirement plan (SERP)
A nonqualified plan that provides retirement benefits in addition to those provided by qualified plans, usually for highly compensated employees.

Nonqualified retirement plans are available as **supplemental executive retirement plans (SERPs)** and nonqualified salary reduction plans. The difference between the plans relates to whether the employer or the participant pays for the benefit.

A plan may be either funded or unfunded, an issue that has implications for participant taxation and security. In a funded plan, the employer sets aside funds specifically earmarked to pay the promised benefits under the plan. While such earmarked funds placed in trust are safe from the company's general creditors, they are taxable to the executive when contributed to the plan

or when the executive becomes vested in the benefit, if later. Because of that, nonqualified retirement plans are usually designed to be unfunded rather than funded plans.

A nonqualified plan is considered unfunded and is not subject to the adverse tax consequences of a funded plan as long as no reserve free from creditor claims is established by the employer to pay benefits. An informally funded plan is considered unfunded even if a reserve is set aside to pay the promised benefits as long as it is subject to the claims of the employer's creditors.

Supplemental Executive Retirement Plans

In a SERP, the plan participant does not defer any of his or her compensation. The employer promises to pay the participant a specified dollar amount for a period of years beginning at the earlier of the participant's death or retirement.

SERPs often act as "golden handcuffs," tying the participant to the employer by including a forfeiture provision that may become operative if the participant leaves the employer's service before a specified number of years, goes to work for a competitor, or opens a competing business.

Salary Reduction Plans

Salary reduction plans are sometimes referred to as "true deferred compensation" plans because plan participants defer compensation until they may be in a lower marginal income tax bracket—at retirement, for example. Although a salary reduction plan may appear to emulate elective deferrals under a 401(k) plan, a significant difference between the two plans relates to the limits applicable to the deferred amount.

Salary reduction plan

A nonqualified plan under which executives may defer compensation until termination of employment to reduce current income tax liability and save for retirement.

Plan participants under a 401(k) plan cannot defer more than the IRC Section 415 limit for elective deferrals of $16,500 (increased by $5,500 for participants age fifty or older). No dollar limit applies to funds deferred under nonqualified salary reduction plans. Because the deferred funds constitute the participant's own money that he or she had a right to receive at the time it was deferred, salary reduction plans do not ordinarily impose a forfeiture condition. See the exhibit "Employer-Sponsored Retirement Plans."

Apply Your Knowledge

Smooth Data, Inc., is a small, regular corporation started five years ago by three retired computer company executives, all age fifty-five. The firm employs thirty younger, moderately paid computer technicians who build and repair computers, printers, and peripherals. The owners want to install a retirement plan to discourage a union from organizing. They also want to ensure that the bulk of contributions and benefits go to their own accounts, enabling them to retain ownership and accommodate periods of low cash flow.

Based on the information provided in this section, what retirement plan would you recommend, and why?

Employer-Sponsored Retirement Plans

Defined Contribution Plans	Defined Benefit Plans	Pension Plans	Profit-Sharing Plans	Qualified Retirement Plans	Nonqualified Retirement Plans
Money purchase pension plan	Traditional pension plan	Traditional pension plan	Traditional profit-sharing plan	Money purchase pension plan	Supplemental executive retirement plan (SERP)
Target benefit plan	Cash balance plan	Cash balance plan	Age-weighted profit-sharing plan	Target benefit plan	Salary reduction plan
Profit-sharing plan		Money purchase pension plan	New comparability plan	Profit-sharing plan	
Thrift plan		Target benefit plan		Thrift plan	
401(k) plan				401(k) plan	
Stock bonus plan				Stock bonus plan	
Employee stock ownership plan (ESOP)				Employee stock ownership plan (ESOP)	
Simplified employee pension (SEP)				Simplified employee pension (SEP)	
Savings incentive match plan for employees (SIMPLE)				Savings incentive match plan for employees (SIMPLE)	
				Traditional pension plan	
				Cash balance plan	

[DA08284]

Feedback: Identifying the appropriate retirement plan or plans requires comparing the client's objectives with characteristics of the various retirement plans. It is impossible to know with certainty just what level and type of retirement benefits will be sufficient to keep union organizing at bay, but, at a minimum, the owners should consider a retirement plan that provides tax benefits to employees—a qualified retirement plan.

In light of the company's need for flexibility with its qualified plan contributions, a defined benefit retirement plan would be inappropriate because it requires annual contributions. Instead, the company should consider a qualified retirement plan under which it could make contributions depending on its cash flow. Three qualified plan possibilities that offer contribution flexibility are an ESOP, a SEP, and a profit-sharing plan.

Under an ESOP, plan participants share ownership of the company, something the owners may wish to avoid because they want to retain complete ownership. An SEP may provide the contribution flexibility the owners want; however, it cannot contain an age-weighting factor that will enable the owners to direct the bulk of contributions to themselves based on their ages. A profit-sharing plan to which they can make discretionary contributions may be the best choice.

An age-weighted profit-sharing plan would allow the owners to allocate the bulk of contributions to themselves because of their older age. Alternatively, a new comparability plan would permit them to allocate a higher percentage of contributions to themselves as members of the top category.

RETIREMENT INCOME CHOICES

Individuals may be unaware of the choices they have regarding accumulating and distributing retirement funds. Advisers who can help clients choose from among the multiple sources of retirement savings and maximize their retirement income are likely to develop loyal followings.

The largest percentage of retirement income is derived from Social Security benefits—37 percent, based on Social Security Administration estimates. Other means of funding retirement often fall short of the amounts needed to maintain retirees' standard of living. Various financial vehicles are available to address these shortages and to help individuals save for retirement.

Multiple Retirement Savings and Income Sources

In addition to part-time earnings in retirement, individuals typically receive retirement income benefits from three principal sources:

- Social Security retirement benefits
- Employer-sponsored retirement plans
- Individually provided retirement plans

The importance of these sources can be expected to change over time. See the exhibit "Income Sources in Retirement."

Social Security Retirement Benefits

Although the maximum monthly Social Security retirement benefit for a sixty-six-year-old worker retiring in 2011 was $2,366, the average monthly Social Security benefit paid in 2011 was about $1,174. For a retired couple, the monthly 2011 retirement benefit amount averaged $1,907.[8]

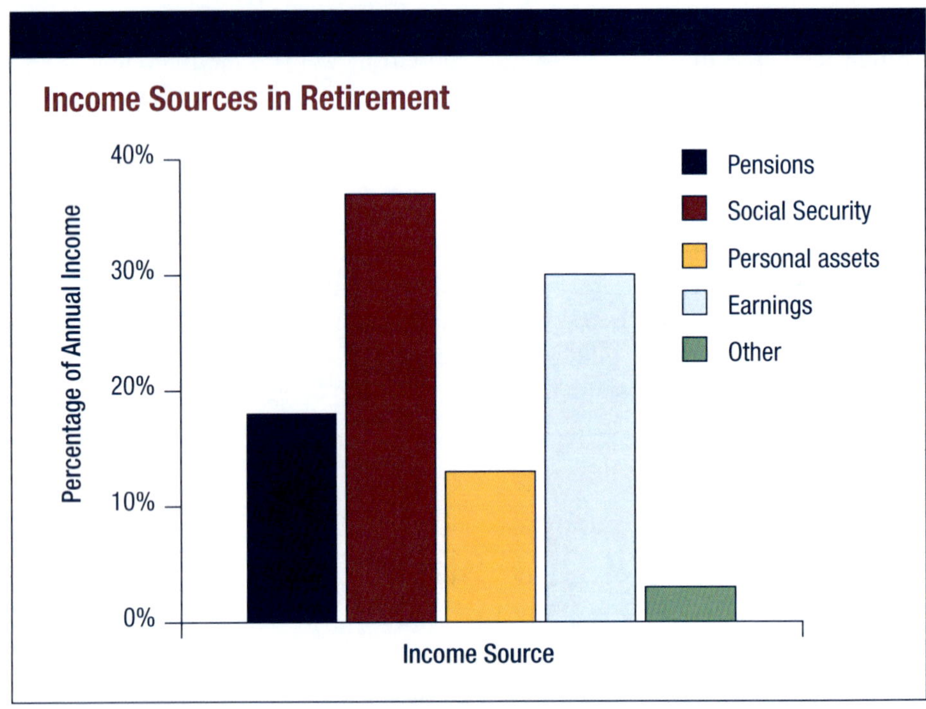

Fast Facts and Figures About Social Security, 2010, Social Security Administration, www.ssa.gov (accessed October 17, 2011). [DA08285]

Both the maximum Social Security retirement benefit and the age at which a retiree can receive full Social Security benefits are increasing. Although sixty-five has long been the normal retirement age for Social Security benefits, the age at which a worker can receive full Social Security retirement benefits depends on his or her date of birth and ranges from sixty-five for someone born in 1937 or earlier to sixty-seven for someone born in 1960 or later.

Employer-Sponsored Retirement Plans

In 2010, 18 percent of retirement benefits were paid under employer-sponsored retirement plans. An individual is generally unable to affect the retirement benefits paid under a pension or profit-sharing plan because the benefits are typically funded entirely by the sponsoring employer.

The principal employer-sponsored plans in which individuals invest are 401(k) plans and 403(b) plans (tax-sheltered annuities).

The Wall Street Journal (WSJ) reports that retirement savings in 401(k) plans are estimated to contain less than one-quarter of the amount of assets needed to maintain retirees' standard of living in retirement.[9] Accordingly, many individuals are making dramatic changes, such as these, in their retirement plans:

- Postponing retirement, by either remaining on the job or working part time
- Moving to less-expensive housing
- Buying less expensive food
- Reducing anticipated travel
- Taking increased risks with their investments in hopes of obtaining larger gains

The *WSJ* article adds that individuals received "too little advice or bad advice" and believed their 401(k) contribution of 6 percent coupled with a 3 percent employer match would provide sufficient retirement income. By the end of 2010, the average 401(k) plan contribution rate was 8.2 percent;[10] however, workers whose primary employer-sponsored retirement benefit is through a 401(k) plan or 403(b) plan need to contribute at least 10 percent of their gross income to produce a more nearly adequate retirement income.

Individually Provided Retirement Plans

Retirees' income from individually provided retirement plans averages only about 13 percent of their entire retirement income, despite the wide range of available plans. Such plans include individual retirement accounts (IRAs), nonqualified annuities, investment funds such as brokerage accounts and mutual funds, and life insurance cash values.

Retirement Income Choices

When individuals retire, or just before that time, they must make a number of important decisions regarding retirement income:

- Whether to purchase an annuity
- How (and whether) to spend down their savings
- When to begin receiving traditional pension payments
- At what age to start receiving Social Security retirement benefits

Purchasing an Annuity

Although rules of thumb abound—such as "Retirement income should be 70 percent of pre-retirement income" and "Spend 4 percent of assets annually"—the method of determining an appropriate retirement income for a client should be based on actual expenses.

To begin, clients should identify what their essential living expenses will be in retirement and then cover those expenses with income sources that are guaranteed. For most clients, only three sources of retirement income are guaranteed: employer-sponsored retirement plans, Social Security retirement benefits, and annuities.

If a client's essential living expenses exceed the total retirement income from employer-sponsored retirement plans, Social Security benefits, and investments, the client should consider purchasing a life annuity. To make this purchase, he or she should take these steps:

1. Annuitize any deferred annuity cash value under a life income settlement option. The gain under a deferred annuity is not taxable at the time of annuitization. Instead, each periodic payment under a nonqualified annuity is deemed to consist partly of the taxable gain and partly of the client's investment in the contract that is tax-free until entirely recovered.
2. Roll over existing IRA, 401(k), or 403(b) balances to an immediate qualified life annuity if additional guaranteed income is required. The amount rolled over is not taxable at the time of the rollover; instead, each periodic payment is taxable in the year received.
3. Consider using taxable assets to fund an immediate life annuity if still more guaranteed income is needed.

For example, a married couple both age sixty-six needing an additional $31,000 in annual income to cover essential expenses would be required to pay $500,000 to purchase an immediate joint and survivor annuity providing monthly periodic payments of $2,596 until the death of both annuitants.

Spend Down Savings

An alternative to purchasing a life annuity is to spend down existing assets. Under a classic spend-down strategy, a retired individual would liquidate 4 percent of assets in the first year. Each year, the amount liquidated in the previous year would increase by the current year's inflation rate. By limiting the amount liquidated in this way, individuals are unlikely to exhaust their assets while they are alive.

Under this strategy, the married couple who requires an additional $31,000 each year to meet essential expenses would need to identify assets equal to $775,000 ($775,000 × 4% = $31,000). Their annual liquidation, assuming a consistent 3 percent annual inflation rate, would be $31,930 in the next year, $32,888 in the following year, and so forth.

For this strategy to work properly, the value of the investment portfolio from which the amounts are liquidated should be able to increase annually by at least the inflation rate. Thus, the portfolio needs to contain some portion invested in equities.

In general, assets should be liquidated in this order to maximize tax benefits:

1. Investments that have been losers. For tax purposes, losses can be used to offset capital gains and up to $3,000 annually of ordinary income.
2. Available cash.
3. Investments that will produce long-term capital gains (taxed at a lower rate than short-term gains).
4. Investments that will produce short-term capital gains.
5. Tax-deferred assets, such as assets in 401(k) and 403(b) plans.

Start Traditional Pension Payments

An individual whose retirement income is insufficient to provide a suitable lifestyle may choose to postpone his or her planned retirement date. Postponing retirement may increase the person's pension benefit, gives him or her an additional period of asset accumulation, and shortens the period during which additional retirement income must be provided using the person's assets.

Decide on the Age to Start Social Security Retirement Benefits

Social Security retirement benefits may begin as early as age sixty-two or as late as age seventy. The individual's age at the time benefits begin can have a significant effect on the monthly benefit amount.

If an individual's full retirement age is sixty-six (that is, the person was born between 1943 and 1954) and he or she begins taking retirement benefits at age sixty-two, the reduction in benefits is 25 percent. If benefits begin at age sixty-three, the reduction is about 20 percent; at age sixty-four, it is about 13.3 percent; and at age sixty-five, it is about 6.7 percent. If full retirement age is greater than sixty-six, the reduction for early commencement of benefits is even greater.

However, if the individual elects to defer the commencement of Social Security retirement benefits, benefits that would have been payable at age sixty-six increase by 8 percent for each year they are deferred. Thus, an individual choosing to defer Social Security retirement benefits the full four years from ages sixty-six to seventy will receive a 32 percent increase in monthly benefits.

A retired widowed spouse of a retiree is eligible to receive the deceased retiree's Social Security retirement benefit if it is greater than the widowed spouse's retirement benefit. Therefore, a person's decision concerning when to commence Social Security retirement benefits can have a dramatic effect on spousal retirement benefits.

For example, suppose a married man age sixty-two expects to have a monthly Social Security retirement benefit of $2,000 if benefits begin at age sixty-six

and of $1,500 if benefits start at age sixty-two. Retirement at sixty-two rather than sixty-six would reduce the widowed spouse's monthly Social Security retirement benefit from $2,000 to $1,500. Deferring Social Security benefits until age seventy would increase the man's monthly benefit—and the benefit his spouse would receive after his death—to $2,640.

Two additional strategies for commencing Social Security retirement benefits may mean additional income for retirees:

- Claiming benefits and then suspending them until age seventy (or another age) to enable a spouse to claim spousal retirement benefits—This strategy allows benefits for the person who has claimed and then suspended them to continue to grow, along with the widowed retirement benefit of the person's spouse.
- Allowing the Social Security benefits of the spouse with the higher benefit to grow beyond full retirement age and instead taking a spousal benefit based on the earnings history of the spouse with the lower benefit. When the spouse with the higher benefit reaches age seventy, he or she begins taking Social Security retirement benefits based on his or her own earnings history.

Apply Your Knowledge

Bob and Ellen, both sixty-six, are a married couple planning to retire within the current year. They need $75,000 in annual income to cover their essential living expenses and expect to need an additional $20,000 each year to cover travel and other discretionary expenses to visit their five children and thirteen grandchildren living throughout the United States.

Their combined pension benefits provide $35,000 in annual income; Social Security retirement benefits add an additional $25,000. They have $350,000 in a 401(k) account, $200,000 in traditional IRAs, and $250,000 in a brokerage account.

What recommendations would you offer to help them retire this year? Explain your answer.

Feedback: The first step is to ensure that the couple's essential living expenses are covered with guaranteed income. Because their essential living expenses amount to $75,000 and their annual income from pensions and Social Security total $60,000, your recommendation should call for the purchase of a joint and survivor annuity that will provide the needed $15,000 for as long as either Bob or Ellen lives. The premium for that annuity would be approximately $240,000. To pay it, Bob and Ellen could roll over $240,000 from the 401(k) account, which would allow them to complete the transaction without recognizing any income. Periodic payments received under the annuity are taxable income in the year received.

The next task is to provide for the $20,000 of annual income the couple expects to need to cover travel and other discretionary expenses. To cover this amount, you could recommend use of the 4 percent withdrawal strategy. After rolling over the annuity premium, the couple would have $110,000 remaining in their 401(k) account, in addition to the $250,000 in the brokerage account and the $200,000 in traditional IRAs. At a combined $560,000, the remaining assets are more than sufficient to provide the needed $20,000 yearly using the 4 percent withdrawal strategy.

Bob and Ellen should withdraw $20,000 from their brokerage account this year, liquidating losing investments first. In the next year, they should withdraw an amount equal to $20,000, increased by the prior year's inflation rate. Each subsequent year, they should withdraw an amount equal to the prior year's withdrawal increased by the prior year's inflation rate. When assets in the brokerage account have been depleted, the couple should withdraw from their 401(k) and traditional IRA balances.

At age seventy and one-half, Bob and Ellen will have to take required minimum distributions (RMDs) from their 401(k) and traditional IRA accounts. If the brokerage account assets have not been exhausted by the time Bob and Ellen reach the required start date for their RMDs, they should withdraw the required amounts from the tax-deferred accounts and take the balance of the annual discretionary withdrawal from the brokerage account.

ELIGIBILITY REQUIREMENTS FOR RETIREMENT BENEFITS

The Employee Retirement Income Security Act (ERISA) was enacted by the United States Congress in 1974 to protect employees' retirement assets.

ERISA establishes eligibility requirements for private industry retirement plans. Although private employers are not obligated to provide retirement plans, those that do (except for government retirement plans and nonqualified retirement plans) are subject to the mandates in ERISA.

Two broad categories of provisions appear under ERISA:

- Standards for retirement plans offered by private industry employers
- Requirements for those who receive benefits from private industry retirement plans

ERISA Minimum Standards for Retirement Plans

ERISA establishes minimum standards for the retirement plans provided by employers in private industries. Among the standards set by ERISA are these:

- When employees are eligible to participate in the plan
- How benefits are accrued

- When an employee is fully vested in the plan
- Length of work time required before an employee has a nonforfeitable interest in benefits
- Whether an employee's spouse is eligible to participate in the plan

Two types of employer-sponsored retirement plans exist:

- Defined benefit plan—The benefit or method of calculating the benefit (such as a percentage of pay or years of service) is provided by the plan. The employer bears the investment risk.
- Defined contribution plan—The plan specifies the amount or percentage of contributions but not the benefit. The employee bears the investment risk.

ERISA requires defined benefit plans to be fully funded. Through the act, the federal government established the Pension Benefit Guaranty Corporation, an insurance program it owns and operates to protect the retirement income of people enrolled in defined benefit pension plans. This protection is not extended to defined contribution plans. See the exhibit "Types of Employer-Provided Defined Contribution Retirement Plans."

Types of Employer-Provided Defined Contribution Retirement Plans

- Cash or deferred arrangements—Internal Revenue Code 401(k)
- Tax-deferred annuities—Internal Revenue Code 403(b)
- Employee stock ownership plans (ESOPs)
- Thrift plans—defined contributions made by employer and employee
- Nonqualified plans—plans that do not qualify under Internal Revenue Code

[DA09055]

Fiduciary responsibility
The obligation to perform duties faithfully, carefully, and diligently.

ERISA includes requirements for **fiduciary responsibility** of administrators of private-employer retirement plans.

An employer-sponsored retirement plan must be accompanied by formal, written documents describing the plan's provisions and how the plan operates. Plans must also regularly provide information about the plan and about benefit accrual to participants.

ERISA Requirements for Receiving Retirement Benefits

ERISA requires that all employees who are twenty-one years of age or older and have at least one year of service with an employer be allowed to partici-

pate in the employer's retirement plan; however, an employer may choose to permit employees under age twenty-one and/or those with less than one year of service to participate. No maximum age can be set for participation in a retirement plan.

ERISA requires employees to be fully vested in their own contributions to retirement plans. Various options are available for vesting in employer contributions, but a plan must fully vest employees after seven years of participation.

A qualified plan is required to allow participants to begin receiving benefits by the latest of these occurrences:

- Age sixty-five or the plan's normal retirement age, if earlier than sixty-five
- After ten years of service
- Upon termination of service

Some retirement plans allow employees to receive early distribution for hardships, and some 401(k) plans permit loans for specific purposes, such as purchasing a home or funding college education.

Distributions from employer-sponsored plans are required to begin no later than April 1 of the year after the year in which the participant reaches age seventy-and-one-half years, unless the participant is still employed by the employer sponsoring the plan. Some employers offer a phased retirement option, in which employees can work part time while receiving retirement plan benefits.

Defined benefit plans are required to provide survivor benefits to employees' spouses unless both the employee and the spouse sign a waiver. In defined contribution plans, the employee can select the beneficiary.

If an employee withdraws funds from a retirement plan prior to reaching age fifty-nine-and-one-half, a tax penalty may be assessed, as well as income tax on the amount of the withdrawal. Some plans permit a lump-sum payment in addition to annuity options for distributions.

PENSION FUNDING

The Pension Benefit Guaranty Corporation (PBGC), an organization of the United States government, is responsible for paying benefits to more than 1.5 million retirees whose pension plans failed. An increasing number of failed pension plans led to enactment of the Pension Protection Act (PPA) in 2006 to strengthen pension funding requirements.

Pension plans are defined benefit plans that promise employees and their beneficiaries a certain income when they retire. Pension plans in private industry are governed by the Employee Retirement Income Security Act (ERISA).

These are the major issues for employers offering defined benefit pension plans to their employees:

- Pension prefunding obligations
- Sources of pension funding
- Postretirement pension funding
- Pension plan termination

Pension Prefunding Obligations

While it is typically desirable for a pension plan to be fully funded up to the amount of its obligations per plan participant, this is frequently not the case, especially during economic downturns. Funding gaps can occur when an employer's contributions into a pension plan are not adequate to cover promised future benefits. A pension plan's actuary is required to develop the amount that the employer must contribute to the pension fund each year—the annual required contribution (ARC). Unless the total ARC is paid into the pension fund each year to cover benefits earned plus past shortfalls, a funding gap can occur.

Funding gaps can occur over time. Pension plans are prefunded, with regular employer contributions made for each participant in the plan over the course of the worker's employment. These contributions are invested, and investment earnings are reinvested into the pension fund on behalf of the participants. However, investments that are not sufficiently diversified, such as investments in the employer's stock, can have a significant negative economic impact on the pension plan if the employer fails.

When a pension plan's assets are exceeded by its obligations, it is said to have an unfunded liability, another term for a funding gap. Additionally, the dollar amounts that ERISA requires for plans to be prefunded, based on the number of plan participants, can be less than 100 percent of the plan's full value.

Sources of Pension Funding

There are three sources of funding for private employers' defined benefit pension plans:

- Employee contributions
- Employer funding
- Investment income

Although employer plans vary by percentage of employee contributions to individual retirement plans, employers bear the responsibility of adequately funding their plans. Employers' current funding obligations can be offset by previous funding, including investment income. However, employers also bear the responsibility for increases in funding resulting from investment losses.

Postretirement Pension Funding

When an employee retires, a defined benefit pension plan typically offers two options for providing the promised retirement benefits to the employee or employee's spouse:

- Lump-sum payment
- Lifetime **annuity**

Annuity
A type of life insurance policy or contract that makes periodic payments to the recipient for a fixed period or for life in exchange for a specified premium.

ERISA requires defined benefit plans to present an annuity option to employees that provides monthly benefits. ERISA also specifies which mortality tables and interest rates must be used to calculate lump-sum payments for employees who elect that option.

Pension Plan Termination

Private employers' defined benefit pension plans can be terminated voluntarily by the employer or involuntarily by the PBGC. There are two types of voluntary employer plan terminations: standard and distressed.

Standard terminations of defined benefit plans are permissible under ERISA requirements only when the plan is fully funded. Plan participants must be notified. Benefits due to participants and beneficiaries must be determined by an actuary. Benefits are then distributed through lump-sum payments or annuities.

Distressed terminations are permitted if one of these conditions is met:

- Employer bankruptcy.
- Employer cannot meet payment obligations unless the plan is terminated.
- Employer has unreasonable pension costs solely as a result of a decline in its workforce.

Further, the PBGC can terminate an employer's pension plan under any of these conditions:

- Funding requirements are not met.
- Plan cannot pay benefits.
- Lump-sum payment is made to a participant who is also a substantial owner of the employer's company.
- Expectation of unreasonable increase in loss to the PBGC.

If a voluntary distressed termination or an involuntary termination of a pension plan occurs, the employer is liable to the PBGC for unfunded liabilities. The liability is due to the PBGC on the plan termination date unless the PBGC has agreed to other repayment terms.

Review Questions

1. Describe the considerations required to effectively plan for retirement.
2. Describe the consequences to individuals of ineffective retirement planning.
3. Explain how a change from defined benefit retirement plans to defined contribution plans affects an individual's retirement planning.
4. Describe the obstacles to adequately funding retirement expenses faced by members of the baby boom generation.
5. Dale and Marge, a Midwestern couple, would like to have their mortgage and other financial obligations paid in full when they retire, and they would like to be able to spend the winter months in Arizona. Describe the point at which these aspirations become factors in Dale and Marge's retirement planning process and how they affect Dale and Marge's retirement plan.
6. Nathan has established his retirement goals, and his insurance adviser is ready to analyze his financial needs for Step 2 of the retirement planning process. Explain what factors they must determine to calculate Nathan's accumulation goal and the additional annual retirement savings needed to achieve that goal.
7. As part of Step 3 of the retirement planning process, arranging financing and control techniques, one factor determines which of the four types of funding vehicles is best to meet an individual's accumulation goal. Name it.
8. Describe how the passage of the Internal Revenue Service's 401(k) plan regulations in the 1980s affected traditional defined benefit pension plans.
9. Contrast qualified retirement plans and nonqualified retirement plans.
10. Describe the tax benefits of a Roth individual retirement account (IRA).
11. Nonqualified employer-sponsored retirement plans offer benefits designed to help employers meet specific business needs. In relation to such plans, describe the following: a. a primary reason an employer would offer a nonqualified retirement plan and b. the characteristic of a nonqualified retirement plan that makes it particularly useful for the reason described in answer a.
12. State which party—the employer or the employee—bears the investment risk in a defined benefit plan, and explain why.
13. Distinguish the primary objectives of a pension plan with those of a profit-sharing plan.
14. Explain how the amounts of an employer's annual contributions to a qualified defined benefit retirement plan are determined.
15. Describe three approaches that may be used for allocating contributions and plan earnings to participants in profit-sharing plans.
16. Contrast the two types of nonqualified retirement plans: supplemental executive retirement plans (SERPs) and salary reduction plans.

17. Explain the income requirements for contributing to a traditional IRA based on whether it is a spousal IRA.
18. Contrast traditional IRAs and Roth IRAs.
19. Contrast direct and indirect rollovers of IRAs.
20. Identify the principal employer-sponsored retirement plans in which individuals invest.
21. List the steps an individual who plans to retire would take to purchase an annuity with retirement income.
22. Describe the retirement income strategy of spending down existing assets.
23. Describe the two major types of retirement plans.
24. Explain the purpose of the Pension Benefit Guaranty Corporation.
25. Explain whether employers may set age limitations for participation in retirement plans.
26. Name the latest date on which retirement plan participants may begin receiving benefits.
27. Identify the three sources of funding for defined benefit pension plans.
28. Describe how defined benefit pension plan participants receive their benefits when they retire.
29. Compare standard and distressed pension plan terminations by employers.

Application Questions

1. Denise, a single woman age forty-five, has sought counsel with an insurance representative on planning for her retirement following a job change. Denise earns $65,000 per year in her current job and has $20,000 per year available for retirement investment. Her disabled daughter is her dependent and requires daily assistance with medical and personal care. Denise would like to have all of her financial obligations, including her mortgage, paid in full when she retires. She would like to be able to travel twice a year to visit other countries in her first five years of retirement and, because her daughter does not enjoy travel, she would like to pay a professional to care for her daughter during those trips. Except for the added travel, Denise would simply like to maintain her current lifestyle after she retires at age sixty-five. Which details from this case would be factors used in Denise's retirement goals? Assume that Denise and her insurance consultant have determined her accumulation funding goal and the additional annual retirement savings she needs to meet her goals. Based on taxation of the four types of retirement savings funding vehicles, which would be appropriate for Denise's needs? Explain your answer.
2. Courtland, Inc., has an employee benefits plan to which it contributes at irregular intervals every few years. Sixty percent of the plan's funds are invested in Courtland stock. On the date of his retirement, Duncan, a manager at Courtland, receives a large lump-sum payment from the plan. What kind of plan does Courtland offer? Explain your answer.

3. Metford, Inc., offers a retirement plan for its employees. The plan has the added benefit of helping finance Metford's growth. What kind of plan does Metford offer? Explain your answer.
4. Anika, who is forty-five, has a traditional IRA to which she has contributed $25,000 in pretax earnings. She is considering converting the traditional IRA to a Roth IRA. Anika, who currently works as an administrative assistant, has been promoted and will assume a management position effective January 1 of the coming year. Explain how Anika's promotion could affect her financial plans.
5. Linda, age sixty-four, makes $60,000 a year. Her employer offers a 401(k) plan that matches up to 6 percent of each employee's annual salary when it is deferred to the plan. Linda defers 10 percent of her salary to the plan. She had intended to retire at age sixty-five but is now considering staying at her job for an additional year. What advantages to her retirement income would the extra year provide?

SUMMARY

Funding for living expenses in retirement requires effective planning in order to accumulate sufficient funds to meeting the costs of living in retirement.

Retirement benefits are provided through three principal sources: employer-sponsored plans, government-sponsored plans, and individual plans. Employer-sponsored plans include qualified plans and nonqualified plans.Government-sponsored plans include Social Security and Railroad Retirement plans. Individual retirement accounts include both traditional IRAs and Roth IRAs. The federal government provides tax incentives to encourage employers, employees, and individuals to actively fund retirement. The tax benefits vary somewhat depending on whether the retirement plan is an employer-sponsored retirement plan or an IRA.

Employer-sponsored retirement plans may be categorized as qualified or nonqualified plans, defined contribution or defined benefit plans, and pension or profit-sharing plans. Qualified plans must meet various IRC requirements; in return, they enjoy important tax advantages. Nonqualified plans, which are not subject to those requirements and advantages, offer employers significant flexibility in developing retirement plans that meet specific business needs. Defined contribution plans require employers to contribute the plan-specified percentage of each participant's income. Defined benefit plans require employers to make annual contributions to ensure their plans' ability to pay promised retirement benefits. Profit-sharing plans offer employers more flexibility than pension plans with respect to annual contributions.

Defined benefit plans, which include defined benefit pension plans and cash balance plans, offer participants a much higher level of benefit guarantees than defined contribution plans. However, defined contribution plans offer employers the opportunity to more effectively manage their qualified plan

costs and, through elective deferrals, to transfer much of the cost to plan participants.

Nonqualified retirement plans, including supplemental executive retirement plans (SERPs) and salary reduction plans, offer employers fairly unlimited flexibility in designing a retirement plan specifically to meet the unique needs of the business and its executive group. The trade-off for such nonqualified plan flexibility is the loss of the special tax advantages enjoyed by qualified plans.

Several strategies are available for individuals approaching retirement who find themselves short of retirement income:

- Purchasing a life annuity to cover essential living expenses
- Withdrawing no more than 4 percent of retirement savings, increased each year by the inflation rate
- Delaying retirement and the commencement of retirement benefits
- Postponing the start of Social Security retirement benefits until later than full retirement age up to as late as age seventy

ERISA is intended to protect retirement income for employees participating in private employer-sponsored retirement plans. The two major types of retirement plans are defined benefit and defined contributions plans. ERISA establishes eligibility requirements that affect employers, plan administrators, and employees.

Private employers' defined benefit pension plans promise certain retirement benefits to employees. ERISA requires employers to prefund benefit obligations in employer-sponsored plans. Funding sources include employee contributions, employer funding, and investments. Retirement benefits are typically provided through either lump-sum payments or lifetime annuities. Defined benefit plans can be terminated voluntarily by an employer or involuntarily by the PBGC.

ASSIGNMENT NOTES

1. "Baby Boom Generation: Retirement of Baby Boomers is Unlikely to Precipitate Dramatic Decline in Market Returns, but Broader Risks Threaten Retirement Security," U.S. Government Accountability Office Report to Congressional Committees, July 2006, p. 4.
2. "Will the Demand for Assets Fall When the Baby Boomers Retire?" Congressional Budget Office, September 2009, p. 10.
3. www.nasaa.org/investor_education/9574.cfm (accessed December 15, 2009).
4. Lindsay M. Howden and Julie A. Meyer, "Age and Sex Composition: 2010," 2010 Census Briefs, U.S. Census Bureau, May 2011, www.census.gov/prod/cen2010/briefs/c2010br-03.pdf (accessed October 12, 2011).

5. Stephen P. McCourt, "Defined Benefit and Defined Contribution Plans: A History, Market Overview and Comparative Analysis," Benefits & Compensation Digest, International Foundation of Employee Benefit Plans, February 2006.

6. Social Security Administration, www.ssa.gov/history/ (accessed October 12, 2011).

7. Railroad Retirement Board, www.rrb.gov/opa/agency_overview.asp (accessed October 12, 2011).

8. Social Security Administration, www.ssa.gov (accessed October 18, 2011).

9. E.S. Browning, "Retiring Boomers Find 401(k) Plans Fall Short," The Wall Street Journal, February 19, 2011, p. A1.

10. "Fidelity Reports Average 401(k) Account Balance Hits 10-Year High at End of 2010," February 23, 2011, www.fidelity.com/inside-fidelity/employer-services/q4-2011-401k-update (accessed October 18, 2011).

Direct Your Learning

15

Mandated/Compulsory Benefits and Social Insurance

Educational Objectives

After learning the content of this assignment, you should be able to:

- Explain the reasons why social insurance programs were established.
- Describe the following with regard to the United States Social Security program:
  - The basic characteristics of OASDHI
  - Covered occupations
  - The eligibility requirements for insured status
  - The types of benefits provided
- Describe the basic objectives and important provisions of unemployment insurance programs.
- Describe workers compensation statutes in terms of these common characteristics:
  - Basic purpose
  - Benefits provided
  - Persons and employments covered

Outline

Social Insurance

Social Security Program (OASDHI)

Unemployment Insurance

Workers Compensation Statutes: Purpose, Benefits, and Persons Covered

Summary

Mandated/Compulsory Benefits and Social Insurance

15

SOCIAL INSURANCE

When modern societies changed from agrarian to industrial and from rural to urban, the need for **social insurance** became apparent.

Social insurance

A program administered or mandated by government to provide coverage for economic hazards.

The Triangle Shirtwaist factory fire in New York City in 1911, in which hundreds of young female garment workers were injured or died, led New York to enact workers compensation insurance. Within several years, most states passed their own workers compensation insurance legislation, thereby implementing the first social insurance program in the United States.

The Great Depression of the 1930s raised awareness of the population's vulnerability to economic hardship. People had little if any protection from hazards related to unemployment that resulted from unavailability of work or inability to work because of disability or age. Social insurance programs to provide unemployment and Social Security benefits were enacted to address these concerns.

Overview and Scope

Industrialized nations differ significantly in the scope of social insurance programs. German social insurance covers healthcare, injury, disability, unemployment, retirement, and long-term care. In contrast, the U.S. until 2010 had no social insurance program to provide healthcare for all of its citizens. The healthcare program established in 2010 is mandated by government but provided by private insurers, except for those who qualify for coverage under Medicare or Medicaid programs.

Distinction Between Social Welfare and Social Insurance

As with other types of insurance, social insurance is based on premiums or similar financial contributions. For example, workers compensation coverage is provided by employers paying premiums to private or state-owned insurers. Injured workers receive a portion of their income based on their wages prior to injury. Social Security premiums are paid by employee and employer taxes, and workers receive retirement benefits based on their contributions and years worked.

In contrast, social welfare is based on financial need rather than financial contribution. Supplemental Security Income (SSI), Medicaid, and Aid to Families with Dependent Children (AFDC) are examples of social welfare programs in the U.S. Unlike social insurance, which is funded at least in part by contributions from program participants and employers, social welfare programs are funded by taxes collected by government sponsors of the programs.

Society's Responsibility

The movement of industrialized societies toward social insurance began in Europe in the 19th century, with the philosophy that an advanced society's responsibilities include helping protect its citizens from risks of hardship. This movement coincided with an increase in the types and availability of private insurance, such as homeowners insurance. Both social and private insurance are based on an underlying concept that modern economies require insurance against risks that could undermine individual and commercial enterprises.

Fortuitous event

An event occurring by chance.

Social insurance is intended to provide protection against risks that may not be **fortuitous events**. For example, retirement is something that can be foreseen and for which individuals can plan. Certain risks covered by social insurance programs can be catastrophic for an individual or for society. For example, unemployment reached catastrophic levels during the Great Depression. Private insurance, although it may play a role in social insurance programs, cannot respond effectively to the types of economic risks covered by these programs.

Social Insurance Attributes

Social insurance, similar to private insurance, is intended to provide coverage for individuals and families against economic hazards. A major difference between social and private insurance is that the coverage provided by social insurance is determined by law, whereas the coverage provided by private insurance is determined by a contract between the insurer and the insured. Another significant difference between social and private insurance is that social insurance is mandatory, while private insurance typically is not. However, this distinction has become increasingly blurred. Workers compensation insurance is provided by private insurers in most states. Private insurers provide coverage for Medicare Part B programs and, beginning in 2014, will provide most health insurance coverage under the Affordable Care Act.

Social insurance programs have these attributes:

- Compulsory
- Prescribed benefits
- Conditional benefits based on specific requirements
- Minimum floor of protection provided to ensure that individuals and communities do not fall below a threshold

- Often include government-subsidized benefits
- Required contributions from participants
- Usually based on employment
- Limited advance funding
- Often involve unpredictable losses

SOCIAL SECURITY PROGRAM (OASDHI)

Most individuals who work a minimum time period and pay Social Security taxes are eligible for benefits through Social Security. Family members of an eligible worker may also receive certain benefits. The benefits provided by Social Security are minimal, however, and other sources of retirement income, disability income, and insurance are suggested to supplement Social Security payments.

The United States federal Social Security program, also known as OASDHI (old age, survivors, disability, and health insurance system), was designed to provide benefits to qualified individuals upon their retirement or if they become disabled and are unable to work, and to supplement medical care. Most occupations are covered; however, some are not. Eligibility for insured status under OASDHI extends not only to covered workers; benefits may also be provided to their families. Most Social Security benefits that are paid are retirement benefits; however, additional benefits can include survivors death benefits, disability benefits, and Medicare benefits.

Basic Characteristics of OASDHI

Most working individuals are covered under the Social Security program for some benefits, and most are currently paying or will pay Social Security taxes based on their earnings. Workers are entitled to Social Security retirement benefits if they were fully insured at the age at which they retired. Social Security defines "fully insured" as having earned forty quarters of coverage. A quarter of coverage is earned for each quarter of a year that an individual works. Effectively, an individual is fully insured after ten full years of work; the quarters do not have to be consecutive as long as forty quarters are earned.

Calculation of Social Security benefits is complicated; however, the Social Security Administration mails a benefit estimate statement to insured individuals every year. It also offers a website with tools to help individuals estimate their future financial needs, to identify the Social Security programs for which they might be eligible, to learn how their age at retirement and other types of earnings and pensions affect their Social Security benefits, and to answer many other questions. The website also offers planners and calculators for disability and survivors benefits, and individuals can apply for Social Security benefits through a link from the Social Security Administration website.[1]

Covered Occupations

Individuals in most occupations, including self-employed individuals who earn $400 or more in one year, pay Social Security taxes and earn Social Security benefits. Certain occupations have special rules for calculating Social Security taxes and benefits. Some types of work or workers are not covered, including federal workers; foreign agricultural workers; students performing service for a school, college, or university; nursing students; Job Corps workers; work not in the course of the employer's trade or business; newspaper delivery workers; work covered by the Railroad Retirement Act; and employment by a foreign government, an international organization, or an instrumentality of a foreign government.

Eligibility Requirements for Insured Status

Individuals must be insured under the Social Security program to receive retirement, survivors, or disability benefits. To receive any Social Security benefits, an individual must have insured status. "Fully insured status" is one requirement for particular types of benefits; however, some benefits may apply if the individual qualifies as "currently insured." To qualify for disability benefits, an individual must have "disability-insured status."

The government uses an individual's lifetime earnings record, reported under his or her Social Security number (SSN), to assign Social Security credits for a specified amount of work (a quarter) and to determine insured status. Alien workers (those who are not U.S. citizens or nationals) are subject to special rules for determining insured status.

To be fully insured, an individual must have at least six credits and meet certain age requirements based on various dates at the time of retirement; however, no more than forty credits are required, regardless of the individual's birth date. An individual may earn no more than four credits in a year. The full retirement age is currently sixty-six. However, in 2003, the full retirement age began increasing from sixty-five to sixty-seven starting with individuals born in 1938. See the exhibit "Age to Receive Full Social Security Benefits."

An individual who has currently insured status can receive certain Social Security benefits. To qualify for currently insured status, he or she must have at least six Social Security credits during the full thirteen-quarter period that ends the year he or she dies, most recently becomes entitled to disability benefits, or becomes entitled to retirement insurance benefits. Periods of disability are generally not counted when computing Social Security credits.

An individual who has disability-insured status qualifies for certain disability benefits. To qualify, the individual must have at least twenty credits during a forty-calendar-quarter period (called the 20/40 rule). The forty-calendar-quarter period ends in the quarter the individual is determined to be disabled, and he or she is fully insured in that calendar quarter. Individuals who are disabled before age thirty-one can qualify for disability insurance benefits as an option

Age to Receive Full Social Security Benefits

Year of Birth	Full Retirement Age
1937 or earlier	65
1938	65 and 2 months
1939	65 and 4 months
1940	65 and 6 months
1941	65 and 8 months
1942	65 and 10 months
1943–1954	66
1955	66 and 2 months
1956	66 and 4 months
1957	66 and 6 months
1958	66 and 8 months
1959	66 and 10 months
1960 and later	67

Social Security Administration, "Age to Receive Full Social Security Retirement Benefits," Retirement Age, May 29, 2009, www.ssa.gov/pubs/retirechart.htm (accessed December 21, 2009). [DA05713]

to the 20/40 rule, called "special insured status." Blind workers who are fully insured are not required to meet the 20/40 rule or the requirements for special insured status.

Types of Benefits Provided by Social Security

Social Security provides several possible benefits to insured individuals and/or their dependents. These benefits are most often provided under the Social Security law:

- Retirement (old age) benefits are paid to insured workers and their eligible dependents.
- Survivors (death) benefits are paid to surviving dependents of insured workers.
- Disability benefits are paid to insured workers and their eligible dependents.
- Health insurance benefits (Medicare) are paid to insured persons age sixty-five or older and to certain other beneficiaries.

Except for Medicare, Social Security benefits are based on the individual's primary insurance amount (PIA). The PIA is calculated by applying a formula to the worker's average monthly earnings over a specified number of years. A

family maximum benefit (FMB) is also calculated from the PIA to limit the benefit amount that may be paid to a worker and his or her eligible dependents. These calculations are complicated, but the amounts are provided on an individual's annual Social Security statement.

Retirement (Old Age) Benefits

An individual can receive retirement (old age) benefits when he or she reaches age sixty-two and has attained fully insured status. The retirement insurance benefit equals the individual's PIA. In certain cases, a special minimum benefit is provided to some individuals who have had low earnings.

For workers born in 1937 and earlier, the full-benefit retirement age is sixty-five. Starting with workers born in 1938, the full-benefit retirement age gradually increases to age sixty-seven for workers born in 1960 and later. A fully insured worker may begin receiving retirement benefits at age sixty-two, but the benefit amount would be permanently reduced. Optionally, a worker can elect to delay retirement until age seventy and receive increased benefits starting at age seventy. See the exhibit "Percentage of Social Security Benefits Gained With Delayed Retirement."

Percentage of Social Security Benefits Gained With Delayed Retirement

Year of Birth	Yearly Rate of Increase	Monthly Rate of Increase
1933–1934	5.5%	11/24 of 1%
1935–1936	6.0%	1/2 of 1%
1937–1938	6.5%	13/24 of 1%
1939–1940	7.0%	7/12 of 1%
1941–1942	7.5%	5/8 of 1%
1943 or later	8.0%	2/3 of 1%

Note: If you were born on January 1, you should refer to the rate of increase for the previous year.

Social Security Administration, "Delayed Retirement Credits," Retirement Planner, January 6, 2010, www.ssa.gov/retire2/delayret.htm (accessed January 7, 2010). [DA05714]

The spouse of a retired worker who has reached age sixty-two can receive a lifetime reduced retirement benefit that is 50 percent of the fully insured worker's PIA, up to the FMB. If the worker retires at age sixty-five, the full spousal retirement benefit can be paid to the spouse. If the spouse is entitled to a personal retirement benefit, then the spouse would receive the larger of his or her personal benefit or his or her spousal benefit.

If the spouse cares for any unmarried child, stepchild, or grandchild of the worker under age sixteen or for a disabled child, stepchild, or grandchild of the worker, additional benefits may also be provided for each qualified dependent on the worker's retirement until the FMB has been met.

Survivors (Death) Benefits

Survivors (death) benefits may be paid to the surviving spouse and other qualified dependents of a deceased worker who was fully insured at the time of his or her death.

The surviving spouse qualifies for survivors benefits if he or she is at least age sixty or is disabled and at least age fifty. The surviving spouse can receive 100 percent of the deceased worker's survivor PIA if that spouse is full-benefit retirement age. The benefit amount is reduced for younger surviving spouses.

Unmarried children and qualifying grandchildren of a deceased worker can receive a child's monthly survivors benefit. This benefit is generally 75 percent of the deceased parent's PIA. The child must be under age eighteen, or eighteen and an elementary or a secondary student, or eighteen or older but disabled before age twenty-two. Certain limitations apply.

A parent who was dependent on the insured worker before his or her death and who has reached age sixty-two can also receive a survivors benefit. If only one parent is entitled to benefits, the surviving parent's benefit is generally 82.5 percent of the deceased worker's PIA. If two parents are entitled to surviving parent's benefits, the benefit amount is generally 75 percent of the deceased worker's PIA.

Additionally, the surviving spouse who cares for an eligible child or grandchild receives a mother's or father's surviving spouse benefit. This benefit is generally 75 percent of the deceased worker's PIA. Note that all of these benefits combined are subject to the FMB.

Finally, a lump sum death benefit may be paid to the survivors of a worker who dies having met the fully insured or currently insured status. This lump sum of $255 is paid in addition to any monthly survivors benefits. Certain restrictions can apply—for example, if the survivor was convicted for the felony homicide of the qualified worker or the qualified worker was granted tax exemption as a member of a religious group.

Disability

The Social Security disability income (SSDI) Monthly Cash Benefits are designed to replace a portion of a wage earner's income for a short period of time if the wage earner becomes disabled because of an injury or illness. A five-month waiting period applies before any benefits will be paid. Auxiliary benefits may be paid to the spouse and other dependents of the injured worker.

Establishment of a Social Security disability period is essential for determination of numerous Social Security benefits. A "period of disability" under the Social Security law is a continuous period during which an individual is disabled. The established period of disability is not counted when determining an individual's insured status under Social Security and is not counted in determining the monthly benefit amount payable to the worker and his or her dependents. This period of disability is also used in determining other types of Social Security benefits for the worker's family.

Health Insurance (Medicare)

Under Social Security, people age sixty-five or older, those under sixty-five with certain disabilities, and people of all ages with specified medical conditions can qualify to receive federal Medicare health benefits including hospital insurance, medical insurance, and prescription drug coverage. Medicare beneficiaries can also choose to take advantage of Medicare Advantage plans that offer higher benefit levels and include managed-care plans and private fee-for-service plans.

UNEMPLOYMENT INSURANCE

Unemployment insurance provisions in the United States were first enacted in Wisconsin in 1932 during the Great Depression, and Congress included provisions for unemployment insurance in the federal Social Security Act of 1935. These unemployment programs were implemented during this time because national unemployment exceeded 20 percent, causing widespread hunger and homelessness.

Unemployment insurance is a partnership between the federal and state governments. Federal law mandates the program, but it is administered under state law.

Unemployment insurance has several basic objectives and contains important provisions at both the federal and state levels in terms of how related programs are operated.

One basic objective is to protect employees, employers, and society from some of the economic hazards of unemployment. Another objective is to serve as a social insurance program, providing temporary financial assistance to people who lose their jobs through no fault of their own.

Thus, unemployed individuals are able to at least minimally support themselves and their families while they look for work. Employers have the benefit of knowing that their employees will receive financial assistance during a reduction in their workforce. The economy, including all employers, benefits when people spend their unemployment allotments. Government studies estimate that $1.60 in economic benefits results from each $1.00 in unemployment benefits. Additionally, unemployment insurance helps to avoid the type of displacement of individuals and families that occurred during the

Great Depression, when large numbers of homeless people migrated across the nation in search of work.

Unemployment insurance programs, while federally mandated, are administered at state levels. Important provisions regarding the programs include those relating to administration, employee eligibility, available benefits, and sources of funding:

- Administration—Unemployment insurance benefit programs are administered by the states. An unemployed individual files a claim with his or her state unemployment agency, which is usually a division of the state labor department. Claims can usually be filed in person, by telephone, or electronically. Each state has a procedure in place for approving or denying claims for unemployment benefits. Either the employee or employer can contest a decision made by a state department of unemployment. Appeals are usually heard in an informal administrative forum.
- Eligibility—To be eligible for unemployment benefits, an employee must have worked a specific number of weeks for a covered employer. The number of weeks is specified by each state. Additionally, the employee must have lost the job through no fault of his or her own. To continue receiving unemployment benefits, employees must be available to work and actively looking for work. Unemployed individuals can usually work part time and take a deduction in their benefits without becoming ineligible. Achieving permanent employment at a rate of pay equal to or greater than the employee's weekly benefit amount will end eligibility for unemployment benefits.
- Available benefits—The number of weeks for which an employee is eligible for benefits is based on that employee's length of employment. The basic program, run by the states, typically provides up to twenty-six weeks of benefits to unemployed workers. The benefit amount, subject to the state maximum, is a percentage of the employee's wages. The federal government has occasionally passed legislation to extend unemployment benefits at certain times when the unemployment rate is high. For example, benefits were extended for individuals who lost their jobs as a result of Hurricane Katrina. Additionally, there have been several extensions of benefits passed by Congress since the financial crisis of 2008, in response to the high level of unemployment. In addition to providing financial benefits, state and federal governments assist unemployed individuals with job searches and job training.
- Sources of funding—Funding for unemployment insurance comes from taxes paid by employers in all but three states, in which employees also contribute toward the tax. When the federal government extends the number of weeks of unemployment benefits, additional federal assistance is typically provided to the states.

WORKERS COMPENSATION STATUTES: PURPOSE, BENEFITS, AND PERSONS COVERED

Insureds with employees that must be covered under state workers compensation statutes need producers, underwriters, claim representatives, and risk management professionals who know the important common characteristics of what causes an employer's loss exposures, what benefits are payable, and who is eligible for payment.

Workers compensation statutes differ by state but share several common characteristics, including these:

- Basic purpose
- Benefits provided
- Persons and employments covered

Basic Purpose

In the United States, before the enactment of workers compensation statutes, workers injured in industrial accidents could, under the common law, sue their employers for damages resulting from the injury. It was up to the employee to establish that the employer was at fault for the injury. The following defenses were among those available to employers:

- The employee contributed to the accident.
- The employee assumed the risk of injury when he or she took the job.
- A fellow worker was responsible for the accident.

It was difficult for employees to overcome these defenses, and the majority of injured workers received no compensation.

Workers compensation statute

A statute that obligates employers, regardless of fault, to pay specified medical, disability, rehabilitation, and death benefits for their employees' job-related injuries and diseases.

To address this problem, individual states enacted workers compensation statutes, starting with New York in 1910 and Wisconsin in 1911. Today, every state, the District of Columbia, Puerto Rico, Guam, the U.S. Virgin Islands, every Canadian province, and some other nations have enacted **workers compensation statutes**. These laws provide no-fault protection by removing the right of employees to sue their employers for injuries covered by the applicable workers compensation statute while obligating employers to compensate injured employees even if employer negligence is not involved. In return for definite payment, the employer's liability is limited (but not eliminated) by statute. Recovery under the applicable workers compensation law is thus often called the employee's "exclusive remedy" against the employer. The workers compensation system effectively guarantees injured workers prompt payment while reducing costs and court workloads arising out of litigation.

Benefits Provided

Workers compensation statutes provide benefits for medical expenses and wage loss resulting from either occupational injury or **occupational disease**.

Occupational disease
Disease thought to be caused by work or the work environment.

To be covered under a workers compensation statute, an injury or disease must (in most states) arise out of and in the course of employment. That is, the cause of the injury or disease must be related to the employment, and the occurrence must take place while the employee is engaged in work-related activities. For example, the statute would cover an employee who was injured falling from a ladder while changing a light bulb in his office because the injury arose out of and in the course of employment.

Generally, an employee is covered for any work-related injury sustained while at his or her place of employment or while traveling for the employer. Injuries occurring while traveling to or from work at a fixed location are typically not covered by the statute.

All U.S. workers compensation laws also include benefits covering occupational diseases. Most occupational diseases become evident during employment or soon after an employee's exposure to injurious conditions, although for some exposures the disease may be latent for a long time. Consequently, many states provide extended periods of time for the discovery of these slowly developing diseases. Although some states cover only occupational diseases specifically named in the law, the majority provide coverage for all occupational diseases.

Not all diseases contracted in the course of an occupation can be attributed to the work or occupational exposure. For example, the common cold is usually not a covered disease. In general, a cause and effect relationship must exist between the occupation and the disease for coverage to apply.

A typical workers compensation statute imposes absolute liability on employers for the benefits it provides. (Absolute liability is liability imposed without regard to fault.) This allows an employee to be at least partially compensated for expenses and loss of earnings incurred as a result of an occupational injury or disease. The benefits payable under the various state workers compensation laws generally include medical benefits, disability income benefits, rehabilitation benefits, and death benefits. See the exhibit "Workers Compensation Benefits."

Medical Benefits

In most instances, the workers compensation law provides full and unlimited medical expense benefits for a covered injury or disease. These benefits include medical, hospital, surgical, and other related medical care costs, including physical therapy and prosthetic devices. First-dollar benefits are ordinarily provided; no deductible or coinsurance provisions are imposed on the employee as under most medical insurance plans. Depending on state

Workers Compensation Benefits

Medical Benefits:

- Medical
- Hospital
- Surgical
- Related medical care costs, such as physical therapy and prosthetic devices

Disability Income Benefits:

- Wage loss subject to a waiting period deductible
- Payments for scheduled injuries

Rehabilitation Benefits:

- Medical rehabilitation
- Vocational rehabilitation

Death Benefits:

- Burial expense
- Partial replacement of the worker's former weekly wage

[DA07863]

law, the injured employee may have the right to select his or her own doctor or may be limited to a choice from a list of physicians designated by the employer or its insurer.

Disability Income Benefits

Workers compensation statutes typically use four disability classifications:

Temporary partial disability (TPD)

A disability caused by a work-related injury or disease that temporarily limits the extent to which a worker can perform job duties; the worker is eventually able to return to full duties and hours.

Temporary total disability (TTD)

A disability caused by a work-related injury or disease that temporarily renders an injured worker unable to perform any job duties for a period of time.

- **Temporary partial disability** is a disability caused by a work-related injury or disease that temporarily limits the extent to which an employee can perform job duties for a period of time (such as thirty or sixty days). After that period, the worker is expected to be able to resume all job duties.
- **Temporary total disability** is a disability caused by a work-related injury or disease that temporarily renders an injured employee unable to perform any job duties for a period of time (such as thirty or sixty days). After that period, the worker is expected to be able to resume all job duties.
- Permanent partial disability is a disability caused by a work-related injury or disease that impairs the injured employee's earning capacity for life. The employee is able to work at reduced efficiency.
- Permanent total disability is a disability caused by a work-related injury or disease that renders an injured employee unable to ever return to gainful employment.

Disability income benefits are intended to compensate an injured employee for wage loss in any of these categories. Unlike medical benefits, income benefits are payable subject to a deductible in the form of a waiting period. Disability benefits do not begin until the waiting period has expired. The waiting period generally varies from three to seven days, depending on the

state. If disability continues beyond a specified number of days, most laws provide for payment of benefits retroactive to the date of injury.

The benefit is payable weekly and is expressed as a percentage of the employee's average weekly wage at the time of disability. Maximum and minimum weekly benefit amounts vary widely from state to state.

State laws also require compensation for a specific number of weeks for the loss (or loss of use) of specific body parts, such as fingers. These injuries are referred to as "scheduled" injuries because the injuries and corresponding benefits are listed in a document called a schedule. Scheduled injuries do not generally cause permanent total disability, but the resulting permanent impairment is assumed to produce long-term loss of wages. As a result, the benefits for scheduled injuries are payable without regard to actual wage loss. All but the lowest paid or part-time workers generally qualify for the maximum compensation. In most states, the compensation for scheduled injuries is in addition to any other temporary disability benefits payable.

Rehabilitation Benefits

Because rehabilitation of injured workers is a goal of the workers compensation system, most state laws include some rehabilitation benefits. The primary rehabilitation benefit required is the payment of expenses for complete medical treatment and medical rehabilitation. Vocational rehabilitation may also be required by law. Most workers compensation laws provide a maintenance allowance to injured workers during rehabilitation in addition to other compensation benefits.

In addition, insurers provide rehabilitation services extending beyond the requirements of the law. For example, an insurer might include payment of expenses to customize a car or van to accommodate the physical disabilities of an injured worker in order to allow the employee to more easily return to light duty work.

Often, rehabilitation can reduce the cost of a workers compensation claim by shortening the length of time that the injured employee is disabled. Consequently, all parties benefit from rehabilitation. The employer and its insurer often save loss costs, and the injured worker returns to productive employment. Thus, rehabilitation also benefits society as a whole.

Death Benefits

Death benefits include a flat amount for burial expense and partial replacement of the worker's former weekly wage. The burial expense allowance varies among the states. The percentage of wage loss payable also varies by state and depends primarily on the number and types of dependents. Some states provide a maximum benefit expressed as either a total amount or a time period.

Apply Your Knowledge

Sam was employed as a producer at an insurance agency. He was traveling to a prospective customer's office for a sales call when he was involved in an auto accident. Sam was injured in the accident, breaking bones in one foot and fingers on both hands. He was immediately taken to the hospital and treated for his injuries. He had temporary total disability. Because of good medical care, Sam has no residual disability and will be able to resume all of his duties at work, without further treatment, after eight weeks. What workers compensation benefits is Sam eligible for?

Feedback: Sam's hospital, medical, surgical and related medical care costs, such as physical therapy, if needed, will be paid for by his employer's workers compensation insurer. After the waiting period deductible expires, Sam will be paid a percentage of his lost wages, including the wages he lost during the waiting period. Since Sam fully recovered from the accident, his lost wages benefit will end when he returns to work in eight weeks. He will not be paid for any rehabilitation expenses as they were not incurred. Sam, or his estate, will also not receive any death benefits, as he did not die as a result of the accident.

Persons and Employments Covered

Workers compensation statutes apply to virtually all industrial workers and most other kinds of private employment. The statutes of some states exempt employers with fewer than a stipulated number of employees, and many statutes specifically exclude certain employments such as farm labor, domestic workers, and casual employees. (A casual employee is one hired for only a short period, usually to accomplish a particular task.)

Many states provide workers compensation protection for all or certain classes of public employees. Some employees are excluded because alternate plans are provided for them. For example, federal statutes govern the rights of various classes of employees to recover benefits or damages from their employers for occupational injury or disease. Examples of such classes of employees are federal government workers, maritime workers, and interstate railroad workers.

Employees and Independent Contractors

Entitlement to benefits under a workers compensation law depends on whether a person qualifies as an **employee** according to the law.

Employee
A person hired to perform services for another under the direction and control of the other party, called the employer.

Independent contractor
A person (or organization) hired to perform services without being subject to the hirer's direction and control regarding work details.

The distinction between employees and **independent contractors** is not always clear. Unlike employees, independent contractors are not subject to direction and control regarding the details of the work. They agree to perform a task meeting the specifications stipulated in the contract but are free

to use their own judgment and methods in performing the task. They may also employ others to perform the task, but they remain responsible under the contract for its completion.

Employment status is a question of fact, not of law. If doubt arises concerning whether an individual is an employee or an independent contractor, a court or an administrative body decides the issue on the basis of the facts. The legislative mandate generally calls for the workers compensation law to be applied liberally. Therefore, the courts have interpreted the definition of an employee broadly to provide protection to those who seek it.

An independent contractor might also employ others. An independent contractor, like all other employers, must provide workers compensation benefits for its employees. In many states, if the contractor does not provide workers compensation insurance, the responsibility and the expense fall on the principal (the firm that uses the contractor's services). Furthermore, if a firm does not have certificates of insurance from the contractors it uses, its workers compensation insurer may require it to pay workers compensation insurance premiums based on the cost of the work sub-contracted. To be certain that the contractor has workers compensation insurance in force, the principal usually requires the contractor to provide a certificate of insurance as evidence of the insurance in force when the certificate was issued.

Leased Employees and Temporary Employees

Many organizations use leased employees, temporary employees, or both. Leased employees differ from temporary employees. Temporary employees are hired for short-term assignments to cope with peak loads or to replace an employee who is on sick leave or vacation. The firm supplying the temporary employee provides workers compensation for temporary employees; the temporary employee is an employee of the providing firm, not the firm that is using his or her services.

In contrast with temporary employees, leased employees have all the outward appearance of regular employees. They work continuously for the same firm and are subject to control by the firm just as they would be if they were its direct employees. Technically, however, they are co-employees of the client company and the leasing contractor, sometimes referred to as a professional employer organization (PEO). Sometimes a firm will transfer its employees to a PEO and then lease them back. The PEO is responsible for all payroll taxes, employee benefits, and workers compensation coverage. Generally, a separate workers compensation policy is written showing the names of the PEO and the client company, although the requirements imposed by law vary from state to state.[2]

Review Questions

1. Contrast social insurance programs with social welfare programs.
2. Describe a major difference between social insurance and private insurance.
3. List the attributes of social insurance programs.
4. Describe what qualifies an individual for "fully insured" status with Social Security, assuming other requirements are met.
5. Describe circumstances under which a self-employed individual's occupation is considered a covered occupation under Social Security.
6. Name the requirements for an individual to qualify for currently insured status under Social Security.
7. State when an individual can receive Social Security retirement (old age) benefits.
8. List two basic objectives of unemployment insurance.
9. Describe how unemployment benefits are administered.
10. Explain how an individual's unemployment benefits are determined.
11. Identify the funding sources for unemployment benefits.
12. Name two Social Security survivors (death) benefits a surviving wife might qualify for if she cares for an eligible child.
13. Describe the purpose of Social Security disability income (SSDI) Monthly Cash Benefits.
14. Name the basic benefits that are provided under Social Security health insurance (Medicare).
15. Explain the basic requirements for an injury or a disease to be covered for workers compensation benefits.
16. Briefly explain the types of benefits included under these categories: a. medical benefits, b. disability income benefits, c. rehabilitation benefits, and d. death benefits.
17. Identify the employees and the types of employment that are frequently excluded from state workers compensation statutes.
18. Why is it important for a principal to verify that its independent contractors carry valid workers compensation insurance on their employees?

Application Questions

1. Fran was attending a training class on behalf of her employer at a professional training center in a bordering state. She had rented a car to get to and from her hotel room and the training center. While driving to the training class, she was rear ended. She suffered injuries requiring medical care and incurred lost wages (as she was unable to work for several weeks).

What benefits are payable to Fran under her employer's workers compensation coverage?

2. Steve was employed by a temporary employment agency and was assigned to a department store during the Christmas shopping season. While lifting a heavy box, he strained his back and then required medical care and rehabilitation. He also incurred a month of lost wages. Which employer's workers compensation policy, if any, will provide benefits for Steve's injury?

SUMMARY

Social insurance programs evolved as modern nations transformed from agrarian to urban-centered, industrial societies. The purpose of social insurance programs is to provide protection for working individuals and their families from economic hardship resulting from injury, illness, age, or unemployment. Unlike social welfare programs, social insurance programs require contributions from participants and/or their employers. Although private insurers may offer social insurance programs, they are typically unable to do so without some level of government subsidy because of the nature of the related risks.

The United States federal Social Security program, also known as OASDHI, was designed to provide benefits to qualified individuals upon their retirement, if they become disabled and are unable to work, and to supplement medical care. Benefits may also be provided to the families of qualified individuals. Social Security benefits include retirement, survivors (death), disability, and health insurance.

Unemployment insurance is a social program in the U.S. representing a federal-state partnership. The purpose of this program is to provide financial assistance to eligible employees who lose their jobs through no fault of their own. This assistance benefits employers and the economy by enabling unemployed people to support themselves and contribute financially to the economy. Unemployment insurance is administered by the states. Each state determines eligibility criteria for employees along with benefit durations and levels. Funding is typically provided by taxes on employers and, in a few states, employees.

These are three common characteristics found in workers compensation statutes:

- Their basic purpose, which is to guarantee injured workers prompt payment for occupational injury or disease while reducing costs arising out of litigation
- Benefits provided, which are medical benefits, disability income benefits, death benefits, and rehabilitation benefits
- Persons and employments covered, which include employees (subject to some exceptions) but not independent contractors

ASSIGNMENT NOTES

1. Social Security Administration, Social Security Online, January 4, 2010, www.ssa.gov (accessed January 7, 2010).
2. For more information on PEOs, see The National Association of Professional Employer Organizations' Web site at www.napeo.org (accessed July 24, 2011).

Index

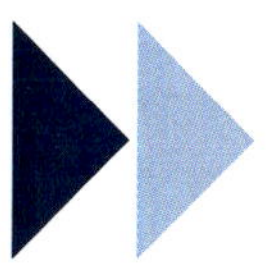

Page numbers in boldface refer to pages where the word or phrase is defined.

SYMBOLS

401(k) Plans, **14.18**–14.19
403(b) Plans, 14.19

A

Ability to Administer the Retention Plan, 6.16
Ability to Control Losses, 6.15
Ability to Diversify, 6.15
Access to Group Pricing, 12.7
Accumulating Sufficient Retirement Funds, 14.4
Achieve Collateral Social Purpose, 9.46
Actual cash value (ACV), **10.3**
Actual Injury or Damage, 3.17
Actuarial Equity Compared With Social Equity, 9.19
Additional insured endorsement, **6.24**
Advantages and Disadvantages of Group Insurance, 12.13–12.17
Adverse Selection, 9.16–9.20, **12.9**
Agency captive, **6.27**
Aging Population, 14.4–14.5
Alternative probability, **4.24**
Amount subject, **4.33**
Annuity, **14.33**
Application of Risk Control Techniques, 5.19–5.23
Asset Exposed to Loss, 2.25
Association captive, **6.26**
Attract and Retain Employees, 12.7
Avoidance, **5.3**–5.4

B

Bailee, **3.17**
Balance sheet, **2.28**
Basic Characteristics of OASDHI, 15.5
Basic Issues Facing Healthcare, 13.3
Basic medical expense coverage, **13.6**
Basic Purpose, 15.12
Basic Purpose and Scope of Risk Management, 2.3–2.4
Benefits for an Organization, 2.5–2.8
Benefits for the Economy, 2.9–2.10
Benefits of Insurance, 8.10–8.14
Benefits of Risk Management, 2.4–2.10
Benefits Provided, 15.13–15.16
Breach of contract, **3.11**
Breach of Duty, 3.14–3.15
Business Continuity Management, 5.23–5.29
Business Continuity Plan, 5.25–5.29
Business Continuity Process, 5.24–5.25
"But for" rule, **3.16**

C

Cafeteria Plans, 12.16–12.17
Calculating Alternative Probabilities, 4.24–4.28, 4.27–4.28
Capacity to Assume New Business, 9.8
Capital Asset Pricing Model and the Worry Factor, 7.16–7.17
Cash Balance Plans, **14.16**, 14.17–14.18
Categories of Employer-Sponsored Retirement Plans, 14.11–14.15
Cause of Loss, 2.25
Ceding commission, **9.51**
Central tendency, **4.11**
Characteristics of an Ideally Insurable Loss Exposure, 9.21–9.28
Characteristics of Employee Benefits Plans, 12.8–12.10
Civil law, **3.9**
Civil Law and Criminal Law, 3.9
Classification of Hazards, 1.10
Coefficient of variation, **4.22**–4.24
Coinsurance, 11.12–11.18, **13.15**
Coinsurance Clause, 11.14
Coinsurance Formula, 11.15–11.18
Coinsurance Overview, 11.13
Common carriers, **3.15**
Common law (case law), **3.13**
Comparing Actual Results With Standards, 2.17
Comparing Employer-Sponsored Retirement Plans, 14.16–14.23
Compel Insurance Purchase, 9.45–9.46
Competitor to Private Insurers, 9.48
Compliance Review, 2.33
Comply With Legal Requirements, 5.16, 6.7
Concurrent causation (concurrent causation doctrine), **3.16**
Conflict Between Goals, 2.24
Consumer-Directed Health Plans, **13.9**–13.11
Continuation of Health Care Coverage Under COBRA, 12.15
Continuity of Operations, 2.21–2.22
Contract, **3.11**, 3.13
Contract of indemnity, **8.8**–8.9
Contracting for Services, 6.19
Contracts, 2.29–2.30
Contractual liability, **3.12**
Contribution by equal shares, **11.5**
Conversion From Group Insurance to Individual Insurance, 12.14–12.15
Core Operations, 6.15

Correcting Substandard Performance, 2.17–2.18
Cost of Residual Uncertainty, 1.13–1.15
Cost of risk, **2.5**
Covered Occupations, 15.6
Credit risk, **1.6**
Criminal law, **3.9**
Cross-Sectional Risk Transfer, 9.26–9.27
Current-loss funding, **6.11**

D

Damages, **10.6**
Death, 9.36–9.37
Death Benefits, 12.4, 15.15–15.16
Decide on the Age to Start Social Security Retirement Benefits, 14.27–14.29
Defendant, **3.12**
Defined Benefit Pension Plans, 14.17
Defined benefit plan, **14.6**, **14.14**
Defined Contribution or Defined Benefit Plans, 14.13–14.14
Defined contribution plan, **14.13**
Definite, 9.24–9.25
Definite and Measurable, 9.24–9.25
Depreciation, **10.3**
Designated Roth 401(k) account, **14.19**
Disability, 15.9–15.10
Disability Benefits, 12.4
Disability Income Benefits, 15.14–15.15
Disaster recovery plan, **5.8**
Disclaimer of Warranties, 6.23
Disclaimers, 11.8
Discrete and Continuous Probability Distributions, 4.9–4.11
Dispersion, **4.20**
Distinction Between Social Welfare and Social Insurance, 15.3–15.4
Diversifiable and Nondiversifiable Risk, 1.8–1.9
Diversifiable risk, **1.8**
Diversification, **5.12**
Document Analysis, 2.26–2.33
Duplication, **5.11**–5.12

E

Earnings Stability, 2.23
Economic Issues Related to Insurance Pricing, 9.15–9.20
Economic View of Insurance, 9.3–9.15
Economically Feasible Premium, 9.28
Economy of Operations, 2.19
Effect of Inflation, 14.5–14.6
Effect of Risk Control Measures, 5.18
Elements of a Loss Exposure, 2.25–2.26
Elements of Negligence, 3.12–3.17
Eligibility and Participation, 12.8
Eligibility Requirements for Insured Status, 15.6
Eligibility Requirements for Retirement Benefits, 14.29–14.31
Empirical probability (a posteriori probability), **4.3**
Empirical Probability Distributions, 4.7–4.9
Employee, **15.16**
Employee benefits, **12.3**
Employee Stock Ownership Plans, 14.19
Employees and Independent Contractors, 15.16–15.17
Employer-Funded Employee Benefits, 12.3–12.5
Employer-Sponsored Retirement Plans, 14.7, 14.24–14.25
Enabling Efficient Use of Resources, 8.11
Ensure Business Continuity, 5.17
Enterprise Risk Management by Organizations, 3.21–3.24
ERISA Minimum Standards for Retirement Plans, 14.29–14.30
ERISA Requirements for Receiving Retirement Benefits, 14.30–14.31
Escape Clauses, **11.6**–11.8
Establishing Standards of Acceptable Performance, 2.16
Evaluating Standards That Have Been Substantially Exceeded, 2.18
Evolution of Retirement Funding, 14.6–14.7
Excess coverage provision, **11.4**
Exclusions, 11.7–11.8
Exclusive control, **3.18**
Exclusive Insurer, 9.47
Exclusive provider organization (EPO), **13.8**
Exculpatory clause (exculpatory agreement), **6.21**
Exoneration, **6.21**
Expected Cost of Losses or Gains, 1.12–1.13
Expected value, **4.12**–4.13
Expenditures on Risk Management, 1.13
Expertise Within and Beyond the Organization, 2.34–2.36
Exposure unit, **4.30**
Externalities, 5.19

F

Federal Compared With State Programs, 9.48
Fiduciary responsibility, **14.30**
Fill Unmet Needs, 9.45
Financial Condition, 6.15
Financial Consequences of Loss, 2.26
Financial Consequences of Risk, 1.12–1.15
Financial Considerations, 2.14–2.15
Financial Impact of Retirement, 14.3–14.6
Financial Statements and Underlying Accounting Records, 2.28–2.29
Financial Status, 9.14
Financing Issues, 12.9
Fire, 9.30–9.31
Flexible Spending Accounts (FSAs), 12.16
Flood, 9.33–9.34
Flowcharts and Organizational Charts, 2.31–2.32
Foreseeability rule, **3.16**
Fortuitous, 9.23–9.24
Fortuitous event, **15.4**
Fortuitous loss, **9.23**
Frequency, **1.10**
Funding Retained Losses, 6.11
Futures contract, **6.10**

G

Government Insurance Programs, 9.44–9.48
Government-Provided Health Insurance Plans, 13.11–13.17
Government-Sponsored Retirement Plans, 14.7–14.8
Group captive, **6.26**
Group Insurance Structure Versus Individual Insurance Structure, 12.9–12.10
Growth, 2.23–2.24
Guarantor, **6.20**

H

Hazard, **1.10**
Hazard analysis, **2.34**
Health Expense Benefits, 12.3
Health Insurance (Medicare), 15.10
Health Insurance Plans, 13.5–13.11
Health Loss Exposures, 9.43
Health maintenance organization (HMO), **13.7**
Health reimbursement arrangement (HRA), **13.9**
Health savings account (HSA), **13.9**
Healthcare Fee-for-Service Indemnity System, 13.3–13.4
Hedging, **6.9**
Hold-Harmless Agreement, **2.30**, 3.11, 6.9, 6.23–6.24
Holistic Risk Management, 2.8
Homogeneity, 4.30–4.33
Homogeneous, **4.30**
How Actual Cash Value Supports the Principle of Indemnity, 10.3–10.4
How Insurable Interest Supports the Principle of Indemnity, 10.4
How Insurance Reduces Risk, 8.3–8.8
How Insurance Uses Pooling, 8.5–8.8
How Pooling Reduces Risk, 8.3–8.5
How Subrogation Supports the Principle of Indemnity, 10.6–10.7
How Utmost Good Faith Supports the Principle of Indemnity, 10.5

I

Identifying Loss Exposures, 2.26–2.36
Implement Effective and Efficient Risk Control Measures, 5.13–5.16
Importance of Insurance to Value, 11.11
Improved Allocation of Productive Resources, 2.8
Income statement, **2.28**
Incorporation, 6.17–6.18
Increase Employee Productivity, 12.7–12.8
Indemnification, **2.30**
Indemnitee, **6.23**
Indemnitor, **6.23**
Indemnity, **6.21**
Indemnity plan, **13.6**
Independence, **4.32**–4.33
Independent, 9.27
Independent and Not Catastrophic, 9.27–9.28
Independent contractor, **15.16**
Individual retirement account (IRA), **14.8**
Individual Retirement Plans, 14.8
Individual- or Organization-Specific Characteristics, 6.14–6.16
Individually Provided Retirement Plans, 14.25
Inflexible Group Insurance Benefits, 12.15–12.17
Insolvency risk, **9.8**
Insurability of Commercial Loss Exposures, 9.28–9.39
Insurability of Personal Loss Exposures, 9.40–9.44
Insurable interest, **10.4**
Insurance, **6.9**
Insurance Demand, 9.12–9.15
Insurance Mandates and Regulation, 9.12–9.13
Insurance Policies, 2.30
Insurance risk, **9.50**
Insurance Supply, 9.6–9.11
Insurance to value, **11.9**–11.12
Intangible property, **3.3**
Intelligent Risk Taking, 2.7
Intentional tort, **3.11**
Intertemporal Risk Transfer, 9.27
Intervening act, **3.16**
Introduction to Retirement Funding, 14.6–14.10
Investment Opportunities, 9.9

L

Large Number of Similar Exposure Units, 9.26–9.27
Law of large numbers, **4.4**
Leased Employees and Temporary Employees, 15.17–15.19
Leasehold, **6.18**
Leasing, 6.18
Legal and Regulatory Requirements, 2.8
Legal duty, **3.13**
Legal hazard, **1.10**
Legal liability, **3.9**
Legal Liability Based on Contracts, 3.11
Legal Liability Based on Statutes, 3.12
Legal Liability Based on Torts, 3.10–3.11
Legal Liability: Torts, Contracts, and Statutes, 3.9–3.12
Legality, 2.19–2.20
Less Expensive, 12.14
Level of Government Involvement, 9.47–9.48
Liability, 9.34–9.36, 9.41
Liability loss, **3.9**
Liability Loss Exposures, **3.4**, 5.21–5.22
Life Loss Exposures, 9.43
Life safety, **5.18**
Life, Health, and Retirement, 9.42–9.44
Limitation of Liability, 6.22
Loss exposure, **2.25**
Loss Exposure Characteristics, 6.13–6.14
Loss Frequency and Loss Severity, 5.17–5.19, 11.9–11.10
Loss Histories, 2.33
Loss Matrix: A Structured Approach to Identifying Outcomes, 7.3–7.6
Loss prevention, **5.5**–5.6
Loss reduction, **5.6**–5.8

M

Maintain an Appropriate Level of Liquidity, 6.6–6.7
Major medical insurance, **13.6**
Manage Cash Flow Variability, 6.6
Manage Downside Risk, 2.6–2.7
Manage the Cost of Risk, 6.5
Managed-Care Plans, **13.7**–13.9
Managing Cash Flow Uncertainty, 8.10
Maximize Profitability, 2.7
Maximum Possible Loss, 4.33
Maximum Probable Loss, 4.34–4.36
Mean, **4.13**
Measurable, 9.25
Median, **4.13**
Median and Cumulative Probabilities, 4.13–4.15
Medicaid, **13.15**–13.17
Medical Benefits, 15.13
Medicare, **13.12**
Medicare Advantage (MA) plans, **13.9**
Medicare Advantage (Part C), 13.12–13.14
Medicare Advantage plans, **13.12**
Medicare Prescription Drug Coverage (Part D), 13.14–13.15
Medicare Supplement Insurance (Medigap), 13.14
Meeting Legal Requirements, 8.10
Minimizing Insurance to Value Problems, 11.12
Mix of Retention and Transfer, 6.12–6.13
Mode, **4.15**–4.18
Moral and Morale Hazard, 9.18
Moral hazard, **1.10**
Morale hazard (attitudinal hazard), **1.10**
Multiple Hazards, 1.11
Multiple Retirement Savings and Income Sources, 14.23–14.25
Mutually Exclusive Events, 4.25

N

Named insured endorsement, **6.25**
Nature of Probability, 4.3–4.4
Negligence, **3.10**, 3.12, 3.12–3.18
Negligence per se, **3.17**
Net Income, 9.38–9.39, 9.42
Net Income Loss Associated With Liability Losses, 9.39
Net Income Loss Associated With Property Losses, 9.38–9.39
Net Income Loss Exposures, **3.6**–3.9, 5.23
Nondiversifiable risk, **1.8**
Nonfinancial Considerations, 2.15
Noninsurance risk control transfer, **6.16**, 6.17–6.23
Noninsurance risk financing transfer, **6.17**, 6.23–6.25
Noninsurance risk transfer, **6.9**–6.10
Nonmutually Exclusive Events, 4.26–4.27
Nonqualified Retirement Plans, **14.7**, 14.11, 14.20–14.23
Not Catastrophic, 9.27–9.28

O

Objective risk, **1.8**
Objectives and Decision Making Rules, 7.6–7.12
Obligee, **6.20**
Obtain Efficiency and Provide Convenience, 9.46
Occupational disease, **15.13**
Offsets, 11.8
Operation of the Law of Large Numbers, 4.30
Organizational Policies and Records, 2.31
Original Medicare, 13.12
Other-Insurance Provisions, 11.3–11.8
Outcomes of a Properly Constructed Probability Distribution, 4.5–4.9
Overview and Scope, 15.3

P

Parties to a Healthcare Transaction, 13.4
Partner With Private Insurers, 9.47
Pay for Losses, 6.4
Paying for Losses, 8.10
Pension Funding, 14.31–14.36
Pension or Profit-Sharing Plans, 14.14–14.15
Pension Plan Termination, 14.33–14.36
Pension Prefunding Obligations, 14.32
Personal Inspections, 2.33
Personal loss exposure, **3.5**
Personal property, **3.3**
Personnel, 9.36–9.38
Personnel Loss Exposures, **3.4**–3.5, 5.22–5.23
Persons and Employments Covered, 15.16–15.19
Physical hazard, **1.10**
Plaintiff, **3.12**
Planning Effectively, 14.3
Point-of-service (POS) plan, **13.8**
Policyholders' surplus, **9.8**
Pooling, 8.3
Possibility and Probability, 1.4–1.5
Post-loss funding, **6.11**
Post-loss goals, **2.18**, 2.21–2.24
Postretirement Pension Funding, 14.33
Preferred provider organization (PPO), **13.8**
Pre-loss funding, **6.11**
Pre-loss goals, **2.18**, 2.19–2.20
Premises and Operations Liability, 9.35–9.36
Premium base, **4.30**
Premium-to-surplus ratio, or capacity ratio, **9.8**
Premium-to-Surplus Ratio, 9.8–9.9
Primary coverage provision, **11.4**
Primary insurer, **9.50**
Primary/Excess Provisions, 11.4
Principal, **6.20**
Principle of indemnity, **8.9**, 10.3, 10.3–10.7
Private fee-for-service (PFFS) plans, **13.14**
Probabilities Estimated, 7.7–7.12
Probabilities Not Estimated, 7.6
Probability, **1.4**
Probability analysis, **4.4**
Probability distribution, **4.5**

Problems Associated With Insurance to Value, 11.12
Production Costs, 9.10
Products Liability, 9.36
Profitability, 2.22
Profit-Sharing Plans, **14.14**, 14.18
Prohibitions, 11.6–11.7
Promote Life Safety, 5.16–5.17
Promoting Risk Control, 8.11
Property, 9.29–9.34, 9.40–9.41
Property Loss Exposures, **3.3**, 5.19–5.20
Proportional other-insurance provision, **11.4**
Proportional Provisions, 11.4–11.6
Protected Cell Company, **6.28**–6.29
Providing Source of Investment Funds, 8.12
Providing Support for Insured's Credit, 8.11
Proximate cause, **3.15**–3.16
Purchasing an Annuity, 14.25–14.26
Pure and Speculative Risk, 1.6–1.7
Pure risk, **1.6**, 2.3, 9.22–9.23

Q

Quadrants of Risk in an Organization, 3.23–3.24
Qualified Defined Benefit Retirement Plans, 14.16–14.18
Qualified Defined Contribution Plans, 14.18–14.20
Qualified or Nonqualified Plans, 14.11–14.13
Qualified retirement plan, **14.7**, 14.11

R

Rationale for Employer-Provided Benefits, 12.6–12.8
Rationale for Government Involvement, 9.44–9.46
Real property (realty), **3.3**
Real Services Rendered, 9.14
Reasonable person test, **3.14**
Reduce Cost of Hazard Risk, 2.5
Reduce Deterrence Effects of Hazard Risks, 2.5–2.6
Reduce Downside Risk, 2.6
Reduced Systemic Risk, 2.10
Reduced Waste of Resources, 2.9
Reducing Social Burdens, 8.12–8.14
Regulatory Environment, 9.10–9.11
Rehabilitation Benefits, 15.15
Reinsurance, **4.33**
Reinsurance agreement, **9.50**
Reinsurance and Its Functions, 9.50–9.53
Reinsurance Basics, 9.50–9.51
Reinsurance Functions, 9.51–9.53
Reinsurance premium, **9.51**
Reinsurer, **9.50**
Rent-a-captive, **6.27**
Replacement cost, **10.3**
Required Proof of Negligence, 3.17–3.18
Res ipsa loquitur, **3.18**
Retention, **6.10**–6.11, 9.50
Retirement, 9.37–9.38
Retirement Benefits, 12.3
Retirement Funding Categories, 14.7
Retirement Income Choices, 14.23–14.29, 14.25–14.29
Retirement Loss Exposures, 9.44, 14.3–14.6
Retirement (Old Age) Benefits, 15.8–15.9
Retrocedent, **9.51**
Retrocession, **9.51**
Retrocessionaire, **9.51**
Risk appetite, **2.7**
Risk Assessment Questionnaires and Checklists, 2.27–2.28
Risk Classifications, 1.5–1.9
Risk control, **5.3**
Risk Control Goals, 5.12–5.17
Risk Control Techniques, 5.3–5.12
Risk financing, **6.7**
Risk Financing Goals, 6.3–6.7
Risk Financing Techniques: Transfer and Retention, 6.7–6.11
Risk management, **2.3**, 3.20
Risk Management for Individuals and Organizations, 2.3–2.4
Risk management process, **2.4**, 2.10–2.18, **3.20**
Risk management program, **3.20**
Risk Management Program Goals, 2.18–2.24
Risk Management Tools and the Worry Value, 7.15–7.16
Risk Maps, 3.22–3.23
Risk retention group, **6.27**
Risk Tolerance, 6.14–6.15, 9.13

S

Salary Reduction Plans, **14.21**–14.23
Sale-and-lease-back (sale-and-lease-back arrangement), **6.18**
Savings incentive match plan for employees (SIMPLE), **14.20**
Scope of Business Continuity Management, 5.24
Section, **14.18**
Section 401(k) plan, **14.6**
Segregation, **6.18**
Selecting Appropriate Risk Financing Measures, 6.12–6.16
Selecting the Proper Tools, 7.3–7.17
Separation, **5.9**–5.11
Severity, **1.10**
SIMPLE Plans, 14.20
Simplified Employee Pension Plans, **14.20**
Single-parent captive (pure captive), **6.26**
Single-Parent (or Pure) Captive, 6.26
Social insurance, **15.3**–15.5
Social Insurance Attributes, 15.4–15.5
Social Insurance Provided Through Employers, 12.5
Social Responsibility, 2.20, 2.23
Social Security Program (OASDHI), 15.5–15.10
Social Security Retirement Benefits, 14.23–14.24
Society's Responsibility, 15.4
Sources of Pension Funding, 14.32
Special needs plans (SNP), **13.9**, **13.14**
Speculative risk, **1.6**, 2.3
Spend Down Savings, 14.26–14.27
Standard deviation, **4.21**–4.22
Start Traditional Pension Payments, 14.27
Statement of cash flows, **2.28**
Static and Dynamic Risk, 1.9
Statute, **3.12**, 3.13

Step 1: Identifying Loss Exposures, 2.10
Step 2: Analyzing Loss Exposures, 2.11–2.12
Step 3: Examining the Feasibility of Risk Management Techniques, 2.12–2.13
Step 4: Selecting the Appropriate Risk Management Techniques, 2.13–2.15
Step 5: Implementing the Selected Risk Management Techniques, 2.15–2.16
Step 6: Monitoring Results and Revising the Risk Management Program, 2.16–2.18
Strict liability (absolute liability), **3.11**
Subjective and Objective Risk, 1.7–1.8
Subjective risk, **1.8**
Subrogation, **6.21**, **10.6**
Substantial factor rule, **3.16**
Supplemental Executive Retirement Plans, **14.20**, 14.21
Supply and Demand, 9.4–9.6
Surety, **6.20**
Suretyship and Guaranty Agreements, 6.20–6.21
Survival, 2.21
Survivors (Death) Benefits, 15.9
Systemic risk, **1.9**, 2.5

T

Tangible property, **3.3**
Tax Advantages, 12.6–12.7
Tax Advantages for Retirement Funding, 14.8–14.10
Tax Incentives, 9.14–9.15
Tax Treatment of Disability Income insurance, 12.12–12.13
Tax Treatment of Employer-Provided Benefits, 12.11–12.13
Tax Treatment of Group Term Life Insurance, 12.12
Temporary partial disability (TPD), **15.14**
Temporary total disability (TTD), **15.14**
Theoretical probability, **4.3**
Theoretical Probability and Empirical Probability, 4.3–4.4
Theoretical Probability Distributions, 4.5–4.7
Tied to Employment, 12.14–12.15
Timing, 9.20
Tolerable Uncertainty, 2.19
Tort, **3.10**, 3.12
Tortfeasor, **3.12**
Traditional Health Insurance Plans, 13.6
Traditional Risk Management, 3.21
Traditional Risk Management and Enterprise-Wide Risk Management, 2.4
Traditional Risk Management Contrasted With ERM, 3.25–3.27
Traditional Risk Management Versus Enterprise Risk Management (ERM), 3.19–3.27
Transfer, 6.9–6.10
Transfer of Risk to the Transferee's Insurer, 6.24–6.25
Types of Benefits Provided by Social Security, 15.7–15.10
Types of Captive Insurance Plans, 6.25–6.29
Types of Contractual Risk Transfer, 6.16–6.17, 6.16–6.25
Types of Loss Exposures, 3.3–3.9

U

Uncertainty and Possibility, 1.4
Understanding and Quantifying Risk, 1.3–1.5
Understanding Hazards, 1.9–1.11
Understanding Loss Severity, 4.33–4.36
Understanding the Law of Large Numbers, 4.29–4.33
Unemployment Benefits, 12.4–12.5
Unemployment Insurance, 15.10–15.11
Using Central Tendency, 4.11–4.18
Using Dispersion, 4.19–4.24
Using Probability Distributions, 4.5–4.11
Utmost good faith, **10.5**

V

Valued policy, **8.9**
Vesting, **14.11**

W

Waiver, **6.21**–6.22
Waiver of subrogation, **6.22**
Whose Worry Value?, 7.16
Windstorm, 9.31–9.33
Workers compensation statute, **15.12**
Workers Compensation Statutes: Purpose, Benefits, and Persons Covered, 15.12–15.19
Worry Method, 7.13–7.17
Worry Method and No Probability Information, 7.14–7.15
Worry Method and the Insurance Method, 7.16
Worry Method and Why a Person Might Purchase Insurance, 7.13–7.14
Written premiums, **9.8**